The Enabling Power of Assessment

Volume 2

Series editor
Claire Wyatt-Smith Faculty of Education and Arts, Australian Catholic University, Brisbane, Queensland, Australia

This series heralds the idea that new times call for new and different thinking about assessment and learning, the identities of teachers and students, and what is involved in using and creating new knowledge. Its scope is consistent with a view of assessment as inherently connected with cultural, social practices and contexts. Assessment is a shared enterprise where teachers and students come together to not only develop knowledge and skills, but also to use and create knowledge and identities. Working from this position, the series confronts some of the major educational assessment issues of our times.

More information about this series at http://www.springer.com/series/13204

Shelleyann Scott • Donald E. Scott
Charles F. Webber

Editors

Assessment in Education

Implications for Leadership

 Springer

Editors
Shelleyann Scott
Werklund School of Education
University of Calgary
Calgary, AB, Canada

Donald E. Scott
Werklund School of Education
University of Calgary
Calgary, AB, Canada

Charles F. Webber
Faculty of Continuing Education
    and Extension
Mount Royal University
Calgary, AB, Canada

ISSN 2198-2643   ISSN 2198-2651   (electronic)
The Enabling Power of Assessment
ISBN 978-3-319-23397-0   ISBN 978-3-319-23398-7   (eBook)
DOI 10.1007/978-3-319-23398-7

Library of Congress Control Number: 2015953103

Springer Cham Heidelberg New York Dordrecht London

Printed on acid-free paper

Springer International Publishing AG Switzerland is part of Springer Science+Business Media (www.springer.com)

Contents

Contributors

Art J. Aitken Faculty of Education, University of Lethbridge, Lethbridge, AB, Canada

E. Nola Aitken Faculty of Education, University of Lethbridge, Lethbridge, AB, Canada

Johanna de Leeuw Founder & President, Instructional Design & Assessment, Visible Assessment for Learning Inc., Calgary, AB, Canada

Jens Dolin Department of Science Education, University of Copenhagen, Copenhagen, Denmark

Don A. Klinger Faculty of Education, Queen's University, Kingston, ON, Canada

Constance Magee Lindbergh Middle School, Long Beach, CA, USA

David F. Philpott Faculty of Education, Memorial University of Newfoundland, St. John's, NL, Canada

Maria Luz Romay School of Physical Therapy, University of the Incarnate Word, San Antonio, TX, USA

Charles L. Slater College of Education, California State University, Long Beach, CA, USA

Donald E. Scott Werklund School of Education, University of Calgary, Calgary, AB, Canada

Shelleyann Scott Werklund School of Education, University of Calgary, Calgary, AB, Canada

Xiaomei Song Office of Institutional Effectiveness, Georgia Southern University, Statesboro, GA, USA

Charles F. Webber Faculty of Continuing Education and Extension, Mount Royal University, Calgary, AB, Canada

Dianne Yee Director, Area III, Calgary Board of Education, Calgary, AB, Canada

About the Editors and Contributors

Editors

Dr. Shelleyann Scott is a Professor in the Leadership, Policy, and Governance specialisation in the Werklund School of Education, University of Calgary. She has held numerous leadership roles in Canada and Australia including most recently Associate Dean, Professional and Community Engagement and Director of Graduate Programmes. Shelleyann's work experience spans the contexts of business, government, and medical research and includes tertiary and secondary contexts, professional development, quality assurance, district school leadership, and includes serving in the capacity of business and government consultant. Her research interests include capacity building of leaders, educators, staff, and organisations within the contexts of K-12 and higher education, and promoting instructional capacity that encompasses pedagogical strategies, assessment approaches and practices, and learning technologies. Shelleyann has published numerous articles and book chapters and serves on a number of editorial boards.

Dr. Donald E. Scott is EdD Programme Coordinator for Leadership in Post-secondary Contexts, Werklund School of Education, University of Calgary. He is an Assistant Professor in the Leadership, Policy and Governance specialisation. His professional experience includes serving as a university educator, school teacher, and school network administrator. His research interests encompass post-secondary teaching and learning, professional development of teachers and faculty, school and university leadership development, and ICT integration within educational environments. He has authored many journal papers and chapters and is on the editorial board of a number of journals.

Dr. Charles F. Webber is Professor and Dean, Faculty of Continuing Education and Extension, Mount Royal University, Calgary, Alberta, Canada. His current research interest focuses on the influences of school leaders on student achievement and on cross-cultural leadership development including technology-mediated leadership development. During his career as an educator he has served as a classroom teacher, curriculum consultant, principal, professor, associate dean, and dean. His work appears in international and national journals and he has served as invited presenter in conferences, seminars, and workshops in North America, Europe, Asia, Africa, the Middle East, New Zealand, and Australia. He has previously served as academic editor of *Educational Forum*, a scholarly journal published by the American educational honour society *Kappa Delta Pi* based in Indianapolis.

Contributors

Art J. Aitken is a life member of the College of Alberta School Superintendents (CASS), having been a school system executive for 12 years. Dr. Aitken is an acknowledged expert in the fields of educational leadership, instructional supervision, student assessment, and teacher evaluation. He has written extensively and presented frequently on these and other leadership topics.

Art spent the most recent years of his career as a university instructor at The University of Lethbridge devoting his time to the educational leadership masters' programme and to teacher preparation. While serving as Superintendent of Prairie Land Regional School Division, Art and his senior leadership partner worked with his board to enhance learning and strengthen community partnerships in Prairie Land. Before coming to Prairie Land in 1997, Art served as the Superintendent of the former Rangeland School Division for 3 years.

At the school level he was a secondary principal for 9 years, a junior high principal for 4 years, an elementary principal for 3 years, and an assistant principal in five different Alberta schools. He has also done school system evaluation work and has served as a consultant in South Africa. Art worked as a teacher and educational leader for 47 years.

Art is enjoying retirement with his wife Nola, splitting his time between Phoenix and Lethbridge, Alberta. He enjoys golf, duplicate bridge, and he likes to maintain his fitness level.

E. Nola Aitken began her career as a schoolteacher teaching students from Kindergarten to Grade 9 for over two decades. Following her teaching career she was a Mathematics Test Development Specialist and was further involved in the Diagnostic Mathematics Programme for 5 years at the Student Evaluation Branch, Alberta Education, Canada. Following her work in those two areas, she taught assessment and evaluation of student learning in undergraduate and graduate programmes from 1992 to 2011 in the Faculty of Education at the University of Lethbridge, Alberta. Nola's research areas were student assessment, mathematics education, and higher education.

Nola has received several research grants including an award of a $40,000 research grant to serve as Director to establish the Centre for Assessment Research in Education (CARE). In addition, she received a $43,000 Social Sciences and

Human Research Count grant for her study on *Native Reserve Students' and Native Public School Students' Ways of Knowing and Doing Mathematics.* Also, Nola was part of a tri-university research team funded by Alberta Education to investigate assessment practices in Alberta.

Nola has published two co-edited books and several journal articles and book chapters on assessment, mathematics education, and higher education.

Since she retired as Professor Emerita in 2011, Nola has continued to write in the education field and has pursued recreational activities such as music, art, and golf in Alberta and Phoenix.

Jens Dolin is Head of Department of Science Education at the University of Copenhagen. His research areas are teaching and learning science (with focus on the development of competencies) and organisational change (reform processes, curriculum development, and teacher conceptions). He has participated in and been leader of a number of Danish and international science education research projects (including FP7-projects such as S-TEAM and Mind The Gap about inquiry based science education) and is member of a number of Danish and international boards and organisations. After a long career as a high school teacher in physics and geography (involving development work and part-time teaching at university), he gradually drifted into research and employment in higher education and involvement in educational policy with emphasis on science education.

Johanna de Leeuw is the Director and Assessment Research Consultant for Visible Assessment for Learning Inc., a professional learning organisation dedicated to promoting innovative inquiry and student peer and self-assessment strategies in critical thinking and writing. Johanna completed her Ph.D. in assessment and instructional design and her MA on musically gifted adolescents at the University of Calgary where she is teaching a winter session graduate course in Gifted Education. For Calgary Board of Education (CBE), Johanna held positions as System Assistant Principal (where she coordinated the CBE's Alberta Initiative for School Improvement Cycle 5 project), Research Specialist, English Curriculum Leader, humanities teacher, music and fine arts specialist. She has had over 30 years of teaching experience at all grade levels, both with the Calgary Board of Education and Mount Royal Conservatory of Music (now University) Calgary. Johanna continues her professional development throughout Alberta in cross-jurisdictional, collaborative assessment practices at the high school level. Johanna has presented at numerous refereed (Canadian Society for the Study of Education, John Hattie's Visible Learning[plus] in Australia, Alberta Assessment Consortium) and non-refereed conferences on the assessment of writing. Johanna is currently designing and developing *PeerVision®*, a formative assessment software application for self and peer assessment.

Don A. Klinger is a Professor in Assessment and Evaluation at the Faculty of Education at Queen's University, Kingston. He has a strong background in quantitative research methods and psychometrics, including Classical Test Theory, Item

Response Theory, Generalisability Theory, and Hierarchical Linear Modelling. Dr. Klinger is particularly interested in the methods we use to evaluate students and the subsequent decisions, practices, and policies that arise from these assessment practices. His research also explores the evolving conceptions of formative and summative assessment, the uses of classroom assessment to inform teaching and learning, and the ways in which large-scale assessments and databases are used to inform educational policy and practice. Ongoing funding and research projects have enabled Dr. Klinger to work on building stronger research collaborations and communication between the research community and practising educators. Dr. Klinger is a founding member of the Assessment and Evaluation Group at Queen's University. He is the co-chair of the task force revising the Classroom Assessment Standards on behalf of the Joint Committee on Standards for Educational Evaluation.

Constance Magee is the principal at Lindbergh Middle School in Long Beach and teaches part-time in the Education Administration programme at California State University, Long Beach. She has been a middle school principal in Long Beach for the past 8 years. She has also served the district as a mentor principal, an assistant principal, curriculum coach, and classroom teacher. She received her Ed.D. and M.A. from the California State University, Long Beach, and her B.A. from University of California, Irvine.

Her dissertation was condensed into a book chapter in collaboration with Dr. Charles Slater, and was recently published in *Advances in Educational Administration*, vol.19.

Her research has focused on the experiences of new principals and the change processes needed to improve struggling urban schools. She has also explored administrative mentoring relationships and support systems for new principals.

David F. Philpott can best be described as a tireless advocate for vulnerable children and their families, having enjoyed a 30-year career in education and community activism. In his activities ranging from involvement in the closure of Exon House, the province's last residential facility for children with disabilities in the mid-1980s to recent pan-Canadian research projects, he has been at the forefront of informing societal approaches to supporting families with exceptional children. He joined MUN's Faculty of Education in 2000 following a 15-year career in the public education system. He has served in a wide range of teaching and management positions in special education, including private consulting/counselling and educational assessment. He was promoted to Full Professor at Memorial University in 2011 and also maintains Adjunct Professor status with the Faculty of Medicine, University of Calgary, where he teaches child-centred, family-focused support planning. His research has informed provincial and territorial models of special services, including Nunavut's approach to inclusive education and Newfoundland's recent review of support services. He led the project that resulted in the Innu's attainment of self-government and the development of a bi-cultural model of education for their children. He has been involved in countless provincial and national organisations and is an international speaker on approaches to supporting children and families and a recognised advocate for vulnerable youth. He was actively involved in a 2011 national report on early child care (Early Years Study 3) through his involvement with private family foundations. His latest work with vulnerable children has led to his involvement in Memorial Universities Teaching and Learning Framework as lead researcher on supporting academically at-risk students. While his contribution to knowledge creation and dissemination has been outstanding, he continues to maintain a private practice working with children, which grounds him in the reality of families and directs his research and teaching. He holds degrees in Education, Special Education and Educational Psychology from Memorial University and a Doctorate of Education from the University of Calgary.

Maria Luz Romay is currently an Associate Professor at the University of the Incarnate Word in San Antonio, TX. She previously taught in several institutions of higher education in Mexico, notably at Iberoamericana University (1986–1996) and the National Polytechnic Institute (1984–1993), both located in Mexico City. She has also collaborated with universities at the international level, conducting seminars and workshops in Honduras, Peru, Taiwan, and the USA. She received her Ph.D. from Loyola University of Chicago, her Masters in Educational Research from Iberoamericana University, and her B.A. from the National University of Mexico (UNAM).

Her professional career has focused on teaching in diverse graduate programmes both in education and business, where she taught courses related mainly to research methodologies, planning and evaluation in education, organisational development, and curricular planning and evaluation. Dr. Romay has worked in research projects at the national level in Mexico, and has collaborated as a consultant for public and private organisations and community programmes.

She has published several articles and book chapters related to topics such as programme evaluation, leadership in educational institutions, assessment of faculty performance, and accreditation processes, as well as theory and practice of administration in social and educational organisations. Her latest academic work has been in collaboration with Dr. Isaias Alvarez, a book in Spanish entitled *Challenges for Developing a Culture of Evaluation in Educational Institutions*, which is still in process for publication.

Charles L. Slater is Professor of Educational Leadership at California State University, Long Beach. He previously served as a professor at Texas State University, San Marcos, and was superintendent of schools in Texas and Massachusetts. He received his Ph.D. from the University of Wisconsin-Madison, his MAT from Occidental College, Los Angeles, and his B.A. from the University of Minnesota.

He has published widely on educational leadership including articles in: the *Educational Administration Quarterly*, the *Journal of Educational Administration*, the *Educational Forum*, *Revista Iberoamericana sobre Calidad, Eficacia y Cambio en Educación*, the *Journal of School Leadership*, *Education and Society*, the

International Journal of Leadership in Education, Educational Management and Leadership, and *Revista Mexicana de Investigación Educativa*.

His research has focused on what is needed for successful leadership in the USA, Mexico, Costa Rica, and Spain with special attention to educational administration preparation. Much of this work has been conducted with the International Study of Principal Preparation (ISPP), a collaboration of researchers in 13 countries.

Xiaomei Song is a Senior Research Associate and Instructor in the Office of Institutional Effectiveness at Georgia Southern University. She undertook her doctorate at the Faculty of Education, Queen's University, Ontario, Canada. Before her academic studies at Queen's University, she worked as a university professor in China and was intrigued by the complex interplay between assessment and student achievement in the Chinese context, where testing played a major role in the classroom as well as high-stakes decision-making involving admission, aptitude, and certification. Stimulated by her observation and experience, she pursued a Master's and Doctorate in Educational Psychology at Queen's University with the major in Educational Assessment and Evaluation. Her primary research interests include validity and fairness of internal and external assessment activities, the role of testing, assessment, and educational programmes in academic and professional settings, learner characteristics on learning outcomes and performance, and research methodologies. She has been particularly interested in exploring concrete ways in which quantitative and qualitative methods of inquiry can be used in concert to inform a deep understanding of the testing culture in China and in other countries. Her research has led her to be aware of, acknowledge, and pursue the epistemological implications in the use of different research methodologies, especially in the area of testing. She has published articles in the *Journal of International Migration and Integration*, *Asia-Pacific Journal of Teacher Education*, and *Language Assessment Quarterly*.

Dianne Yee has been with the Calgary Board of Education (CBE) since 2004 and is currently the Director of Area III. During her career she has worked in five school districts in Alberta and Saskatchewan, serving as a teacher, resource teacher, counsellor, assistant principal and principal. In addition, Dianne has worked as a sessional instructor for the University of Regina, the Saskatchewan Institute for Applied Science and Technology, and the University of Calgary. She began her work with CBE as principal of Lord Beaverbrook High School and has held CBE district positions as System Principal for Secondary Schools, Director of Instructional Design and Assessment and Director of Area I. Her academic credentials include a Bachelor of Education, a Master of Education in Educational Psychology and Counselling, and a Doctor of Philosophy in Educational Leadership and Educational Technology.

Part I
Assessment in Education:
Implications for Leaders

Chapter 1
Student Assessment in a Civil Society

Charles F. Webber and Shelleyann Scott

Abstract A rigorous public education system is crucial in supporting and nurturing a strong civil society and assessment is a key component of teaching and learning within any education system; however, assessment is also one of the most contentious and politicised dimensions within societies. Assessment data at all levels of an education system informs decision making, policy and practices, as well as individual student achievement and careers. The importance of assessment therefore cannot be debated but there must be appropriate and sound debate regarding assessment issues with stakeholders working together to balance the needs of students with the other purposes and uses of assessment information. When stakeholders constructively engage with each other for the advancement of teaching, learning and assessment they demonstrate multidimensional perspectives, thereby strengthening the fabric of a civil society. Conversely, when partisan politics prevails and unidimensional thinking abounds – displaying limited role conceptualisations thereby restricting opportunities to improve their educational systems – it places at risk the robustness of a civil society and reinforces stagnation and the maintenance of the status quo. Hence, a tenet of a democratic civil society is the preservation of respectful, open dialogue among divergent voices with the aim of producing a better educational system for all young people within that society.

Keywords Civil society • Democracy • Assessment • Leading assessment • Multidimensional perspectives • Unidimensional perspectives • Politics • Stakeholders • Tensions and opportunities • Assessment within teaching and learning

An abbreviated version of this chapter was previously published in Emerald's *Journal of Management Development* in 2012. Emerald has provided copyright approval for this expanded version.

C.F. Webber
Faculty of Continuing Education and Extension, Mount Royal University, Calgary, AB, Canada
e-mail: cfwebber@mtroyal.ca

S. Scott (✉)
Werklund School of Education, University of Calgary, Calgary, AB, Canada
e-mail: sscott@ucalgary.ca

1.1 Introduction

Educational institutions contribute to the creation and sustenance of a civil society. This reality has long been recognised in the Canadian context as evidenced by Edgerton Ryerson's creation of a particular kind of educational system in Upper Canada (Nixon, 2006). Ryerson's vision for schooling included "centralized free compulsory education … [with] a standardized curriculum, the printing of textbooks by Canadian authors, the training, examination and inspection of teachers, pedagogical conventions, libraries" (Nixon, p. 95). Ryerson's cultural and religious background led him to posit that the stability of a nation depended in large part upon institutions such as the family, church, and school (Pearce, 1988). Ryerson also advocated for the recognition of teaching as a profession (Danylewcyz & Prentice, 1986). Certainly his worldview reflected his time and culture and promoted what now can be argued to be a narrow view of education. For example, his desire to provide Aboriginal communities with an education intended to integrate young people into the dominant English agricultural economy (Pettit, 1997) is perceived in the twenty-first century to be a colonising and highly disruptive influence on Canada's First Nations people. Nonetheless, Ryerson understood the power of education to shape and maintain social order.

Today, the construct of *civil society* in Canada, similar to the United Kingdom, Australia, and New Zealand, includes the notions of open debate, respect for diversity, religious freedom, the right to vote, and access to health care (Macfarlane, 2008). The education system also has evolved so educators are expected to be advocates for social justice and, indeed, address concerns such as racism in the attempt to maintain what Lund (2003) called a "democratizing influence in schools and communities" (p. 266). In contrast to Ryerson's perspective on education in First Nations communities, Canadians are exercising their desire to regain a sense of cultural identity and to improve curricula in "a manner that honors the knowledge, principles, and values the communities regard as integral to who and what they are" as a people (Lewthwaite & Renaud, 2009, p. 154).

Consistent with Macfarlane's (2008) understanding of civil society, Beets' (2012), writing in a post-apartheid South African educational context, described *ubuntu* (p. 80) as a Zulu expression that highlights the understanding that members of a society are responsible for the welfare of themselves and everyone around them: "This means that when one person's circumstances improve, everyone gains but if one person is treated unjustly, everyone is diminished" (p. 80). Unfortunately, the fragility of a civil society is underscored when the overall welfare of a society is ignored or intentionally trampled, as illustrated during the Ceauşescu era within Romania (Kligman, 1990), jeopardising the attainment and sustenance of a civil society for generations, and as Fukuyama (2001) indicated "civil society serves to balance the power of the state and to protect individuals from the state's power" (p. 11).

Table 1.1 Assessment in the service of civil society

Assumption	Ontology	Epistemology
Every child deserves access to quality teaching and learning	A threshold of knowledge and skills is necessary for full participation in a democratic civil society	Education based upon a class structure that reflects socio-economic or cultural capital is unacceptable
Assessment data are used as planning tools by educators and policy makers	Curriculum and instruction should be planned and structured deliberately	A common curriculum, adaptable to local contexts, serves a civil society
Assessment is a shared responsibility among educational stakeholders	Teaching and learning affects both individuals and their communities: classroom, school, district, ministry, and nation	No individual or group is a neutral cultural force
Quality student assessment practices are complex and difficult	Assessment knowledge and skills need to be taught explicitly	Expectations for assessment evolve and develop constantly
Assessment is political	Assessment policies and practices will be contested publicly and regularly	Emotions associated with individual student success and achievement will permeate policy and practice

1.2 Conceptual Framework

This chapter about leading student assessment is premised upon a conceptual framework that includes several basic assumptions about the role of assessment in teaching and learning. Table 1.1 outlines the chapter assumptions and their related ontological and epistemological foundations.

1.3 Access to Teaching and Learning

The UNESCO stand on the right of every child to education articulates one of the basic assumptions for this chapter:

> There is a growing consensus that human development must be at the core of any development process: that in times of economic adjustment and austerity, services for the poor have to be protected; that education – the empowerment of individuals through the provision of learning – is truly a human right and a social responsibility. (Inter-Agency Commission, 1990, p. 1)

Further,

> The task of education is to give everyone the opportunity to play an active role in shaping the future of society ... The aim is not to teach moral principles as rigid rules, in an indoctrination-like way, but to introduce democratic practices into the school. Drawing on practical examples, the aim is for pupils to learn and understand their rights and responsi-

bilities and how their own freedom is limited by the rights and freedoms of others … Given
that teaching and understanding democracy cannot be restricted to the period in which
children receive formal education, it is also essential for families and other members of
society to be integrated into the process. (UNESCO, 1997, p. 50)

We also subscribe to the description of democracy endorsed by Laguardia and
Pearl (2009), a society characterised by inclusion in political decision making, guar-
anteed human rights, equality, universal access to high quality learning, and "equal
availability to the understanding required for deliberating the most serious challenges to democracy and livability" (p. 353). We are hesitant to agree with Laguardia
and Pearl's suggestion that such a democracy is unattainable, though we understand
that they described an ideal democratic state and cautioned that there are significant
ongoing challenges to democracies. We also understand schooling can be both a
liberating and colonising initiative (Zamudio, Rios, & Jaime, 2008). However, consistent with Cowie, Jones, and Otrel-Cass (2011) perspective that students must
develop the knowledge and skills needed to engage with societal challenges and
possibilities, we suggest full participation in a democracy depends upon achieving
a threshold of knowledge and skills that should be accessible to all, regardless of
cultural or socioeconomic background.

1.4   Assessment as a Planning Tool

Effective planning is a critical element in the success of any educational initiative.
Planning depends to a large degree upon access to information about what has been
done and what could or should be done. Many researchers have asserted that student
assessment is necessary for monitoring quality instruction (Elmore, 2005; Popham,
2008; Reeves, 2002; Rogers, 1991). Others (e.g., Delaney, 2009), have highlighted
the importance of developing assessment literacy across the roles of educators, academics, and policy makers. Delaney also emphasised the value of benchmarking
and understanding the influence of the external environment. Clearly, student
assessment is an important element in making decisions about student learning and
programming (Webber, Aitken, Lupart, & Scott, 2009).

If quality teaching and learning is supported by good assessment practices then
it is essential the assessment be planned and structured deliberately. Delaney (2009)
advised that planning include (1) attention to developing a conceptual model for
assessment based on principles of effective assessment, (2) identification of
organisational barriers to assessment, and (3) creation of policies that promote success. Similarly, Boudett, City, and Murnane (2005) stressed the importance of
organising for collaborative work and building assessment literacy as part of the
cycle of assessment planning.

There is merit in the use of a common curriculum. Halstead (2007) noted a common school experience leads to set of shared values, a heightened sense of citizenship, and appreciation for diversity. He also cautioned that not all groups – e.g.,

minorities, religious groups, or members of some social classes—wish to assimilate to the same extent with the larger society. Further, how individual school communities organise learning can exclude some, for example, Muslim students during Ramadan, leading to possible alienation from society. Thus, the potential value of a common curriculum lies in how sensitively and knowledgeably it is applied in local communities. Shaker and Grimmett (2004) posited, from a western Canadian perspective, the curriculum in a good public school attends to students' various learning differences and cultural origins. Shamah and MacTavish (2009) and Tupa and McFadden (2009) emphasised the importance of including place-based knowledge in school curricula so community values and experiences can be validated.

1.5 Assessment as a Shared Responsibility

Assessment has traditionally been perceived as the primary responsibility of educators who evaluate students' performance for the purpose of planning, teaching, and reporting to parents (Earl & Katz, 2006; Heldsinger, 2012). As reasonable as this perspective is, there is a wider set of purposes and, therefore, responsibilities for assessment. Webber, Lupart, and Scott (2012, p. 285) described the "spectrum of influence" of educational assessment, beginning with individual students and classrooms but also pervading communities and societies and extending to the international, global village level. Due to the widespread influence of educational assessment it is essential that all stakeholders have a voice in the assessment process, beginning with students and parents (Aitken, Webber, Lupart, & Scott, 2011). Other groups, such as community and government leaders (Alberta Education, 2008), also have a responsibility to support and use student assessment data appropriately.

Given the potentially powerful impact of assessment on the lives of individual young people and their capacity to participate fully in society, it is necessary for all educational stakeholders to recognise the ways they shape the form and function of assessment. That is, educators can position classroom and external assessment as oppositional in purpose, or they can use both to provide a more informed set of learning experiences for students. Parents can accept uncritically the assessment data educators provide to them or they can strive to be partners in the analyses of data and in the resultant decision making processes. Moreover, parents and educators can recognise the value of the perspectives and opinions of students by involving them in the establishment of assessment criteria for example, or they can continue the traditional practice of imposing assessment on students which typically has a disempowering effect. In short, the merit of assessment policies and practices is based to a large extent upon the capacity of stakeholders to recognise how they can work together in the best interests of students, communities, and the larger society.

1.6   Complexity of Assessment

Assessment skills are complex and, in the case of educators, must be taught explicitly (Webber et al., 2009). Classroom assessment is influenced by variability in assessment standards (Wyatt-Smith, Klenowski, & Gunn, 2010) and by a dearth of strategies for meeting the needs of diversity, e.g. English-as-a-second-language learners (Inbar-Lourie & Donitsa-Schmidt, 2009; Wolf & Leon, 2009), Aboriginal students, and special needs learners (Webber et al., 2009).

Unfortunately, a clear understanding of how to navigate assessment complexity is not widespread in society. That is, educators tend to value assessment data that focus on their classrooms and individual students, while downplaying the importance of school and system data in informing macro-level decision making processes. Local policy makers may focus on comparative data about schools in their districts without adequately recognising the value in national and international comparisons. Other community leaders may want only to know if they are getting sufficient return on their educational investments. Given the wide range of information needs and varying capacities to interpret assessment data, it is clear that open dialogue and community education initiatives are necessary components of the assessment process.

1.7   Politics of Assessment

Given the range of stakeholders with differing perspectives and motivations related to assessment, it is not surprising that assessment is a politicised topic (Aitken et al., 2011). Indeed, assessment is possibly the most contentious educational issue of all, one that generates polarised debates among stakeholders and in the media. Parents are normally concerned about the educational well-being of their child, and the emotional attachments that they have with their progeny can result in extreme reactions to school assessment reports. Teachers and their unions often link student assessment with teacher accountability, resulting in defensive posturing that can impede educational progress in schools and systems. The media use publicly accessible assessment data to rank schools and districts without sufficient attention to demographic variables or to the possibility of highlighting schools performing beyond or below expectations. Policy makers at all levels understandably focus on big picture assessment issues and fail to give adequate attention to micro-level concerns of individual students and teachers.

Therefore, it is to be expected that assessment policies and practices will be contested publicly and regularly by stakeholders. Also, the heightened emotions and tensions inherent in discussions of assessment should be expected and navigated respectfully. The ability of stakeholders to harness their emotions productively will advance or impede the capacity of schools to provide access for all children to high quality teaching, learning, and assessment.

1.8 The Tensions of Professional Assessment Practices in a Civil Society

Promotion of a civil society, as noted earlier, is premised upon open debate, tolerance, attention to social justice, and recognition that assessment is complex and political. Therefore, it is to be expected that tensions exist within this politically charged context. However, in order for innovation and positive change to occur, the tensions need to be directed in such a way that it nurtures opportunities and creates synergies for the benefit of all students and their societies.

Observations of different stakeholder interactions during the Alberta Student Assessment Study (Webber et al., 2009) have led to the conceptualisation of a framework for understanding reactions and stances, while navigating a pathway through the tensions inherent in the assessment landscape. In the continuum from negative to positive dynamics there are *unidimensional perspectives* that demonstrate limited role conceptualisations and restricted opportunities to improve educational systems. In contrast, stakeholders with *multidimensional perspectives* manifest the capacity to engage cognitively in a broader and more inclusive manner, thereby overcoming tensions, engaging in productive dialogue, and promoting increased opportunities.

Stakeholders with multidimensional perspectives are able to address and ameliorate the *role-related tensions* that invariably arise in politicised and emotionally charged interactions. Further, multidimensional perspectives increase the likelihood that *assessment opportunities* can be realised (See Table 1.2).

1.9 Unidimensional Perspectives

Unidimensional perspectives are evident within the roles related to educational assessment. This orientation is characterised by a restricted viewpoint that privileges a particular stakeholder group to the exclusion of others. Even though we acknowledge there is a strong need for advocacy of specific roles within society, when this is carried to the extreme it impedes productive dialogue and effective decision making about educational assessment. For example, teacher professionalisation clearly must be respected but it is counterproductive when educators assume the position that they are the professionals and their opinions are the only ones that matter. Similarly, educational leaders who demonstrate a unidimensional perspective operate on the assumption that they are solely responsible for shaping school assessment and reporting practices, thereby silencing the voices of their community stakeholders. Also within the sphere of the school, parents may operate as if their child's needs supersede those of other children and privilege parental knowledge over that held by any other stakeholder. As understandable as this orientation may appear initially, it actually works against inclusive practices in schools that are established upon democratic, social justice principles. Other individuals who may

Table 1.2 Framework for navigating assessment tensions

Role in a civil society	Unidimensional perspectives	Multidimensional perspectives	Tensions	Opportunities
Teacher	Teacher is professional and opinions are to be trusted on that basis alone	Parents know more about their children Information from other professionals – psychologists, doctors, physiotherapists – is necessary	Perception that assessment challenges educators' professional judgment, credibility, and autonomy	Richer decisions, enhanced learning, more opportunities for young people, greater professional credibility
Educational leader	Leaders are superordinate, solely responsible for shaping school assessment and reporting	Leaders share information gathering and data analyses Facilitate educative development of teachers, parents, and community members around assessment	Resistance to decisions based on assessment data. Autocratic behaviour Insensitive interactions among educational stakeholders Ineffective communication Stagnant personal and professional development Power struggles	Distributed leadership Community support Enhanced loyalty and trust Transparent assessment and decision making processes Increased understandings about assessment and its purposes
Parent	"My child's needs are paramount" "No one knows my child better than I do"	Multiple role allegiances Respect for professionalism and expertise of educators, health care workers, social workers, and elders	Home-school conflict Overly strong advocacy for children Fear and mistrust of school Partisan views Disengaged parents	Shared responsibility for the achievement of individual young people Productive partnerships among home, school, and community Holistic care for children and families

Union representative	Protecting educators' working conditions is the primary focus	Opportunities for professional growth in assessment knowledge	Inappropriate advocacy for one role in society	Provision of time for professional growth
	Overemphasis on professional knowledge about assessment		Resistance to educator accountability	Maintain standards of work environments
				Protect from exploitive working conditions
				Articulate workers' perspectives about assessment to employers and community
Professional association representative	Primary loyalty is to the profession and not individual educators	Negotiating the interests of the profession and those of learners, educators, and larger community	Need to garner respect for classroom assessment practices	Increased credibility of the teaching profession
			Misperceptions of the teaching profession	Heightened professionalism among educators
				Holding individual educators accountable for their professional judgments about children

(continued)

Table 1.2 (continued)

Role in a civil society	Unidimensional perspectives	Multidimensional perspectives	Tensions	Opportunities
Department of Education personnel	Focus is on the educational system and its assessment policies and procedures	Integration of varying stakeholder perspectives related to assessment policies and procedures	Assessment focus is too closely aligned with accountability	Coherence across curriculum, teaching, learning, and assessment
			Accountable to political leaders for administering assessment policies that may be unpopular or questionable	Consistency of assessment practices across schools and districts
			Motives are questioned	Common standards for learning and assessment
			Perceived as too removed from the classroom	Comparability of students, schools, and systems
				Public accountability for educational system
Academic researcher/practitioner	Primary focus on assessment knowledge acquisition and dissemination	Collaborate and create partnerships among stakeholders	Knowledge for knowledge sake rather than social justice	Informed professional practice
			Self-promotion	Evidence-based decision making
			Paradigmatic tension between perceived merits of qualitative versus quantitative data	Increased professionalism among educators
				Development of educators with increased professional capacity in assessment

Informal community leader	Informal advocate for particular cultural or interest groups in relation to assessment practices	Recognition of the range of appropriate assessment practices	Exclusive advocacy for personal demographic group	Community cohesion
		Willingness to negotiate culturally-sensitive assessment	Conflict among stakeholders	Interest group collaboration
				Promotion of tolerance and inclusion in assessment
				Common social identity
				Culturally-appropriate assessment
Local politician	Quality of schooling for local electorate is the primary objective	Representation of the assessment interests of the entire electorate	Conflicting issues	Community cohesion
			Competing interests	Use of assessment data to create common allegiance to community, schools, educators, and students
			Questioning of motives, leading to overly personalised interactions	Strong sense of place based upon a common understanding of assessment data

(continued)

Table 1.2 (continued)

Role in a civil society	Unidimensional perspectives	Multidimensional perspectives	Tensions	Opportunities
Provincial or territorial politician	System rather than individual student focus is paramount	Cross-role understanding of assessment influences	Balancing individual, professional, and provincial/state perspectives	Evidence-based decision making
		Leadership and facilitation of cross-role dialogue about assessment policies	Partisan conflicts	Development of a high quality education system
			Budgetary concerns vis-à-vis assessment programs	Highly functioning professional educators
			Inappropriate cross-cultural borrowing of assessment policies and terminology	Constructive relationships among stakeholders
				Tolerance of variable stakeholder perspectives related to assessment
National politician	National assessment concerns restricted to their country	Assessment data must facilitate national and international comparisons	Unreasonable emphasis on international rankings	Sharing of assessment information among nations
		National assessment data support international competitiveness and reports on the educational quality of individual nations	Unreasonable expectations for educational system	National and international improvements
			Partisan conflicts	Evidence-based policy development
			Inappropriate cross-cultural borrowing of assessment policies and terminology	

strive to shape educational assessment include informal community leaders. When informal community leaders demonstrate a unidimensional perspective they may advocate for their particular cultural or interest group to the exclusion of counterparts or the school as a whole. Finally, another individualistic role is that of the academic researcher whose primary focus may tend to be on knowledge acquisition and dissemination with insufficient consideration of stakeholder collaboration and field-based practice.

The preceding paragraph focuses on individual behaviours but unidimensional perspectives can be exhibited by stakeholder groups such as unions, professional associations, and department of education personnel. Unions, by their very nature, are established to protect their members' working conditions and remuneration packages. These are laudable and necessary functions. However, when the focus on protection of workers' interests is at the expense of other stakeholder groups then a more balanced stance is required. Unions also may perceive the assessment knowledge of their members as something that must be protected and exclusive to the profession. The perception is that all worthwhile knowledge about assessment is held in the school and that outside dialogue and/or external professional expertise is intrusive. The professional association's loyalty is to the profession in general and not necessarily to individual educators. The result may be that the nuances of context may be lost. A similar organisational perspective may be demonstrated by department of education personnel when they implement assessment policies and procedures in a top-down, bureaucratic approach.

At the macro level, a civil society is dependent upon the governance and oversight of its elected representatives. These include local politicians, such as school board members and municipal councillors or aldermen, who are responsible for the quality of schools and educational infrastructure. Politicians at this level may, and in fact should, appreciate the responsibilities of more senior levels of government. However, their duties and interests are primarily at the local level. At the provincial and territorial political levels, elected representatives have educational systems, rather than individual students, paramount in educational decision making. At the national level, unidimensional perspectives would be demonstrated by national assessment concerns restricted to their nation's interests alone. While none of these political stances are necessarily inappropriate, it is possible for elected officials to manifest a singular focus that fails to recognise sufficiently the needs and interests of all citizens.

1.10 Multidimensional Perspectives

The framework presented in Table 1.2 makes it explicit that a multidimensional perspective of educational assessment offers greater potential for individual and social good. It facilitates broader and more inclusive orientations that promote tolerance and support for the educational aspirations of all stakeholders. Educators operating within the multidimensional domain acknowledge and value the information that other stakeholders have about students, including parents, psychologists, doctors, physiotherapists, police, social workers, elders, and community liaison officers. Educational leaders who hold a multidimensional perspective include other stakeholders in the decision-making processes and can use and share data effectively. Within this perspective, parents understand and respect the multiple role allegiances of educators, health care workers, social workers, and community elders and leaders. Similarly, informal community leaders recognise a range of appropriate assessment practices and demonstrate a willingness to negotiate culturally-sensitive assessment. Academic researchers use their knowledge to promote collaboration and to support partnerships among stakeholders for the benefit of the larger educational community.

Unions that demonstrate a multidimensional perspective value opportunities for their members to access professional development programs relating to assessment. This viewpoint recognises that increasing the quality of assessment knowledge and expertise is a professional obligation and is a correlate to accountability. This benefits all members of the educational community, including the union membership as it garners greater respect and credibility within society. Similarly, professional associations with this broader stance negotiate the assessment interests of the profession and those of learners, educators, and the larger community. Department of education personnel, who exhibit a multidimensional approach to educational assessment, integrate widely varying perspectives into a coherent portfolio of policies, procedures, and resources.

Moving again to the governance level, politicians at all levels—local, provincial, and national—increase the responsiveness of assessment policies to community and societal needs. They demonstrate cross-role understandings of assessment influences and facilitate dialogue across stakeholder groups related to assessment policies. At the national level, useful assessment data supports national and international comparisons designed to increase the international competitiveness of educational systems.

1.11   Tensions and Opportunities

Educational assessment is rife with tensions but it also presents opportunities to enhance the quality of the educational experience for all concerned. Attending only to tensions represents a unidimensional approach to assessment while adopting a multidimensional orientation opens opportunities for individual and system enhancement. For example, perceiving assessment, particularly external assessment, as a challenge to educators' professional judgment, credibility, and autonomy is a major tension throughout the Western world. This denies the capacity for richer decision making, enhanced learning for young people, and opportunities for greater professional credibility. Unidimensional leaders frequently experience tensions related to teachers' resistance to decision making based on assessment data and, in response, the leaders may resort to autocratic styles of leadership. When this occurs, insensitive and ineffective communication is likely, resulting in power struggles and lost opportunities for personal and professional growth. On the other hand, leaders with multidimensional perspectives are prepared to distribute the leadership load among capable educators, thereby engendering increased community support, plus enhanced loyalty and trust. Transparent assessment and decision making processes promote increased understandings about assessment and its purposes. Leaders utilising a multidimensional approach are able to work effectively with parents with a tendency to be overly strong advocates for their children, causing disruption to home-school harmony due to partisan views. Leaders may also encounter disengaged parents or those who fear or mistrust educators and school systems. If such unidimensional parents can be encouraged by leaders to adopt a more multidimensional perspective, then there is the possibility of sharing responsibility for the achievement of students, more holistic care for children and families, and more productive partnerships among home, school, and community. In the same way, informal community leaders can be motivated to collaborate with the school and, in this way, contribute to tolerance and the sustenance of a common social identity with the school and the community it serves. Very important, these external partnerships can result in culturally-appropriate assessment. The contributions of academic researchers ideally should lead to more informed professional practice rather than knowledge for knowledge sake alone or personal self-promotion. The acknowledgement by academic researchers of the merits of both qualitative and quantitative data can overcome paradigmatic tensions. These data can provide foundations for evidence-based decision making and heightened levels of professionalism among educators.

Unions throughout the Western world tend to be united in their opposition to some forms of assessment, particularly external assessments which are interpreted by unions as forms of imposed accountability. It can be argued union resistance to external assessment demonstrates a lack of understanding of the role of standardised tests in meeting the information needed at macro levels of a civil society. Unions are unidimensional almost by definition in that they are formed to advocate for educators' rights to reasonable working conditions and accountability frameworks. However, it is possible for union personnel to protect educational workers from exploitive working conditions while also using assessment and accountability frameworks to negotiate time for professional growth and to voice educators' perspectives about assessment to employers and community members. Somewhat different from the profile of unions, professional associations tend to focus on societal respect for the profession as a whole and to hold individual educators accountable for their practices in schools and systems. Done well, this leads to increased assessment consistency in classrooms and greater credibility of the teaching profession generally. The unfortunate dominance of perceptions among educators of assessment-as-accountability too often demonises the personnel from departments of education who are responsible for implementing and disseminating assessment policies. Their motives are questioned by unions for example, and they may be portrayed as too removed from the classroom to have realistic and educationally valid perspectives. However, within the context of civil societies, departments of education serve the purpose of facilitating coherence and consistency across curriculum, teaching, learning, and assessment. They translate societal expectations into pragmatic common standards for learning and assessment that provide comparability and accountability for schools and systems. This fulfils the responsibilities departments of education have to their political masters within civil societies.

Politicians at local, provincial, and national levels share the responsibility of facilitating community cohesion and tolerance of varying community perspectives about educational assessment. They are constrained by the need to provide sufficient funding across a range of educational programs. Politicians' knowledge base about assessment may be dependent upon the advice provided to them by bureaucrats but they are informed by the educational expectations of their constituents. By their very nature, political systems are open to partisan conflicts but within functioning democracies politicians are able to acknowledge varying beliefs while creating high quality education systems serving the interests of all members of society. In an era of globalisation, politicians may borrow policies that are perceived to be working well in other cultures. Even though it is important for policy makers to keep informed about policy development and implementation in other nations, it is important that assessment policies are not borrowed indiscriminately from other cultural and political contexts. In the end, politicians at all levels of a civil society are charged with ensuring national and international competitiveness in the quality of their educational system and nurturing the professionalism of their educators.

1.12   Leading Assessment in a Civil Society

The role of educational leaders in a civil society is complex and difficult. However, societal leaders "should have a role in ensuring that accountability frameworks and support structures are properly focused on the present and future needs of the world, with the range of stakeholders holding proportionate control" (Davies, 2006, p. 53). In addition, leaders are expected to foster professional growth of teachers who possess varying levels of assessment expertise and diversity of professional judgment (Bolt, 2011). At the same time, leaders are required to monitor and evaluate the assessment practices of teachers who are concurrently professionals and public servants. These dual leadership responsibilities need not be conflicting, but in some situations they do become oppositional due to the mistaken perception that professionalism equates to complete autonomy. Such a lens disregards the legal obligations of educators accredited as professionals within a thriving civil society. Understanding the legal and moral implications of being a professional educator can be uncomfortable and potentially fraught with conflict, as noted by Beets (2012) who highlighted the importance of asking if "the assessment practices of teachers are morally appropriate" (p. 69).

The following vignette illustrates the discomfort but also the opportunities that can emerge from a leader who refused to accept a less than ideal status quo. This is a story of exceptional leadership within a senior high school in the province of

Alberta. The story was told not by the leader but by one of the grade 12 English teachers in the school, an individual who had 20 years of teaching experience at the time of the interview. The account was framed in a discussion of assessment and the professional development processes within the school designed to support enhanced teacher assessment practices.

> Assessment has changed dramatically for me over the past five years, primarily because of what's gone on in this school. Five years ago I had an English class where marks were 10 % lower than the provincial average. In [a previous province there were] no departmental exams, no formalised feedback [about] how students were doing compared to others. At that time I thought I was leaving the land of authentic assessment [and coming] to the land of standardised testing.

The principal encouraged the teacher to compare the grades she had assigned students, with those that they achieved on the grade 12 provincial standardised exit examination.

> My class marks were not reflective of [students'] true ability as measured by diplomas (standardised grade 12 exit examinations). I looked in the mirror and said, "What's going on here?" There was no reason that my students were 10 % lower than anyone else. Kids are who they are no matter where they are. It's the adults in the building who determine the success of learning, the students, and the school. I knew those kids knew the information but what I was reporting wasn't accurate.
> What made the difference is that [a new principal] came to our school. I'm indebted to him. You can hear the emotion in my voice. He had a vision and it was that learning is the focus, not teaching. It's about improved student learning. We've clarified that vision to – all students will learn at high levels. [He's made the difference in] two years so there was a high degree of urgency.

She went on to state that the principal described learning in the following way…

> [He spoke figuratively stating] "We should not step over dead bodies. We don't ignore a student lying in the hall with a heart attack so we can't ignore students dying [academically] in our classrooms. Every kid in our classroom belongs to someone. I don't want anyone stepping over my kid".

She reflected on his words…

> It didn't click but he's not going away nor are the four questions [that he keeps asking us].
>
> 1) What do you want them to learn?
> 2) How do you know when they've learned it?
> 3) How do you know if they don't?
> 4) What will you do after they've learned it?
>
> I scrawled the four questions down and put them on my computer monitor and it's been there ever since, in my face.
> Before [this principal] I'd had about 20 administrators. He's the first one who made it about learning and gave us the tools to make it happen. Prior to him it was about generating numbers, needing to improve performance by 2 %. How do I deal with that? Then [the principal] came along and he focused on the learning.

What did this principal do that influenced you and your colleagues?

> No other principal set the stage for current best practice to play a role. No other principal asked me to be better. They walked by my room and thought, "That's [teacher's name], kids like her class, she's getting good results" and they left me alone. He [the new principal]

hasn't left anyone alone. I was working hard to be a good teacher, and I was, but I didn't know why things were working or why things could be better.

The principal linked professionalism to teacher professional growth plans and accountability.

> Administrators put out a lot of energy that is sucked up by the mediocre teacher. As [our principal said], put your energy into the superstar. Check with your superstar and see if the idea is a good one. If you can't get the superstar to do something then how can you get others to participate?
>
> You can't argue with student learning [as a rationale for teacher professional growth]. If someone wants to argue with that then that's an admin job.
>
> There were a few templates for individual professional growth plans floating around. He [the principal] designed a very deliberate template. Previously, people would hand in a paragraph on a napkin and call that a professional growth plan. Now we complete a set form and meet three times a year with the principal.
>
> Personal and professional growth plans are different. Professional growth is being current in your practice and influencing student learning. We have to do those reflections.

The principal established expectations for embedded professional development.

> We had curricular conversations about assessment, cross-curricular conversations. It removed the subject matter and focused on assessment and learner outcomes. [The principal] knows that leadership isn't built on compliance. It's on commitment. Leadership is a choice, not a position. As learning coaches, we have the opportunity to direct conversations in this building toward learning. It is not coming from top-down administration but from four learning coaches in the building.
>
> All English teachers have common preparation time. In my 20 years of teaching I've never had such rich, DAILY conversations about learning outcomes and assessment strategies.
>
> In that first year, since his arrival, we did basic current best practice, graphic organisers, brain-based learning, gender differences, and technology. My entry point to all of this was the brain-based learning. I went to [several local and international professional development sessions].
>
> Then came the 'Aha!' moments. That's why the success. I had it coming from that. The teacher professional growth plan's focus was brain-based learning. There were huge significant results in learning. Students said "I learned. You got into my head. I don't know how you did it."
>
> My entry point is through instruction. Then I'm able to affect change in learning.
>
> Now that I'm continuing to perfect my craft, that's what the assessment journey is with formative assessment coming to the forefront.
>
> The Alberta Initiative for School Improvement is the 'King of the World' for letting me see the world. It's been an awesome ride. I love what I do.
>
> We have a long way to go. We are not ready for [the principal] to go. He's pissed people off along the way. He's sarcastic and that can turn people off. But sarcasm and ridicule can bring about change. He addressed little things that could be avoided but turn into big stupid issues. He's tenacious with his commitment to do what is right for kids. He will not step over a dead body. It's about kids stepping up to the plate. Some teachers didn't know where their curriculum guide/programme of studies was. Some of the younger teachers now say, "This is what we do here," but they worry [about the differences in assessment practices] if they go to another school. But I tell them to stay and live in the rain forest. It's lush here.

The teacher described how her practice changed.

Initially the most significant component was incomplete assignments and zeroes. I was getting roughly a 75 % assignment completion compared to 98 % now. It was a lot of hard
work. What I did was adopt the bottom line that opting out is not an option. Now students have to work hard to get a zero.

One strategy that was introduced to address incomplete school work was a common study
hall from Monday to Thursday from 11:15 to 12 o'clock. This is a random group of kids
in a common grade with a focus on the learning. It can be homework completion. It's
about learning. Kids start working together without banging on the math teachers'
doors. There is now a heightened cross-curricular awareness of what kids are doing.

That was a painful part in our journey, people grappling with second chances, alternatives
to zeroes… it still goes on but not as much. There are lone individuals in departments
who are still doing that.

My assignments originally asked students to complete busy work and sometimes they were
assignments that were not aligned to curricular outcomes. Late marks were deducted so
at some point students thought, "What's the point in handing it in?"

At that time, I had [merged] behaviour and attendance components and so now assignments
are aligned with curricular outcomes and now I love the students in the lower level
English classes. They knew what being nickeled and dimed is and now they know
what's authentic. I ask them things that are going to hit a number of curricular targets in
one fell swoop. .... My mark sheet is focused on curricular outcomes, not on attendance
or behaviour components. I still offer non-graded components indicating when dead-
lines were met such as when they put it in their portfolios. There is a reflection on non-
graded elements but they are not being penalised for [things like late assignments]. … I
read a piece and offer formative feedback, to get a sense of it being appropriate, satisfac-
tory, or not. It's about the learning … A number doesn't have to be attached to everything to mean something.

I walked into a lower track grade 12 English classroom where there was a young man
expressing dismay and annoyance with his assignment. He did a first draft. I highlighted
in orange to indicate that, if you're going to change it, here's a hot spot or a confusing
idea. Good work was highlighted in green. When I give the first draft back there is a lot
of formative feedback. Orange areas lead to conversations with kids and/or teachers …
The young man didn't want to revise and resubmit. Kids were defending what we were
doing. However, one young lady said, "Look at how much I've learned." That normally
doesn't happen, but it did! So I knew I was on the right track. You see the growth in that
level of class where there is a bigger gap. The more academically oriented kids will do
well whether I'm there or not. They will learn in spite of us. With the lower level classes
you have to go in the back door.

How sustainable is the teacher learning that's occurred?

We have a lot of things to do. We're not ready for [the principal] to go yet. When he goes …
we have to get to a place where the new guy [principal] has to honour the culture that
has been established. If that's not possible then we need to scream bloody murder.

Each person is in their own place. My entry point is instructional strategy. Some teachers
are on journey but pulled into a parking lot.

It was [the principal's] leadership that made the difference. Everyone else let me be and he
didn't let me be. There was nothing wrong with what I was doing but it became better.
As teachers we have to look in the mirror. It's about the kids.

The scenario above, gathered as part of the Alberta Student Assessment Study
(Webber et al., 2009), illustrates several key leadership lessons. First, educational
leaders must operate with a clear conceptual framework for their professional practice. Part of the framework is an understanding that the culture of sound assessment
is fragile and needs to be nurtured. Another central component of the framework is

the basic fact that good assessment cannot exist in the absence of compelling leadership. Further, if leaders are to promote good assessment practices then they must know what these are and how to nurture them.

Second, leadership is value laden. Leading assessment requires an overt focus on all learners within a school community, both students and adults. The focus also includes articulating a vision for student learning, understanding the impact of assessment on students, and separating the assessment of learning from student behaviour. Another value is the relentless seeking of academic excellence and the refusal to accept an unsatisfactory status quo and mediocrity. Seeking excellence includes embracing the principle that good teachers can be better. In addition, excellence means having the courage and tenacity to challenge longstanding practices that simply are pedagogically unsound.

A third lesson for educational leaders is that they must possess a portfolio of strategies for establishing sound teaching, learning, and assessment practices. The predominant strategy is to establish sound contextually-relevant professional development. This means using assessment data to create and embrace the cognitive dissonance needed to promote individual and collective readiness to engage with change. Another strategy is the promotion of both discipline-alike and cross-disciplinary dialogue and reflection. A straightforward strategy for facilitating professional development is to design school timetables that include common preparation time for teachers of the same subject or grade. It also means nothing short of insistence on professional growth that is followed up with a structured process for monitoring and evaluating teacher performance.

This vignette demonstrates the role that leaders and classroom teachers can play in the ongoing development of an educational system supporting a thriving civil society. It highlights the importance of supporting student learning and the role good assessment practices play in that process.

1.13 The Way Forward

Strong public education is essential in the creation of a thriving, democratic, civil society. Quality student assessment policies and practices constitute a significant factor in the construction of a strong education system. Assessment data is essential for evidence-based decision making within the classroom and larger educational system, and at policy-making governance levels. Assessment must be responsive to the diversity within society and demonstrate educational monitoring that respects differences in ability, culture, language, religion, and gender. Similarly, the indiscriminate borrowing of assessment policies and terminology from different cultures and contexts can be problematic and potentially damaging. Therefore, cross-cultural policy borrowing should occur only in conjunction with careful critical analyses of intended and unintended consequences.

Democracy and the realisation of a civil society are fragile and so too is the maintenance of a quality education system. Therefore, stakeholders must avoid the vili-

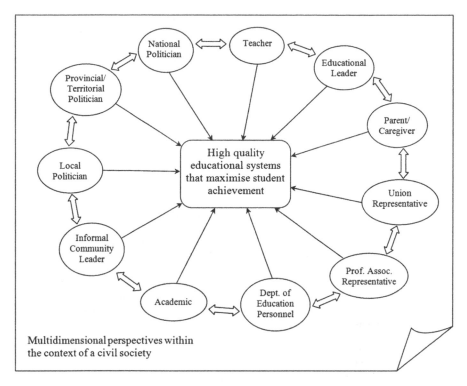

Multidimensional perspectives within the context of a civil society

Fig. 2.1 Multidimensional interactions in the interest of a civil society

fication of others with the view to preserving the fragile balance among competing interests. The media play a role in the maintenance of the freedoms inherent in a civil society but they also must assume liability for responsible reporting of assessment data to ensure they do their part in the dissemination of information in the interest of the public good. Assessment is a highly politicised issue and will remain so.

However, if a civil society is to be maintained then educational partners must endeavour to build trusting relationships, to work together, and to acknowledge the expertise that other stakeholders hold (See Fig. 2.1). That is, a tenet of a democratic civil society is the preservation of respectful, open dialogue among divergent voices with the aim of producing a better educational system for all young people.

References

Aitken, N., Webber, C. F., Lupart, J. L., & Scott, S. (2011). Assessment in Alberta: Six areas of concern. *Educational Forum, 75*(3), 192–209. doi:10.1080/00131725.2011.576803.

Alberta Education. (2008). *General information bulletin: Introduction to the achievement testing program 2008*. Retrieved from http://education.alberta.ca/media/946688/02-achgib-2008-09_%20introduction%20&%20revisions.pdf

Beets, P. A. D. (2012). Strengthening morality and ethics in educational assessment through "Ubuntu" in South Africa. *Educational Philosophy and Theory, 44*(2), 68–83. doi:10.1111/j.1469-5812.2011.00796.x.

Bolt, S. (2011). Making consistent judgements. A professional development program based on using teacher judgement to assess student attainment of systemic achievement targets. *Educational Forum, 75*(2), 157–172. doi:10.1080/00131725.2011.552694.

Boudett, K., City, E., & Murnane, R. (Eds.). (2005). *Data wise: A step by step guide to using assessment results to improve teaching and learning.* Cambridge, MA: Harvard Education Press.

Cowie, B., Jones, A., & Otrel-Cass, K. (2011). Re-engaging students in science: Issues of assessment, funds of knowledge and sites for learning. *International Journal of Science and Mathematics Education, 9,* 347–366.

Danylewcyz, M., & Prentice, A. (1986). Teachers' work: Changing patterns and perceptions in the emerging school systems of nineteenth- and early twentieth century Canada. *Labour/Le Travail, 17,* 58–80.

Davies, T. (2006). Creative teaching and learning in Europe: Promoting a new paradigm. *Curriculum Journal, 17*(1), 37–57. doi:10.1080/09585170600682574.

Delaney, A. M. (2009). Institutional researchers' expanding roles: Policy, planning, program evaluation, assessment and new research methodologies. *New Directions for Institutional Research, 143,* 29–41. doi:10.1002/ir.303.

Earl, L. M., & Katz, S. (2006). *Rethinking classroom assessment with purpose in mind: Assessment for learning, assessment as learning, assessment of learning.* Crown in Right of Manitoba, Minister of Education, Citizenship and Youth. Manitoba Education, Citizenship and Youth, School Programs Division. Retrieved from http://www.edu.gov.mb.ca/k12/assess/wncp/rethinking_assess_mb.pdf

Elmore, R. F. (2005). *School reform from the inside out: Policy, practice and performance.* Cambridge, MA: Harvard Education Press.

Fukuyama, F. (2001). Social capital, civil society and development. *Third World Quarterly, 22*(1), 7–20. doi:10.1080/01436590020022547.

Halstead, J. M. (2007). In place of a conclusion: The common school and the melting pot. *Journal of Philosophy of Education, 41*(4), 829–842.

Heldsinger, S. (2012). Using a measurement paradigm to guide classroom assessment processes. In C. F. Webber & J. L. Lupart (Eds.), *Leading student assessment* (pp. 241–262). Dordrecht, The Netherlands: Springer.

Inbar-Lourie, O., & Donitsa-Schmidt, S. (2009). Exploring classroom assessment practices: The case of teachers of English as a foreign language. *Assessment in Education: Principles, Policy, & Practice, 16*(2), 185–204. doi:10.1080/09695940903075958.

Inter-Agency Commission. (1990). *Meeting basic learning needs: A vision for the 1990s.* New York: UNICEF House. Retrieved from http://unesdoc.unesco.org/images/0009/000975/097552e.pdf

Kligman, G. (1990). Reclaiming the public: A reflection on creating civil society in Romania. *East European Politics and Societies, 4,* 393–438. doi:10.1177/0888325490004003002.

Laguardia, A., & Pearl, A. (2009). Necessary educational reform for the 21st century: The future of public schools in our democracy. *Urban Review, 41*(4), 352–368.

Lewthwaite, B., & Renaud, R. (2009). Pilimmaksarniq: Working together for the common good in science curriculum development and delivery in Nunavut. *Canadian Journal of Science, Mathematics, and Technology Education, 9*(3), 154–172. doi:10.1080/14926150903118334.

Lund, D. (2003). Facing the challenges: Student antiracist activists counter backlash and stereotyping. *Teaching Education, 14*(3), 265–278. doi:10.1080/1047621032000135177.

Macfarlane, E. (2008). Terms of entitlement: Is there a distinctly Canadian "rights talk"? *Canadian Journal of Political Science, 41*(2), 303–328. doi:10.1017/S0008423908080451.

Nixon, V. (2006). Egerton Ryerson and the old master copy as an instrument of public education. *Journal of Canadian Art History, 27,* 94–113.

Pearce, C. D. (1988). Egerton Ryerson's Canadian liberalism. *Canadian Journal of Political Science, 21*(4), 771–793.

Pettit, J. L. (1997). *"To Christianize and civilize": Native industrial schools in Canada.* Unpublished doctoral dissertation, University of Calgary, Calgary, AB, Canada.

Popham, W. J. (2008). *Transformative assessment.* Alexandria, VA: Association for Supervision and Curriculum Development.

Reeves, D. (2002). *The daily disciplines of leadership: How to improve student achievement, staff motivation, and personal organization.* San Francisco: Jossey-Bass.

Rogers, W. T. (1991). Educational assessment in Canada: Evolution or extinction? *The Alberta Journal of Educational Research, 37*(2), 179–192.

Shaker, P., & Grimmett, P. (2004). Public schools as public good: A question of values. *Education Canada, 44*(3), 29–31.

Shamah, H. D., & MacTavish, K. (2009). Rural research brief: Making room for place-based knowledge in rural classrooms. *The Rural Educator, 30*(2), 1–4.

Tupa, M., & McFadden, L. (2009). District, know thyself. *Phi Delta Kappan, 90*(8), 563–566.

UNESCO. (1997). *Learning: The treasure within. UNESCO report for education for the 21st century.* Berlin, Germany: German UNESCO Commission.

Webber, C. F., Aitken, N., Lupart, J. L., & Scott, S. (2009). *The Alberta student assessment study: Final report.* Edmonton, AB, Canada: Government of Alberta.

Webber, C. F., Lupart, J. L., & Scott, S. (2012). The ecology of student assessment. In C. F. Webber & J. L. Lupart (Eds.), *Leading student assessment* (pp. 283–296). Dordrecht: Springer.

Wolf, M. K., & Leon, S. (2009). An investigation of the language demands in content assessments for English language learners. *Educational Assessment, 14*(3–4), 139–159. doi:10.1080/10627190903425883.

Wyatt-Smith, C., Klenowski, V., & Gunn, S. (2010). The centrality of teachers' judgement practice in assessment: A study of standards in moderation. *Assessment in Education: Principles, Policy & Practice, 17*(1), 59–75. doi:10.1080/09695940903565610.

Zamudio, M., Rios, F., & Jaime, A. M. (2008). Thinking critically about difference: Analytical tools for the 21st century. *Equity and Excellence in Education, 41*(2), 215–229. doi:10.1080/10665680801957378.

Chapter 2
Assessment as a Dimension of Globalisation: Exploring International Insights

Donald E. Scott

Abstract This chapter explores assessment as a dimension of globalisation, particularly linking themes of the knowledge economy, impacts of technologies, and international-national competitiveness. An inductive analysis was undertaken to explore international themes of assessment examining similarities and differences across nations. The themes to emerge involved the impact of globalisation in terms of the inter-relatedness of national economies, which has elevated the importance of transparency for accountability and national competitiveness. Additionally, the pursuit of quality education is discussed particularly in relation to standardised testing, classroom assessment practices, and teacher professionalism. Debates and controversies encompassed: the purposes of assessment, high stakes testing, what is valued is assessed, cultural sensitivity, teachers philosophical orientations, and societal trust and teacher accountability. Socio-cultural aspects were identified in terms of student diversity. The media also emerged as influencing the debates about assessment and public support for education.

Keywords Globalisation • National competitiveness • Standardised tests • Teacher accountability • System accountability • Professionalism • Politicisation of assessment • Moderation • Professional development • Teacher judgement • Socio-cultural diversity • Purposes of assessment • Media influences • Cultural sensitivity • Beliefs, ethics and relationships • Assessment debates

2.1 Introduction

During the reading and editing of this text I became fascinated with the similarities and differences that were evident in themes surrounding assessment, which led me to ponder whether or not these were universal. As this book was designed for an international audience I decided to undertake an inductive approach to exploring a

D.E. Scott (✉)
Werklund School of Education, University of Calgary, Calgary, AB, Canada
e-mail: descott@ucalgary.ca

© Springer International Publishing Switzerland 2016
S. Scott et al. (eds.), *Assessment in Education*, The Enabling
Power of Assessment 2, DOI 10.1007/978-3-319-23398-7_2

sample of assessment related papers from different countries to gain insights about aspects of possible alignment and interesting differences.

Not surprisingly, globalisation appears to have had a significant impact across many aspects of education, and assessment and evaluation have not escaped this trend. The term 'globalisation' frequently denotes the linked nature of the world and this has been borne out through the inter-relatedness of national economies wherein the failure of one nation's economy affects others. Similarly, these globalised linkages across various nations place many in positions of competition, sometimes fighting for supremacy within very small margins. Competition usually filters directly down to education systems wherein quality of outcomes, teaching, and leadership are main accountability indicators, highlighting the importance of assessment and evaluation data in monitoring and reporting on 'quality', and making decisions that will positively influence national education systems, and in turn, national economies.

Another feature of globalisation which has emerged is the movement of workers and displaced or disenfranchised peoples seeking better lives in more stable countries. This transience has resulted in greater diversity in schools including: racial, ethnic, linguistic, intellectual, physical, and religious diversity. Diversity represents greater complexity for educators in supporting the learning of all and devising appropriate assessments to support learning and ascertain student outcomes.

With globalisation the culture of accountability has emerged: accountability of the politicians and economists to ensure the security and stability of optimal lifestyles for their citizens, accountability of leaders for institutional outcomes, filtering down to accountability of educators to ensure students reach their potential becoming engaged and productive citizens. Hence, within this atmosphere of accountability, or at least the perceptions of responsibility, educators must create and use assessment data to make informed decisions and guide pedagogical approaches.

Linked to the conceptions of accountability and responsibility is that of professionalism. Educators are expected to maintain and enhance their professional knowledge and capacities and yet when they demonstrate a lack of understanding, misuse data, practice unfair or inequitable approaches, or are unable or unwilling to innovate their assessment approaches this creates a loss of societal confidence in educators' professionalism. Hence, educators have an inherent responsibility to remain abreast of, and engaged with, trends and innovations in assessment thus ensuring their competence to engage in informed debates. This highlights the pivotal importance of educator preparation and ongoing professional development.

An emergent theme is the influence and uses of the media. We know that a key dimension of globalisation has been the virulent influence of technology which has impacted educational systems in multitudinous ways. For example, educators use technology for teaching, learning, administration, communication, collaboration, and research. Technology-facilitated media can be a powerful influence on societal and governmental perceptions, particularly when they use assessment data to create awareness, useful debate, or controversy, and with current sophisticated technological forums, the media's influence is almost limitless.

The aforementioned themes have emerged from the literature across different national contexts and they serve as the foundational themes for this chapter which examines assessment as it pertains to various dimensions of globalisation.

2.2 Evidence-Based Approach

This chapter presents an inductive analysis of a selection of research studies reporting on 'assessment' in its many and varied forms across different nations. Once a wide range of sources had been collated an inductive activity was conducted whereby key points from each paper (representing an assessment/evaluation issue from a particular country) were selected and clustered according to similar themes, while noting significant differences between various cultural contexts. Each paper was colour coded to enable the tracking of country and individual study. The themes that emerged served as the framework for the chapter and enabled deeper discussion and exploration of the nuances of difference across national settings. A distinct limitation of this approach was that not all papers on assessment from each country were selected although an effort was made to see if the assessment issue was relatively prevalent or representative, that is, were many authors writing about the same or similar issues.

2.3 Impact of Globalisation

In this inductive analysis the conceptualisation of globalisation came to the fore. Globalisation is a ubiquitous term that appears to be used in many different fields to explain any manner of issue or contention. Hence, it was important to identify what globalisation is and how it may be influencing nations, education systems, and ultimately assessment in its many forms.

Rajagopal (2009) described globalisation as "the combined influences of trade liberalization, market integration, international finance and investment, technological change, the increasing distribution of production across national boundaries and the emergence of new structures global governance (sic)" (pp. 1–2). He also noted the significant impact of technology in driving change: "by accelerating communication, transport and travel, drives the world toward a converging commonality" (p. 1); while Winter (2011) identified technology as influencing the "knowledge economy" (p. 298). Clearly technology means greater and easier access to information which equates to power, particularly when information can be harnessed to drive innovation thereby gaining advantage within this global consumer society.

Toakley (2004) explored globalisation in terms of the intersection between international economics, sustainability, political influences, environmental impacts, technologies, and the role of universities within a knowledge economy. From his extensive discussion of globalisation I extracted the key elements of: technology, linked international economies and marketisation, migration, and the knowledge economy to illustrate how the world has changed from the Industrial Revolution to the present. Although there are many other factors linked with globalisation, such as sustainability and environmental issues, these are not within the scope of this chapter.

> Globalization is a natural outcome of the sustained technological and economic growth, which originated with the Industrial Revolution in Britain during the 18th Century. This path to continuing economic growth spread initially to continental Europe and North America, and brought with it the creation of large towns and substantial social change. (p. 311) ... At the beginning of the 21st century, virtually all of the command economies have collapsed and capitalism is in its ascendancy .... Globalization ... has involved the expansion of markets from local, national and regional to an international context. (p. 314) ... there has been another transition where a substantial section of the workforce is involved in processing information [now encapsulated within 'the knowledge economy']. (p. 315) ... Migration from developing countries (whether legal or illegal) will not solve [developing nations'] problems of overpopulation, and it also results in the loss of valuable skilled labour. However, it can contribute to solving the skilled and unskilled labour problems of developed countries with declining and aging populations. As can be seen from recent events in Europe, the migration of substantial numbers of people can be a source of cultural tension, and in the case of United States the ingress of large numbers of migrants from Mexico has depressed unskilled labour wage levels (p. 316). (Toakley, 2004, pp. 311–316)

Not all scholars are proponents of globalisation as some countries fear the pace of change and are struggling to compete with their larger, wealthier, and more powerful counterparts, while some nations are disturbed with the contentions that arise due to migration of populations, and yet others are worried about the imposition of:

> a deadening cultural uniformity ... that local cultures and national identities are dissolving into a cross-regional consumerism. That cultural imperialism is said to impose American values as well as products, promote the commercial at the expense of the authentic, and substitute shallow gratification for deeper satisfaction. (Rajagopal, 2009, p. 4)

Similarly, technology is creating dramatic change with "new hybrid cultures" (Rajagopal, 2009, p. 5) emerging, the English language arising as the predominant information medium, and cross-border collaborations and recreation purposes (socialising and gaming activities) now possible. However, technology can also produce national security threats, youth subcultures which conflict with previous generational mores, and demand for greater literacy in English potentially depreciating the value of native lingualism.

The aspect of globalisation that was directly relevant to education systems was the implication from the knowledge economy which translates into national competitiveness frequently manifested in national testing that governments use to monitor educational quality. Emerging from the inductive analysis was the theme of national competitiveness arising from the inter-relatedness of global economies' encompassing international comparisons, and the politicisation of assessment and the movement towards greater system accountability. Associated with the politically-charged aspects were societal debates related to teacher accountability and educator professionalism underlining the importance of effective preservice preparation and subsequent ongoing professional development. Concomitant with the migration of peoples were the themes of socio-cultural diversity and the influence of the media. These various themes within the frame of globalisation are explored in the subsequent sections.

2.4   Global Economies – International Competitiveness

As Toakley (2004) described, nations now compete on the global economic stage, where many are not equal players. Rajagopal (2009) stated, "Open trade, competitiveness and emergence of global markets for standardized consumer products are the new commercial reality which has driven the developing nations with a high magnitude of change in the economy and consumer culture" (p. 1). As a result, government leaders seek to improve their country's position in this globalised market and education is frequently perceived to be a significant factor in manoeuvring their workforce and industries into more competitive positions. With education systems factoring into governmental conversations about quality and 'skilled' workers, it is hardly surprising that national testing programmes such as the Organisation for Economic Cooperation and Development's (OECD) Programme for International Student Assessment (PISA), the International Association for the Evaluation of Educational Achievement's (IEA) Trends in International Mathematics and Science Study (TIMSS), and the Progress in International Reading Literacy Study (PIRLS) assessments take on such importance. PISA assesses reading, mathematics, and science across 65 countries with approximately 510,000 students participating across the globe (OECDa, n.p.). TIMMS assesses the mathematics and science knowledge of 4th and 8th grade students which roughly equates to children aged 9–10 and those 13–14 years of age, respectively; while PIRLS assesses reading and literacy of 4th grade students (IEA). The most frequently cited national or international test is the PISA test. This is possibly because the OECD, established in 1961, is an internationally focused organisation with 34 member countries, and its mission "is to promote policies that will improve the economic and social well-being of people around the world (OECDb, n.p.) … [and] to build a stronger, cleaner, fairer world" – arguably highly desirable goals to most nations (OECDc, n.p.). The value of these tests for many governments includes the capacity to monitor the quality of their own education system (Eurydice, 2009; Pepper, 2011; Ross, Cen, & Zhou, 2011; Zhang & Kong, 2012), to explore similarities and differences between countries (Eurydice, 2009; Schleicher, 2011), and to potentially learn from high performing countries with the view to initiating reforms and/or innovations (Sarjala, 2013; Schleicher, 2011; Schleicher & Stewart, 2008). These comparative approaches have even extended to the development of dynamic databases designed to track the different 'quality indicators' in education across various countries to facilitate more accurate and aligned comparisons (Poliandri, Cardone, Muzzioli, & Romiti, 2010).

2.4.1   International Comparisons

Zhang and Kong (2012), commenting on the Shanghai context identified that in the 1980s politicians linked education to national economics so it is not surprising that national tests were of interest to governments. Acar (2012) in Turkey, Matsuoka (2013) in Japan, and Ross et al. (2011) in China specified that PISA data enabled the tracking of international competitiveness by examining student outcomes in line with curriculum modifications that were designed for greater alignment with the expectations of knowledge-based economies. This is even more pertinent for the European Union (EU) with its lowered borders, inter-related economies, and more mobile citizenry; as The Education, Audiovisual and Culture Executive Agency (Eurydice, 2009) reported:

> Improving the quality and efficiency of education is at the centre of education policy debate at both national and EU level. It has a crucial role to play in Europe's Lisbon strategy to build its future prosperity and social cohesion. It lies at the heart of the EU's goals for education and training in the period up to 2020. (p. 3)

Likewise, China is responding to international competition in the quality education agenda by instituting "another wave of reform ... defining and redefining educational quality" (Ross et al., 2011, p. 34). Sarjala (2013) from Finland reported that national testing like PISA enabled the cross-national comparison of student learning approaches. Schleicher and Stewart (2008) noted differences between high and low performing countries. Their analysis revealed high performing countries invested in the professional development of teachers, recruited strong teacher candidates, promoted educators' discipline knowledge, and abandoned "traditional factory model" conceptualisations of teaching wherein educators were at the "bottom of the production line receiving orders from on high" in pursuit of contemporary conceptualisations of professionalism whereby teachers were considered "knowledge workers" (n.p.). Ungerleider (2006) from Canada reflected that many countries are now aiming for more coherent assessment systems which are multi-layered from classroom to schools to entire districts or regions and on to the national and international levels.

Another potential use of international comparisons is the capacity to explode common myths. Schleicher and Stewart (2008) continued their comparison noting that data from Japan, Korea, Finland, and Canada revealed improvement was possible even in disadvantaged socio-economic status (SES) localities, refuting counter claims from the US. They also stated that the prevalence of immigrant student populations did not correlate to poor performance in PISA; nor was performance simply a matter of education funding reflecting that only Luxembourg, Switzerland, and Norway spend more per student than the US and yet the US was not competitive with countries like Finland or Alberta, Canada (Schleicher, 2011). Similar to Schleicher and Stewart's (2008) commentary, Ungerleider also noted that high quality education systems and their equally professional educators did not use diversity in school populations as an excuse for poor performance.

"Knowledge is seen as a codifiable commodity which is produced, measured, marketed, sold and distributed in the market place: 'productive knowledge is believed to be the basis of national competitive advantage within the international marketplace'" (Ozga & Lingard, 2007, p. 71). Winter, reflecting on the UK school system, drew upon the World Bank (2005, cited Winter, 2011) comments to note that the knowledge economy required schools to reject the traditional conceptualisations of curriculum subject specialisation to one of 'knowledge as skills' "toward broader curriculum areas, skillcentred approaches, and non-academic sources of relevant knowledge, with the aim of constructing more relevant and inclusive secondary curricula" (pp. 300–3001). Hence, international comparisons are more likely to influence policies (macro level) rather than practices (micro level).

2.4.2 Cautions with National Testing Data

Even with the potential for international comparisons Zhang and Kong (2012), Cowie, Jones, and Otrel-Cass (2011) and Wainer (2011) offered cautionary insights about the conclusions that can be drawn from national testing data. Zhang and Kong indicated that findings from Shanghai's PISA data may not be representative of China as a whole, while Cowie, Jones, and Otrel-Cass reflected that high PISA scores in New Zealand masked concerns with Māori and Pacifica students' achievement. Methodologically, Wainer recommended those using test data should be more familiar with the inherent strengths and weaknesses of particular testing instruments and administration approaches. Similarly, Garner (2013) from the US stated that while data were important, equally important were informed consumers of test data, highlighting the need to "educate consumers" to become …

> critical, knowledgeable consumer[s] of statistics who can ask the right questions about the numbers and make a judgment about the validity of the numbers and how appropriately they were used … we should keep in mind how tests are received by innumerate users and factor in this consideration as we explore more thoroughly indirect and even direct uses of tests. (p. 39)

2.4.3 Exploring Contemporary Issues

Another purpose of national testing programmes is to provide data that enables the exploration of contemporary internationally-relevant issues. For example, Brunello, Rocco, Ariga, and Iwahashi (2012) examined the efficiency of tracking or streaming students in the European Union, while Sarjala (2013) noted the importance of stakeholder cooperation throughout the education sector in Finland in order to create educational equality as an economic necessity. Commeyras and Inyega (2007) and Vikiru (2011) in Kenya, and Gove and Wetterberg (2011) in Liberia utilised systematic testing programmes to provide data for informed decision making regarding the all-important issue of English language literacy in East and West Africa, which was articulated as crucial to educational success and students' personal career options, as well as national–international competitiveness.

Another contemporary issue was the skills agenda, which was particularly pervasive across the European Union potentially due to the movement of workers across its 28 member states. Raisanen and Rakkolainen (2009) discussed the importance of assessing key competencies such as "learning-to-learn skills, communication skills, social skills and entrepreneurship ... skills required in the labour market" (p. 36) in vocational programmes in Finland, while the wider Finnish education system also focused on media skills in addition to the previously cited ones (Eurydice, 2009). Similarly, the Scottish system assessed problem-solving, team work, and information communication skills, and Winter (2011) identified that in England new curriculum and policy guides emphasised "thinking and social and emotional skills", particularly, higher order thinking skills including metacognition, as important in preparing students for future careers (p. 300). Drawing upon UNESCO and OECD documents Winter highlighted the need for students to acquire "'knowledge-how' (or skills/competency-based knowledge)" (p. 301) rather than fact-based knowledge that the teaching of discrete subjects in secondary schools currently provides. Shafiq's (2011) shocking discussion of the "skills crisis" in Jordan and Tunisia – literacy skills, higher order thinking, and individual responsibility – indicated their skills shortage has suppressed economic growth and development and was also linked to "the surge of youth participation in extremist activities such as violent protests and suicide bombings" (Krueger, 2007, cited in Shafiq, 2011, p. 1). "Queen Rania of Jordan, for example, refers to the situation as a 'ticking time bomb' and stresses the urgency of adopting skill-enhancing policies" (p. 1). Clearly, the skills agenda in these Arab nations is not simply a matter of promoting career success but is also a matter of stability, peace, and national security. Across all these countries the concern was expressed that many teachers were ill-prepared to teach and assess skills which creates a further dilemma in integrating these pivotal twenty-first century skills expectations into school curricular and instructional practices.

If the expectation is then to remain competitive, nations must have high quality education systems that support knowledge and skill development; and it is also just as important to evaluate their systems and to have assessments that can inform and report on students' outcomes in line with national and state/provincial curricular goals (Raisanen & Rakkolainen, 2009).

2.5   National Scene – Politicisation of Assessment

The previous section explored the international comparative uses of student data such as PISA, TIMMS, and PIRLS in order to monitor competitiveness within the international arena. National testing also serves individual governments in their accountability mandate to their societies (Hulpia & Valcke, 2004). With increasing calls from the public for transparency in reporting on the quality of systems, along with the justification to society for government spending on education, national examinations were deemed to be an appropriate measure of everything from the adequacy of the curriculum to teacher effectiveness to student achievement (Poliandri et al., 2010). Indeed, the vast majority of nations across the globe have introduced some form of national testing. During the 1960s–1970s Sweden, France, England, Wales and Northern Ireland introduced national testing. Moreover, the years 1990–2010 saw the wholesale introduction of national testing in Latvia, Estonia, Spain, Belgium's French community, Romania, Belgium's Flemish community, Lithuania, Poland, Slovakia, Austria, Norway, Germany, Bulgaria, Cyprus, Denmark, and Italy, in chronological order. In noting the prevalence of national testing in the EU it was interesting to find that in 2008/2009 only Belgium's German-speaking community, the Czech Republic, Greece, Wales, and Liechtenstein did not administer national tests (Eurydice, 2009). Aside from the EU other countries have commenced national testing for example, New Zealand (1995), and Australia (2008) after their introduction of a national curriculum. Similarly, Song's chapter in this book describes China's long history of national testing commencing with the Imperial Examination administered by the Emperor around the year 606 and national testing being re-instituted with the National Matriculation Entrance Examination in the early 2000s. Similarly, the US instituted Scholastic Aptitude Tests (SATs) in 1926 while the prevalence and value placed on standardised testing dramatically increased with the No Child Left Behind Act in 2001.

In the information age, society and governments have become more informed and more aware of the need to monitor and be accountable for student success, with education perceived to be a key measure of the likelihood of national competitiveness and prestige; and as Barber (2004) noted discussing accountability in the UK: "We want to raise the bar and narrow the gap. This means we want a system of strong external accountability which can make a decisive contribution to the achievement of that widely shared moral purpose" (p. 7). Therefore, national tests have assumed considerable importance to parents, leaders, education and system leaders who are charged with the responsibility for their system performance. Governments must respond to their society's perceptions of educational quality; for example, Ross et al. (2011) stated that even though China is emerging as a strong international player, "the Chinese public has expressed consistent dissatisfaction with educational quality" (p. 24). Similarly, Matsuoka (2013) indicated that testing masked underlying societal issues within Japan explaining that their education system reinforced status differences where only the wealthy could afford to provide additional tutoring to ensure the success of their children leading "to the unequal distribution of learning opportunities" (p. 65). Griffiths, Vidovich, and Chapman (2008) in Australia also discussed the importance of parents as a voice in education reforms, referring to them as "customers in the education marketplace" (p. 167) further emphasising our increasingly marketised society. In contrast, Finland's commitment to the tenets of a democratic civil society, with its notions of responsibility, is demonstrated by ensuring the welfare of its students through complimentary lunch programmes, seamless support throughout schooling, access to services for no cost (Sahlberg, 2012), greater flexibility to move between vocational programmes and academic streams (Raisanen & Rakkolainen, 2009), and investment in the professionalism of their educators. All of these commitments to educational quality have yielded success in the PISA rankings (Schleicher & Stewart, 2008).

Accountability also relates to monitoring the impact of reforms. Zhang and Kong (2012) discussed how the Shanghai government uses PISA data "to establish very specific targets for change … to make accurate decisions, to deepen reform and development and to promote education equity and excellence and promote 'the lifelong development of each student'" (p. 158). Other reforms that were cited in the literature included Kenya's English and Kiswahili literacy reforms (Commeyras & Inyega, 2007), reforms to support differentiation for Aboriginal students in Australia (Fenwick, 2012), and the outcomes-based education (OBE) reform movement in Western Australia (Griffiths et al., 2008). Additionally, the development of standards usually accompanies the accountability movement as these are deemed to be useful in assisting leaders to determine how closely the system and its stakeholders are aligning with the criteria for success, with expectations for action to address lower performance. In Hungary for example, since 2008 schools that do not perform well in the national tests have to prepare an improvement action plan to address their low performance. The focus on improving schools has led to school authorities in Belgium's French community, Estonia, Hungary, Slovenia, England,Scotland, and Iceland, requiring schools to carry out internal critical analyses of their exam results to identify appropriate action (Eurydice, 2009). So one can argue that some form of accountability at the system level is a force for positive action; however, the outcomes of these accountability measures are largely dependent on educational stakeholders genuinely engaging with enhancement initiatives to make a difference to student outcomes. As Sahlberg (2012) identified, "The equitable Finnish education system is a result of systematic attention to social justice and early intervention to help those with special needs, and close interplay between education and other sectors – particularly health and social sectors – in Finnish society" (p. 21). This is similar in Alberta (Canada) and the EU (Eurydice) where many stakeholders including ministry personnel, parent councils, professional developers, leadership associations, university professors, and union officials come to the table around policy decisions and professional development initiatives, which has resulted in high performance in the PISA rankings.

2.6   Debates and Controversies

Although it is readily acknowledged that accountability is an embedded element of any society within our globalised world, there are many issues that surround this concept. For example, Wang, Beckett, and Brown (2006) from the US noted that no assessment – standardised or teacher-developed – is perfect, which is why there is so much controversy surrounding assessment. Debates continue surrounding misunderstandings of the purposes and uses of different assessments and how these can be high stakes for various stakeholders. As well as these issues, this section examines the values that underpin assessment in terms of what is assessed is valued, ensuring cultural sensitivity, and teachers' beliefs, ethics, and relationships.

2.6.1 Purposes of Assessment

One hotly debated topic is the purpose and uses of assessment data. This issue encompasses whether or not important stakeholders understand the different purposes of various assessments, ensuring the "fitness-for-purpose" of different forms of assessment (Eurydice, 2009, p. 63), and being vigilant that resultant data are used for the purposes for which the assessment was originally designed to prevent misaligned or misguided decisions. An associated issue is ascribing value or worth to various types of assessment (James & Pedder, 2006). A current trend across the world is to demonise summative forms of assessment due to misconceptions of the negativity associated with labelling students, reducing them to numbers, or placing them into a ranking hierarchy; and conversely, elevating formative feedback due to perceptions of its value in informing teaching and learning and its potential to motivate students. This type of "evil versus good" debate in assessment repudiates the needs of different stakeholders to have various forms of data to make decisions at different levels of society (Sahlberg, 2012).

2.6.2 High Stakes

Volante and Beckett (2011) commented on the concerns with the high stakes associated with large-scale testing programmes in North America, particularly in the US, where schools can be closed, and teachers and school leaders fired or demoted due to poor school performance. Even though these punitive measures are not enacted in Canada provincial exams are high stakes for students in their final year of school as they serve as a gatekeeping mechanism for eligibility for entry into post-secondary programmes. Along the high stakes theme Katsiyannis, Zhang, Ryan, and Jones (2007) also discussed their concerns about students with special needs sitting high stakes testing in the US. They found that students with disabilities are "particularly vulnerable" if they fail to achieve "proficient levels" in these exams and suffer the consequences if they make schools "look less effective" which raises the stress students' experience in taking these tests (p. 164).

2.6.3 What Is Assessed Is Valued

Another debate of large-scale testing programmes is that what is tested is valued, which in turn can influence teaching behaviours. It may be argued that a test is evaluating the learning outcomes of students in alignment with curriculum standards and so teachers teaching to the test will by default be teaching to the curriculum standards. Even so, Barber recognised that systems must reinforce the teaching and assessment of broader educational outcomes, not simply those tested through standardised tests. Provided that all curriculum areas are included in standardised tests there can be little criticism if teachers teach to the test. An additional issue now arising around the world, particularly noted across Europe, is what assessments are necessary for evaluating students' development of skills. One may question whether standardised pen and paper tests validly assess all skill development, and if they do not, this then elevates the importance of innovations in assessment, such as performance and authentic assessment, which should be teacher-led. Therefore, what is valued is assessed but there must be clarity regarding what is valued and what forms of assessment can most effectively assess these diverse criteria.

Encompassed within the political nature of large-scale testing are suspicions about how these data are used or portrayed. Garner (2013) commented, "statistics can be misunderstood … perverted, or misused (p. 36) … there are those who cynically manipulate numbers and report numbers purely to achieve their own goals, just as some politicians use test scores to forward their agenda, whether the test score is appropriately used or not" (p. 38). Drawing upon Best's thoughts (2001, cited in Garner) Garner states that "many bad statistics are produced by 'selective, self-righteous efforts to produce numbers that reaffirm principles and interests that their advocates consider just and right'" (p. 38). Thus there is the potential for distressing and destructive relationships between those who manipulate numbers and those who uncritically accept numbers.

2.6.4 Cultural sensitivity

Ungerleider (2006) indicated that system administrators must examine the appropriateness of standardised tests for different populations. For example, he pondered the suitability of a test for Aboriginal and non-Aboriginal students, students situated in rural and metropolitan localities, girls and boys, immigrants and native born students, as well as linguistically diverse student groups. Reiterating Ungerleider's concern, Volante and Beckett (2011) in Canada identified that standardised testing programmes can be culturally inappropriate for indigenous students who are unable to interpret or misinterpret the test questions due to differences in cultural understandings. As an interesting example they posited a test question that required students to identify the deleterious effects of smoking, while pointing out that for many Canadian indigenous groups smoke and smoking are inherent aspects of sacred ceremonies – hence, students' cultural filters would impede their capacity to fully respond to the question in the way the test developer expected. Likewise, Friesen and Ezeife (2009) recommended greater collaboration with "Aboriginal Elders and other leaders in order to develop appropriate assessments founded on culturally responsive instructional and assessment practices" (p. 35) and for teachers to consider students' social and cultural backgrounds when formulating their assessment tasks to ensure a "high degree of cultural validity" (p. 31). Commeyras and Inyega (2007) iterated similar sentiments but applied to the Kenyan context. Fenwick (2012) in Australia explored the potential for performance assessment as a more suitable assessment strategy for indigenous students. Similarly, in New Zealand, Harris and Brown (2009) proposed that teachers "consider divergent stakeholder interests when selecting assessments for [Māori and possibly Pacifica] students, balancing the needs of the society, the school, and the pupil" (p. 365). They also stressed that Māori students should not be considered a homogenous group as they too represent diversity within their own cultural cluster, similar to the diversity among Australian Aborigines and the North American First Nations groups.

2.6.5   Beliefs, Ethics, and Relationships

Another controversy revolves around teachers' beliefs about assessment, their ethical stance in assessing particular students, and the relationship they have with students. Cowie et al.'s (2011) New Zealand study reported on the broad impact of teachers' assessment practices recounting this in terms of social, emotional, cognitive dimensions:

> The assessment relationships students have with the teacher, tasks and one another shape their opportunities to learn and they impact on the identities students develop as learners and knowers ... This is the case irrespective of whether the assessment is summative and of learning or assessment is formative and for learning. (p. 354)

Even though most teachers choose to enter the teaching profession for altruistic reasons – helping children and young people to learn – we must recognise they are human beings with biases. One of the main reasons for parents' and society's concerns with trusting teacher judgements is because many of us have personally encountered poor assessment, been the subject of teacher bias, or have not had positive relationships with teachers. Harlen (2005) in the UK discussed these issues and identified that many studies reported teacher bias directly related to student characteristics, such as "behaviour (for young students), gender, special educational needs; overall academic achievement and verbal ability" which influenced teachers' judgements in assessing specific skills (p. 262). Harlen's analysis was further corroborated in the Alberta Student Assessment Study where students and parents reported concerns with teacher bias in relation to inappropriate coalescence of behaviour with academic achievement, gender – wherein boys were graded more harshly frequently due to teachers' concerns with their behaviour, while teachers themselves acknowledged issues in assessing students with cultural and linguistic diversity, and students with special needs, particularly those of the gifted and talented (Scott, Webber, Lupart, Aitken, & Scott, 2013). Likewise, Green, Johnson, Kim, and Pope (2007) from the US articulated their concerns with the variability of teachers' ethical behaviour with assessment. They highlighted Strike's (1990, cited in Green et al., 2007, p. 1009) suggestion that moral concepts should be addressed in preservice education, particularly related to the principles of "Do No Harm" and "Avoid Score Pollution". Do no harm relates to how poor assessment can damage students indicating that this could also be related to Payne's (2003, cited in Green et al., p. 1000) concept of "Assess As Ye Would Be Assessed"; however, do no harm may actually be a passive concept where active engagement with the ethical issues may be required. For example, teachers may need to actively interrogate their biases towards certain groups of students i.e., special needs or indigenous students and address their inaccurate or inappropriate assessment approaches. "Avoid score pollution", which may on initial glance appears to highlight the inappropriateness of conflating behaviour with academic achievement judgements, is actually a deeper principle. Drawing upon Popham's (1991, cited in Green et al.) and Haladyna and his associates' (1991, cited in Green et al.) premises, Green et al. suggest:

> any practice that improves test performance without concurrently increasing actual mastery of the content tested produces score pollution. That is, the score on the test does not represent actual student achievement in the content area and is 'polluted' by factors unrelated to academic attainment. If scores do not reflect mastery then harm has been done. This situation is akin to lying. For example, practicing beforehand with actual test content would produce score pollution. In essence, this is a validity issue. Test scores no longer measure generalized mastery but simply ability to memorize specific test items. (p. 1001)

Therefore avoiding score pollution includes teaching to the test that involves teachers only teaching the test items rather than the full curriculum content.

An interesting aspect of the ethical and moral dimensions of assessment was explained by Friesen and Ezeife (2009) in Canada and Saunders and Vulliamy (1983) in their comparative study of Papua New Guinea and Tanzania, where they pointed out that parents will frequently reward or punish their child or allocate resources for tutoring or further educational opportunities based upon teachers' assessments of students' capacities. Hence when viewed through this lens, teacher assessment can be perceived as just as "high stakes" as standardised tests. Friesen and Ezeife continued stating that biased teachers can actually perpetuate the cycle of failure for indigenous students rather than promoting positive educational experiences that can create productive futures for these students.

Beets (2012) in South Africa explored the importance of teacher-student relationships and described this in terms of the morality of teachers' practice where assessment should be utilised to "enhance both teaching and learning in the interests of each learner and ultimately society" (p. 81). He identified that positive relationships with students implied high levels of trust which could only be founded upon "unconditional caring with the sole intention to scaffold and guide the learners' journey" (p. 80). He continued by stating:

> Supporting learners through educational assessment practices to reach their potential level of development implies a relationship of trust – a deep human engagement between a more knowledgeable other (in this case, a teacher) and learners who commit themselves regardless of differences at various levels to use the processes inherent to, and insights gained from, assessment retrospectively (feedback) and prospectively (feedforward) to enhance learning. (p. 79)

Green et al. (2007) also emphasised the importance of trust, reporting that the teacher-student relationship could be irreparably damaged by assessments and practices students perceive as "unfair or unfounded" (p. 1009). An aspect of creating a trusting relationship is effective communication. This was implied in Griffiths et al.'s (2008) Australian study where they identified the demotivation that students experienced when they were not progressing through the outcome levels within each year, which led them to posit that teachers were not providing sufficient ongoing feedback to students regarding the differentiation contained by standard descriptors within the levels, and their achievement in relation to these standards. Vikiru's (2011) Kenyan study found that "students found it strange to be involved in the planning and assessment of their own learning" (p. 134) which again indicated teachers were not overtly facilitating student empowerment with assessment. All of these studies reinforced the importance of communication in building positive relationships around assessment.

This brief foray exploring some studies that touch upon teachers' beliefs about assessment, teachers' ethics in assessment and the ethic of care and relationships they create with students underpins some of the concerns that parents and society have with trusting teachers to make in accurate and fair judgements about their children. Of course this has implications for teacher preparation programmes and for professional development in addressing these concerns, which can in turn have a significant influence on societal perceptions of the credibility and professionalism of educators.

2.6.6 Accountability of Teachers – Societal Trust in the Profession

A sometimes confused debate is conceptualisations of accountability of systems and schools versus accountability of teachers and leaders. This confusion entails systems versus people and as such gives rise to passionate debate and inflammatory rhetoric as illustrated by Beets' comment that teachers' concerns with "their own performativity in terms of the stated performance indicators and their accountability towards the education authorities have a higher priority than the interests of learners, their parents and ultimately society" which he felt constituted an ethical dilemma (p. 71). As I have previously identified, it is reasonable and necessary for governments to want to monitor the quality of their educational systems and effectiveness of schools/jurisdictions as transparency is a key responsibility in meeting societal demands for accountability. This is why standardised testing is prevalent and useful for checking the pulse of the nation's systems and international competitiveness; while teacher assessment is valuable and influential for guiding and promoting learning, informing teaching decisions, and reporting on student outcomes. Therefore, even though standardised testing in many countries is not designed to scrutinise individual teacher's behaviours it is aimed at monitoring the effectiveness of the curriculum and whether or not standards are being maintained for all; whereas Ungerleider (2006) stated that these tests "must be predicated on enabling teachers rather than controlling or 'fixing' them" (p. 879). Standardised test data can inform curricula development, policies, resourcing decisions, and highlight particular needs of vulnerable groups in society (e.g., indigenous and/or gifted and talented students), which is generally outside the sphere of influence of individual teachers. If standards fall or quality indicators are found to be declining then it is hardly surprising that policy makers will query what is happening at the micro level, that is, between teachers and students, as this constitutes the baseline data.

While many rail against teacher accountability using terminology like "neo-liberal" (Winter, 2011), and "managerial and market" accountability (Griffiths et al., 2008), educators cannot escape societal expectations that as public servants they too, like police, nurses, doctors, and the military, are accountable for the work they do in the service of society. Harris and Brown (2009) found New Zealand's teachers were highly critical and suspicious about government imposed testing programmes as they perceived these to be irrelevant to their work with students and "clashing with their personal beliefs about effective assessment" (p. 370). Harlen (2005) indicated policy makers in England, Wales, and Scotland were increasingly willing to reduce the impact of large-scale testing programmes and considered "making greater use of teachers' judgements for summative assessment" (p. 246). On a counterpoint though, Harlen reported that the review by no means constituted "a ringing endorsement of teachers' assessment [as] there was evidence of low reliability and bias in teachers' judgements" (p. 245). Bolt (2011) and Klenowski and Wyatt-Smith (2010) identified a range of issues in Australia in supporting teachers to be more consistent in judging students' work against curriculum standards. They found that without moderation and school communities of practice to continue professional development efforts, teachers were less able to make consistent judgements even with well-articulated standard guides. Klenowski and Wyatt-Smith proposed that "standards intended to inform teacher judgement and to build assessment capacity are necessary but not sufficient for maintaining teacher and public confidence in schooling" (p. 21). Wang et al. (2006) sought the middle ground stating "If used prudently, standardized tests can complement teacher-made tests to provide a more comprehensive description and valid assessment of student achievement" (p. 321). Similarly within the Canadian context, Ungerleider (2006) endorsed Wang et al.'s notions about finding a middle ground where teacher's suspicions about standardised testing can be allayed through greater involvement in acquiring useful information about teaching and learning, analysing results and planning implementation of improvements in instruction. He stressed that leaders have a significant role to play working with teachers to identify the connections between teacher and school data and policies and practices.

Aside from the tensions surrounding teacher judgement, there are also concerns with teacher assessment knowledge. There can be no doubt that while many teachers have a broad understanding of instructional approaches, many lack the knowledge of and expertise with a variety of alternative assessment approaches (Geçer & Özel, 2012; Scott, Webber, Aitken, & Lupart, 2011). This deficit leaves them feeling uncomfortable in defending their judgement to parents and highlights the need for assessment related professional development. Gove and Wetterberg (2011) found that many teachers did not know how to teach and assess reading and they recommended professional development to increase teacher expertise in Liberia. Harlen indicated that teachers in the UK failed to take advantage of their autonomy from standardised testing; however, they tended to emulate standardised tests within their routine continuous assessment. This indicated that they lacked expertise in varied and innovative forms of assessment and misinterpreted the ways to include formative feedback.

Garner (2013) further identified concerns in US teachers' perceptions of value ascribed to formative over summative assessment. She stated that there is a tendency for teachers to believe testing imposed from external sources (summative) "is bad" as they …

> insist that it is possible to reduce children to mere numbers (with the incorrect assumption that the purpose of testing is to reduce children to numbers). … If teachers, administrators, and parents don't believe that testing can improve schooling, they ignore the test or design clever ways to circumvent or even undermine the test. How can any direct or indirect uses of testing operate under such disbelief and resistance? (p. 37)

Griffiths et al. (2008) discussed the problems of implementing policy reforms in Australia without providing teachers with the necessary professional development to be able to understand how to change their assessment practices in line with OBE legislation:

> With no clear and substantive unpacking of how assessment becomes part of a productive pedagogy, teachers find it difficult to understand that assessment can fulfil purposes other than producing a mark against which learners will be promoted or kept back in a specific grade. (p. 70)

They noted the problems with outdated teacher knowledge which compounded the difficulties they encountered in assessing within a new paradigm. Clearly, there is the need for professional development of teachers in relation to not only expanding their assessment repertoire to more innovative forms, but also in gaining a deeper understanding of the purposes of different forms of assessment and the impacts these may have on different stakeholders who require the information that these assessments yield.

A more pertinent question is not whether or not teachers should be accountable, rather … What resources and professional development are in place to enhance educator capacity and professionalism in carrying out this important role? (Schleicher, 2011) The question of teacher responsibility is emerging more strongly now as many systems are moving towards greater weighting for teacher assessments. For example, Denmark and Finland have recognised the importance of teachers and their assessment capacities and are focusing on building professional capacity and "confidence in professional accountability" using external school performance measures as data that serves "to encourage teachers and schools to develop more supportive and productive learning environments" (Schleicher & Stewart, 2008).

2.7 Professionalism and Professional Development

Increasingly there are discussions within society about the professionalisation of educators (Schleicher, 2011) with some arguing that teachers are merely technicians while others promote notions of professionalism as an ideology to drive positive change. Drawing upon Webber and Scott's (2013) discussion of the conceptualisation of professions and professionalism, they used Brandeis' (1912) early three-point definition of what constitutes a profession. First, professions require "preliminary training" that is "intellectual in character" and involves the development of understandings instead of simply focusing on skill development alone. Second, professions entail the pursuit of altruism rather than simply self-serving, while the third point encompasses notions of the rejection of performance or success measured purely in terms of financial gain. Webber and Scott continued, describing 'professionalism' using Parsons' (1968, cited in Webber & Scott, p. 115) definition that encompassed "fiducial responsibilities ... with a 'service orientation'"; that is, the trust that society places in educators to ensure the wellbeing and care of students, as well as Torstendahl's (2005, cited in Webber & Scott, p. 115) complementary characteristics of responsibility to the institutional arrangements of their employers and the responsibility "to discuss among their colleagues how to perform their duties".

It is pivotal to note that definitions of professionalism relate to education and training that is intellectual in nature with the view to ensuring best practice in the service of students and ultimately society. Schleicher (2011) endorsed these sentiments when he explored the differences between high and low performing education systems, reporting that in high performing systems there was a shared commitment to professionalised teaching, the application of "evidence-based practices", and a sense of "professional pride" (p. 62). Additionally, attention was paid to the selection of high quality teacher candidates who were provided with excellent preparation and induction, as well as subsequent on-the-job professional growth opportunities. Rewards and recognition were integrated into systems so that the pursuit of excellence was promoted with the expectation that all teachers would be well equipped for facilitating the effective learning of students under their care. He identified that the Singaporean system allows for multiple career pathways including master teacher, content specialist, or principal.

Ungerleider (2006) discussed further issues with ensuring effective preservice preparation where he asserted that university professors were going to have "to operate in a changed milieu" whereby they must collaborate with their colleagues in order to identify what knowledge, skills and attitudes or beliefs teachers must develop for contemporary school contexts (p. 882). Therefore, teachers must gain knowledge of alternative and authentic assessments (Cowie et al., 2011; Fenwick, 2012; Friesen & Ezeife, 2009; Geçer & Özel, 2012; Griffiths et al., 2008; Raisanen & Rakkolainen, 2009), as well as how to make consistent judgements supported by systematic moderation processes (Bolt, 2011; Harlen, 2005; Hulpia & Valcke, 2004; Klenowski & Wyatt-Smith, 2010; Sahlberg, 2012; Vikiru, 2011), and embed into their pedagogical philosophy an ethic of care and high moral process with a clear understanding of how these beliefs and values would be demonstrated in assessment practices (Beets, 2012; Green et al., 2007; Harris & Brown, 2009; Katsiyannis et al., 2007; Scott et al., 2013; Webber & Scott, 2013). Volante and Beckett (2011) though were concerned that many educators look to university programmes for their professional preparation and development, however, all too often assessment is not encompassed in programmes, or the content is outdated, or too theoretical to be of much use. Scott et al. (2011) recommended university professors and leaders must engage with the contemporary issues of assessment by reviewing the currency, innovativeness, and pragmatism within their preservice and graduate programming to address these deficits.

2.7.1 Moderation

Klenowski and Wyatt-Smith (2010) offered this description of moderation:

> teachers' judgement practice in the context of standards-driven reform with a focus on how the stated standards are used by teachers … The processes and social interactions that teachers rely on to inform their decisions have been identified. The ways in which these teachers talked through and interacted with one another to reach agreement about the quality of student work in the application of standards have been analysed with evidence of differences in the way that they make compensations and trade-offs in their award of grades dependent on the subject area they teach. … moderation meetings … are designed to reach consistent, reliable judgements. (pp. 22–23)

Moderation emerged as a crucial approach in promoting more consistent and valid teacher judgements about students' work particularly when aligned with standards and criteria. Klenowski and Wyatt-Smith (2010) and Bolt (2011) in Australia, and Harlen (2005) in the UK, all discussed the merits of moderation approaches. The advantages of moderation were described by Klenowski and Wyatt-Smith as "intrinsic to efforts by the profession to realise judgements that are defensible, dependable and open to scrutiny" (p. 21), while Harlen indicated that it is a leader's responsibility to enhance the dependability of teachers' assessment by "protecting time for planning assessment, in-school moderation (p. 267) … for teachers to meet and to take advantage of the support that others, including assessment advisers, can give" (p. 262). Naturally, moderation has leadership implications as teachers must be released from the classroom in order to participate in these collaborative moderation processes.

2.8 Socio-cultural Issues – Diversity in Schools

At this juncture it is relevant to return to the overarching theme of this chapter – globalisation and its influence on education and assessment. As previously noted, globalisation has influenced the socio-cultural dimensions of schools due to the migration of peoples which has resulted in significant changes to the demographics of school populations around the world. Additionally, due to government policies addressing children with special needs, many students with exceptionalities now have greater access to mainstream education. This means educators have an increasingly complex task in supporting the learning of a wide range of students who have varied learning needs. This section explores the assessment issues for students with special needs, as well as those in lower socio-economic status situations, and acknowledges the concerns for indigenous students which were discussed in the section under "cultural sensitivity".

The term 'inclusion' has arisen to represent the more diverse classroom and the expectation that teachers will differentiate their instructional and assessment strategies in order to meet all students' learning needs (Jordan, 2007). Differentiated assessment entails modifying an assessment to enable students to access and engage with the task. This may include altering the wording of tasks, including accommodations to assist students to understand and engage with the task, changing the task altogether by raising or lowering the cognitive demand, considering the cultural dimensions, and/or allowing students to demonstrate their understandings in a variety of ways and using a range of media or technologies. The following sections examine the literature that emerged from different nations regarding socio-cultural diversity in schools.

2.8.1   Students with Special Education Needs (SEN)

The Eurydice report (2009) stated that across Europe there was variability as to whether or not SEN students were included in standardised testing programmes or if their inclusion was optional. Indeed, including SEN students in standardised tests has been highly controversial in the US where some students have been excluded from testing because they can influence the school results and this is can have negative consequences for all stakeholders (Katsiyannis et al., 2007). SEN students in Slovenia have modified tests or can take the test using accommodations including audio visual aids, braille, more time or breaks allowed during testing, "assistants on hand to offer support", and the use of technology or "specially adapted equipment or resources" (p. 40).

France has diagnostic assessments which enable teachers to modify their instructional approaches and personalise their assistance to SEN students (Eurydice, 2009). Wang and his associates (2006) in the US felt that adaptive technologies held real promise in meeting the individualised learning needs of SEN students. Lebeer et al. (2012) reported on the concerns of assessment for children with special education needs (SEN) across various countries in Europe. They felt that assessment for these students was particularly important due to the potential motivation and esteem issues that could arise from poor assessment practices. They indicated that in Romania accessing psychological assessments was difficult and protracted, which was exacerbated by the high demand for these assessments resulting in overload on psychological services. Additionally, they expressed concern with the "too negative" formulation of the psychological assessments, and in the Virgin Islands there was a lack of pragmatic guidance for teachers within these assessments (p. 82). Not surprisingly they reported these assessments "should be formulated in an optimistic way, giving clear indications as to the construction of an academically and socially challenging individual educational programme" (p. 89).

2.8.2 Other Socio-culturally Diverse Students

Other socio-culturally diverse students that were cited as at-risk due to poor or inappropriate or insensitive assessments were those in low socio-economic status locales, English language learners, and gifted and talented students. Friesen and Ezeife (2009) emphasised the issue of validity where students have no experience with the aspects in a test which can apply to any of these socio-culturally diverse students. Fenwick warned that when standards and assessments were devised with lower expectations for students in low SES areas or other socio-culturally diverse demographics, this actively impeded these students from rising above their circumstances as low expectations became a self-fulfilling prophecy. Low SES students were the focus of a major Australian government funding and research initiative with the view to avoiding and addressing low expectations (MCEETYA, 2008). In the UK, teachers are able to assess ELL students through teacher assessment rather than placing them into the national testing programmes before they are ready (Eurydice, 2009). De Boer, Minnaert, and Kamphof (2013) reported that the Netherlands government had made gifted and talented education a priority with the view to enhancing national competitiveness.

2.9 Media Influences

A surprising dimension to emerge from many countries, namely Australia, Finland, Liberia, the Netherlands, UK, and US was the influence of the media on education policies and assessment debates. The media has had a significant role in our globalised society largely due to the influence of technology facilitating the ease and speed of information dissemination. This analysis revealed that the media can be a force for positive action or a highly destructive one depending on how it is harnessed, how succinct and accurate the reporting is, and whether or not the issue at hand has the capacity to be sensationalistic.

The research from Liberia showed the influence of the media can be a two-edged sword. The education system effectively utilised the media to garner public curiosity over a reading initiative, disseminating the purposes and processes involved, and garnered support for the project. Leaders publicised a competition and gained support from influential members of the community to gain funding for the project – a positive outcome from media support. However, Gove and Wetterberg (2011) reported that the necessity for the English language project was not simply a matter of student learning, rather, they highlighted the pivotal role the media had played in inciting people to violence after the election of 2007–2008, which was exacerbated by tribal rivalries inherent in linguistic difference. Hence, this project was significant in using the media in promoting peace and tolerance.

Unfortunately, the media is about selling papers and maintaining or increasing readership; hence, it is in their best interest to devise stories that provoke controversy and contentious debate rather than to simply serve the informational needs of the public. Garner described Best's (2001, cited in Garner, 2013) lament about the media's sometimes erroneous or skewed reporting of educational statistics:

> the media like to report statistics because numbers seem to be factual, little nuggets of truth. The public tends to agree; we usually treat statistics as facts. In part, this is because we are innumerate. Innumeracy is the mathematical equivalent of illiteracy. (p. 38)

Erroneous reporting can arise due to the conflation, ambiguity, or incertitude regarding the purposes of different types of assessments which can lead to applications of data for which the assessment was never designed. Therefore, the media can play on the ignorance of the public regarding sectors or industries in society about which they have little or no insider knowledge which limits their capacity to make informed judgements about the merits of a debate; and education is an easy target because everyone has gone to school.

Barber (2004) in the UK identified the importance of positive self-marketing to the media from within the public service sector where he cautioned that overt criticism from within the sector tends to negatively colour the thinking of the public about that sector as a whole. Similarly, in the Netherlands, Segers and Tillema (2011) found students and their parents were confused and disillusioned about the high stakes examinations due to the "vivid debate on the quality of examinations" that was widely publicised in the media (p. 53). Sarjala (2013) noted the media scepticism regarding governmental policy directions, even though these were largely uncontested within the parliament. The media in Australia has had a long and very contentious relationship with education policy, frequently portraying teachers in a poor light, and lambasting curriculum and assessment reforms to the point where parents and the public doubt the quality of their school system, openly question teacher judgements, and curriculum and assessment implementation efforts. Griffiths et al. (2008) reported this as the media "steering from a distance … [having] symbolic power over policy processes" (p. 170). They continued stating this has seriously damaged teachers' professional self-belief and confidence and has made educators resistant to further change.

Potentially the most contentious and damaging educational report is 'annual league tables' where school rankings are reported with little explanation or discussion of the criteria used in the ranking process (Schagen & Hutchison, 2003). Unfortunately, there are usually fewer reports about schools who have improved their effectiveness in student achievement than those which have lost ground due to various factors. While acknowledging parental rights to select schools and make choices based on the information that is available – frequently those of league tables – the ramifications for schools where parents move their children can have serious consequences in terms of funding, which exacerbates opportunities for students in those schools who are unable to move (Eurydice, 2009; Griffiths et al., 2008). Unless governments take action to provide more support to poorer performing schools, league tables or similar ranking systems can reinforce status differences within civil societies (Schleicher, 2011). Even though censorship of the school data is not desirable in a civil society, it is important to consider the potential damage that can be wrought from indiscriminate or misleading conclusions that can be drawn from 'selected' data. It is then important for school and system leaders to be proactive in educating the public regarding these school data, as well as in presenting positive portrayals of exemplary educators and schools, thereby providing the opportunity for balanced public perceptions of educators and the sector (Schagen & Hutchison, 2003).

2.10 Concluding Thoughts

There can be no denying that globalisation has changed and continues to change the world we live in and the fabric and expectations of society. Assessment with its overt flavour of accountability and politicisation is a modern-day reality for everyone but particularly for students, educators, and leaders. Curiously, this inductive analysis revealed debates and discussions that focused on the political dimensions of assessment, accountability of systems and teachers but only peripherally included leaders in these debates. The leadership focus tended to be on political leaders or system leaders, but little on school leaders or jurisdictional leaders. Therefore this book, with its emphasis on leadership for enhanced assessment in schools and across districts, seeks to address the dearth of literature about the assessment leader. I hope that readers will find valuable theoretical and practical insights into leadership for enhanced assessment.

References

Acar, T. (2012). The position of Turkey among OECD member and candidate countries according to PISA 2009 results. *Educational Sciences: Theory & Practice, 12*(4), 2567–2572.

Barber, M. (2004). The virtue of accountability: System redesign, inspection, and incentives in the era of informed professionalism. *Journal of Education, 185*(1), 7–900.

Beets, P. A. D. (2012). Strengthening morality and ethics in educational assessment through "Ubuntu" in South Africa. *Educational Philosophy and Theory, 44*(2), 68–83. doi:10.1111/j.1469-5812.2011.00796.x.

Bolt, S. (2011). Making consistent judgements. A professional development program based on using teacher judgement to assess student attainment of systemic achievement targets. *Educational Forum, 75*(2), 157–172. doi:10.1080/00131725.2011.552694.

Brandeis, L. D. (1912). *Business — A profession*. Retrieved from: http://louisville.edu/law/library/specialcollections/the-louis-d.-brandeis-collection/business-a-profession-chapter-1

Brunello, G., Rocco, L., Ariga, K., & Iwahashi, R. (2012). On the efficiency costs of de-tracking secondary schools in Europe. *Education Economics, 20*(2), 117–138.

Commeyras, M., & Inyega, H. N. (2007). An integrative review of teaching reading in Kenyan primary schools. *Reading Research Quarterly, 42*(2), 258–281. doi:10.1598/RRQ.42.2.3.

Cowie, B., Jones, A., & Otrel-Cass, K. (2011). Re-engaging students in science: Issues of assessment, funds of knowledge and sites for learning. *International Journal of Science and Mathematics Education, 9*(2), 347–366.

De Boer, G. C., Minnaert, A. E. M. G., & Kamphof, G. (2013). Gifted education in the Netherlands. *Journal for the Education of the Gifted, 36*(1), 133–150. doi:10.1177/0162353212471622.

Eurydice. (2009). *National testing of pupils in Europe: Objectives, organisation and use of results* (pp. 1–109). Brussels, Belgium: Education, Audiovisual and Culture Executive Agency, P9 Eurydice. doi:10.2797/18294.

Fenwick, L. (2012). Limiting opportunities to learn in upper-secondary schooling: Differentiation and performance assessment in the context of standards-based curriculum reform. *Curriculum Inquiry, 42*(5), 629–651. doi:10.1111/j.1467-873X.2012.00609.x.

Friesen, J. B., & Ezeife, A. N. (2009). Making science assessment culturally valid for Aboriginal students. *Canadian Journal of Native Education, 32*(2), 24–37.

Garner, M. (2013). Lies, damn lies, and tests. *Measurement: Interdisciplinary Research and Perspectives, 11*(1–2), 36–39.

Geçer, A., & Özel, R. (2012). Elementary science and technology teachers' views on problems encountered in the instructional process. *Educational Sciences: Theory & Practice, 12*(3), 2256–2261.

Gove, A., & Wetterberg, A. (2011). *The early grade reading assessment: Applications and interventions to improve basic literacy*. Research Triangle Park, NC: RTI International.

Green, S. K., Johnson, R. L., Kim, D.-H., & Pope, N. S. (2007). Ethics in classroom assessment practices: Issues and attitudes. *Teaching and Teacher Education, 23*, 999–1011. doi:10.1016/j.tate.2006.04.042.

Griffiths, J., Vidovich, L., & Chapman, A. (2008). Outcomes approaches to assessment: comparing non-government and government case-study schools in Western Australia. *Curriculum Journal, 19*(3), 161–175. doi:10.1080/09585170802357470.

Harlen, W. (2005). Trusting teachers' judgement: Research evidence of the reliability and validity of teachers' assessment used for summative purposes. *Research Papers in Education, 20*(3), 245–270. doi:10.1080/02671520500193744.

Harris, L. R., & Brown, G. T. L. (2009). The complexity of teachers' conceptions of assessment: Tensions between the needs of schools and students. *Assessment in Education: Principles, Policy & Practice, 16*(3), 365–381. doi:10.1080/0969594090331974.

Hulpia, H., & Valcke, M. (2004). The use of performance indicators in a school improvement policy: The theoretical and empirical context. *Evaluation & Research in Education, 18*(1–2), 102–119. doi:10.1080/09500790408668311.

James, M., & Pedder, D. (2006). Beyond method: assessment and learning practices and values. *Curriculum Journal, 17*(2), 109–138. doi:10.1080/09585170600792712.

Jordan, A. (2007). *Introduction to inclusive education*. Mississauga, ON: John Wiley & Sons Canada, Ltd.

Katsiyannis, A., Zhang, D., Ryan, J. B., & Jones, J. (2007). High-stakes testing and students with disabilities. *Journal of Disability Policy Studies, 18*(3), 160–167. doi:10.1177/10442073070180030401.

Klenowski, V., & Wyatt-Smith, C. (2010). Standards-driven reform years 1–10: Moderation an optional extra? *Australian Educational Researcher, 37*(2), 21–39.

Lebeer, J., Birta-Szekely, N., Demeter, K., Bohacs, K., Candeias, A. A., Sonnesyn, G., et al. (2012). Re-assessing the current assessment practice of children with special education needs in Europe. *School Psychology International, 33*(1), 69–92. doi:10.1177/0143034311409975.

Matsuoka, R. (2013). Learning competencies in action: Tenth grade students' investment in accumulating human capital under the influence of the upper secondary education system in Japan. *Educational Studies in Japan: International Yearbook, 7*, 65–79.

Ministerial Council on Education, Employment, Training and Youth Affairs (MCEETYA). (2008). *Measurement Framework for National Key Performance Measures.* Victoria, Australia: Ministerial Council on Education, Employment, Training and Youth Affairs.

Organisation for Economic Co-operation and Development (OECDa). *Programme for International Student Assessment (PISA).* Retrieved from http://www.oecd.org/pisa/keyfindings/pisa-2012-results.htm

Organisation for Economic Co-operation and Development (OECDb, n.p.). *About the OECD.* Retrieved from http://www.oecd.org/about/

Organisation for Economic Co-operation and Development (OECDc, n.p.). *Members and partners.* Retrieved from http://www.oecd.org/about/membersandpartners/

Ozga, J., & Lingard, B. (2007). Globalisation, education policy and politics. In B. Lingard & J. Ozga (Eds.), *The RoutledgeFalmer reader in education policy and politics* (pp. 65–82). Abingdon, Oxon: Routledge.

Pepper, D. (2011). Assessing key competences across the curriculum – and Europe. *European Journal of Education, 46*(3), 335–353.

Poliandri, D., Cardone, M., Muzzioli, P., & Romiti, S. (2010). *Dynamic database for quality indicators comparison in education.* Paper presented at the bordering, re-bordering and New Possibilities in Education and Society, Istanbul. doi:10.2139/ssrn.1639398.

Raisanen, A., & Rakkolainen, M. (2009). Social and communicational skills in upper secondary vocational education and training. *US-China Education Review, 6*(12), 36–45.

Rajagopal. (2009). *Globalization thrust: Driving nations competitive.* Hauppauge/New York: Nova Science Publishers Inc.

Ross, H., Cen, Y., & Zhou, Z. (2011). Assessing student engagement in China: Responding to local and global discourse on raising educational quality. *Current Issues in Comparative Education, 14*(1), 24–37.

Sahlberg, P. (2012). A model lesson: Finland shows us what equal opportunity looks like. *American Educator, 36*(1), 20–27.

Sarjala, J. (2013). Equality and cooperation: Finland's path to excellence. *American Educator, 37*(1), 32–36.

Saunders, M., & Vulliamy, G. (1983). The implementation of curricular reform: Tanzania and Papua New Guinea. *Comparative Education Review, 27*(3), 351–373. doi:10.2307/1187742.

Schagen, I., & Hutchison, D. (2003). Adding value in educational research – the marriage of data and analytical power. *British Educational Research Journal, 29*(5), 749–765. doi:10.1080/0141192032000133659.

Schleicher, A. (2011). Is the sky the limit to education improvement? *Phi Delta Kappan, 93*(2), 58–63.

Schleicher, A., & Stewart, V. (2008). Learning from world-class schools. *Educational Leadership, 66*(2), 44–51.

Scott, S., Webber, C. F., Aitken, N., & Lupart, J. (2011). Developing teachers' knowledge, beliefs, and expertise: Findings from the Alberta Student Assessment Study. *The Educational Forum, 75*(2), 96–113. doi:10.1080/00131725.2011.552594.

Scott, S., Webber, C. F., Lupart, J. L., Aitken, N., & Scott, D. E. (2013). Fair and equitable assessment practices for all students. *Assessment in Education: Principles, Policy & Practice.* doi:10.1080/0969594X.2013.776943.

Segers, M., & Tillema, H. (2011). How do Dutch secondary teachers and students conceive the purpose of assessment? *Studies in Educational Evaluation, 37*, 49–54.

Shafiq, M. N. (2011). Do school incentives and accountability measures improve skills in the Middle East and North Africa? The cases of Jordan and Tunisia. *Review of Middle East Economics and Finance, 7*(2), 1–28. doi:10.2202/1475-3693.1279.

Toakley, A. R. (2004). Globalization, sustainable development and universities. *Higher Education Policy, 17*(3), 311–324.

Ungerleider, C. (2006). Reflections on the use of large-scale student assessment for improving student success. *Canadian Journal of Education, 29*(3), 873–883.

Vikiru, L. I. (2011). From assessment to learning: The teaching of English beyond examinations. *Educational Forum, 75*(2), 129–142. doi:10.1080/00131725.2011.552685.

Volante, L., & Beckett, D. (2011). Formative assessment and the contemporary classroom: Synergies and tensions between research and practice. *Canadian Journal of Education, 34*(2), 239–255.

Wainer, H. (2011). *Uneducated guesses: Using evidence to uncover misguided education policies.* Princeton, NJ: Princeton University Press.

Wang, L., Beckett, G. H., & Brown, L. (2006). Controversies of standardized assessment in school accountability reform: A critical synthesis of multidisciplinary research evidence. *Applied Measurement in Education, 19*(4), 305–328. doi:10.1207/s15324818ame1904_5.

Webber, C. F., & Scott, S. (2013). Principles for principal preparation. In C. L. Slater & S. Nelson (Eds.), *Understanding the principalship: An international guide to principal preparation* (Vol. 19, pp. 95–124). Bingley, UK: Emerald.

Winter, C. (2011). School curriculum, globalisation and the constitution of policy problems and solutions. *Journal of Education Policy, 27*(3), 295–314. doi:10.1080/02680939.2011.609911.

Zhang, M., & Kong, L. (2012). An exploration of reasons for Shanghai's success in the OECD Program for International Student Assessment (PISA) 2009. *Frontiers of Education in China, 7*(1), 124–162. doi:10.3868/s110-001-012-0007-3.

Chapter 3
Monitoring, Accountability, and Improvement, Oh No! Assessment Policies and Practices in Canadian Education

Don A. Klinger

Abstract Public education in Canada is under the jurisdiction of provincial and territorial governments that oversee policies, procedures, practices, curriculum, funding structures, and public accountability. This chapter explores the shifting methods that provinces use to monitor student achievement and demonstrate educational accountability. Large-scale testing programmes provide a central measure of educational accountability at the district, school, and even teacher level. However, these Canadian accountability models do not impact teachers' salaries, teacher promotion or school funding. Rather, they appear to reflect a level of trust in educators' professionalism to work to improve student achievement. This overview of the large-scale, K-12 assessment programmes across Canada highlights the common structures and practices that exist across the country, while also summarising the links between these testing programmes and accountability. The emerging trends in large-scale testing and educational accountability also underscore current debates and movements. Hence large-scale tests serve a growing number of purposes, and alternative data sources are being promoted to support accountability. "Assessment For Learning" is now prevalent throughout provincial assessment policies and practices. These accountability practices and trends to support student achievement raise a number of questions. Of these emerging questions, we must ask if accountability should be the lightning rod for school improvement?

Keywords Educational accountability • Large-scale testing • Education policy • Assessment for learning • K-12 education • Public education • Canadian education

3.1 Introduction

Public education in Canada is not under the jurisdiction of the federal government. Rather, each provincial or territorial government has a separate Ministry or Department of Education that is responsible for overseeing education policies,

D.A. Klinger (✉)
Faculty of Education, Queen's University, Kingston, ON, Canada
e-mail: klingerd@queensu.ca

© Springer International Publishing Switzerland 2016   53
S. Scott et al. (eds.), *Assessment in Education*, The Enabling
Power of Assessment 2, DOI 10.1007/978-3-319-23398-7_3

procedures, practices, curriculum, funding structures, and public accountability. Regional school boards or school authorities are tasked with the actual operation of schools in the province with the responsibility of ensuring the provincial/territorial educational mandates are implemented. This includes the hiring of teachers and administrators, and the maintenance of students' records. The result of the provincial territorial model is that Canada does not have a single model of public education. In some provinces, both public and separate (typically Catholic) schools are fully funded (e.g., Alberta, Ontario). In other provinces, private and religious schools are either partially funded by the Ministry of Education, or not funded at all. Public schooling typically begins in kindergarten (Ontario provides 2 years of kindergarten) and ends after Grade 12 (Grade 11 in Quebec). The transition from elementary to secondary school also varies not only across provinces but also within provinces.

Despite the differences in the manner in which education is delivered across the country, there are strong similarities across provinces and territories with respect to the purposes of education. The overall goals of education tend to focus on maximising opportunities for children to find success, meet individual learning needs, and prepare for inclusion into adult society. As an example, Gerard Kennedy, the Ontario Minister of Education in 2004 stated "The contemporary mission of publicly funded education and our moral purpose in schools is to ensure that all children and youth are educated to high levels of intellectual, practical and social competence" (Ontario Ministry of Education, 2004). More recently, the Alberta Department of Education Ministerial order stated that the "fundamental goal of education in Alberta is to inspire all students to achieve success and fulfilment, and reach their full potential by developing the competencies of Engaged Thinkers and Ethical Citizens with an Entrepreneurial Spirit, who contribute to a strong and prosperous economy and society" (Alberta Department of Education, 2013c).

The intention of provincial governments is to develop curriculum that will help children meet these educational goals. Once again, each province has distinct curriculum documents; however, these documents are almost entirely subject based, with the subjects themselves being very similar along with the expected learning outcomes within each subject. Students graduating from schools across Canada are expected to demonstrate skills in English or French, math, science, social studies, participate in physical education programmes, and follow their own specialised interests, for example, the arts, technology, or languages.

Of interest to my work have been the shifts in the manner in which provinces monitor the educational outcomes of students to demonstrate that public education is meeting its goals. Public education in Canada tends to have the broad support of the public, although growing concerns and declines in the public's confidence can be traced to the 1990s through more recent years (e.g., Dunleavy, 2007; Guppy & Davies, 1999). While several provinces have historically monitored and reported on educational outcomes, the decline in public confidence reported above may have created new models of educational monitoring and accountability across the country. It is no longer sufficient for a provincial Ministry or Department of Education to report on educational outcomes. Rather, promises are made to increase students' graduation rates and academic achievement, demonstrate higher levels of performance on international measures (e.g., PISA, or TIMMS), or to increase public trust in education. My interest has been in the common use of large-scale provincial examination (assessment) programmes to monitor overall student achievement and guide school improvement efforts. These provincial assessment programmes exist in every province and two of the three territories; however, the manner in which these examination programmes are implemented and used highlight a "low-stakes" approach to educational accountability that characterises the Canadian context (e.g., Klinger, DeLuca, & Miller, 2008; Klinger & Rogers, 2011; Klinger & Saab, 2012).

3.2 The Heart and Soul of School Accountability Models

With the published criticisms of public education in North America in the late twentieth century (e.g., National Commission on Excellence in Education, 1983; Nikiforuk, 1993), governments throughout North America enacted procedures to not only better track the educational achievement of children but also on ways to communicate the results to the general public. Accountability entered the common vocabulary of education policy. Naturally, methods and tools were required to provide an objective measure of educational achievement, and the real or perceived criticisms of education made it difficult to justify the use of teachers' assigned grades and summaries of student achievement. Large-scale, standardised tests were quickly viewed as a solution. These had long been used to measure student achievement (Klinger & DeLuca, 2009; Nagy, 2000; Taylor & Tubianosa, 2001). For example, the SATs had been used for the purposes of university admission for over 100 years in the United States, and externally administered school examinations had been in place on and off in Canada since the mid-1800s (Gidney & Harris, 1990; Putman, 1912). Hence methods and historical precedence were already in place for the use of external student achievement measures, with the need only to rationalise the use of these measures to direct accountability initiatives. There was also some precedence here as well, given the Tennessee Value-Added Assessment System (TVAAS) introduced in 1993. Imagine the likely conversation:

> We use large-scale, standardised examinations to individually measure student achievement and encourage students to work harder to meet educational outcomes. Let's expand the purposes of these examinations to also get teachers and school systems to work harder as well. There are already a few examples in place. All we have to do is promote the use of examinations at key educational grades, and modify the reporting methods so that overall student achievement results are publically reported.

The rest as they say "is history."

Policy makers believed these large-scale testing and assessment programmes would focus educators' attention, improving instruction and student achievement (Elmore, 2004; Mazzeo, 2001). Further, these examination programmes were argued to provide a relatively efficient, visible, and more fair measure of overall student achievement for the purposes of comparison across schools and years (Linn, 2000). Statistical methods were already in place to "account for" differences due to context, and mathematical equating methods could be used to compare annual results. Subsequently, the United States passed the No Child Left Behind (NCLB) Act (2002) that stressed the use of high-stakes testing to advance accountability goals in K-12 education (Brennan, 2006). The more recent Race to the Top (RTTT) legislation served to further support the fundamental tenets of NCLB (United States Department of Education, 2009). Certainly, the United States was not alone in the use of large-scale testing models to direct accountability efforts. Examples can be found across international jurisdictions including Australia, China, Denmark, Chile, Japan, Sweden, and the United Kingdom (Johnson, 2009; Phelps, 2000).

Armed with the "tool" of large-scale tests, an increasing number of centralised education jurisdictions adopted, refined, or developed large-scale testing and reporting models to use these student achievement measures to monitor overall achievement results at the district, school, and even teacher levels. This allowed the identification of districts and schools that, and teachers who, had student performance above or below expectations (using statistical modelling). Educators were increasingly held accountable to demonstrate the value of their efforts to not only contribute, but also improve student performance. In many contexts, the consequences for poor performance continue to be high for teachers and schools. Teachers' salaries and promotion may be based on student achievement on these examinations, and schools may be sanctioned or shut down if poor student performance persists.

Welcome to the evolution, or as some would claim, the devolution of large-scale achievement testing. From the humble beginnings to provide a "fair measure" of student achievement and skills (e.g., The Imperial Examinations in ancient China), we now have models of educational accountability linking educators' salaries and the continued operation of schools to student performance on external large-scale examinations (assessments). The purpose here is not to critique the foundations for these educational accountability models, and the use of large-scale testing to support these models; suffice it to say that there are a plethora of arguments for (e.g., Roderick & Engel, 2001; Sanders & Horn, 1998) and against (e.g., Delandshere, 2001; Ravitch, 2010; Wilbrink, 1997) previous and current accountably models. The negative position recently espoused by Diane Ravitch is particularly interesting given her earlier central role in the NCLB legislation. Of greater importance for my work are the conspicuous differences that exist within the Canadian context.

3.3   The Canadian Model of School Monitoring and Accountability

As with many other educational jurisdictions, there is a long history of large-scale educational testing of Canadian youth. And the absence and presence of these testing programmes can be linked to the changing educational, political, and social perspectives of the country and of each province/territory (Klinger & DeLuca, 2009; Klinger et al., 2008). Historically, and with few exceptions, these examinations served to provide an external and "more objective" measure of student achievement. Interestingly, even in the 1800s, such examinations were used to monitor and direct educators, and these "examination programmes became particularly important mechanisms of central control and authority" (Klinger & DeLuca, 2009, p. 5; see also Gidney & Harris, 1990, Putman, 1912). External monitoring programmes that used large-scale assessments appeared in the 1970s, likely influenced by the National Assessment of Educational progress (NAEP) in the United States that began in the late 1960s. For example, the province of British Columbia introduced the Provincial Learning Assessment Programme (PLAP) in 1976. The Council of Ministers of Education, Canada (CMEC) administered the School Achievement Indicators Programme (SAIP) between 1993 and 2004. The Pan-Canadian Assessment Programme (PCAP) has since replaced SAIP. These assessments were and are typically given to samples of students at key grades or ages, with the primary purposes to inform educators and the public about the strengths and weaknesses of the education system. The PLAP monitored students' learning over time to guide the British Columbia Ministry of Education, school districts, and schools with respect to curricula and the allocation of resources. SAIP and PCAP allow for some form of interprovincial comparisons.

The shift from monitoring to accountability began to occur when existing or new testing programmes were expanded to include all students rather than a sample of students. The inclusion of all students enabled the reporting of more stable, school level estimates, and this provided both a measure for between and within (across time) school comparisons. Increasingly, high-stakes examinations (typically administered in Grade 12 academic subjects) were also reported at the school level. As a result, there has been a growing need for test security and measurement models that allow horizontal equating (the same grade over time) of test results from year-to-year. There is little doubt that large-scale educational assessment programmes across Canada now serve purposes related to accountability along with the long-standing purposes of measuring and monitoring individual student achievement or broad educational outcomes as a whole. However, the accountability models are a strong contrast to those found in other jurisdictions. I have previously termed Canadian approaches to educational accountability as low-stakes accountability frameworks (e.g., Klinger & Rogers, 2011; Klinger & Saab, 2012).

The accountability models that exist in Canadian education do not link large-scale assessment results to teachers' salaries, teacher promotion or school closures as supported by NCLB or RTTT. The perspective that teacher quality and effort along with administrator leadership are key determinants of student achievement remains. However, the Canadian perspective appears to reflect a level of trust in educators' professionalism to work to improve student achievement, perhaps in recognition of the overall public confidence in public education. Teachers and principals are expected to use the results to review their instructional practices and, based on the performance of their students in the examination, make needed changes that are designed to maintain learning/teaching strengths and address weaknesses. The logic here is that by so doing, student performance in the next year will increase, thereby increasing the level of performance of the schools (see also Klinger & Saab,

2012). The effect of the changes made is then determined by the performance of the students in a comparable form of the examination in the next year. The public reporting of results is largely considered a sufficient level of accountability. As a further example of the vast differences in the Canadian approach to accountability, the Ontario Ministry of Education, through its Literacy and Numeracy Secretariat (LNS) has used several procedures to provide lower performing schools with additional funding and resources to support improvement efforts. Other provinces (e.g., British Columbia, Alberta, and Nova Scotia) have used school directed, internal accreditation or accountability frameworks to support explicit school improvement efforts.

3.4   A Closer Look at Provincial Assessment Policies and Practices

In spite of the provincial levels of control of public education, the large-scale examination and assessment programmes in Canada are very similar. Every province and territory in Canada has at least one large-scale examination programme in its K-12 public education system. The *explicit* purposes of all of these examination programmes tend to include at least one of three major purposes: (1) describing the individual achievement of students (used for monitoring or grading); (2) describing the overall quality and effectiveness of education (monitoring); and (3) focusing school improvement efforts (accountability) (e.g., Hodgkinson, 1995; Klinger, DeLuca & Miller, 2008; McEwen, 1995; Nagy, 2000; Wolfe, Childs, & Elgie, 2004). The word explicit is highlighted, as there appear to be many implicit purposes for many of the examination programmes as well. There are also many purposes attributed to these examination programmes claimed by various stakeholders (e.g., Klinger & Rogers, 2011), some based on misinformation, others based on anecdotal evidence. Yet other attributed purposes are based on actual "non-approved use" of these examination programmes, most notably those reported by external organisations in which comparative rankings of schools are made (e.g., Johnson, 2005).

Most commonly, the explicit purposes focus on improving students' learning and system improvement. As an example, two of the key purposes of the Assessment for Learning Programme administered by the Saskatchewan Ministry of Education are to "raise the level of student learning and achievement for all students" and "strengthen the capacity of teachers, schools and school divisions to use data to inform decision making" (Government of Saskatchewan, 2012, www.education. gov.sk.ca/AFL/AFLProgram). Similarly, the elementary examination in Quebec is intended to describe the competency levels attained by students at the end of elementary school, and also "offer guidance to teachers who seek to inform themselves about the effectiveness of their classroom practices" (Ministère de l'Éducation, du Loisir et du Sport, 2007, p. 3).

The commonalities across examination programmes extend beyond purpose. Similarities can be found in the structure, timing, administration, curriculum examined, teacher involvement, and reporting (e.g., Klinger et al., 2008; Klinger & Saab,

2012). The administration pattern typically has examinations separated by 3 years starting in primary and continuing until early secondary school. A common starting point is either Grade 3 or Grade 4. The variations in starting times and the intervals between examinations are primarily due to differences in academic divisions across the provinces/territories (Grade 6 marks the end of elementary school in Alberta, while Grade 7 marks the end of elementary school in British Columbia) rather than the cognitive developmental stages of students. Examinations and assessments in the elementary grades have no direct consequences for students, and are typically administered in April or May. Some provinces administer these assessments earlier to further direct subsequent instructional practices (e.g., Nova Scotia). High-school examinations exist in most provinces and these are more likely to have direct impact on students, with the examination scores contributing to a student's final course grade. These high school examinations may be administered in the early high-school grades, with the scores contributing a relatively small percentage (10–20 %) towards students' grades, or as Grade 12 academic course examinations with the scores providing a substantial contribution to students' grades (30–50 %). These examinations are administered at the end of the course, with multiple administrations in those provinces having different school schedules (full year, semester, quarter). Interestingly, the use of such provincially administered, Grade 12 examinations is declining. British Columbia stopped administering all but the Grade 12 Language Arts in the early 2000s. Nova Scotia stopped administering its Grade 12 Mathematics examinations in 2012/2013.

Throughout Canada, language/literacy (reading and/or writing) and mathematics are the most commonly assessed subjects. Reading and writing skills typically define literacy examinations. The range of mathematics topics and skills is somewhat more varied. For example, the topics typically include one or more of number sense and numeration; measurement; geometry; patterning and algebra; trigonometry; and data management and probability, while the skills typically include computation, problem solving, and communication. Ontario and New Brunswick administer a high school literacy test that students must successfully complete prior to graduation (Education Quality and Accountability Office, 2013; New Brunswick Department of Education and Early Childhood Development, 2013). Alternatives are in place to support those students who are unable to successfully complete this test prior to Grade 12.

One of the important and surprisingly unique aspects of the examination programmes in Canada is the level of teacher involvement. Teachers are typically involved in many aspects of the development, administration, and marking processes. For example, the examinations are commonly marked in central locations by trained teacher markers, although there has been a recent shift towards school district marking centres, or marking guidelines provided by the province's Ministry (Department) of Education to teachers.

Lastly, examination reports are most commonly produced at the student, school, school board, and provincial levels, and less commonly at the classroom level. Centrally scored reports tend to be released in the late summer or early in the subsequent school year. School and school board reports are distributed in a manner that protects the anonymity of individual students and teachers. Hence the general public and policy makers have access to school, district, and provincial results, but only the students, parents, teachers and school administrators have access to individual student results. When reports are published, caveats are provided noting the limitations and errors of measurement.

3.5   Emerging Trends

While education accountability remains an important topic in public education throughout Canada, the examination programmes used to inform those accountability frameworks have been changing somewhat. In provinces such as British Columbia and Nova Scotia, the Grade 12 examination programmes have been substantially reduced, while new examination programmes have been added in earlier grades. Accountability models are also beginning to rely on other forms of data, including teacher grades, absenteeism, graduation rates, diagnostic assessments, and internal educator developed measures intended to monitor school improvement efforts. The School Effectiveness Framework in Ontario provides an extensive set of guidelines for school and district improvement efforts that promote the use of other educational outcomes (Ontario Ministry of Education, 2013).

There is also a developing trend to support improved educational outcomes through alternative assessment practices in the classroom. For example, curriculum and assessment documents from the Ontario Ministry of Education continually state, "the primary purpose of assessment and evaluation is to improve student learning" (e.g., Ontario Ministry of Education, 2010, p. 6). There has been a growing recognition of the value of formative classroom assessment practices to enhance students' learning. These assessment practices reflect more current conceptions of classroom assessment that are purposefully integrated with teaching and learning, and represented through such phrases as Assessment "Of", "For" and "As" Learning (e.g., Earl, 2003; Wiliam, 2006; Wiliam, Lee, Harrison, & Black, 2004). Provincial curriculum and assessment documents increasingly refer to these three phrases (e.g., Manitoba Education, 2010; New Brunswick Department of Education and Early Childhood Development, 2013; Ontario Ministry of Education, 2010, 2013). Further, provincial initiatives such as the Alberta Initiative for School Improvement and various projects from the Literacy and Numeracy Secretariat in Ontario provide funding to improve teachers' skills in using Assessment "*For*" and "*As*" Learning strategies (Alberta Department of Education, 2013a; Ontario Ministry of Education, 2011). While these efforts to support teachers' assessment practices are intended to support teaching and learning, there is also an aspect of professional accountability and responsibility underlying such initiatives and supports.

The "Assessment for Learning" focus can also be found within large-scale testing programmes. As described previously, Saskatchewan Learning's Assessment For Learning provincial examination programme is designed to provide information to: "help students learn more and promote greater learning" among other purposes and objectives (Saskatchewan Ministry of Education, 2007, p. 2). Perhaps even more interesting, Alberta, arguably Canada's most conservative province, is planning on replacing its long established Provincial Achievement Tests with Student Learning Assessments (SLAs) (Alberta Department of Education, 2013b). These SLAs will be administered at the beginning of the school year "to identify areas where kids might need some extra attention and get them the support they need to succeed." These Assessment For Learning assessment programmes are intended to support teachers' efforts to improve student learning; however, they also fulfil a public accountability purpose. As an example, the Assessment For Learning assessment programme in Saskatchewan includes amongst its purposes to "Strengthen the ability of school divisions to report to the public on student learning and school effectiveness"(Saskatchewan Ministry of Education, 2007, p. 3). The Alberta Department of Education Acknowledges that "the new assessments will continue to provide accountability information" (Alberta Department of Education, 2013d).

The Assessment for Learning trend underlies a shift in thinking regarding the types of students' educational outcomes that should be the focus of teaching efforts and monitoring. As Darling-Hammond notes, there is a need to focus on other educational outcomes, including critical thinking, collaboration, problem solving, reflection, and working independently. Students need "to learn to learn: to be able to learn new things on one's own, to be self-guided and independent in the learning process" (Umphrey, 2009, p. 18). The beginnings of this shift are already in place in Saskatchewan (Assessment for Learning programme) and in Manitoba. Manitoba includes an assessment of student engagement (Manitoba Education, 2010). Future shifts are in place for Alberta and British Columbia is beginning to explore new forms of large-scale assessments to measure important learning skills.

3.6 Final Thoughts

Canada has not been immune to the growing demands for educational accountability. Throughout Canada, the provincial/territorial ministries or departments of education describe the explicit purposes of their examination programmes using a language of professional accountability, first for raising student achievement, and second for improving professional practice. Nevertheless, our perceptions of accountability in Canadian education reflect a low-stakes approach that attempts to promote professional responsibility and accountability (e.g., Klinger & Rogers, 2011; Klinger & Saab, 2012). As Klinger and Saab note:

> Schools are not sanctioned for poor performance, and there are no legislated negative consequences to schools or teachers who are unable to meet educational targets. Instead, accountability frameworks throughout the provinces and territories are typically framed to be a responsibility of educators. School boards, administrators, and teachers are expected to use the results from large-scale assessments to inform and guide board and school improvement efforts. (p. 81)

Admittedly, it is not clear that the Canadian approach to educational accountability has had a positive impact on overall student achievement. National and international comparisons can be made using results from the Programme for International Student Assessment (PISA) or from the recently introduced Pan Canadian Assessment Programme (PCAP). There is some evidence that the Province of Ontario has made improvements relative to the provinces of British Columbia, Alberta and Quebec on the PISA assessments (Bussière, Cartwright, & Knighton, 2004; Council of Ministers of Education, Canada, 2011; Knighton, Brochu, & Gluzynski, 2010). Through the Literacy and Numeracy Secretariat and other initiatives, the province of Ontario has made increased student achievement an important educational mandate. Nevertheless, these same PISA results suggest that although Canada remains a high performing country educationally, Canadian students may have declining results relative to other high-performing countries. Yet, even in Ontario, the evidence of improvement in student achievement on large-scale assessments is not unequivocal. The provincial achievement results published by the Education Quality and Accountability Office (EQAO) illustrate, using equated scores, that the proportion of students meeting provincial standard in reading and writing is increasing but the proportion meeting the provincial standard in mathematics is declining (2013, 2014). And this is in spite of recent provincial initiatives focused on mathematics.

Perhaps more importantly, large-scale assessment programmes throughout Canada interweave system monitoring, professional accountability, and increasingly, formative diagnosis of student learning. There is little evidence these multiple and increasing purposes can be met (see also Klinger & Rogers, 2011; Klinger et al., 2008). Hence it is possible that the provincial and territorial large-scale examinations and assessments being used for these purposes cannot support such purposes.

It is also possible that the central underlying tenet of these examination programmes is problematic. Over the last 20 years, the number and types of provincial, large-scale examinations in Canada have increased dramatically. The increasing use of these examinations in Canada underlies a belief that these examination programmes can affect changes in policy, curriculum, and practice to improve student achievement and school performance, a generally untested hypothesis (e.g., Delandshere, 2001; Madaus & Kellaghan, 1992; Ontario Royal Commission on Learning, 1994; Ryan, 2002). Regardless, the data from the vast majority of large-scale assessments rarely provide specific information that would directly inform subsequent instruction. Similarly, the foundational aspects of "Assessment For Learning" and "Assessment As Learning" require a much stronger research foundation. Lastly, my recent and ongoing work with schools and school districts further highlights the difficulty in supporting educators' efforts to actually use data to inform instruction (e.g., Klinger, Maggi, & D'Angiulli, 2011).

Educational accountability in Canada continues to make explicit use of large-scale examinations to demonstrate an ongoing commitment to improving the educational outcomes for our youth. These examinations shape and guide instruction, curriculum, and policy. Given the importance of such assessment policies and programmes, there needs to be careful forethought and informed debate about their accuracy, viability, and use. Such debate needs to include policy makers and practitioners along with the academic community if shared progress is to be made. The following questions provide a foundation for subsequent debate, discussion, and research:

1. Should accountability be the lightning rod for school improvement?
2. Is it sufficient to use models of professional responsibility and accountability to improve overall student learning?
3. Can the current procedures support the monitoring, and subsequent instructional diagnoses being promoted?
4. What are the consequences for assessment results? Are these appropriate?
5. Can the assessment programmes support the increasing purposes for which they are being used?
6. What is the role of the provinces and territories to develop subsequent assessment policies and practices for teachers and boards?
7. Can such policies ensure consistent expectations and reporting?

References

Alberta Department of Education. (2013a). *AISI: Improving student learning.* http://education.alberta.ca/teachers/aisi.aspx
Alberta Department of Education. (2013b). *Alberta empowers more students to succeed.* http://alberta.ca/NewsFrame.cfm?ReleaseID=/acn/201305/3413389E6F172-A58E-3543-821C27F503CDA92B.html
Alberta Department of Education. (2013c). *Department of education ministerial order (#001/2013).* Retrieved from: http://education.alberta.ca/media/6951645/skmbt_c36413050707450.pdf
Alberta Department of Education. (2013d). *FAQ – Student learning assessments.* Retrieved from: http://education.alberta.ca/media/7380300/faqstudentlearningassessments.pdf
Brennan, R. L. (2006). Perspectives on the evolution and future of educational measurement. In *Educational measurement* (4th ed., p. 1–16). Westport, CT: Praeger Publishers.
Bussière, P., Cartwright, F., & Knighton, T. (2004). *Measuring up: Canadian results of the OECD PISA study: The performance of Canada's youth in reading, mathematics and science: 2003 First results for Canadians aged 15.* Toronto, ON, Canada: Human Resources and Skills Development Canada, Council of Ministers of Education, Canada and Statistics Canada.
Council of Ministers of Education, Canada. (2011). Pan-Canadian assessment program PCAP-2010: Report on the Pan-Canadian assessment of mathematics, science, and reading. Toronto, ON, Canada: Council of Ministers of Education, Canada.
Delandshere, G. (2001). Implicit theories, unexamined assumptions and the status quo of educational assessment. *Assessment in Education, 8,* 113–133.
Dunleavy, J. (2007). *Public education in Canada: Facts, trends and attitudes.* Toronto, ON, Canada: Canadian Education Association.
Earl, L. M. (2003). *Assessment as learning: Using classroom assessment to maximize student learning.* Thousand Oaks, CA: Corwin.
Education Quality and Accountability Office. (2013). *Educator resources.* Retrieved from www.eqao.com/Educators/educator.aspx
Education Quality and Accountability Office. (2014). *Highlights of the provincial results.* Retrieved from http://www.eqao.com/en/assessments/results/communication-docs/provincialreport-highlights-elementary-2014.pdf
Elmore, R. F. (2004). The problem of stakes in performance-based accountability systems. In S. F. Furman & R. F. Elmore (Eds.), *Redesigning accountability systems for education* (pp. 274–296). New York: Teachers College Press.
Gidney, R. D., & Harris, W. P. J. (1990). *Inventing secondary education: The rise of the high school in nineteenth century Ontario.* Montreal, QC, Canada: McGill-Queen's University Press.

Government of Saskatchewan. (2012). *Assessment for learning program.* Retrieved from http://www.education.gov.sk.ca/AFL/AFLProgram

Guppy, N., & Davies, S. (1999). Understanding Canadians' declining confidence in public education. *Canadian Journal of Education, 24,* 265–280.

Hodgkinson, D. (1995). Accountability in education in British Columbia. *Canadian Journal of Education, 20,* 18–26.

Johnson, A. W. (2009). *Review of objectifying measures: The dominance of high-stakes testing and the politics of schooling.* Philadelphia, PA: Temple University Press.

Johnson, D. (2005). *Signposts of success: Interpreting Ontario's elementary school test scores. C. D. Howe Institute.* Ottawa, ON: Renouf.

Klinger, D. A., & DeLuca, C. (2009). *The history of large-scale achievement testing in Ontario's education system.* Toronto, ON, Canada: Elementary Teachers' Federation of Ontario.

Klinger, D. A., DeLuca, C., & Miller, T. (2008). The evolving culture of large-scale assessments in Canadian education. *Canadian Journal of Educational Administration and Policy, 76.* Retrieved from http://www.umanitoba.ca/publications/cjeap/articles/klinger.html

Klinger, D. A., Maggi, S., & D'Angiulli, A. (2011). School accountability and assessment: Should we put the roof up first. *The Educational Forum, 75*(2), 114–128.

Klinger, D. A., & Rogers, W. T. (2011). Teachers' perceptions of large-scale assessment programs within low-stakes accountability frameworks. *International Journal of Testing, 11,* 122–143.

Klinger, D. A., & Saab, H. (2012). Educational leadership in the context of low-stakes accountability: The Canadian perspective. In L. Volante (Ed.), *School leadership in the context of standards-based reform: International perspectives* (pp. 73–96). Dordrecht, Netherlands: Springer.

Knighton, T., Brochu, P., & Gluzynski, T. (2010). *Measuring up: Canadian results of the OECD PISA study: The performance of Canada's youth in reading, mathematics and science: 2009 First results for Canadians aged 15.* Toronto, ON, Canada: Human Resources and Skills Development Canada, Council of Ministers of Education, Canada and Statistics Canada.

Linn, R. L. (2000). Assessments and accountability. *Educational Researcher, 23*(9), 4–14.

Madaus, G. F., & Kellaghan, T. (1992). Curriculum evaluation and assessment. In P. W. Jackson (Ed.), *Handbook of research on curriculum* (pp. 119–154). New York: Maxwell Macmillan International.

Manitoba Education. (2010). Middle years assessment of key competencies in mathematics, reading comprehension, expository writing, and student engagement. Retrieved from www.edu.gov.mb.ca/k12/assess/docs/my_policy/document.pdf

Mazzeo, C. (2001). Frameworks of state: Assessment policy in historical perspective. *Teachers College Record, 103*(3), 367–397.

McEwen, N. (1995). Accountability in education in Canada. *Canadian Journal of Education, 20,* 1–17.

Ministère de l'Éducation, du Loisir et du Sport. (2007). Information document: Compulsory examination, English language arts. http://www.mels.gouv.qc.ca/DGFJ/de/pdf/2007/ela3_07.pdf

Nagy, P. (2000). The three roles of assessment: Gatekeeping, accountability, and instructional diagnosis. *Canadian Journal of Education, 25,* 262–279.

National Commission on Excellence in Education. (1983). *A nation at risk: The imperative for educational reform.* Washington, DC: U.S. Government Printing Office.

New Brunswick Department of Education and Early Childhood Development. (2013). *Framework for provincial assessments.* Retrieved from http://www.gnb.ca/0000/results/pdf/AssessmentFrameworkDocument.pdf

Nikiforuk, A. (1993). *School's out: The catastrophe in public education and what we can do about it.* Toronto, ON, Canada: Mcfarlane & Ross.

No Child Left Behind Act. (2002). *Public Law No. 107–10.* United States Federal Education Legislation.

Ontario Ministry of Education. (2004). *Building the Ontario education advantage: Student achievement. Mini-discussion paper prepared for the education partnership table.* Retrieved from www.edu.gov.on.ca/eng/document/nr/04.03/building.pdf

Ontario Ministry of Education. (2010). *Growing success: Assessment, grading, and reporting in Ontario schools*. Toronto: Queen's Printer for Ontario.

Ontario Ministry of Education. (2011). *Initiatives and professional learning*. Retrieved from www. edu.gov.on.ca/eng/literacynumeracy/about.html

Ontario Ministry of Education. (2013). *School effectiveness framework: A support for school improvement and student success*. Toronto: Queen's Printer for Ontario.

Ontario Royal Commission on Learning. (1994). *For the love of learning: A report of the Royal Commission on Learning* (Vols. 1 & 2). Toronto: Queen's Printer for Ontario.

Phelps, R. P. (2000). Trends in large-scale testing outside the United States. *Educational Measurement: Issues and Practices, 19*, 11–21.

Putman, J. H. (1912). *Egerton Ryerson and education in upper Canada*. Toronto, ON, Canada: William Briggs.

Ravitch, D. (2010). *The death and life of the great American school system: How testing and choice are undermining education*. New York: Basic Books.

Roderick, M., & Engel, M. (2001). The grasshopper and the ant: Motivational responses of low-achieving students to high-stakes testing. *Educational Analysis and Policy Analysis, 23*(3), 197–227.

Ryan, K. (2002). Assessment validation in the context of high-stakes assessment. *Educational Measurement: Issues and Practice, 21*(1), 7–15.

Sanders, W. L., & Horn, S. P. (1998). Research findings from the Tennessee Value-Added Assessment System (TVAAS) database: Implications for educational evaluation and research. *Journal of Personnel Evaluation in Education, 12*(3), 247–256.

Saskatchewan Ministry of Education. (2007). *Saskatchewan learning: Assessment for learning program: Supporting data-guided decision-making to improve student learning*. Assessment for Learning Conceptual. http://www.education.gov.sk.ca/adx/aspx/adxGetMedia.aspx?DocID =11401,11400,1,Documents&MediaID=20000&Filename=Assessment+for+Learning+Conc eptual+Framework+Sept+2007+_web_.pdf

Taylor, A. R., & Tubianosa, T. (2001). *Student assessment in Canada: Improving the learning environment through effective evaluation*. Kelowna, BC: Society for the Advancement of Excellence in Education.

Umphrey, J. (2009). Toward 21st century supports: An interview with Linda Darling-Hammond. *Principal Leadership, 10*(1), 18–21.

United States Department of Education. (2009). *Race to the top program: Executive summary*. Washington, DC: U.S. Department of Education.

Volante, L. (2007). Educational quality and accountability in Ontario: Past, present, and future. *Canadian Journal of Educational Administration and Policy*, (58).

Wilbrink, B. (1997). Assessment in historical perspective. *Studies in Educational Evaluation, 23*(1), 31–48.

Wiliam, D. (2006). Assessment for learning: Why what and how? *Orbit, 36*(2), 2–7.

Wiliam, D., Lee, C., Harrison, C., & Black, P. (2004). Teachers developing assessment for learning: Impact on student achievement. *Assessment in Education: Principles, Policy, & Practice, 11*, 49–65.

Wolfe, R., Childs, R., & Elgie, S. (2004). *Final report of the external evaluation of EQAO's assessment processes*. Toronto, ON, Canada: Ontario Institute for Studies in Education of the University of Toronto.

Chapter 4
Fairness in Educational Assessment in China: Historical Practices and Contemporary Challenges

Xiaomei Song

Abstract Chinese education is historically examination-oriented. For centuries, high-stakes public examinations have been used as the primary assessment tool to make decisions on learning outcomes, educational upward movement, and social mobility. In present day China, various initiates have been adopted to address issues related to the deeply entrenched testing-oriented practices. Regardless, testing continues to play a major role in education and educational assessment, in particular, for admission, progressing, and accountability purposes. To have an indepth understanding of such a situation, this chapter explores social-cultural factors which influence the determination of the fairness in a high-stakes test. This chapter first reviews the historical development of educational assessment in China and illustrates the significant influence of testing on classroom teaching and learning, followed by an introduction of four major, large-scale educational testing systems. Following that, the chapter focuses on one test in one of the testing systems and explores students', teachers', and administrators' perceptions about the fairness of this test. Results found that the participants endorsed such a testing-oriented system for various reasons, including the fair testing process, the merit-based value, the testing-oriented tradition, and pursuit of efficiency. Finally, the study questions whether fairness, driven by cultural and political ideology, serves to impede the development of fairness for those in the least advantaged positions in China. Dangers remain in treating testing as a predominantly fair and legitimate tool. As formative learning models gain impetus in the twenty-first century, educational policies and practices need to consider balanced and aligned assessment that represents the real benefits and interests of all students.

Keywords Educational assessment • Chinese educational system • Testing • Fairness • Historical development • Chinese testing system • Graduate School Entrance Examination • Imperial Examination • Testing culture • Chinese high-stakes testing

X. Song (✉)
Office of Institutional Effectiveness, Georgia Southern University, Statesboro, GA, USA
e-mail: xsong@georgiasouthern.edu

© Springer International Publishing Switzerland 2016   67
S. Scott et al. (eds.), *Assessment in Education*, The Enabling
Power of Assessment 2, DOI 10.1007/978-3-319-23398-7_4

4.1   Introduction

Concerns about fairness among stakeholders are paramount in educational assessment especially with the recent worldwide trend towards using testing for standards-based educational reform (Davis, 2009; Klenowski, 2013). Although researchers and educators have criticised the use of testing due to the potential negative consequences and lack of consideration of learners' differences and diversity in learning opportunities and outcomes (Cizek, 2001; Harrison, 2013), testing remains firmly entrenched in the Chinese educational system. The Chinese educational system is historically examination-oriented. For many years, summative, high-stakes tests have served as the major assessment tool to make judgments on learners' performance. In present day China, testing continues to play a key role in Chinese educational assessment, despite the implementation of various educational reforms which are intended to address problems related to deeply entrenched testing-oriented practices (Han & Yang, 2001).

To provide background information, this chapter first reviews the historical development of educational assessment in China and illustrates the significant influence of testing on classroom teaching and learning. The chapter then introduces four major, large-scale, high-stakes testing systems in today's China. After that, the chapter focuses on one particular test in one testing system and examines students', teachers', and administrators' perceptions about the fairness of this test. As formative learning models gain impetus in the twenty-first century, educational policies and practices in China need to consider fair, balanced, and aligned assessment tools that represent the real benefits and interests of groups and individual students.

4.2   The Imperial Examination

The Chinese educational system is historically examination-oriented. It can be traced back to the Imperial Examination when ancient China selected capable candidates for Imperial positions thousands of years ago. The system is often regarded as starting around the year 606 in the Sui Dynasty (589–618) (Yu & Suen, 2005). The Imperial Examination is called the *KeJu* in Chinese (科举). *Ke* means "function" and *Ju* means "many persons gathering in one room and sharing" (Zhang & Zhong, 2003, p. 254). In the Song Dynasty (907–1276), more and more candidates attempted the Imperial Examination. The number increased from less than 30,000 in the early eleventh century to about 400,000 test takers when the Song dynasty ended (Ebrey, 2010). By the time of the Ming Dynasty (1368–1644), the examination system, which consisted of three progressive levels over 3 years, was fully developed. Candidates went through the three levels of examinations from local, prefecture, to palace testing. Those who succeeded at local and regional levels would be summoned to the imperial palace for the final examination by the Chinese emperors. Successful candidates in palace testing would be identified to initially serve as scholars in the imperial secretariat known as the Hanlin Academy (翰林院). From those positions, the scholars might be promoted to serve as "district magistrates, prefectural governors, provincial governors, national departmental ministers, or even prime ministers/grand councillors" (Yu & Suen, 2005, p. 19). With such positions came legal privileges, power, reputation, and financial rewards for the candidate and their entire extended family. The system grew until finally almost anyone who wished to become an official had to prove his worth by passing the Imperial Examination.

The Imperial Examination ruled almost every aspect of teaching and learning through tested knowledge, format, and skills. For example, the major domain tested in the Imperial Examination was Confucian philosophy, which was covered by the Four Books and Five Classics (四书五经). These Confucian classics formed the standard curriculum. Composition writing, one of the major tested skills, had to be written according to a strict pattern called the "eight-legged essay" (Baguwen, 八股文), with introduction, exposition, argumentation, and conclusion, both in two sections (Berry, 2011). Each "leg" had to be written in words that paralleled its counterpart in the corresponding section. Even the total number of characters in composition writing was regulated. The "eight-legged essay" later became synonymous with pedantry or triteness. The Imperial Examination had significant impact on teaching and learning at the schools, which were often run privately for those who could afford to pay for education and examinations. Passing the exams was the final goal of learning. The whole society only valued knowledge and skills that were tested in the Imperial Examination. The Imperial Examination was the focus of the centralised, bureaucratic system and test-driven education in Ancient China for many decades.

During the three levels of testing, extremely rigorous procedures were used such as double marking, scrutiny for examiners' personal conflicts of interest, candidates being locked in separate examination cells for 3 days, and test scripts with candidate's name being concealed and scripts copied so that handwriting could not be recognised (Cheng, 2010; Yu & Suen, 2005). The Imperial Examination promoted the ideal of equality through identical treatment in testing across the whole country, regardless of candidates' social class (He, 2012). The high-stakes Imperial Examination was the key aspect of educational testing in Ancient China till almost the end of Qing Dynasty (1664–1911). Historically, the exam-oriented system helped the Chinese government choose the talent for governmental positions, promoted justice and equality through identical treatment of candidates, and prepared a large number of scholars and professionals for its pre-modern development (Hu & Seifman, 1987). The Imperial Examination was considered fair because the selection was based on test performance and merit, not blood or family connections. All test takers took the same test under the same conditions. Testing seemed to provide a level playing field. Such a testing system was derived from a firm philosophical belief in fairness which promotes equality based on test performance as opposed to family connections, socio-economic status, and sponsorship (Lee, 1985). Testing was viewed as a meritocratic solution to the widespread problems of favouritism, bribery, and corruption in the nomination system (Yu & Suen, 2005). Clearly, the appeal and acceptance of such a testing system was that tests were identical for every candidate who took them, though, of course, those candidates were generally limited to males whose families could afford to pay for education and examinations.

4.3   Educational Assessment After the Imperial Examination

By the nineteenth century, the Imperial Examination had gradually lost its vitality
and hindered the social and economic development of China (Ebrey, 2010). With
scientific development and industrialisation in Europe and North America, the
Imperial Examination was regarded as outdated and inadequate when the country
and its officials faced the task of modernising China. Since the contents of the
Imperial Examinations were narrow and stereotypical and examinations did not
identify candidates who could help to modernise the country, the Imperial
Examination was officially abolished in 1905 (Ebrey, 2010). It was replaced by a
three-level national examination system at the end of the three major stages of
schooling: primary, junior, and senior secondary education (Berry, 2011). Guided by
"*Presented School Regulations*" (奏定学堂章程) enacted in 1904 – the first educational regulation issued by the Chinese government – five types of tests within
schools were administered, including "non-regular tests, during term time, mid-term
examinations, end-of-year examinations, graduate examinations and entry examinations for further education" (Berry, 2011, p. 50). Although public education with a
Western-type curriculum was promoted, the testing-centred system remained. In
comparison with the Imperial Examination, educational assessment in Modern
China made limited progress, which was, in particular, due to the social environment
where China was confronted with dramatic challenges resulting from the military,
political, and economic invasion of Western countries and the Chinese Civil Wars
during this period of time. Despite developments such as the introduction of educational measurement theories and techniques (e.g., the book *Methods of Intelligence
Testing* by Liao and Chen in 1921), examinations were still used as a major tool to
drive learning and make judgments of learning outcomes (Berry, 2011).

A new educational system was established shortly after the founding of the
People's Republic of China in 1949. As a member of the Socialist Bloc, the educational system and assessment policies were structured following those of the Soviet
Union (Feng, 2006). The system was operated in a highly centralised way and public education became much more accessible. Moves towards formative assessment
and assessment *for* learning made a fleeting appearance in the 1950s. For example,
schools used a five grade marking system — Poor (1), Fail (2), Pass (3), Good (4),
and Distinction (5) (Feng, 2006). A variety of classroom assessment methods were
encouraged, such as observation, questioning, written assignments, quizzes, and
exams (Dong, 1998). Regardless, the influence of testing on classroom learning and
teaching remained. This was partially due to the adoption of one of the educational
policies—the "key school" mechanism, which influenced assessment practices
(Gang, 1996; Han & Yang, 2001). Given substantive financial difficulties and the
need to make the most of limited educational resources, a small number of schools
and universities were designated as key schools and universities. The Chinese
Government allocated quality educational resources to select schools from the
beginning of the 1950s. The "key school" scheme was introduced into secondary
education in 1953, higher education in 1954, and primary education in 1962 (Gang,

1996). The main purpose of the "key school" scheme was to give a small number of schools, colleges, and universities priority in allocating limited human and material resources, so that the training of the needed top-level manpower for China's development could be carried out more efficiently (You, 2007; Yuan, 1999). This policy was abandoned during the Cultural Revolution (1966–1976) when most school activities were cancelled. The "key school" scheme has been restarted since the adoption of the "Open Door Policy" in 1979 (Gang, 1996; You, 2007). There were, for example, 194 key secondary schools in 1953, making up 4.4 % of the total number of secondary schools across China. In 1963, there were 487 key secondary schools, about 3.1 % of the total number. In 1981, there were 4016 key secondary schools, about 3.8 % of the total number (China Great Encyclopaedia Publishing House, 1984). Despite the large increase in the total school numbers over the decades, secondary schools with the "key school" title remain a very small portion, and students have to compete for enrolment in these key schools. Because key schools and universities have better material conditions, a large number of qualified teachers, lower teacher-student ratios, and higher rates of students progressing to higher level schools than those in the remaining (normal) schools, students and parents fiercely compete for entry to those key schools.

Since 1979, China has adopted the "Open Door Policy", shifting the country from a planned economy to a market economy. In education and educational assessment, many unintended consequences related to the exam-oriented system became increasingly evident. Teachers focused on memorising facts and tested knowledge instead of providing opportunities to enhance students' skills and develop their positive attitudes and other non-cognitive attributes toward learning (Wu, 1994). Schools only concentrated on tested subjects, and some schools reduced or even cancelled the teaching of untested subjects (Wu & Luo, 1995; Yang, 1993b, 1993c). Classroom assessment tools highly resembled high-stakes testing in terms of test items, tasks, and formats. Strong washback of high-stakes testing led to a situation of "what to examine, what to teach" (Yang, 1992, p. 5).

One of the major initiatives to minimise the role of testing was restructuring the curriculum documents with the intention of moving the focus away from the testing-centred education system (Ministry of Education & the People's Republic of China, 1990, 1993). The curriculum document, *Instructional Plans for Syllabi of Full-Time Students at Primary School and Junior Middle School in Compulsory Education* (九年义务教育全日制教学大纲) was published in 1989 (People's Education Press, 1989). It emphasised *quality education*, which meant to move away from testing-oriented education toward one that developed the qualities of all citizens, served all students, and holistically enhanced students' qualities in morality and ethics, culture and sciences, labour and applied skills, as well as physical education, and psychological and emotional capacities (Lo, 2000). The revised curriculum intended to cultivate rounded, well-developed citizens who were more creative, independent, and capable of dealing with challenges in the increasingly competitive world. It highlighted that proficiency and success should not be based exclusively on students' test scores; instead, and more importantly, students' attitudes towards society, social intelligence, and many other non-intellectual qualities should be considered in a more comprehensive assessment of students' abilities (Yang, 1993a, 1997a, b). There were some changes due to the implementation of the 1993 curriculum document, such as the abandoning of the entrance examinations for Junior Secondary Schools (Grade 7) (Gang, 1996). In addition, the "key school" title in primary education has almost disappeared, although substantive differences among schools still exist (Gang).

Generally speaking, little evidence showed any success of the reform in shifting away from the testing-oriented system (Han & Yang, 2001; Luo & Wendel, 1999). Testing continued to be used as a major tool in day-to-day classroom teaching and learning (Yang, 1997a, b). Since the results of examinations were also linked to teachers' performance as an indicator of teaching effectiveness, teachers focused on tested knowledge in their classroom instruction (Dong, 1998; Man, 1997). The "key school" scheme continued to significantly influence school education and educational assessment. In more recent years, the "key school" scheme has been used to boost performance in external exams, showcase government achievements in promoting education, or both (Gang, 1996; Suen & Yu, 2006). Large-scale, entrance examinations were implemented at all levels, except primary level, to decide whether students could enter key schools. To be successful in the entrance examinations, students had to do a lot of scholastic drills and exercises. They were examined weekly, at the middle and end of the term, all of which placed great pressure on them. The policy of the "key school" mechanism had intensified examination-oriented education. At this stage, assessment was still a synonym of testing and carried considerable connotations of selecting and comparing. China's educational assessment reform was still far from reaching the aim of quality education, as evidenced in China's continuing reforms in the new century.

4.4   Educational Assessment in the Twenty-First Century

With the economy burgeoning and political reforms speeding up, China's educational reforms have moved forward. In the new millennium, the new education curriculum has been introduced in the wake of dramatic economic and social transformations that took place in the 1990s (Ministry of Education, 1999). The National Curriculum Standards (国家课程标准) was drafted in 2001 for trial in some designated schools, and the official document was published nationwide in 2003 (Ministry of Education & the People's Republic of China, 2001, 2002). The National Curriculum Standards states that the ultimate goal of education is to achieve broad and balanced moral, intellectual, physical, and aesthetic development and a high level of character building for students. The National Curriculum Standards underlines the significance of assessing learning processes with the following specific major elements (Ministry of Education & the People's Republic of China, 2001, p. 2):

- Focusing on quality education and giving equal emphasis to both learning processes and outcomes;

- Variety and flexibility of learning objectives;
- Learner-centred instruction and recognising individual differences;
- Task-based teaching approaches;
- Encouraging formative assessment, self-, peer-, and parental assessment in addition to teachers' assessment; and
- Encouraging the use of technology to enrich the new curriculum.

Signals have been sent from the central government that the educational assessment system should change from being over-reliant on the selection function of assessment and assessment should be used to enhance teaching and support learning (Chang, 2002; Zhu, 2007). The documents have made significant improvements in elaborating on specific assessment strategies and suggestions. The Chinese Ministry of Education has introduced an agenda to reform entrance examinations at various levels including the one with the highest stakes—the National Matriculation Entrance Examinations (more information will follow in the next section). To achieve the goals stipulated by the central government, the provincial and local districts and schools have responded in a variety of ways. For example, Jiangsu, Education Department, and City of Taicang (2007) has proposed "Six seriousnesses in teaching" (教学六认真) to help to strengthen teaching qualities. Teachers are required to adopt changing practices in six areas: designing student assignments, selecting appropriate types of assignments, marking student assignments, giving feedback, acknowledging achievements, and improving student learning.

Regardless of these many attempts, empirical results seem to show that high-stakes testing continues to play a major role in educational assessment (Liu & Wu, 2006; Ren, 2011). Testing is still very powerful and routinely used to make educational decisions. Testing directs what to teach and learn in the classroom for at least two reasons: unpreparedness of formative assessment among teachers and students, as well as the influence of the "key school" scheme. First, empirical studies found that teachers were generally unprepared for formative assessment and they did not know how to integrate formative assessment into teaching and learning (Wang, 2008). Their understanding of formative assessment was limited; as a result, they did not see the value of formative assessment for teaching and learning. Likewise, students did not seem to be interested in the new assessment initiatives stipulated in the education reforms. There were very few assessment activities designed to support learning processes, and the quality of the assessment tools and activities was generally low (Jing, Hang, & Zhang, 2007). Second, the "key school" scheme continues to be used and external examinations continue to play a major role in deciding who may enter those key schools and universities (You, 2007). By 2011, about 10 % of universities and colleges and 5 % of senior secondary schools had the "key" title (Berry, 2011). At this point, educational assessment in China is conceptually and practically synonymous with examinations, and testing is a major tool to measure success.

4.5   High-Stakes Testing and the Current Study

In present day China, primary education starts at age 6 (Grade 1) till 12 years old
(Grade 6), followed by 3 years of junior secondary education (Grade 7–9) and 3
years of senior secondary education (Grade 10–12). Higher education institutions
comprise universities which offer both 4-year undergraduate and/or graduate degree
programmes as well as short-cycle (usually 2- or 3-year) colleges without degree
programmes. Throughout these various stages, students have to take a number of
high-stakes tests at the municipal, provincial, and national levels. These tests are
used to decide whether students can enter a higher level of education or graduate
from the current level of schooling. In the following section, I introduce four major,
large-scale, high-stakes testing systems in the current Chinese educational system,
followed by a description of the current study.

4.5.1   Entrance Examinations to Senior Secondary Schools (EESS)

In China, 9-year compulsory education ends at the junior secondary level. At the
end of Grade 9, all students take the EESS, which is the summative assessment of
the previous 9-years of compulsory education, and more importantly, the entrance
examination to senior high school (Wu, 2012). The EESS is developed and administrated by municipal/district/county education bureaus (Gang, 1996). Tested subjects and formats vary from one municipality to another. The major purpose of the
EESS is to provide information on junior secondary school students' achievement in
the required subjects (Ministry of Education of China, 2005). The results of the
EESS also decide whether students go to key senior secondary school, ordinary
secondary school, or vocational school. In other words, the result of the EESS has
two functions. One is to evaluate whether or not students have reached standards for
graduation from junior secondary schools, while the other is for the screening purpose of deciding which types of school students can enter. The total raw scores are
used as the main criterion for selection. Students are enrolled according to their
performance and application preference. Usually, the entry scores for key senior
secondary schools are the highest, and the vocational schools the lowest. This reinforces the status differences between academic/professional and applied tracks.

4.5.2   High School Certificate Examinations (HSCE)

The HSCE is a nationally regulated, provincially designed and administered exam.
The HSCE is relatively new compared with other testing systems (Yang, 1993d). It
was first introduced in Shanghai in 1985; in 1993, it was finally introduced in Tibet.

The HSCE is an end-of-course examination and is spread over 3 years of senior secondary school studies. The major functions of the HSCE are to establish standards for classroom learning, evaluate teaching effectiveness, and award certificates to those who successfully reached the standards (Gang, 1996). It generally covers nine subjects – Chinese, mathematics, foreign languages, politics, history, geography, physics, chemistry, and biology. In some provinces, school-based tests of laboratory skills and technology (working skills) are also conducted. The results of the HSCE are based on four or five grades (A-D or E) instead of percentiles. The HSCE is different from other high-stakes tests in that it is based on a criterion-referenced scoring system. The passing rate of a single subject is usually high, about 90 %. If a student fails in one subject, he or she will have a chance to retake it, but the result is only reported as pass or fail. A certificate of the HSCE records the grades of all examinations that a student sits.

4.5.3 National Matriculation Entrance Examinations (NMET)

The NMET, often nicknamed the "Footslog Bridge", is one of the testing systems with the highest stakes in China (Davey, Chuan, & Higgins, 2007). It is designed for admission to undergraduate programmes of higher educational institutions across the whole country. There are millions of test takers every year, for example, 10.1 million in 2007 (Liu, 2010). The NMET was introduced in 1952 as a national examination, replacing the practice of entrance examinations run by individual higher education institutions before the founding of the People's Republic of China. There have been some significant changes since the 1990s, particularly related to tested subjects. Currently, the NMET is regulated by the National Education Examination Authority (NEEA). While the NEEA decides tested subjects and designs tests for some provinces, examination boards in other provinces decide and design their own tests. In other words, different provinces may adopt different testing systems by testing different subjects and using different tests. However, the NMET is designed and administered uniformly within each province. The "3 + X" is one of the systems which is used the most widely. Students take both "3" and 'X". "3" refers to Chinese, mathematics, and a foreign language. Each of the three subjects accounts for 150 points in total. "X" means two tracks: Social Science (including the three subjects of Politics, History, and Geography) and Natural Science (including the three subjects of Physics, Chemistry, and Biology), with a total score of 300 points in each track. Based on individual interests and preferences, students choose one of the tracks and are tested accordingly. Beside the NMET, there are other criteria for admission decisions. However, academic excellence is usually the most important factor (Liu & Wu, 2006).

4.5.4 The Graduate School Entrance Examinations (GSEE)

The GSEE is a testing system which determines whether or not candidates can gain annual admission into a Master's programme (Liu, 2010). The total number of GSEE applicants, for example, reached approximately 1.2 million in 2008 (Liu). There have been some changes in the GSEE since its restart in the 1980s. The current GSEE includes the first round of preliminary examinations and the second round of re-examinations. While the first round of preliminary, national examinations is set and arranged in a unitary way by the Ministry of Education (MOE) and NEEA, the second round is determined by individual institutions, including important testing decisions such as time, place, content, and subjects. The first round of preliminary examination includes four tests: foreign languages (English, Japanese, or Russian), political science, and two other subject areas. Each year, the NEEA prepares test papers for foreign languages, political science, and some other subject areas (e.g., computer science). Test takers who surpass cut-off scores set by the MOE or select universities on all the four tests in the first round may enter the second round. Except for 34 universities, whose Master's programmes have the flexibility to set up their own cut-off scores independently, all the other universities, over 900, have to adopt national cut-off scores. After the first round of preliminary examinations, individual institutions take responsibility for the second round and make admission decisions.

Overall, high-stakes testing continues to play a prominent role in deciding achievement, admission, and graduation in China, in the past and at present. Passing tests has important benefits for individuals, such as progressing to higher level schools, admission to universities and colleges, and the attainment of a diploma qualification. Failing, on the other hand, has significant disadvantages, such as losing further learning or employment opportunities or not being able to graduate on time. Research has documented the negative impact on classroom teaching and learning, for example, the tendency to have limited vision in knowledge and skills, undermining critical thinking, neglect of teaching aspects not covered by tests, and diminishing students' self-esteem (Cheng, 2008). Top-down educational policies have been adopted to encourage a shift from the test-oriented system. However, testing continues to be a dominant feature in Chinese education and educational assessment.

4.5.5 The Current Study

Fairness is one of the important goals in the Chinese educational assessment system. In the following section, I investigate the fairness through delineating perceptions as expressed by students and teachers/administrators on one test — the Graduate School Entrance English Examinations (GSEEE) within the testing system of the GSEE. The GSEEE has two purposes: to measure English proficiency of test takers and to provide information for educational institutions for selecting candidates for master's programmes (He, 2010). According to the GSEEE test specifications, the GSEEE examines students' English language abilities, including knowledge of the language (grammatical competence, textual competence, and sociolinguistics competence) and language skills in reading and writing (NEEA, 2012).

This study, a part of a large-scale research project, examined implicit, underpinning reasons which influenced perceptions of students and teachers/administrators on the fairness of the GSEEE. In particular, the study focused on investigating students', teachers', and administrators' beliefs and values related to the GSEEE. Investigations of cultural beliefs, values, and assumptions are of great importance since students' and teachers' beliefs and values influence their expectations and behaviour towards classroom learning and teaching. Through discussions with students and teachers/administrators about their perceptions on the fairness of the GSEEE, the research may identify what students and teachers believe to be fair assessment, as well as how their underlying socio-cultural beliefs, values, and assumptions influence such a determination.

4.6   A Socio-cultural Perspective

This study is underpinned by a socio-cultural view of learning and assessment. The view generally defines fairness as equity (Gipps & Stobart, 2009; Stobart, 2005) and social justice (Kunnan, 2008). Kunnan's work highlights the importance of value implications and social consequences. He proposes a test fairness framework (TFF) and a test context framework (TCF), which examine a wide context in order to fully determine whether and how the test is beneficial or detrimental to society. The wide context includes four aspects: (1) the political and economic, (2) the educational, social and cultural, (3) the technological and infrastructure, and (4) the legal and ethical considerations. The TCF requires fairness investigations of the whole system including various political, economic, socio-cultural, technological, and legal considerations. Similar to Kunnan's work, Gipps and Stobart argue that twenty-first century assessment should consider the contexts of assessment, and social and cultural issues (Gipps & Stobart, 2009; Stobart, 2005). Fairness in assessment involves "both what precedes an assessment (for example, access and resources) and its consequences (for example, interpretations of results and impact) as well as aspects of the assessment design itself" (Gipps & Stobart, 2009, p. 105). They use equity interchangeably with fairness, which they believe is socially embedded and can only be fully understood by taking account of social and cultural contexts along with technical characteristics. They consider the pursuit of fairness in assessment and opportunity for the individual as two major and ongoing challenges for educational assessment. Fairness and equity cannot be assumed, but must be carefully investigated in any assessment environment by looking at its social and cultural context.

According to the socio-cultural perspective, whether assessment is fair is mediated culturally, socially, and historically within a context. Fairness investigations may include many aspects and various social, cultural, educational, political, economic, and philosophical features (Moss, Pullin, Gee, Haertel, & Young, 2008). This perspective contends that knowledge and skills are not only related to mental function and information processing within test takers' minds, but also result from social interactions between test takers and their larger learning environments. Fair assessment of students' knowledge and skills does not just include testing practices that are mind and body engaged but also culturally acceptable. As pointed out by Moss et al. (2008), this type of work needs the study of the context, in particular, related to the social cultural forces that have shaped the current practices. The emphasis is on acquiring an indepth understanding of how a particular context shapes the complexity and dynamics of fairness. The application using the socio-cultural perspective for fairness investigations has been widely used in classroom assessment in various contexts such as Australia, Canada, and New Zealand (Klenowski, 2013; Webber & Scott, 2012). However, the socio-cultural approach has been rarely used in examining the fairness of high-stakes testing, since high-stakes testing is traditionally influenced by statistical models and psychometric theories (Moss et al.). This study intends to address the following research questions: (1) what are the overall perceptions of students and teachers/administrators regarding the fairness of the GSEEE? and (2) what are their major beliefs and values for such determinations on the fairness of the GSEEE?

4.7   Methods

To understand students' and teachers' perceptions on the fairness of the GSEEE, interviews were conducted with 20 students and 10 teachers/administrators. Students were recruited from one large-scale university in China. This university has a large number of undergraduate students from across China applying for its Master's programmes every year. Those who attended the GSEE in 2012 were invited to participate in the study. Five focus group interviews, involving 20 students in total, were conducted, with each group consisting of two to six students. Among the 20 students, there were 10 males and 10 females. They came from a variety of academic backgrounds including Mathematics, Computer Science, Electrical Engineering, Economics, Business, Pharmacy, Chinese Medicine, and Political Science. The students ranged from 23 to 28 years old.

Eleven teachers/administrators were recruited for one-to-one interviews. All the participants were classroom teachers, teaching disciplinary subjects or English.[1] They all played a leading role in classroom teaching and learning in their own

---

[1] Based on the *Syllables for Non-English Major Master's Students (1992)*, Master's students have to obtain certain credits in language learning (e.g., English) at the Master's level to obtain a Master's degree across the country of China, unless specified otherwise.

department or school. At the time of the study, all the participants held administrative positions as unit head, department head, dean, or associate dean at the graduate school or graduate programme, for example, School of Foreign Languages, College of Economics and Management, and College of Computer Science. There were seven males and three females, and their age ranged from 40 to 60 years of age.

The interview protocol included two sections concerning students' and teachers' perceptions of the GSEEE. The first section was related to their background/teaching/working experience, and the second section to their overall perceptions on the fairness of the GSEEE and the major factors influencing their perceptions. Considering the participants' language background, all the interviews were conducted in Chinese. Several steps were followed in analysing the interview data. First, to organise and prepare the data for analysis, I transcribed them verbatim in Chinese. Then, using NVivo 8, I began with open coding to help inductively build ideas, followed by axial coding through selecting, categorising, synthesising, and interpreting the interview data. Finally, selective coding was performed and the major themes developed from the open coding and axial coding guided data analysis. Quotations that best represented categories were included in the findings. When I reported the findings, the quotations used were translated into English and verified by a native speaker.

4.8 Results

The focus group and one-on-one interviews were analysed and commonalities were found among the participants' responses. Those responses were coded and grouped together by five themes: (1) the fair testing process, (2) the merit-based value, (3) the testing-oriented tradition, (4) usefulness, and (5) practicality. First, the participants had consensus that the GSEEE was a fair test because all students "took the same test at the same time, under the same scoring scheme". The GSEEE provided students with equal opportunity to take the test under standardised administration processes, being assessed and scored under the same scoring scheme. The test had appeal, particularly related to its standardised administration procedures and objectivity in item design (e.g., multiple choice items). In the GSEEE, cheating was typically perceived as a random occurrence, while in other tests or testing systems (e.g., the NMET), cheating was often described as "prevalent" and "systematic". The participants showed limited confidence in other testing formats such as performance assessment due to issues of "subjectivity". They noted there was "no better alternative choice" to replace testing in the current Chinese system.

Second, the participants highlighted the importance of meritocracy and test performance in deciding further educational opportunities. The participants believed the test provided a chance of "upward mobility" for those who had limited access to quality education. The selection was based on test performance rather than family connections. The GSEEE promoted equality based on performance and academic merit instead of class, wealth, race or political affiliation. As one of the teachers/administrators explained:

The only thing you can fight is this score. And once the cut score is drawn, you are either in or out. No one can help you. For those who do not have any background, this is the only chance they can climb up ... .There is a huge gap between the rich and poor in China now. How could you give those poor kids an opportunity to compete against those guan er'dai, fu er'dai, if testing is cancelled?

The Chinese term *guan er'dai* (官二代) could be translated into English in numerous ways, and possibilities might include "sons and daughters of government officials" or "official offspring". The term is used in conjunction with the term *fu er'dai* (富二代), or "progeny of prosperity", which refers to the sons and daughters of rich, powerful businessmen, who are similarly afforded tremendous opportunity. Both terms are widely used in the current Chinese context, implying growing inequality due to differences in educational opportunities, social connections, and economic status in China, which has put power and wealth in the hands of a relatively small number. To combat such inequality, testing such as the GSEEE was used to provide a level playing field for all test takers. The participants in this study believed that the Chinese government provided such a chance of "upward mobility". There was a strong belief that educational opportunities should be assigned to individuals based upon their merits, which was measured by testing such as the GSEEE.

Third, the participants stated that they accepted the GSEEE because of the strong influence of the test-oriented tradition. The participants pointed out that high-stakes testing had been used for thousands of years in China ever since the Imperial Examination. The heavy weight of testing in the overall education system was evident in that "no matter what you are doing, from young to old, you have to take the test, from the entrance of secondary school, college, university, Master programme, and PhD programme". These participants, students in particular, described the existence of the testing as "just like the existence of an apple". They believed "everything in existence was reasonable" and the test was immune to critique and reflection. The participants expressed their sense of "affective commitment" and showed acceptance of the GSEEE's configuration. The participants believed that the test held an important, symbolic value due to the test-centred tradition in China.

Fourth, when discussing their views, the participants recognised the usefulness of the GSEEE in achieving the "selection" purpose. The students explained that the role of "differentiation" was much more important than proficiency, and it was difficult for proficiency to "be evaluated by a single score". The GSEEE was seen by the teachers/administrators as a useful, effective way to achieve the goal of screening. Deciding admission status was a tedious, difficult, yet very important task at the institutional level. The GSEEE provided a relatively quick, prima facie applicable method to screen applicants and decide who could enter the second round of re-examinations. The teachers/administrators mentioned that students' GSEEE scores were actually "unknown" to most regular classroom teachers and classroom teaching was "primarily based on the specific teaching environment not the GSEEE scores". Overall, the societal use of the GSEEE to stream and weed out applicants was highly valued while the purpose of English proficiency was often ignored.

Fifth, the participants believed that a fair test should take practicality into account, and the GSEEE met this consideration. The large-scale GSEEE was administered to over one million students every year with various constraints in human and material resources. Considering the present constraints on equipment and time, the participants believed that the GSEEE provided a relatively appropriate, balanced opportunity for students in terms of test design, administration, and scoring. As one teacher/administrator explained:

> Chinese education has a very large population, much larger than graduate programmes in other countries … Chinese universities, at similar ranking like us, enrol 5000 or 6000 master's students ever year. Our university is quite selective, but still there are about 3000 spaces, and it takes forever to complete the selection of qualified candidates for our master's programmes.

Given the large number of applicants and current financial limitations, the one-shot, standardised testing had tremendous administrative appeal and could be cost-effective when proceeded with large amounts of applicant information. The GSEEE provided a "practical, efficient approach" at the institutional level. The GSEEE strengthened itself as a relatively convenient method for screening applications. The GSEEE affected much more than admission decisions. The teachers/administrators mentioned that the GSEEE scores were used to determine placement, whether students can go on to combined "Master and PhD" programmes, or whether some credits can be waived. These unwarranted uses were introduced simply because they provided a great deal of efficiency, practicality, and administrative utility. Despite "not being absolutely fair", the participants recognised that the MOE "took one step after another" toward the path of fairness. Various new practices had been used to balance the interests of different groups and individuals. The participants believed that fairness would be improved further and progress could be pursued in the long run.

4.9 Discussion

Although the interview results represent solely the perspectives of 20 students and 11 administrators/teachers, they do point toward critical issues for continued fairness inquiry. Overall, these results show that the students and teachers/administrators were still very deeply steeped in the examination culture. The participants regarded the exam as sacred, fair competition for students. The GSEEE was first and foremost about academic merit, which was assessed based on equal treatment in testing. This type of large-scale high-stakes test organised by the central government was a tradition carried on for thousands of years through many dynasties. The GSEEE provided a practical, efficient approach for the selection purpose. The participants did not want to have the tradition changed, but work to improve it.

Results provide direct evidence that, within the context of this study, the test enjoys acceptance and recognition as a fair means to success. The GSEEE is considered as fair for two major reasons. The first reason is related to the testing process with the fundamental feature that individual students are treated identically and equally. This perception remains the same with the key element of the Imperial Examination, that is, all test takers sit the same test under the same conditions with the same scoring procedure (Suen & Yu, 2006). This is a quite narrow view of test fairness due to two considerations. Researchers and educators in North America and Europe have increasingly found ostensible differences in test performance due to different access to quality education and they have raised 'fairness' concerns for groups of test takers who are placed in a disadvantaged position (Cowie, 2013; Harrison, 2013). In a paper entitled "This test is unfair", Walpole et al. (2005) investigated urban African and Latino high school students' perceptions, test preparation, information sources, and strategies towards college admission standardised tests such as Scholastic Aptitude Tests (SATs). Findings showed that the African American and Latino students generally lacked information and resources to pay for tests and test preparation. Overall, fair assessment needs to consider accessibility and learning opportunities, especially for under-represented groups. In addition, the literature has overwhelmingly pointed out the importance of accommodating and meeting the special needs of specific individuals during the testing process (Sculte, Elliott, & Kratochwill, 2000). Since disability interferes with students' opportunity to demonstrate their knowledge and skills, test accommodation practices offer opportunities, remove barriers, increase access, and provide a more accurate description of performance of disabled students. Such needs-based accommodations often result in different treatments such as providing extended time, providing large-type versions of tests, or reading aloud some or all of the items without changing the actual format of test items (Thurlow, Thompson, & Lazarus, 2006). Accommodation practices, which have been recommended over the last two decades, are increasingly perceived as an important, valuable aspect to promote social justice and test fairness (Pitoniak & Royer, 2001). Some countries even mandate test accommodations and the inclusion of students with disabilities in large-scale testing. For example, in the United States, the Individuals with Disabilities Educational Act of 1997 was the first piece of legislation that required the inclusion of students with disabilities in assessment systems (Lazarus, Thurlow, Lail, & Christensen, 2009). However, these values were not evident in this Chinese context. As Fan and Jin (2012) reported, there was a lack of provision of reasonable test accommodations in Chinese high-stakes testing programmes.

Apart from the testing process, the second reason is that the determination of the fairness of the GSEEE among the participants of this study was driven by social, cultural, and economic considerations. Within the context of the study, the influential beliefs and values can be summarised as: the merit-focused value, the testing-centred tradition, and the pursuit of efficiency. Meritocracy is still a valued ideal among the participants in this study. Meritocracy, as the term implies, advocates that rewards should be given to individuals based on merit or achievement (Walton, Spencer, & Erman, 2013). There was an assumption among the participants that the GSEEE provides all the students with the same starting point when they take tests. After testing results were aggregated, compared, and publicised, those who were selected were revealed in terms of their attributes and norms. For the participants, individuals were rewarded based on their test performance; hence, the results were fair and just. Fairness was demonstrated through a norm-referenced system with the focus that every individual student was treated identically. The result of the merit-focused value suggested that Chinese society may be organised in a way where students' endowments such as test performance are used to determine if society should invest scarce resources in training them for certain desirable life chances.

The acceptance of the GSEEE is also influenced by the testing-centred tradition. Such a tradition, as discussed in the introduction, can be traced back to the Imperial Examinations (606–1905). In present day China, high-stakes entrance examinations are implemented at all levels from secondary schools to graduate programmes (Gang, 1996). Paper-and-pencil exams are widely accepted as the important indicator of proficiency, achievement, and promotion in every corner of current society. The tradition has become so deeply entrenched in Chinese culture and such testing is highly endorsed among the participants. Testing has become commonplace and frequently begins very early in a person's life so that few participants in this study questioned its legitimacy. The study results showed that the GSEEE is perceived as a symbolic representation of knowledge and skills, and has tremendous appeal to the students and teachers who were accustomed to, and obsessed with, numerical measures of proficiency. The fairness of the GSEEE is taken at face value as legitimate for these participants.

Finally, the GSEEE was perceived to be fair among the participants, partially because it met two considerations: (1) usefulness in terms of the major goal of selection under the national agenda, and (2) practicality which considers constraints at the institutional level. These two considerations can be summarised as the pursuit of efficiency. Given the various constraints in human and material resources, there are limited resources for many GSEEE test takers. Test results provide a tidy, quick solution to the administrative challenge of selection for the administrators/teachers. The issue of usefulness, practicality, and efficiency has been discussed in the fairness literature. Willingham (1999) believes that the social justification of a test sits on the three-legged stool of "fairness, usefulness, and practicality" (p. 227). Fair practices should be supported by reasonable rationales within the limits of feasibility and acceptability (ALTE, 2001). Bachman and Palmer (2010) contend that assessment is a process to consider trade-offs, meaning to "reduce the importance of one or more qualities of a claim in order to maintain or increase the qualities of another claim, either in response to competing values of different stakeholders, or in order to make the assessment practical" (p. 266). Decisions on key issues should be supported by reasonable economic, social, and educational rationales. Obviously, there are no universal trade-offs which can be applied in all testing contexts. In the current trend of standards-based education reform, the increasing use of testing has expanded exponentially around the world (Moses & Nanna, 2007). Efficiency seems to have its appeal in China and other parts of the world.

In conclusion, there is complex interaction between the fairness of the GSEEE and the culture in which it occurs and is accepted as legitimate. The beliefs and values of students, teachers, and administrators with regard to the fairness of the

GSEEE reflect the important influences of the social-cultural context. These underlying considerations become ideological, and are known "only tacitly, remain unspoken, and are very difficult to formulate explicitly" (Apple, 1990, p. 126). High-stakes testing such as the GSEEE becomes a powerful, symbolic object of representation that is given unwarranted epistemic endorsement. The legitimising forces of policy makers, institutionalised policies, societal acceptance, as well as students', teachers' and administrators' endorsement, combine together within this culture to perpetuate existing symbolic roles of testing. From this perspective, the GSEEE is justified to the extent that it is connected to an underlying symbolic system that is seen as fair, useful, practical, and legitimate within Chinese culture.

4.10   Implications for Leadership

Possessing the world's largest educational system, China merits the attention of global scholars, policy makers, and educators. Pursuing fairness is among the most important endeavours in education and educational assessment. The use of the GSEEE received acceptance among the students, teachers, and administrators in this research, and such use seems to be aligned with their values and beliefs. Such alignment, however, cannot conceal the potential of competing interests, especially of those test takers who are in the least advantaged positions.

Neglect of group differences and gaps may bring conflict and instability. Currently, the Chinese society and education system faces accelerating polarisation and many challenges such as a huge population, minority issues, east–west-region economic disparities, an urban/rural divide, and a growing income gap (Postiglione, 2006). These problems have become an untenable situation when applied to education. There are a range of groups that can be categorised as disadvantaged resulting from unbalanced learning opportunities and resources, for example, ethnic, low social-economic, marginalised (migration workers moving from less developed areas to developed areas), and disabled groups (Wang, 2011). However, some of these groups are largely ignored in Chinese education and educational assessment. In spite of being predominantly emphasised in the literature, students with disabilities in China remain the most vulnerable, invisible group in China. The lack of educational accessibility (Human Rights Watch, 2013) and reasonable accommodations in testing (as shown in this chapter) present great barriers to these groups. There is still a great deal to be accomplished in order to truly realise participation and inclusivity for those who are in a disadvantaged position, including disabled students. It is imperative to ensure access in every school and classroom to an intellectually rich engagement for all students, especially those who have been denied that access in the past.

Prolonged values and traditions may lead to the naturalisation of unfairness. Within the context of this study, the merit-based, testing-oriented test seems to have become so deeply ingrained in Chinese society that it was difficult for stakeholders (e.g., the students and teachers/administrators in this research) to identify alternative selection activities other than testing. I believe that there are dangers in treating the GSEEE (and testing in general) as a predominantly fair, legitimate, and justified criterion for decision-making. For thousands of years, the Chinese nation has been accustomed to examinations, and has culturally accepted high-stakes examinations as a means to determine their future prospects and learning opportunities. Assessment practices in schools are often teacher-led with a strong emphasis on getting students to prepare for exams (Jing et al., 2007). Teachers are unprepared for formative assessment and students are not interested in the new assessment initiatives using formative practices (Wang, 2008). The findings of the study have demonstrated that, when this kind of ingrained system is perceived as a natural, socially-accepted phenomenon, societies develop conceptual, political, and ideological ignorance that resists other options.

As Klitgaard (1985) pointed out in his thought-provoking book, *Choosing Elites*, the "first question to ask about selective admissions is why it should be selective at all" (p. 51). Klitgaard noted that we, as a society, have mixed feelings about selectivity. On one hand, we think it "has unpleasant connotations of elitism, unfairness, snobbishness, and uniformity [while on the other hand, we] ... laud excellence, recognize its scarcity and utility, and endorse admissions on the basis of merit" (p. 51). To deal with this dilemma, Howe (1994) highlights a shift from summative testing that serves institutions to formative testing that serves individual needs, as well as substantial changes in education itself. Achieving such a goal in China would require considerable support at the political, economic, social, and cultural level. The recognition of the various potentials of students, coupled with an appreciation of equal educational accessibility among all individuals and reasonable test accommodations for some groups, creates a new conceptual space from which policy makers, professionals, and other persons might compassionately consider their roles in admission decisions. It is only through ongoing discussions among stakeholders and continued improvements that assessment tools can be enriched and the goal of formative assessment that serves individual needs can be accomplished.

4.11 Future Directions for Proactive Policies and Practices

Although there has been progress in reforming assessment policies and examination systems since 1990, educational assessment in China is still in the shadow of the examination-oriented system. To shift away from such a system, transformation of its stakeholders' beliefs and values is needed. There are a number of important topics to be tackled, particularly:

1. Opening discussions and conversations about the goal of quality education and assessment practices to achieve this goal;
2. Increasing public understanding and appreciation of formative assessment;
3. Increasing emphasis and education on formative assessment in teachers' preservice and inservice training

4. Reforming the "key school" scheme and continuing to reform admission practices at all levels of education; and
5. Investigating and minimising negative consequences of high-stake testing.

4.12   Conclusion

Historically, the test-oriented system assisted the Chinese government in choosing the best talent for government positions and preparing a large number of scholars and professionals (Hu & Seifman, 1987). However, with societal changes and economic development, more and more negative consequences of such an examination-oriented system have been identified. Although the Chinese government has formulated policies with the intention of reducing excessive use of examinations and has encouraged the use of formative assessment, the reform is far from reaching its goal. This may be related to some deeply-entrenched values and beliefs, which are embedded in Chinese society, and endorsed by students and teachers, as shown in this study. Despite a series of educational reforms, the ultimate goal for quality education is continually unmet. On the whole, moving away from test-oriented educational assessment needs discussion and reconsideration of beliefs, values, polices, and practices in order to achieve the full potential of each individual student. When this happens, education and educational assessment may reach its goal to develop "the qualities of all citizens, serve all students, and comprehensively enhance students' qualities at all the aspects" (Ministry of Education & the People's Republic of China, 2001, p. 1).

References

Apple, M. (1990). *Ideology and curriculum*. New York: Routledge.
Association of Language Testers in Europe. (2001). *ALTE principles of good practice for ALTE examinations*. Retrieved from https://www.testdaf.de/fileadmin/Redakteur/PDF/TestDaF/ ALTE/ALTE_good_practice.pdf
Bachman, L. F., & Palmer, A. S. (2010). *Language assessment in practice*. Oxford, UK: Oxford University Press.
Berry, R. (2011). Educational assessment in Mainland China, Hong Kong and Taiwan. In R. Berry & B. Adamson (Eds.), *Assessment reform in education: Policy and practice* (pp. 49–61). Dordrecht, Netherlands: Springer.
Chang, X. (2002). *A comparison between the outlines and the teaching guidelines*. Sichuan: Sichuan Province Chengdu Oriental Bilingual Publication House.
Cheng, L. (2008). The key to success: English language testing in China. *Language Testing, 25*(1), 15–38.
Cheng, L. (2010). The history of examinations: Why, how, what and whom to select? In L. Cheng & A. Curtis (Eds.), *English language assessment and the Chinese learner* (pp. 13–25). New York: Routledge.
China Great Encyclopaedia Publishing House. (1984). *Educational yearbook 1949–1981*. Beijing, China: China Great Encyclopaedia Publishing House.

Cizek, G. J. (2001). More unintended consequences of high-stakes testing. *Educational measurements: Issues and practices, 20*(4), 19–27.

Cowie, B. (2013). *Fairness in assessment in primary science classrooms in New Zealand*. Paper presented at the annual conference of AERA, San Francisco.

Davey, G., Chuan, D. L., & Higgins, L. (2007). The university entrance examination system in China. *Journal of Further and Higher Education, 31*(4), 385–396.

Davis, A. (2009). Examples as method: My attempts to understand assessment and fairness (in the spirit of the Later Wittgenstein). *Journal of Philosophy of Education, 43*(3), 371–389.

Dong, Y. (1998). *An analysis of teaching in China*. Beijing, China: People's Education Press.

Ebrey, P. (2010). *The Cambridge illustrated history of China*. Cambridge, UK: Cambridge University Press.

Fan, J., & Jin, Y. (2012). *Developing a code of practice for EFL testing in China: A data-based approach*. Paper presented at the annual conference of LTRC, Princeton, NJ.

Feng, D. (2006). China's recent curriculum reform: Progress and problems. *Planning and Changing, 37*(1&2), 131–144.

Gang, W. (1996). Profiles of educational assessment systems world-wide: Educational assessment in China. *Assessment in Education, 3*(1), 75–88.

Gipps, C., & Stobart, G. (2009). Fairness in assessment. In C. Wyatt-Smith & J. Cumming (Eds.), *Educational assessment in 21st century: Connecting theory and practice* (pp. 105–118). Dordrecht, the Netherlands: Springer.

Han, M., & Yang, X. (2001). Educational assessment in China: Lessons from history and future prospects. *Assessment in Education, 8*(1), 5–10.

Harrison, C. (2013). *Walking the tightrope: How UK teachers manage classroom assessment*. Paper presented at the annual conference of AERA, San Francisco.

He, L. (2010). The graduate school English entrance examination. In L. Cheng & A. Curtis (Eds.), *English language assessment and the Chinese learner* (pp. 145–157). New York: Routledge.

He, W. (2012). *In the name of justice: Striving for the rule of law in China*. Washington, DC: The Brookings Institution.

Howe, K. R. (1994). Standards, assessment, and equality of educational opportunity. *Educational Researcher, 23*(8), 27–33.

Hu, S. M., & Seifman, E. (Eds.). (1987). *Education and socialist modernization: A documentary history of education in the People's Republic of China, 1977–1986*. New York: AMS Press.

Human Rights Watch. (2013). *"As long as they let us stay in class": Barriers to education for personal with disabilities in China*. Retrieved from http://www.hrw.org/sites/default/files/reports/china0713_ForUpload.pdf

Jiangsu Province, Education Department, City of Taicang. (2007). *Opinions on the implementation of "Six Seriousnesses in teaching" to strengthen teaching and learning in City of Taicang*. Retrieved from http://www.tcldxx.cn/sms/news/readnews.jsp?id=1992

Jing, L., Hang, S., & Zhang, C. (2007). Investigation and analysis of implementation of assessment in primary English teaching. *Teaching and Management, 18*(6), 18–22.

Klenowski, V. (2013). *An exploration of fairness in classroom assessment in Australia*. Paper presented at the annual conference of AERA, San Francisco.

Klitgaard, R. E. (1985). *Choosing elites*. New York: Basic Books.

Kunnan, A. J. (2008). Towards a model of test evaluation: Using the test fairness and wider context frameworks. In L. Taylor & C. Weir (Eds.), *Multilingualism and assessment: Achieving transparency, assuring quality, sustaining diversity* (pp. 229–251). Cambridge, UK: Cambridge University Press.

Lazarus, S., Thurlow, M., Lail, K., & Christensen, L. (2009). A longitudinal analysis of state accommodations policies: Twelve years of change, 1993—2005. *The Journal of Special Education, 43*(2), 67–80.

Lee, T. H. C. (1985). *Government education and examinations in Sung China*. Hong Kong, China: Chinese University Press.

Liao, S., & Chen, H. (1921). *Methods of intelligence testing.* Beijing, China: Business Printing House.

Liu, H., & Wu, Q. (2006). Consequences of college entrance exams in China and the reform challenges. *KEDI Journal of Educational Policy, 3*(1), 7–21.

Liu, Q. (2010). The national education examinations authority and its English language tests. In L. Cheng & A. Curtis (Eds.), *English language assessment and the Chinese learner* (pp. 29–43). New York: Routledge.

Lo, L. N. K. (2000). Educational reform and teacher development in Hong Kong and on the Chinese mainland. *Prospects, 30*(2), 237–253.

Luo, J., & Wendel, F. C. (1999). Preparing for college: Senior high school education in China. *NASSP Bulletin, 83*(609), 57–68.

Man, Q. (1997). Educational despair and quality education reform. *Chinese Education & Society, 30*(4), 21–25.

Ministry of Education. (1999). *Decisions of the Central Committee of the Communist Party of China and the State Council on deepening education reform and advancing essential-qualities-oriented education in an all-round way.* Beijing, China: People's Press.

Ministry of Education, the People's Republic of China. (1990). *Provisional regulations for senior secondary schools educational assessment.* Beijing, China: Ministry of Education.

Ministry of Education, the People's Republic of China. (1993). *The outlines of China's educational reforms and developments.* Beijing, China: Ministry of Education.

Ministry of Education, the People's Republic of China. (2001). *The outlines for basic Educational reform (Pilot).* China: Ministry of Education. Retrieved from http://www.being.org.cn/ncs/index.htm

Ministry of Education, the People's Republic of China. (2002). *Evaluation policies on subject teaching in regular secondary schools.* Beijing, China: Ministry of Education.

Ministry of Education of China. (2005). *The guidelines on the reform of junior high school graduation examination and senior high school enrolling system of experimental areas of basic curriculum reform.* Retrieved from http://www.moe.gov.cn/publicfiles/business/htmlfiles/moe/moe_711/201001/xxgk_78374.html

Moses, M. S., & Nanna, M. J. (2007). The testing culture and the persistence of high stakes testing reforms. *Education and Culture, 23*(1), 55–72.

Moss, P. A., Pullin, D. C., Gee, J. P., Haertel, E. H., & Young, L. J. (2008). *Assessment, equity, and opportunity to learn.* Cambridge, UK: Cambridge University Press.

National Education Examination Authority. (2012). *GSEEE syllabus.* Beijing: Higher Education Press.

People's Education Press. (1989). *Syllabus for full-time compulsory education at primary school and junior middle school.* Beijing, China: People's Education Press.

Pitoniak, M. J., & Royer, J. M. (2001). Testing accommodations for examinees with disabilities: A review of psychometric, legal, and social policy issues. *Review of Educational Research, 71,* 53–104.

Postiglione, G. A. (2006). School and inequality in China. In G. A. Postiglione (Ed.), *Educational and social change in China: Inequality in a market economy* (pp. 3–24). New York: M.E. Sharpe, Inc.

Ren, Y. (2011). A study of the washback effects of the College English Test (band 4) on teaching and learning English at tertiary level in China. *International Journal of Pedagogies and Learning, 6*(3), 243–259.

Sculte, A. A. G., Elliott, S. N., & Kratochwill, T. R. (2000). Educators' perceptions and documentation of testing accommodations for students with disabilities. *Special Services in the Schools, 16*(1), 35–56.

Stobart, G. (2005). Fairness in multicultural assessment. *Assessment in Education: Principle, Policies, and Practices, 12*(3), 275–287.

Suen, H. K., & Yu, L. (2006). Chronic consequences of high stakes testing? Lessons from the Chinese Civil Service Exam. *Comparative Education Review, 50*(1), 46–65.

Thurlow, M. L., Thompson, S. J., & Lazarus, S. S. (2006). Considerations for the administration of tests to special needs students: Accommodations, modifications, and more. In S. M. Downing & T. M. Haladyna (Eds.), *Handbook of test development* (pp. 653–676). Mahwah, NJ: Lawrence Erlbaum.

Walpole, M., McDonough, P. M., Bauer, C. J., Gibson, C., Kanyi, K., & Toliver, R. (2005). This test is unfair: Urban African American and Latino high school students' perceptions of standardised college admission tests. *Urban Education, 40*(3), 321–349.

Walton, G. M., Spencer, S. J., & Erman, S. (2013). Affirmative meritocracy. *Social Issues and Policy Review, 7*(1), 1–35.

Wang, H. (2008). Reflection on classroom assessment. *Journal of Agricultural University of Hebei (Agriculture and Forestry Education Edition), 10*(4), 142–145.

Wang, H. (2011). Access to higher education in China: Differences in opportunity. *Frontiers of Education in China, 6*(2), 227–247.

Webber, C. F., & Scott, S. (2012). Student assessment in a Canadian civil society. *Journal of Management Development, 31*(1), 34–47.

Willingham, W. (1999). A system view of test fairness. In S. J. Messick (Ed.), *Assessment in higher education: Issues of access, student development, and public policy* (pp. 213–242). Mahwah, NJ: Lawrence Erlbaum.

Wu, W. (1994). *Comparative pedagogy*. Beijing, China: People's Education Press.

Wu, W., & Luo, D. (1995). Combat in "Black July". *Chinese Education & Society, 28*(2), 9–38.

Wu, Y. (2012). *The examination system in China: The case of Zhongkao mathematics*. Retrieved from http://www.icme12.org/upload/submission/2034_F.pdf.

Yang, X. (1992). Effects and difficulties of giving the general examination for students. *Chinese Examinations, 1*(1), 4–6.

Yang, X. (1993a). A major reform in the examination system. *Chinese Education & Society, 26*(5), 77–96.

Yang, X. (1993b). On reforming the college and university entrance examinations. *Chinese Education & Society, 26*(5), 6–30.

Yang, X. (1993c). Proposals regarding the college-university examination taking place after the upper middle school general gradation examination. *Chinese Education & Society, 26*(6), 27–37.

Yang, X. (1993d). The general upper middle school graduate examination. *Chinese Education & Society, 26*(6), 15–26.

Yang, Y. (1997a). An exploration of several theoretical problems concerning quality education. *Chinese Education & Society, 30*(6), 8–12.

Yang, Z. (1997b). Examinations, coping with examinations, and the relationship between examination-oriented education and quality education. *Chinese Education & Society, 30*(6), 15–18.

You, Y. (2007). A deep reflection on the "key school system" in basic education in China. *Frontiers of Education in China, 2*(2), 229–239.

Yu, L., & Suen, H. (2005). Historical and contemporary exam-driven education fever in China. *KEDI Journal of Educational Policy, 2*(1), 17–33.

Yuan, Z. (1999). *On Chinese educational policy transformation: Case studies on equality and efficiency of key-point middle schools in China*. Guangzhou, China: Guangdong Educational Press.

Zhang, H., & Zhong, Q. (2003). Curriculum studies in China: Retrospect and prospect. In W. F. Pinar (Ed.), *International handbook of curriculum research* (pp. 253–268). Mahwah, NJ: Lawrence Erlbaum Associates.

Zhu, M. (2007). Recent Chinese experiences in curriculum reform. *Prospects: Quarterly Review of Comparative Education, 37*(2), 223–235.

Chapter 5
Concerns with Using Test Results for Political and Pedagogical Purposes: A Danish Perspective

Jens Dolin

Abstract Testing – classroom based as well as large-scale testing for comparative purposes – is becoming an increasingly important factor in educational policy in Denmark as in the other Nordic countries. Test results are attracting headlines in the media, often because these results disturb the national self-image of being among the best in the world, and improvement in these tests is established as a political goal. Especially high-stakes and large-scale tests affect both the national educational policy and the teaching in the classroom – not necessarily directly, but increasingly indirectly through the values and the discourse they impose on the school and society. These effects will be illustrated through the results from two larger research projects in which the author participated. The first is a Danish Clearinghouse study on the pedagogical consequences of high-stakes tests, showing the negative influence of these tests on teaching and on student behaviour. The other is a research project validating the PISA test in a Danish context, showing how the PISA tests, as an example of large-scale, comparative tests, have become a lever for dramatic changes in the Danish educational policy, without building on a valid justification. On a general level, these examples are seen as confirming the overall shift driven by global test systems, from a 'bildung/didaktik' approach (traditionally undertaken in the Nordic/Central European countries) towards a curriculum/policy driven approach (Anglo-American tradition) within education. Finally, the article will draw from the demonstrated tendencies to present some leadership and policy implications.

Keywords Standardised tests • PISA • Bildung • Denmark • Nordic leadership • Validity • Assessment • Assessment paradigm • Didaktik • Curriculum • School leadership • Educational policy

J. Dolin (✉)
Department of Science Education, University of Copenhagen, Copenhagen, Denmark
e-mail: dolin@ind.ku.dk

© Springer International Publishing Switzerland 2016
S. Scott et al. (eds.), *Assessment in Education*, The Enabling
Power of Assessment 2, DOI 10.1007/978-3-319-23398-7_5

5.1 Introduction

With the establishment of one global market and one dominating political-economic discourse, education has for better or for worse become subjected to the same driving forces as the rest of society. Accountability, comparability, and organisational models taken from the corporate world have to a large degree become the framing factors for education. Trust is replaced with control, dialogue with political decisions – to push it to extremes. This tendency can seem natural, more or less 'business as usual', in many countries in the Anglo-American part of the world. But in Denmark and the other Nordic countries, this is signalling a dramatic shift in the conditions for teaching and for schooling, for the teaching profession and for being a school leader. Even if the tendencies have not fully penetrated all spheres of the educational system and we still have important domains with traditional, Nordic approaches to education – and I will later come back to what is understood by that – these overall societal values and discourses occupy our minds and affect our actions. They have a profound influence on the way educational politicians think and act on all educational levels and they influence, both directly and indirectly, classroom practice and the possibilities for exercising leadership.

These overall tendencies will be examined via exemplary cases from evaluation and assessment practices and the leadership implications will be concluded from these examples. The assessment and evaluation culture is a good yardstick for the whole educational system. Assessment consolidates what is central knowledge and competences within a given subject or domain – and is in this respect one of the best expressions of the system itself. In his construction of a post-modern mode of analysing organisations, Robert Chia (1995) replaced the traditional emphasis on organisational forms and attributes with an examination of the local manifestations which all together make up the social reality of the organisation:

> the examination system in the university, how it is carried out, the examination protocols and processes of marking, etc., tell us more about the aims of the university than explicitly stated aims such as the 'pursuit of truth'. (p. 600)

This chapter deals with summative assessments that are external to the classroom in the sense that they are standardised and not adapted specifically to the classroom in which they are used. Within different forms of assessment, the big difference is between the formative and summative purposes and uses of assessments and there is a good reason to call formative assessment 'assessment for learning' and summative assessment 'assessment of learning' (Gardner, 2006). Formative uses of assessment have three distinct features that differentiate them from summative uses of the same assessment: the formative assessment judges the students with both curriculum- and student-based criteria, the assessment process is designed and carried out in collaboration between teacher and student, and the results are used to enhance the student's learning (Harlen, 2013). Some summative uses of assessment can have formative features but the arguments in this chapter pertain only to assessments without the characteristics of formative assessments. This implies that they normally will be standardised, i.e., designed in order to assess some standards established outside the classroom. They will in this context mostly be named tests. The tests can be high-stakes or low-stakes or have no stake at all. Research shows that when external tests are introduced, even without any stakes involved, teachers change their teaching in a direction that ensures good test results for the students (Schou, 2010) – and not necessarily good learning of the curriculum.

5.1.1 Standardised Testing – Purposes and Use

The use and influence of summative assessment in the form of testing, and especially high-stakes tests, has increased dramatically within the last decades. The increase is not due to pedagogical reasons as such, and not based on teacher formulated needs in classroom contexts, but an overall political wish to increase the quality of the educational system. This process has revealed a tension between the legitimate need for information about the performance of teachers and the educational system to inform policy, and the teachers' and students' use of this information for pedagogical purposes in the classroom. We know well how the policy makers interpret and use the outcomes of such tests, but we know less about how teachers make use of high-stakes tests to inform their pedagogical practice. An important question is whether there is a contradiction between the political system's use of high-stakes tests and teachers' (possible) pedagogical use of these tests. And if that is the case: what is the contradiction based on? The questions are important because these tests are expensive and time-consuming and take time from students' learning if they have no pedagogical use. They might also have a dramatic influence on classroom practice.

These questions are of topical interest in Denmark due to newly introduced national tests. Motivated by the quite heated public debate in Denmark about the national tests and their influence on classroom practice, the Danish Clearinghouse for Educational Research initiated a review of research about the pedagogical use of tests (Nordenbo et al., 2009). The author was one of four Nordic researchers invited to collaborate with the Clearinghouse staff (including librarians, research assistants etc.) and we started by setting up a research model, as shown in Fig. 5.1.

The research group narrowed the research questions in an ongoing process to keep the research literature to a manageable level with the final research questions framed as:

- How does the introduction of tests affect teachers' didactical decisions (question 1 in Fig. 5.1) and the students' learning approach (question 3 in Fig. 5.1)?
- How can primary school teachers' individual and class oriented use of test data enhance teachers' didactical and/or subject specific teaching in classes without special needs students (question 2 in Fig. 5.1)?

The questions only pertain to test types that form part of national tests in the Nordic countries. The study was based on all published research in the period 1980–2008. Many studies were excluded from the review largely due to the narrowing of

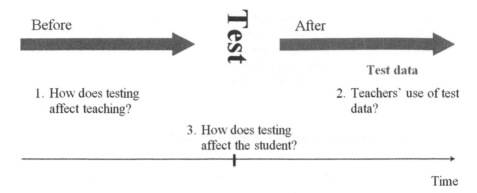

Fig. 5.1 The research model for the research project on the pedagogical use of tests

the research questions, and 5986 references from the first search were reduced to 118 documents of which some, after a more thorough reading, did not fit the criteria. The remaining 61 publications were re-described according to the EPPI Centre (Evidence for Policy and Practice Information and Coordinating Centre) data extraction and coding tool for education studies v2.0 (EPPI, 2002). This lists 87 categories to describe a research project, covering the project's purpose, context, design, method, results, and research and report quality. For each study these categories were completed in a very fixed template, which made it possible to extract the research evidence for each category. The tool could be criticised for its relatively rigid approach to research (Bennett, Lubben, Hogarth, & Campbell, 2005) but it gives a systematic overview of the research within a specific area. Based on quality criteria, some publications were excluded and the project ended up with a narrative synthesis based on 43 research projects.

The review revealed most evidence on question 1, about how the tests as such (i.e. the fact that testing is taking place) affect the teachers' pedagogical decisions. It concluded, in accordance with the general understanding amongst educational researchers (for instance Au, 2007; Smith, Hounshell, Copolo, & Wilkerson, 1992), that:

- tests do affect the teacher's instruction in the intended way; but
- the effects are not uniquely positive.

The review revealed considerable negative effects of introducing centrally administrated tests:

- a narrowed down or distorted realised curriculum: professional lines of thought are simplified, facts and mechanical skills are emphasised on behalf of creative and aesthetic perspectives;
- teaching time allocated to test issues on behalf of not test issues;
- teaching becomes addicted to 'teaching to the test' and 'rote learning'.

As regards the question of the teachers' pedagogical use of test data (question 2 in Fig. 5.1), none of the studies dealt with the teacher's interpretation of the information embedded in test data. So we really do not know whether teachers understand test results in accordance with the test developers' intentions. One finding to emerge however was that teachers'sense of ownership of the tests seemed to play a central role in'successful systems' (Dolin, 2012). Teachers preferred tests adapted to the actual class and teachers preferred tests with multifaceted results – but these relations were vaguely investigated in the research literature. One study showed that the very fact that a test had taken place could completely overshadow the teacher's openness for a pedagogical use of test data.

The announcement of a test in the classroom can have a strong influence on student emotions and motivation (question 3). When a test is announced, it can release emotional reactions like fear and nervousness, and students prepare for the test by rote learning and memorising. High performing students will have an increased motivation for learning while low performers will lose heart. And the test result will determine future motivation and self-efficacy.

Especially the results concerning teachers' possible use of test data for pedagogical purposes in their daily practice is congruent with the results from a study of Danish science teachers' assessment culture (Dolin & Krogh, 2008). This study surveyed and interviewed a representative sample of Danish science teachers. We found the typical science teacher to hold a broad repertoire of active assessment formats, with a combination of individual written tests and dialogical talks with the whole class as the dominant form. The teachers did not teach in order to enhance a test performance (the study compared the Danish teachers' assessment culture with the PISA test format). They taught for more varied goals and they simply used a much broader palette of assessment tools than the PISA formats. Most of the teachers expressed a student oriented aim with their assessments. They had a marked focus on learning and learning potential in their assessments with formative and summative approaches as well, and they evaluated both during and after the teaching sequences. They often made the criteria for the assessment open to the students, and the students always received feedback on the tests and assessments. Like in the Clearinghouse review these teachers also expressed a need to have control over the test items; they wanted them to be designed explicitly for their own classes and aligned with their selected content and problems and their pedagogical style.

This is probably one of the main reasons why standardised and high-stakes tests are so relatively badly received by teachers and difficult to use for pedagogical purposes. The tests are designed by others and not suited to the teachers' own classroom. Not being able to fit the tests to their classroom, teachers compensate by fitting their teaching to the test (Sturman, 2003)! On top of this the results of these tests are often used against teachers: students perform badly equals teachers do a lousy job with potentially dramatic consequences for teachers and even schools.

These distorting effects of standardised and high-stakes tests could be acceptable, a necessary evil, for steering the teaching in a wanted direction. But as we will see below, the tests are not testing what society wants.

5.1.2   The Limitations of Standardised Tests

Analyses of current trends in European educational policy point at three general policy trends (Young, 2010, p. 1):

* The building up of a national qualifications framework;
* A shift in curriculum from content to learning outcomes;
* A move from subject-specific learning goals to generic curriculum criteria.

The desired learning outcomes and generic abilities are more and more often described in 'competence' terms. Although there is no generally accepted definition of competence (Weinert, 2001), normally a competence is understood as a combination of skills, knowledge, characteristics, and traits that contribute to performances in particular domains. Hartig, Klieme, and Leutner (2008) described a competence as a complex ability that is closely related to performance in real life situations. In accordance with this, Shavelson (2011) considered with regard to assessment of competences that:

> a competence measure should tap complex physical and/or intellectual skills, produce observable performance on a common, standardized set of tasks with high fidelity to the performances observed in the "real world" ("criterion") situations to which inferences of competence are to be drawn, with scores reflecting the level of performance (mastery or continuous) on tasks where improvement can be made through deliberative practice. (n.p.)

These are quite demanding requirements for an assessment system, reflecting that the more complex the learning goals, the more difficult they are to measure. The understanding of competences as the ability to cope with relatively complex challenges in everyday life means that assessment methods necessarily have to be relatively advanced, flexible, and process oriented.

But formulating these necessary conditions for a viable assessment points to the well-known dilemma in all assessments: the contradiction between high reliability (necessary for justly marking students and establishing the league tables) and high validity (that you actually test what you are interested in, such as competences, and not some proxy variable) – in a system with limited economic resources. Any summative and comparative test must be reliable and is therefore forced to compare relatively simple aspects of student performance, while the (valid) test of advanced competencies is complicated and expensive. But advanced competences are what all policy makers want the students to have – like creativity, innovation, flexibility, collaboration abilities etc. combined with advanced professional process competences.

An example of an attempt to change the goals of a discipline in a competences direction could be the dramatic changes in science education during the last 10–15 years. For many reasons many attempts have been made by education policy makers and educationalists to transform school science, from a system transferring a fixed body of canonical knowledge to a system reflecting the knowledge-producing process. There has been pressure as well as strong support to change school science, in the words of Latour (1987), from teaching 'ready-made-science' to involving students in 'science-in-the-making'. Science education researchers have, in partnership with theorists of science, analysed what scientists are doing when they do science, and a whole field of research on 'the nature of science' has emerged (Abd-El-Khalick, 2012; Eijck, 2012). Based on this insight, new frameworks for science education have been formulated, like the US National Academy of Sciences' Framework for K-12 Science Education (Committee on a Conceptual Framework for New K-12 Science Education Standards, 2012). This framework describes school science as using investigations of the real world (through observing, experimenting, measuring, and testing) to develop explanations and solutions (through creative thinking, reasoning, calculating, and planning) with the link established by argumentation. The traditional science competences: experimenting, measuring and so on are integrated with new competences like argumentation, creativity et cetera. A European counterpart is the so-called Rochard report *Science Education Now: A Renewed Pedagogy for the Future of Europe* by the European Commission, 2007. Based on the report's recommendations, the European Commission has heavily funded a large number of projects aimed at implementing a so-called 'inquiry-based science education' in the classroom. This approach to science teaching has many versions, but typically it involves students working with authentic problems, involving experimental procedures, a high degree of student autonomy, and argumentation and communication.

These intentions to prepare students for the future in a global information society, formulated via complex competences, are often entered in the curriculum parallel with or on top of the more traditional curriculum goals – and despite significant teacher professional development programmes, not much has changed in classroom practice. A major reason for this is the fact that most testing systems are not able to meet the new learning goals. Due to limited resources and an often simplistic understanding of learning, they are often restricted to relatively simple drill and multiple choice questions. And as shown above, the assessment forms have a deciding influence on teaching, teachers do teach to the test, and 'traditional' assessment forms will encourage 'traditional' teaching, so most existing assessment and evaluation formats are blocking teaching that makes it possible for students to meet the new learning goals. The only way out of this is to introduce more valid assessment methods that promote these new goals.

The international PISA project (OECD, 1999), testing reading, mathematical and scientific literacy, declares itself an exponent for a test system able to capture these competences essential for future life:

> Although the domains of reading literacy, mathematical literacy and scientific literacy correspond to school subjects, the OECD assessments will not primarily examine how well students have mastered the specific curriculum content. Rather, they aim at assessing the extent to which young people have acquired the wider knowledge and skills in these domains that they will need in adult life. (p. 9)

In order to investigate the limitations of traditional, summative tests, the author, together with Lars B. Krogh, University of Aarhus, designed a research programme 'Validation of PISA in a Danish context' (VAP), examining to what degree a relatively advanced test like the PISA test gives a valid picture of Danish students' scientific literacy (Krogh & Dolin, 2011). The project re-tested, in a more school-like, everyday setting, students who have completed the PISA test. Through a relatively complex methodological design, we were able to compare student performance in the two different situations, using PISA's own standards, and at the same time get a broader knowledge of the students' science competencies than the PISA test makes possible.

The theoretical basis for the project was research showing that student performance is dependent on the mediation in the situation (available artefacts, possibility for dialogue with peers, a relaxed atmosphere etc.) (Schoultz, Saljo, & Wyndhamn, 2001a, 2001b) and that any assessment implies a model of learning (Gipps, 1999). The PISA test, like most summative and all large-scale tests, is based on a post-positivistic approach to learning (explained in detail later), seeing student abilities as constant across different assessment situations. The research project's assessment was more socio-cultural, seeing student abilities as dependent on/linked to the assessment situation.

Some weeks after the PISA 2006 testing was administered, 130 pupils who had completed the PISA 2006 test were randomly selected and subjected to the socio-culturally oriented VAP-test. The sample was stratified and provided by the Danish PISA consortium, which also made the students' original PISA performances available. Three PISA items made up the core of the VAP-validation: a biology item (PISA 2006 # S478, 'antibiotics'), a geographical/physical item (the PISA 2006 # S465, 'different climates') and an experimental task (the PISA 2006 item # S477, 'sunscreens', which imitates laboratory work). The items were chosen because they spanned a range of subjects and competences, were related to core domains of the Danish curricula, and seemed well-constructed.

A number of other items from the same PISA booklets were used to examine possible effects of the re-examination. The students simply answered these items in the original PISA paper-and-pencil format and under the same conditions. We saw no re-testing effect – the students got exactly the same scores in the re-testing as in the original test. This confirms that summative use of tests has no formative effects – the students do not learn anything from summative use of tests!

In accordance with the socio-cultural orientation of VAP, the re-examination was carried out by means of interviews/conversation and the practical task was performed in student pairs. Both situations allowed pupils to make use of relevant artefacts (laboratory equipment), like Petri dishes, pipettes etc. in the antibiotics item, as well as maps, a globe etc. in the climate item, and sunscreens with different protection factors, light sensitive photo paper etc. in the practical tasks. The dialogic assessments were guided by semi-structured interview-protocols, developed from a pilot-study, in order to secure reliability. The PISA item questions were integrated into these protocols to make it possible to determine the change in students' performance if students are (re)tested within a socio-culturally oriented test format using dialogue, mediating artefacts, and practical enactment. But the interview protocols also contained broader questions related to the Danish curriculum, Common Goals, within the domain. The latter was to ensure VAP validity in relation to the requirements of the Danish compulsory school, the Folkeskole ('the people's school' – the Danish compulsory school), and Danish science teaching.

Student science teachers were recruited and trained as research assistants to conduct the interviews, and they were gathered regularly for quality assurance. Typically, 30 min were used for dialogic assessment of "antibiotics" and "different climates", another 30 min for the practical assessment of "sunscreens", and finally some 35 min for the paper-and-pencil test of retest effects. All dialogical oriented sessions were videotaped and processed for subsequent scoring and socio-cultural analysis. The video-recordings were analysed using PISA's scoring criteria and the scorings were compared with the students score in the PISA test. Assessment of performance in relation to the broader domains in Danish Common Goals were made holistically and scored according to these standards and expert-benchmarks. For all analyses several researchers contributed and high inter-rater reliability was ensured.

The differences in student performance in the two tests were quite dramatic: changing the test-format to a richer and therefore more valid one increased students' overall performance on PISA criteria from a mean of 0.54 to an interval 0.68–0.7 – an increase of 26 %! And low performers improved relatively the most. A (traditional) psychometrician would say: 'The socio-cultural oriented test is easier for the student' (due to the artefacts and the dialogue), while a socio-culturally oriented researcher will say: 'Knowing is in context and relative to circumstance'. More interesting was that the students only had a correct understanding according to the Danish learning objectives on 20–35 % vs. 45–75 % correct PISA scores. They were thus able to perform to a mediocre standard in PISA Science test with only a very low fulfillment of the Danish curriculum. A possible explanation for this is that scientific literacy can be defined on different taxonomic levels (Bybee, 1997). The demands in The Danish Common Goals seem to imply scientific literacy on a higher taxonomic level than demanded by the PISA items. PISA simply does not test the degree of conceptual understanding and process mastery that is assumed to be learned in the Danish school according to the Common Goals. So, changing the test-format improved scores on PISA-tested knowledge areas and demonstrated that PISA is not able to capture advanced levels of scientific literacy (like those demanded by the Danish curricular goals); and students with a poor or incorrect understanding were able to perform well on PISA. And maybe the most important point – a lot of relevant knowledge about student competence is not tested by PISA – thus missing didactical directions for improving science education.

As an overall conclusion, it can be stated that even advanced summative assessment methods currently in use are not able to capture competences in the true sense of the concept: students' abilities to cope with complex challenges in varied situations. Traditional test settings and standardised test items like the PISA assessment (OECD, 2004) and end of year examinations can assess subject-specific knowledge and abilities in solving problems in a school-like context. Such knowledge and skills are obviously useful and probably a prerequisite for building proper competences.

Focusing on testing such traditional knowledge and skills might nevertheless block teaching for advanced competences and steer the educational system in a wrong direction. Some research indicates that it might be even worse: high performance in traditional tests might foreshadow low performance in more desired personal competences. Zhao and Meyer (2013) "argue that high achievements on standardised tests may also reflect a school system's efficient functioning as a disciplinary mechanism, representing the absence of independent and creative thinking" (p. 268). They analysed students' performances in China, number one in all three domains of the PISA test in 2009, and Singapore, number two in math, fourth in science and fifth in reading in PISA 2009, for entrepreneurialism, which they see as "a key indicator of a person's ability and willingness to take risks in the pursuit of innovation, and a key prerequisite for economic prosperity" (p. 268). Both countries are educational giants measured by traditional standards but they have very weak entrepreneurial traditions. The same contradictions existed in other high-performing countries like Korea and Japan. Zhao and Meyer investigated the correlation between a country's PISA performance in the 2009 test and the country's rank in the 2011 Global Entrepreneurship Monitor (GEM) report. Thirty-nine countries out of the 54 economies surveyed in the 2011 GEM report also participated in the 2009 PISA testing and the PISA scores in reading, math and sciences were negatively correlated with all entrepreneurship indicators at statistically significant levels. The roots to the apparent contradictions shown here between different goals for education, the teaching carried out in the classroom and the applied assessment systems, are to be found in the different conceptualisations of these fundamental elements of education and the missing alignment between them.

5.1.3 Different Assessment Paradigms and the Necessity of Alignment

Research shows (Dolin & Krogh, 2008; Nordenbo et al., 2009) that teachers prefer tests with multifaceted results, that is, tests with high validity able to capture student performance in an everyday context. From a Danish perspective, this contradiction between external tests and classroom practice is, on a deeper level, an expression of the different theoretical foundations of standardised tests and most teachers' everyday student assessment. The 'Validation of PISA in a Danish context' project established two different paradigms for assessing students (Krogh & Dolin, 2011), based on different understandings of knowledge and learning. PISA, like all standardised tests, identifies student abilities as constant across different assessment situations and in this respect is based on a post-positivistic learning understanding. On the other hand, much teaching is based on a socio-cultural approach, seeing student abilities as dependent on/linked to the assessment situation (Gipps, 1999). The post-positivistic, psychometric oriented test design – standardised and with high reliability – that characterises external and international comparative tests, is in contrast to most teachers' socio-cultural, hermeneutic oriented assessments, classroom adaptable and with high validity (Buhagiar, 2007). In a very schematic form, you can contrast the two assessment paradigms in this way (See Table 5.1):

Table 5.1 Contrasting the two assessment paradigms

Post-positivist assessment	Socio-cultural assessment
Student abilities are seen as constant across different assessment situations	Student abilities are seen as dependent on/linked to the assessment situations
Tests are:	Tests are:
Non-interactive	Interactive
Non-collaborative	Collaborative
Static	Dynamic (upper ZPD-oriented)
Product-oriented	Process-oriented
Limited use of tools (symbolic, physical)	Extended use of tools (symbolic, physical)
Situated in special settings	Embedded in authentic situations

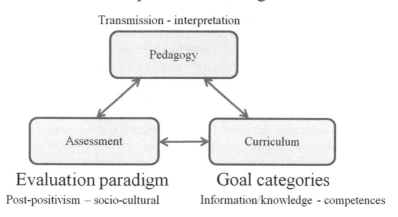

Conceptions of learning

Transmission - interpretation

Pedagogy

Assessment ← → Curriculum

Evaluation paradigm   **Goal categories**

Post-positivism – socio-cultural   Information/knowledge - competences

Fig. 5.2 Elements that need to be aligned for a well-functioning educational system

Seen in this light, it is not surprising that many teachers have difficulties in using standardised tests for pedagogical purposes and often have hostile feelings about them. And it is also evident that traditional tests are not able to assess more advanced competences as they are demanded in modern society.

What is needed is an alignment between the three elements in the chain from the educational goals as they are expressed in the curriculum, the pedagogy implementing the curriculum in the classroom, and the assessment assessing the fulfilment of the goals. This is illustrated in Fig. 5.2. Each of the elements hold a scale of positions representing different attitudes and paradigms and without alignment between positions in each element, the system will malfunction. Thus, in order to make it possible for students to acquire advanced competences as expressed in the curriculum, the teachers must use a certain pedagogy based on a certain conception of learning and the assessment must be based on an assessment paradigm that makes it possible to assess the desired competences. Unfortunately, such coherence between the determining factors of educational systems is very rare. There are many and not very transparent reasons for this but one important cause is national and international comparative testing.

5.1.4 International Competition – Distorting National Development

As shown above, research tells us that standardised testing affects classroom practice directly and even if it has no direct consequences, such testing is often high-stakes for teachers and schools. Some of the driving forces for these tests are control and accountability; the policy levels need proof of student performance and they want to know whether they are getting value for money. These mechanisms reproduce themselves on national and international levels with even wider perspectives, related to education becoming a competitive field. In a (Central/North) European context, education has traditionally been outside the competitive imperative of the market. But on a global level the ever-closer links between knowledge (and competence), education, and competitiveness have played a central role in all educational initiatives over the past 10–15 years and this is also the case in Europe. Competition is the global condition, and at the same time, the answer. The point here is that it is not always economic rationales or human values that are the driving forces, but the mere logic of competition, detached from the concrete reality; competition as an ideology. In this logic of 'competition legitimacy' and the 'self-evident' is the values and understandings of competition – and the rules and framing that gives meaning to competition are market adaptation and comparison. In the fear of falling back in the international horse race, you need to know where you are placed in the field and you will then automatically do what those leading the race are doing and you will run faster along the same track. This is a fatal mistake if the premises for the race and the direction of the field are different from your own goals. You (the politicians) will act without looking to the sides or trying to find other ways or building on other logic than the one driving the international competition. The way the PISA test results have been used in Denmark is a good example of this.

The somewhat disappointing Danish results in the PISA tests have been used by the Danish government as an argument for pursuing their educational goals for more marketisation of education and introducing new educational reforms (Dolin & Krogh, 2010) in the Folkeskole. This process has been indirectly supported by massive media coverage each time a new cycle of PISA tests was released. Newspaper headlines like "Un-acceptable – a national mobilisation is needed to rebuild quality in Folkeskolen" (Bindslev, 2004) and "PISA report says: Folkeskolen fails, once again" (Aarsland, Danielsen, & Winther, 2004) resonated with the Minister of Education's new initiative; as a consequence of the poor performance in PISA, a new system of national tests was introduced! The resulting test-system clearly illustrates the constitutional effects of PISA – Danish/literacy, mathematics, and all science subjects are tested, and most tests are placed around the PISA age-window (8th grade in the Danish school). Tests in the subject of English are the only extension to the PISA domains.

Another fundamental impact of PISA can be seen in the changes in the preamble to the Act on the Folkeskole. The Folkeskole is seen as the prime conduit of Danish identity and culture and up till 2006 the first paragraph expressing the goals of Folkeskole stated its overall aims as to:

> contribute to the all-round personal development of the individual pupil;
> endeavour to create such opportunities that pupils develop awareness, imagination and an urge to learn, so that they acquire confidence in their own possibilities and a background for forming independent judgements and for taking personal action;
> familiarise pupils with Danish culture and contribute to their understanding of other cultures and of man's interaction with nature. The school shall prepare the pupils for active participation, joint responsibility, rights and duties in a society based on freedom and democracy.

This demonstrates a focus on the development of the individual student and the preparation for participation in society. In 2006, the preamble was changed with reference to the poor PISA results. The new first paragraph reads:

> In cooperation with parents the Folkeskole must supply students with knowledge and skills, that will prepare them for further education and motivate them to learn more, familiarize them with Danish culture and History, induce understanding of other nations and cultures, contribute to their understanding of human interaction with nature, and support each student's all-rounded development.

These goals express an increased emphasis on subject-specific skills and on preparation for further education, and subsequently for the labour market. At the same time the government then in power declared that the goal of the educational policy was to see Denmark situated among the top five in the PISA league table!

The PISA project is only one factor contributing to the dramatic change the Danish educational system has gone through during the last 10–15 years. But it is an excellent illustration of how supra national organisations like OECD and EC have imposed market logic on education. Described in educational terms, this trend can be interpreted as a shift from a traditional Nordic/Central European understanding of education toward an Anglo-American understanding.

5.1.5 A Central European/Nordic versus an Anglo-American Approach toward Education

The PISA project and the published PISA results landed Denmark in a conflict between three different goal discourses (Dolin, 2013):

- *bildung* discourse valuing personal and societal development;
- *curriculum* discourse with emphasis on 'traditional' subject-specific content;
- *competence* discourse aiming at giving the students individual capabilities for acting in society.

The first two discourses express the traditional Nordic and Central European dichotomy between education for later use in a job and/or education, etc. and citizenship – the curriculum tradition – and an education for 'life' and 'personality' – the 'bildung' tradition.

The concept of bildung (a German word, Danish: dannelse) is not easy to explain. It has its roots in antique Greek and has developed through history, and the present understanding in Denmark is basically related to the German influence from the first half of the nineteenth century. An education aimed at enhancing the students' bildung will emphasise the general character development of the student. Through the acquisition of subject-specific knowledge in an organised process, the student's mind and whole personality should develop. He or she will establish an emancipatory relation between him/herself and the outside world. It is a process of transformation in which you build your personality ('to build' and 'bildung' probably have the same etymology). The important point here is that the emphasis on bildung has given rise to a specific understanding of teaching, schooling, and the teaching profession – the Didaktik tradition (Westbury, 2000) – spelled in German to distinguish it from the English term 'didactics', which has a rather schoolmaster-like connotation in an Anglo-American context. The didaktik tradition has a different way of thinking about curriculum and teaching than the Anglo-American curriculum tradition:

> In the American case, the dominant idea animating the curriculum tradition has been organizational, focusing on the task of building systems of schools that have as an important part of their overall organizational framework a 'curriculum-as-manual', containing the templates for coverage and methods that are seen as guiding, directing, or controlling a school's, or a school system's, day-by-day classroom work. ... Teachers are ... seen as more or less passive 'conduits' of the system's or district's curriculum decisions. (Westbury, 2000, pp. 16–17)

In opposition to this, the didaktik tradition has another view on the teacher's role:

> the state's curriculum making has not been seen as something that could or should explicitly direct a teacher's work. Indeed, teachers are guaranteed professional autonomy, 'freedom to teach', without control by curriculum in the American sense. The state curriculum, the Lehrplan, does lay out prescribed content for teaching; but, this content is understood as an authoritative selection from cultural traditions that can only become educative as it is interpreted and given life by teachers—who are seen, in their turn, as normatively directed by the elusive concept of Bildung, or formation, and by the ways of thinking found in the 'art' of Didaktik. (Westbury, 2000, p. 17)

Put into a schematic form (Table 5.2).

The bildung tradition paves the ground for pedagogy in the Folkeskole that is student-centred, rather than subject-centred. This does not mean that the Folkeskole does not place emphasis on subject-specific knowledge and skills – only it has another way to professional knowledge, a way that tries to start with the student and which gives room for the student's own interpretation. Traditionally, the Folkeskole has not been an examination-oriented school. Before the introduction of the national tests, no grades were given before lower secondary school, so for many years assessment was almost exclusively informal, formative by nature, and directed towards

Table 5.2 Comparing Central European/Nordic tradition with the Anglo-American tradition

Didaktik/bildung tradition (Central European/Nordic tradition)	Curriculum tradition (Anglo-American tradition)
The government sets up a guiding frame for education in the form of general goals	The government/authorities have the authority to establish standards for the subjects
The teacher is the authority who chooses the content and the pedagogy in order to make it possible for the student to internalise the subject, to form his or her own personal understanding	The role of the teacher is to transmit a certain, pre-defined content to the students, making it possible for the students to learn the prescribed content
Based on a humanistic ideal of bildung, education shall liberate the individual to democratic participation through obtaining personal authority	Based on an instrumental, market oriented ideal of education for society (as a labour force and a democratic citizen)

students and parents. The only high-stakes examinations were placed at the end of the Folkeskole to provide certification for upper secondary school entrance. Promotions to the next class were, and are still, based on holistic teacher judgments rather than testing, and failure to be promoted is an almost non-existent phenomenon. The Danish Folkeskole has traditionally valued inclusion, participation and dialogue between teachers and students, as well as a sense of community instead of tests. The slogan has been: willing hands make light work, and at least by some measures the Danish Folkeskole has been found to succeed: "All in all, in the international comparison, the Danish primary and lower secondary school seems to be succeeding in its object concerning all-round development of students: the students are motivated and have confidence in their academic ability" (English summary, Danish PISA report 2000, cited in Andersen et al., 2001). Similarly, the PISA reports document that Danish students are among the most motivated to learn.

Until the 1990s, the bildung tradition dominated the educational discourse in the Nordic countries, or more precisely, it held the curriculum tradition off. The curriculum tradition was, and is, represented by powerful business and economic interests, often advocating a 'back to basics' movement with emphasis on acquiring fundamental knowledge. The two traditions have approached each other in subject-specific contexts, discussing which content best fulfilled the goals, and with more focus on control and accountability; hence, the bildung tradition has come under pressure.

The competence discourse entered into the Nordic (and European) educational landscape in the late 1990s with the market orientation invading the educational sphere. The competence approach has more or less swept the table by its insistence on action based on knowledge and personal abilities. But the personal qualities embedded in the spectrum of competences are often formulated in management terms like creativity, innovation, entrepreneurship etc., and oriented toward use in a market society – quite far from the traditional bildung understanding. So, many educationalists will talk about competence in metaphors of loss; loss of basic values sacrificed on the altar of economics and management.

PISA, and the wave of testing, tumbled down in the cross field between the three educational discourses. PISA officially oriented itself towards competence logic, but in reality it promoted a curriculum thinking, which certainly did not coincide with a bildung approach. In practice, PISA has thus induced and legitimised radical changes of traditional priorities in the Danish educational landscape.

5.1.6 Leadership Perspectives

Concurrent with the previously described dramatic changes in education, an equally heavy emphasis on leadership and leadership roles has taken place. The educational aims have been directed from democratic involvement and personal development, towards more focus on economy and employability. At the same time new forms of public sector management have emerged under the umbrella term *New Public Management* (Greve, 2002). The philosophy of New Public Management coincided with the ideology behind the educational shifts: the public sector shall be led in the same way as the private sector through competition and consumer choice in an 'educational market'.

Leaders at different levels will necessarily address the issues put forward differently according to their various manoeuvre possibilities and options. Their decisions will also be strongly affected by their different philosophies of leadership providing each leader with diverse tools to manage the different challenges.

On a *national level* members of parliament (MPs) are responsible for the laws setting the overall frame and the overall goals for education. Most of these MPs have no deep understanding of educational problems – although they are always willing to discuss and comment on educational matters, often based on own experiences from school or their children's current school incidents! It is extremely important that these high level politicians establish connections to key national experts in order to be able to have a well-founded national perspective on international trends. Danish politicians have argued for, and voted for, dramatic changes in the educational system based on a decrease in PISA scores that is not even significant! We would avoid such impulsive reactions if politicians followed the conclusions of Zhao and Meyer (2013): "We will stand in the best tradition of western rationalism if we question the authority of global assessments, contextualize their meaning, and delineate their utility, thereby increasing the wisdom of both test-makers and test-consumers" (p. 276). On a more theoretical level, politicians should, to a larger degree, base their decisions on considerations of principle and be careful not to go into blind competition. They should rather build on known strengths. Denmark and the Nordic countries might not perform among the top countries in PISA and many other comparative tests, but despite that, the living conditions in Denmark are among the best in the world (UNDP, 2013), it is the country with the happiest population in the world (Helliwell, Layard, & Sachs, 2013), and it is one of the most attractive countries to invest in for innovative capital (World Economic Forum, 2008, 2009). You could even argue that if Denmark ended among the top five on the

PISA league table, it might be at the expense of the characteristics that have brought Denmark to its present state of wealth and welfare. So it should rather substantiate and consolidate what has led to the present well-functioning educational system instead of trying to win a horse race with too strong competitors. Naturally, you can always learn from others, and you should not let your success be an excuse for doing nothing. But instead of trusting large-scale comparative testing it would be wiser to put resources into developing assessment forms tailored to the Danish educational system and capable of assessing the competences (or bildung!) that we find central for the Danish students.

Most educational leadership is practiced at the *school level* – and with New Public Management the schools have seen a boom in mid-level leaders. Fifteen years ago, a normal Danish school was led by a headmaster helped by one or two deputy heads, who often had some teaching responsibilities as well, and they had support from two to three secretaries. These numbers have increased dramatically in order to meet a large number of bureaucratic procedures for accounting, certification, evaluation, contract fulfilling and so on. This trend goes together with a change in the understanding of school development (Raae, 2013). Some 20 years ago, school development was seen as pedagogical development of the individual teacher, often as continuous pedagogical development or inservice teacher training offered by subject teacher associations or teacher training colleges. This has changed towards development of the school as an organisation. The focus now is more on whole-school programmes about common themes, such as, teacher cooperation, new teaching methods etc., for all teachers at the school. The aforementioned shift from a bildung/didaktik tradition towards a curriculum tradition, therefore, has a parallel in how school development is changing from the individual teacher's own training to the school's implementation of centrally fixed goals. Goals the school is held accountable for. The individual school is organised and run as a private business with strategies for optimising its performance on key indicators like dropout rates, average marks, teacher illness, profit etc., in order to compete for students and be able to attract good teachers.

Now, the question is whether there is a special Nordic school leadership way of managing this global trend? The answer is yes! Sixty school leadership researchers from the Nordic countries have recently completed a 3-year research programme to find out how Nordic educational politics and leadership are influenced by transnational agencies like OECD and EC (Moos, 2013). The researchers compared the Nordic traditions with the UK/US tradition and they started by lining up the different societal backgrounds in the two sets of countries. The more egalitarian Nordic societies were the background for flatter management structures and more collegial relations than in the UK/US where steeper hierarchies were the basis for accepting stronger, more direct leadership than in the Nordic countries (Moos, 2013, p. 7). As part of this, the UK/US societies were more liberal with a deep belief in individual choice and competition in opposition to the Nordic values of community and collaboration. The large majority of the Nordic schools are comprehensive, without streaming. The Nordic welfare society is based on a strong state (the majority of Danish citizens are happy to pay their very high taxes) and a well-regulated labour market. These different backgrounds are reflected in the organisation and leadership of the schools. The Nordic schools have three layers in staff: teacher, middle leader, school leader. UK schools can have eight layers: school leader, deputy, assisting deputy, department leader, deputy department leader, assistant deputy department leader, teacher and assistant teacher (Moos, 2013, p. 8). The fewer layers in the Nordic system make it easier to establish communities of practice and self-governing teams and collaborative leadership in Nordic schools and they give a shorter pathway from leader decisions to classroom practice.

The research reveals three aspects to be common Nordic features in successful school leadership (Moos, 2013, p. 218):

- School leaders' translation and mediation of external demands into local meaning.
- School leaders translate the often contradictory expectations and demands from external stakeholders into a language and a practice suitable and practicable for the staff and the school culture.
- Balancing between different leadership ways of influencing staff.
- Nordic school leaders mobilise both teachers and middle leaders to react on external expectations, while UK/US school leaders more often take over command.
- Strong relations to school environment.
- Nordic school leaders interpret signals and expectations from many stakeholders and balance considerations of local interests with official demands and school possibilities.

These trends might be summed up in this statement:

> While UK/US school leaders tend to be more compliant with external expectations, like high-stake accountabilities, Nordic school leaders try to respond to both short-term accountability and long-term comprehensive education demands. They try to bridge expectations from both welfare state and competitive state governance, when strengthening relations to parents. (Moos, 2013, p. 218f).

Even if the competitive trend in new public management and accountability systems, here exemplified by central testing, is threatening the Nordic bildung/didaktik tradition, it seems as if the Nordic leadership approach is capable of stemming the tide of external influence from global trends. Such a leadership is also necessary if the teachers are to feel comfortable to teach to support students' personal development and advanced competences not necessarily tested in the external examinations but requested by many stakeholders. An unwanted consequence of this seemingly sympathetic and inclusive leadership style might be that some of the accountability pressure is forwarded downwards in the system to the teachers. This gives them a responsibility they should not have. But until now the bildung culture has to a large degree kept the teachers free from direct accountability consequences; it is still only targeting the school and national level.

5.2 Conclusions and Perspectives

This chapter has investigated how summative assessment and standardised tests, be they high-stake or low-stake, are influencing teaching conditions without being able to measure desired competences. They are also affecting national educational policies in a non-appropriate direction for the Danish context. Industry and society demand that schools educate young people in the competences needed to perform in post-modern society. Educational research has designed teaching methods and materials making it possible to fulfil these demands, but the test systems in use are preventing teachers from implementing them. Even worse, international comparative tests such as the PISA test are contributory causes in changing the educational policy in a direction away from encouraging teaching for innovative competences.

The results from the Validation of PISA Project are a warning against using test results from traditional tests as an indicator for more advanced student competences. They demonstrate the necessity of developing assessment formats capable of capturing such learning goals in a reliable way. The project points to the fact that standardised tests are based on different premises than those of teachers' everyday assessment and that there must be an alignment between the requested competences of the student, the instruction, and the assessment paradigm.

What is needed, then, is an assessment system that can give summative results on an individual student level, which can be aggregated to higher levels – for political purposes – and that can be used by teachers for formative purposes.

These systems have not yet been designed in full-scale. But many approaches seem possible. You could for instance extract evidence of student performance from classroom work produced during the course (e.g., electronic portfolios). This could be done using computer-based technologies where substantial research is done to enhance the possibilities for assessing complex competencies. In general, when students are learning online, there are multiple opportunities for gathering data in the course of learning that can be used for assessment. The possibilities for integrating standardised and classroom based assessments exist now. What is needed is research into usable procedures in close collaboration with teachers and policy makers daring to implement them.

A project currently trying to do this is the EU financed research project Assess Inquiry in Science, Technology and Mathematics Education (ASSIST-ME) (http://assistme.ku.dk/). Based on an analysis of what is known about summative and formative assessment of knowledge, skills, and attitudes related to key Science, Technology, and Mathematics competences and an analysis of European educational systems, the project aims to design a range of assessment methods for both formative and summative use. These methods will be tested in primary and secondary schools in different educational cultures in Europe in order to analyse the conditions that support or undermine the uptake of formative assessment related to inquiry processes. What distinguishes this project from most research is that the research process and the results will be evaluated and discussed in national stakeholder panels in order to formulate guidelines and recommendations for policy makers,

Fig. 5.3 Change in assessment practice presupposes a strong collaboration between research, teaching and policy

curriculum developers, teacher trainers, and other stakeholders in the different European educational systems.

Figure 5.3 illustrates the collaboration in ASSIST-ME between the three most important actors in changing assessment practice (apart from the students). The researchers are, together with teachers, developing usable assessment methods; politicians are persuaded to trust teachers to assess their own students in a valid way and researchers must then convince policy makers to change the assessment framework so reasonable assessment and teaching is possible. School leaders will play a key role in mediating between the policy level and the teacher practice, framing the necessary teacheprofessional development and securing good working conditions for teachers.

This triangle of productive collaboration for change is not easy to establish because the three groups involved normally live and work apart from each other, following quite different norms and discourses. The national stakeholder panels established in the ASSIST-ME project are struggling to find a way to balance stakeholder interests. It is often a question of understanding each other and the conditions under which decisions are made. In the ASSIST-ME project researchers are involving teachers as well as politicians in the formulations and the accomplishment of research projects about assessment in order to secure the relevance and the meaningfulness – and potential implementation – of the research. It requires the researchers to renounce traditional research organisations and attitudes and it will require the politicians to hand over some control to the educators. School leaders and teachers must be willing to change their practice according to research results. It is basically about understanding each other and building up trust, which is difficult in systems based on power and interests. The hope is that such common forums can contribute to a meaningful dialogue between key actors and consequently serve as incubators for fundamental change.

References

Aarsland, L., Danielsen, A. B., & Winther, A. (2004, December 7). PISA-rapporten: Ny nedtur for folkeskolen [English: PISA report says: Folkeskolen fails, once again]. *Politiken* (Newspaper), p. 2.

Abd-El-Khalick, F. (2012). Nature of science in science education: Toward a coherent framework for synergetic research and development. In B. J. Fraser et al. (Eds.), *Second international handbook of science education*. Dordrecht, The Netherlands: Springer.

Andersen, A. M., Egelund, N., Jensen, T. P., Krone, M., Lindenskov, L., & Mejding, J. (2001). *Forventninger og færdigheder - danske unge i en international sammenligning* [English: Expectations and skills – Danish youth in an international comparison]. København, Denmark: AKF, DPU og SFI-Survey. (The Danish PISA2000 report – in Danish)

Au, W. (2007). High stakes testing and curricular control: A qualitative metasynthesis. *Educational Researcher, 36*(5), 258–267.

Bennett, J., Lubben, F., Hogarth, S., & Campbell, B. (2005). Systematic reviews of research in science education: Rigour or rigidity? *International Journal of Science Education, 27*(4), 387–406.

Bindslev, M. W. (2004, December 7). Danske elever er middelmådige [English: The mediocre performance of Danish students]. *Kristeligt Dagblad* (Newspaper), p. 1.

Buhagiar, M. A. (2007). Classroom assessment within the alternative assessment paradigm: Revisiting the territory. *The Curriculum Journal, 18*, 39–56.

Bybee, R. (1997). Towards an understanding of scientific literacy. In W. Graeber & C. Bolte (Eds.), *Scientific literacy* (pp. 37–68). Kiel, Germany: Independent Publishers Network.

Chia, R. (1995). From modern to postmodern organizational analysis. *Organizational Studies, 16*(4), 579–604.

Committee on a Conceptual Framework for New K-12 Science Education Standards. (2012). *A framework for K-12 science education: Practices, crosscutting concepts, and core ideas.* Washington, DC: National Academies Press.

Dolin, J. (2012). Using large scale test results for pedagogical purposes. In C. Bruguière, A. Tiberghien, & P. Clément (Eds.), *E-book proceedings of the ESERA 2011 conference: Science learning and citizenship. Part 10* (pp. 16–22). Lyon, France: European Science Education Research Association.

Dolin, J. (2013). Dannelse, kompetence og kernefaglighed (English: Bildung, competence, and core subject specific knowledge). In E. Damberg, J. Dolin, G. H. Ingerslev, & P. Kaspersen (Eds.), *Gymnasiepædagogik* [English: Pedagogy for upper secondary] (pp. 67–86). København, Denmark: Hans Reitzel (In Danish).

Dolin, J., & Krogh, L. B. (2008). *Den naturfaglige evalueringskultur i folkeskolen. Anden delrapport fra VAP-projektet* [English: The assessment culture in the science subjects in the compulsory school. Second report from the VAP project] (INDs skriftserie nr. 17). København, Denmark: Institut for Naturfagenes Didaktik/Københavns Universitet. (In Danish)

Dolin, J., & Krogh, L. B. (2010). The relevance and consequences of PISA science in a Danish context. *International Journal of Science and Mathematics Education, 8*, 565–592.

Eijck, M. V. (2012). Capturing the dynamics of science in science education. In B. J. Fraser et al. (Eds.), *Second international handbook of science education*. Dordrecht, The Netherlands: Springer.

EPPI CENTRE. (2002). *EPPI-Reviewer, version 2.0* (Web edition), EPPI-Centre software. London: Social Science Research Unit, Institute of Education. Retrieved from http://eppi.ioe. ac.uk/cms/

European Commission. (2007). *Science education now: A renewed pedagogy for the future of Europe*. Brussels, Belgium: European Commission.

Gardner, J. (Ed.). (2006). *Assessment and learning*. London, UK: SAGE Publications.

Gipps, C. (1999). Socio-cultural aspects of assessment. *Review of Research in Education, 24*, 355–392.

Greve, C. (2002). *New public management*. København, Denmark: Nordisk Kultur Institut. (In Danish)

Harlen, W. (2013). *Assessment & inquiry-based science education: Issues in policy and practice.* Global Network of Science Academies (IAP) Science Education Programme (SEP). Retrieved from http://www.interacademies.net/File.aspx?id=21245

Hartig, J., Klieme, E., & Leutner, D. (2008). *Assessment of competences in educational contexts.* Göttingen, Deutschland: Hogrefe.

Helliwell, J. F., Layard, R., & Sachs, J. (Eds.). (2013). *World happiness report 2013.* New York: UN Sustainable Development Solutions Network.

Krogh, L. B., & Dolin, J. (2011). PISA 2006 Science testen og danske elevers naturfaglige formåen [English: The PISA 2006 Science test and Danish students' scientific literacy]. *Periodicals from Department of Science Education, 25*, University of Copenhagen.

Latour, B. (1987). *Science in action*. Cambridge, MA: Harvard University Press.

Moos, L. (Ed.). (2013). *Transnational influences on values and practices in Nordic educational leadership. Is there a Nordic model?* Dordrecht, The Netherlands: Springer.

Nordenbo, S. E., Allerup, P., Andersen, H., Dolin, J., Korp, H., Larsen, M.S., et al (2009). *Pædagogisk brug af test – Et systematisk review* [English: Pedagogic use of tests – A systematic review]. København, Denmark: Danmarks Pædagogiske Universitets Forlag.

OECD. (1999). *Measuring student knowledge and skills. A new framework for assessment*. Paris, France: OECD Publications.

OECD. (2004). *Learning for tomorrow's world. First results from PISA 2003*. Paris: OECD Publications.

Raae, P. H. (2013). Skoleudvikling (English: School development). In E. Damberg, J. Dolin, G. Ingerslev, & P. Kaspersen (Eds.). *Gymnasiepædagogik* (English: Pedagogy for upper secondary) (pp. 714–735). København, Denmark: Hans Reitzel. (In Danish)

Schou, L. R. (2010). Test og evaluering: Løsningen eller problemet? (English: Test or evaluation: the solution or the problem?). *Dansk Pædagogisk tidsskrift, 1*(10), 74–81 (In Danish).

Schoultz, J., Saljo, R., & Wyndhamn, J. (2001a). Conceptual knowledge in talk and text: What does it take to understand a science question? *Instructional Science, 29*, 213–236.

Schoultz, J., Saljo, R., & Wyndhamn, J. (2001b). Heavenly talk: Discourse, artifacts, and children's understanding of elementary astronomy. *Human Development, 44*, 103–118.

Shavelson, R. (2011, February). *An approach to testing and modeling competence*. Presentation at the conference on Modeling and Measurement of Competencies in Higher Education, Berlin, Germany.

Smith, P. S., Hounshell, P. B., Copolo, C., & Wilkerson, S. (1992). The impact of end-of-course testing on curriculum and instruction. *Science Education, 76*(5), 523–530.

Sturman, L. (2003). Teaching to the test: Science or intuition? *Educational Research, 45*(3), 261–273.

UNDP. (2013). *Human development report 2013*. New York: United Nations Development Programme (UNDP).

Weinert, F. E. (2001). Concept of competence: A conceptual clarification. In D. S. Rychen & L. H. Salganik (Eds.), *Defining and selecting key competencies*. Göttingen, Deutschland: Hogrefe & Huber Publishers.

Westbury, I. (2000). Teaching as a reflective practice: What might Didaktik teach curriculum? In I. Westbury, S. Hopmann, & K. Riquarts (Eds.), *Teaching as a reflective practice: The German Didaktik tradition* (pp. 15–39). Mahwah, NJ: Lawrence Erlbaum.

World Economic Forum. (2008, 2009). *The global competitiveness report* 2008, 2009. Geneva, Switzerland: World Economic Forum.

Young, M. (2010). Alternative educational futures for a knowledge society. *The European Educational Research Journal, 4*(1), 1–12.

Zhao, Y., & Meyer, H. D. (2013). High on PISA, low on entrepreneurship? What PISA does not measure. In H. D. Meyer & A. Benavot (Eds.), *PISA, power, and policy: The emergence of global educational governance*. Oxford, UK: Symposium Books.

Chapter 6
Redefining Assessment in Contemporary Classrooms: Shifting Practices and Policies

David F. Philpott

Abstract This chapter explores the evolution of assessment for students with individual learning needs in both the Canadian and global context. Assessment practices may have developed to support students with developmental issues but in today's schools they are morphing into approaches for a whole other level of individual learning need. This chapter argues that a singular paradigm of assessment no longer exists and that written policy is struggling to stay abreast of a rapidly evolving school context. While this shift in policy and practice is resulting from a number of issues, two in particular –globalisation and inclusion – each are bringing unique criticism of traditional assessment methods that have held to a "testing and labelling" approach. Contemporary schools are characterised by an ethnically diverse population, heightened student mobility and an evolving paradigm of ability. As a result, the praxis between written and enacted policy for assessment is being re-examined. There is growing recognition of a need to shift assessment away from diagnostic/prescriptive approaches back into the hands of teachers. This chapter discusses the impact of this trend and calls for both a re-examination of teacher readiness for change as well as a re-definition of the role of formally testing children with individual needs. It argues that the contemporary classroom is characterised by an inclusive model of support planning where philosophy blends with practice in identifying and accommodating the needs of all students. The chapter concludes with a discussion of the implications of this paradigm shift for educational leaders.

Keywords Globalisation • Cultural diversity • Contemporary classrooms • Contemporary assessment • Inclusion • Inclusive assessment • Differentiated instruction • Educational leadership

D.F. Philpott (✉)
Faculty of Education, Memorial University of Newfoundland, St. John's, NL, Canada
e-mail: philpott@mun.ca

© Springer International Publishing Switzerland 2016   113
S. Scott et al. (eds.), *Assessment in Education*, The Enabling
Power of Assessment 2, DOI 10.1007/978-3-319-23398-7_6

6.1   Shifting Practice

Diversity has become central to a debate on contemporary education. For many in the field of special education who have struggled for years to have the needs of students with exceptionalities recognised and accommodated, a broader understanding of diversity is most welcome, and in fact, long overdue. Globalisation and inclusion are now entrenched concepts in today's classrooms, and are redefining the profession of teaching, particularly the process of responding to diverse individual needs, whether they be linguistic, cultural or developmental. McCarthy, Rezai-Rashti and Teasley (2009) argued that globalisation trends are changing the very identity of schools:

> Today's dominant form of globalisation is throwing new system-based identity crises onto schools, as educators are confronted with the proliferation of difference and multiplicity. New, complex forms of identity and affiliation are not only defining the lives and lifestyles of immigrant youth outside of schools, but are powerfully impacting their in-school experiences as well. (p. 77)

Driedger (1989) discusses the rapid growth of special education and calls it *The Last Civil Rights Movement* where parents and citizens lobbied for stronger support for individuals with exceptionalities, and fuelled a debate on best practices for identifying and responding to individual differences. Smith, Polloway, Patton and Dowdy (1998) credit this debate to establish best practice as characterising the entire history of special education, which they describe as one long road toward inclusion, after moving through the two previous phases of segregation and integration. However, in contemporary classrooms the concept of inclusion has become much broader than the debate around special education ever imagined. Today, growing cultural diversity, an increasingly mobile population, and expanding religious and sexual diversity are combining to redefine what we mean by diverse learners.

Central to an examination of the issues pertaining to diversity is the very process of identification in the school context: educational testing and assessment. In fact, no issue in the history of the debate around learner diversity has garnered as much criticism as traditional, psychological approaches of testing children and ascribing a label to rationalise intervention (Lipsky & Gartner, 1997; Foucault, 1977; Fulcher, 1989; Skrtic, 1995). In fact, a dominant criticism of special education itself has been an absence of evidence which proves ascribed labels have actually resulted in optimised support or enhanced instruction (Armstrong, Armstrong, & Barton, 2000; Grobe & McCall, 2004; Holdnack & Weiss, 2006; Ysseldyke, Algozzine, & Thurlow, 1991). As schools become more ethnically diverse the criticism of such assessment practices for children of other cultures and languages grows exponentially (Artiles, 2003; Donovan & Cross, 2002; Gersten, Baker, & Pugach, 2001; Gopaul-McNichol & Armour-Thomas, 2002; Samunda, 1998). Today, these criticisms are calling for a re-examination of existing practice and a re-development of policies to guide them.

Perhaps few countries other than Canada can appreciate the urgency of this debate for effective assessment among diverse student populations. With an increasing Aboriginal population, growing immigration rates, increased inter-regional mobility and a national embrace of inclusive education Canada is redefining, out of sheer necessity, a new understanding of assessment of learner diversity. Certainly, practitioners are discovering that in an increasingly pluralistic society a singular approach to assessment does not work. Likewise, inclusive education questions why a student needs prior identification as "disabled" before intervention can begin. Hutchinson (2009) writes:

> Inclusive schools are a natural part of inclusive society, and equitable treatment of students regardless of (dis)ability is closely related to equitable treatment of students regardless of gender, race, and so on. In Canada, if we choose to teach we choose to teach in inclusive settings. (p. xxi)

6.2   Evolving Policy

Subsequently, it is against this backdrop of sceptical practice in an evolving school context that we look to examining policies and practice. In the midst of such a paradigm shift, exploring trends and actual practice might well be more informative than exploring written policy. Many areas such as Newfoundland and Labrador, Ontario, Nova Scotia, and Alberta, have programs that are evolving faster than the written policy reflects. An example of this is the written Special Education Policy in the province of Newfoundland and Labrador which remains dated as "Draft, 1998", despite a 2007 review which heralds a whole new direction (Philpott, 2007a).

Policy and practice have always enjoyed a symbiotic relationship, where policy is developed to guide practice; yet, it is actually practice which moulds and shapes policy. Delaney (2002) discusses this mutual relationship and argues that it is virtually impossible to solidify a rigid implementation of written policy. Wink (2005) views such praxis as "the constant reciprocity of our theory and our practice. Theory building and critical reflection inform our practice and our action, and our practice and action inform our theory building and critical reflection" (p.50). McLaren (1998) defines this reciprocal process as "a way of thinking about, negotiating, and transforming the relationship among classroom teaching, the production of knowledge, the institutional structures of the school, and the social and material relationships of the wider community" (p.45). MacDonald (1981) argues that policy is actually a mixture of three distinct types: what is written, what is stated, and what is actually done. He argues that it is enacted policy which really informs practice as it reflects the experience of parents and educators. Ware (2000), commenting on the effectiveness of written policy, states that "practice may align with the original intent of the law, but it can be argued that the spirit of the law remains elusive and unrealized" (p.45). Such a tendency to move away from written policy is well identified in the literature. Wincott (2006) references it as *policy drift* where it is natural for enacted policy to diverge from implementation.

Policy drift should not be seen as an alternative to notions of policy inertia – it is tempting to suggest that it is society that drifts away from the policy status quo. Strictly speaking, it is social realities that change more than the policies themselves (although the latter may also alter – either insufficiently to keep up with social changes or even be subject to degradation). Policy drift may be best understood as a form of mission drift where social policies lose their normative moorings (Wincott, 2006, p.25).

This chapter will explore this evolution of policy and practice for assessing children with diverse learning needs. While assessment policy began for students with developmental issues, the need to assess individual learning need is now much broader. In the context of rapidly changing classrooms in an increasingly pluralistic world the very nature of diversity is being challenged and redefined. The resultant praxis that is emerging informs an examination of shifting Canadian practices within a global context. As such, the resultant debate affords practitioners, policy writers and educational researchers an opportunity to explore the space that exists between rigid paradigms and actual practice. The chapter posits that instead of arguing for either a diagnostic/prescriptive model of identifying individual need or a philosophical approach to inclusive environments, today's classrooms, more than ever, call for a balance of the two.

We begin this exploration with an examination of how globalisation is changing classrooms and the concerns for the ineffectiveness of assessment practices to inform or support programming. We then seek to understand how the very need to assess children is rapidly changing with the emergence of inclusion, which, in large part, emerged from criticisms of traditional assessment practices. Finally we conclude with an examination of a new paradigm of assessment in Canadian schools which seeks to accept that while complexity accompanies diversity, educators have an alternative.

6.3   Impact of Globalisation

6.3.1   *Shifting Paradigms*

The twenty-first century has brought an interesting, though somewhat predictable, characteristic to contemporary classrooms: ethnic diversity. Gould and Findlay (1994) suggested that increased global migration would result from global economic disparity between developed countries (with low populations) and Third World countries (where the majority of the population lives). They also predicted that the twenty-first century would see a pattern of increase in immigration, not just as a means to escape poverty and exploitation, but as a means to meet labour market demands.

Taylor and Whittaker (2009) build on these observations and outline a number of factors that have resulted in high global migration. While they agree that economic disparity is a dominant cause of migration, they cite internal and international conflicts, human rights concerns, ineffective and collapsing governments, absence of personal security, the rise of multi-national corporations, globalised media and improved travel as also supporting the shifting patterns of immigration. Sassen (1996) also suggested that individual countries are supporting these shifting migration patterns and gave the United Nations partial credit through initiatives such as the 1975 Helsinki Accord, which encouraged countries to ease restrictions on migration, the 1980 Refugee Act, which opened countries to refugee claims, and the 1990 International Convention on Protecting the Rights of Migrant Workers and their Families. Taylor and Whittaker (2009) add more recent initiatives to this list, including the 1999 Programme of Action on Population and Development that encouraged cooperation between an immigrant's country of destination and the country of origin, by focusing on the rights of the person, not the policy of the country. While many factors lead people to want to migrate, such international agreements make it easier for them and their families to do so. As a result, wherever we live on this earth, it is increasingly obvious that we live in diverse communities.

The United Nations now reports that: "We live in a highly mobile world, where migration is not only inevitable but also an important dimension of human development. Nearly one billion – or one out of seven – people are migrants" (United Nations Development Programme, 2009, n.p.). This pattern of migration is witnessed in such countries as the United Kingdom, where Dunnell (2008) reports growing ethnic diversity in the population, especially in urban areas, as well as an increase in religious, linguistic, and sexual diversity and multi-lingual families. She also notes a marked increase in inter-ethnic marriages that further diversify families and communities. Dunnell voices particular concern for the younger age of this newly-emerging ethnic population and the concomitant fallout: living in poverty, coping with poor health, and struggling with academic achievement. Migration Watch UK (2009) predicts that immigration will account for 6 million of the projected 7.2 million population increase between 2004 and 2031.

Similar trends are occurring elsewhere. In New Zealand, the ethnic population is expected to grow dramatically between 2001 and 2021, with its Asian population alone growing by 120 % (Statistics New Zealand, 2004). Australia, too, is experiencing similar growth with immigration accounting for 63 % of its current population growth, a pronounced rise in inter-regional migration, and the expectation that its indigenous population will increase by approximately 75 % by 2021 (Australian Bureau of Statistics, 2009).

In America, an 8 % growth in the school-aged population is projected by 2018, due in large part to internal migration, and both legal and illegal immigration (National Center for Educational Statistics, 2009). The "white population" will account for only 4 % of this growth while the remaining growth will be attributed to: "26 % Blacks, 38 % Hispanic, 29 % Asian, 32 % American Indian, and 14 % non-resident alien" (p. 10).

This brings us to the Canadian context. Canada, a country which defines itself as multi-cultural in nature, is emerging as a leader, not only in support of immigration but in recognition of the important role immigration can play in social and economic development (United Nations Development Programme, 2009). The 2006 census (Statistics Canada, 2007/08) outlined that there are over 200 languages spoken in Canadian schools and 20 % of our population reports a first language other than English. The population is shifting radically toward greater cultural diversity and it is predicted that by 2017, 23 % of Canada's population will be from a visible minority. While two-thirds of this growth is from immigration, the Aboriginal population has exploded with a 45 % increase in the last decade, standing at nearly 1.2 million, with a projected growth rate of 34 % in the next twenty years, 48 % of whom are school-aged youth. Reflecting global trends, Canada is also experiencing greater inter-regional migration as the population shifts from rural settings toward both urban and western regions. Economic and labour market demands are resulting in families moving between provinces (and varying school policies and practices) at an increasing pace (Statistics Canada, 2008).

As globalisation continues to change demographics of countries (and the mobility of citizens within countries), it is poised to redefine the nature of schools and the profession of teaching. McCarthy et al., (2009) argue that such trends are changing the very identity of schools:

> Today's dominant form of globalization is throwing new system-based identity crises onto schools, as educators are confronted with the proliferation of difference and multiplicity. New, complex forms of identity and affiliation are not only defining the lives and lifestyles of immigrant youth outside of schools, but are powerfully impacting their in-school experiences as well. (p. 77)

While the impact of globalisation on our population base is pronounced, the implications (and the young age of the growing ethnically diverse portion of our communities) are central to a discussion of contemporary classrooms. If the identity of schools is being reshaped, and policies reconceptualised to respond accordingly, then traditional practices must evolve as well. School reform initiatives, first initiated with the release of *A Nation at Risk* (National Commission on Excellence in Education, 1983), have challenged schools to raise achievement outcomes. While assessment practices are "an inescapable reality of the educational, social, and economic enterprise of any modern society" (Samunda, 1998, p. 1) the need to change practice in order to reflect diverse, contemporary schools is equally inescapable.

6.3.2 Impact on Assessment Practices

A call to reconceptualise assessment for minority children is hardly new. The literature has long voiced concern for the accuracy of standardised assessment for students of diverse cultural backgrounds (Armour-Thomas, 1992; Cummins, 1984; Gopaul-McNichol & Armour-Thomas, 2002; Lewis, 1998; Samunda, 1975, 1998). Likewise, the literature is equally clear in questioning a blatant over-representation of minority children in special education programmes (Artiles & Trent, 1994; Chinn & Hughes, 1987; Donovan & Cross, 2002; Duren-Green, McIntosh, Cook-Morales, & Robinson, 2005). Gopaul-McNichol and Armour-Thomas (2002) reflect on this over-representation and attribute it to poor assessment practices and inappropriate use of tests. They conclude "that standardized tests are invalid for students of non-dominant cultures" (p. 5). They suggest that the construction of standardised assessment instruments, as well as the research on student performance that uses these instruments is equally biased as it:

> reflects Western/Anglo/Euro epistemological traditions [in which] there is a tendency to generalize findings to other groups that do not share those perspectives. Often, studies do not include operationally definable constructs of culture and when they do, terms like *culturally disadvantaged* or *cultural deprivation* betray an ethnocentric bias. (p. 9)

Lewis (1998) discusses this literature and attributes such blatant misuse of testing processes to "inappropriate test content, inadequate standardisation samples, examiner bias, lack of language facility, lack of predictive validity, differing test-taking strategies and the non-equitable social, educational and vocational opportunities of the testee" (p. 218).

As a result of this wide recognition, the field of culturally-fair assessment has become a growing discipline within the assessment field as publishing houses attempt to develop and market instruments heralded as being specific to testing these students. Lewis (1998) cautions against this and states that:

> the movement to so-called culture-free and culture-fair tests was begun to counteract, or at least neutralize, the culturally loaded information and language items found in standardized tests. Although no test can be considered culture-free, some can be thought of as culture-reduced instruments. The reduction of the influence of culture has been attempted by decreasing the number of test items with culturally-loaded content and by reducing the language components present in the test. (p. 222)

Samunda (1998) cautions, however, that ensuring accuracy of assessment findings for minority children is not as simple as selecting an instrument that is marketed as culture-fair. He states that "even the so-called culture-fair tests are really only culture-reduced because they assume that examinees have been socialized and educated in the culture in which the test originated" (p. 17). He calls for a broader view of assessment practices that move beyond measuring development into facilitating development. While assessment practices play an important role in education, an over-reliance on standardised instruments for children of diverse cultural backgrounds has had a negative effect on culture and identity. An over-representation of minority-group children in remedial programs limits educational opportunities and career possibilities.

The issue of test results and their interpretation extends beyond concerns that relate to their use in the school systems. Tests can have dire social and economic consequences for those individuals who are labelled and placed in minimal curricular programs, and thus curtailed from further secondary or tertiary education. Tests and their results, therefore, can bring disastrous outcomes affecting the lives and aspirations of minorities in any society (Samunda, 1998, p. 3).

Padilla (2001) builds on this concern with specific reference to First Nations populations. He argues for a paradigm shift so that a specific ethnic group is valued for its differences and there is no need to compare them to a dominant population. He states that "Educational research involving ethnic populations should not examine students from the perspective of their failures in the educational system; rather, it should concentrate on how to achieve success regardless of the task or level involved" (p. 23).

While cultural diversity necessitates a need for a paradigm shift in assessment practices as well as the policies that guide them, the very need to be assessing children is also changing. The popularity of inclusion is calling for educators and citizens alike to not merely accommodate diversity but to actually embrace it.

6.4 Impact of Inclusion

6.4.1 Shifting Paradigms

Interestingly, as globalisation creates diverse communities, mounting criticism of the current treatment of diverse students is creating a global shift toward inclusive programs. In many ways it was regard for the rights of minority populations that first voiced concern for the quality of educational services for children with disabilities. The desegregation of American schools validated a parallel human rights argument against segregation based on physical/mental ability (Friend, Bursuck, & Hutchinson, 1998; Smith et al., 1998). In the years following the Civil Rights Movement parents of children with disabilities would effectively lobby governments to create special education and ensure policies and legislation to establish free and appropriate education in least restrictive, non-discriminatory environments (Dworet & Bennett, 2002; Smith, Polloway, Patton, Dowdy, & Heath, 2001; Weber, 1994).

Individual support services and practice, albeit initially focused on students with disabilities, secured a foothold in community schools across North America by the early 1980s, and the succeeding years would witness mounting scrutiny and criticism of practice. Hockenbury, Kauffman and Hallahan (2000) summarise the ensuing criticisms of special education and view it as a system that stigmatises children with a medical label resulting in marginalised placement in a completely separate educational system. Skrtic (1995) makes the observation that special education is anchored in "a theory of human pathology and organizational rationality" (p. 67). The existing model, he argued, is based on a behavioural approach to diagnosing difference in order to rationalise a hierarchical system of fixed knowledge which renders the student a passive recipient of scientific interventions. He questions why we have to label a child in order to qualify for services, all the while knowing the marginalising impact that such labelling will have.

Lipsky and Gartner (1997, 1998) support this criticism of a deficit model and call for an approach that responds to displayed need versus the prescribed label. Fuchs and Fuchs (1995) add to this by questioning the research base upon which special education practices were built. Danforth (1999) cautions that a model promoting heavy use of medical language limits parental involvement and fractures a spirit of collaboration and empowerment. Danforth echoes Foucault's (1977) discussion of the social construct of disability, where "via observation and normalising judgments and examinations" (p. 195) subjects are individualised and thereby stigmatised as disabled. Foucault warned that the process of focusing on students' deficits through assessment creates a model that rationalises stigmatisation and discrimination. Allan (1996), reflecting on Foucault's concerns, summarises these findings, observing that the resultant power which professionals gather further marginalises students and families. Lupart (1999) questions whether such approaches reflect contemporary social values. She cites The National Commission on the Future of Teaching in America (1996) in challenging this archaic perspective of management:

> Today's schools are organized in ways that support neither students nor teaching well. Like the turn-of-the-century industries they were moulded after – most of which are now redesigning themselves – current structures were designed to mimic factories that used semi-skilled workers to do discrete pieces of work in a mass production assembly line. (p. 45)

The School Reform movement would underscore criticisms of a system that would separate students into a regular stream and a special education stream, and raise concern not only for the financial cost of having dual systems, but also for the outcomes of students placed in the latter (Kauffman, 2000; Lipsky & Gartner, 1997; Salend, 2001). Further concern would come with the realisation that the number of children being labelled as "disabled" was growing disproportionate to the population (Lupart, 1999; Philpott & Dibbon, 2008).

6.4.2 Impact on Assessment Practices

As early as the beginning of the 1980s, educators, building on mounting concern about traditional assessment practices, questioned the usefulness of such practices to their work in accommodating students in the classroom. Ysseldyke and Shinn (1981) concluded that only "13.5 % of teachers claimed that these assessments were slightly helpful or better, and 77.3 % claimed that these assessments were not relevant, no help, or detrimental" (p. 23). They concluded that teachers and parents both viewed psychologists' reports as being very difficult to comprehend and, therefore, having little impact on interventions. These concerns have persisted over the years and the very appropriateness of standardised testing has remained a hotly debated issue (Grobe & McCall, 2004; Holdnack & Weiss, 2006; Lipsky & Gartner, 1998). Ashman and Conway (1993) elaborate on the history of this concern:

> These tests have come under considerable criticism over the past two decades because of three characteristics: their bias against minority groups and those with identifiable learning

difficulties; their inability to parcel out the contributions of motivation, personality and setting; and their inability to provide information that can be translated into instructional practice. (p. 25)

McLaughlin (1991) also commented that few tests measure attributes or variables that are directly related to learning, higher order thinking, or problem solving. Because tests do not tap complex cognitive processes, they do not support classroom practices that are directed toward teaching them. Ashman and Conway (1993) concluded:

Clinicians, such as school psychologists and counsellors, spend a considerable part of their professional lives administering and scoring standardized psychological and achievement tests with the objective of identifying, screening and classifying students, and teachers also spend a good part of their professional lives preparing students for assessment, and administering and scoring tests that provide evidence of mastery over the curriculum; it indeed seems that there is an inherent inefficiency in testing for classification and testing again to establish goals for instruction or remediation (p. 25)… [and] … Without doubt, clinicians have been reluctant to involve themselves in classroom remediation or instruction, but teachers also have been less than enthusiastic about the ability of psychologists and counsellors to collaborate with them. (p. 33)

It was this recognition of concern about such diagnostic/prescriptive approaches to label difference that an increasingly diverse society began to shift debate to embracing difference. Subsequently, inclusive education emerged as a philosophy of community development and educational programming that reflect this approach (Sands, Kozleski, & French, 2001; Smith, 1998; Stainback & Stainback, 1992; Thomas, 1997). Support for this democratic view of diversity has come from groups including the World Health Organization (1980) and the United Nations (1989), and has been articulated in UNESCO world conferences (1990 and 1994).

Bloom, Perlmutter and Burrell (1999, cited in Salend, 2001) define inclusion as a philosophy that brings students, families, educators, and community members together to create schools and other social institutions based on acceptance, belonging, and community" (p. 5). Sergiovanni (1994) refers to inclusion as community building, in which values of diversity reflect the social fabric of the community. Noddings (1992) endorses this view of diversity, stressing that schools have a responsibility to promote an "ethic of caring" in communities by way of positive classroom experiences for children. Stainback and Stainback (1992) state:

when schools include all students, equality is respected and promoted as a value in society. Whereas, when schools exclude some students, prejudice is entrenched in the consciousness of many students when they become adults, with the results of increased social conflict and dehumanizing competition. (p. 8)

Globally, inclusive education is gaining favour in countries as diverse as Australia (Slee, 2002), Bangladesh, Denmark, Italy, Lesotho (Mittler, 2000), India (Alur, 2002), Ireland (Shevlin, 2002), New Zealand (McDonald, 2002), and South Africa (Muthukrishna, 2002). Timmons (2002) explores this international perspective on the popularity and growth of inclusive education and views it as mirroring societal transformations that call for a celebration of diversity. She notes that despite differences in actual practice among the countries she studied, commonalities can be identified. She describes a global understanding of inclusion that goes beyond disability status to include religion, culture, and race. Banks et al. (2005) comment on this broader, cultural rationale for inclusive education:

> The ideas of culturally responsive classrooms and inclusive classrooms are not entirely the same, but they are similar. Specifically, both terms suggest that schools and teachers need to develop classrooms that are supportive of children and accepting of difference. Within both of these conceptions, children's strengths are emphasized and differences are considered a positive part of a learning environment because they allow children to share and experience diverse perspectives. In the past … special education was associated primarily with a deficit orientation. (p. 255)

Subsequently, as schools shift practice to embrace difference (whether linguistic, religious or in physical ability) the need to test and label students so as to rationalise accommodations begins to lessen.

6.5 Contemporary Assessment

6.5.1 Diverse and Inclusive Practice

It is against this backdrop of classrooms increasingly characterised by the effects of globalisation and a practice increasingly characterised as inclusive – both of which question traditional assessment practices – that we focus on a new paradigm of practice. In the Canadian context, recent studies have validated the recognition that there is a growing break between theory and practice and that a new paradigm of identifying learner need is required. Klassen (2002) reviewed Canadian educational practice specific to the area of Learning Disabilities (LD) and found that educational policy is not well defined for assessment practice, diagnostic criteria or programme planning procedures. He notes that "among the provinces, a number of different operational definitions are currently in use" and he questions the appropriateness of traditional assessment practices (p. 199). He suggests that "consultation and whole-school intervention approaches may become more germane for school psychologists … teachers may assume a greater role in the assessment and identification process" (p. 214). Klassen, Neufeld and Munro (2005) support this shift toward collaborative assessment and identification, and cite it as a growing preference for psychologists and educators in countries as diverse as Australia, Germany, Japan, and the United Kingdom.

Kozey and Siegel (2008) build on this evolution of understanding of assessment and a resultant praxis between theory and practice among the Canadian provinces. They cite a growing trend in the literature to move away from discrepancies in test scores toward a more functional understanding of disability and they raise concern about written policy. They conclude that "despite the numerous recent policy revisions, the concepts of intelligence and a discrepancy between intelligence and academic achievement have been retained in most provinces, which contrasts with recent research and applied perspectives of LD" (p. 169).

Similarly, Edmunds and Martsch-Litt (2008), in a pan-Canadian review of assessment policies and practices for Attention Deficit/Hyperactivity Disorder (ADHD), found varying practices, few diagnostic guidelines and vague theoretical foundations to inform the field. They voice the almost obfuscated observation that "It is not difficult to hypothesize about the compounding problems that would arise from inconsistent diagnoses due to inconsistent diagnostic perspectives due to inconsistent criteria and nearly non-existent procedural guidelines" (p. 17).

Likewise, Philpott and Cahill (2008) conducted a pan-Canadian review of policy and training for LD and supported significant "interprovincial variability" in both assessment practices and understandings. They report that all of the provinces/ territories reference general special education policy as the only source of guidelines for assessment practices. They recognise that the absence of specific and current policy is problematical and creates ineffective service delivery. Following interviews with key-informants from each provincial Ministry of Education, they question, given the diversity in the country, whether "one policy can be effective for regions as diverse as Nunavut, Toronto, and rural Newfoundland?" (p. 27). Nonetheless, they do identify similar trends: "All regions reported a shift towards "team-based" assessments as their preferred practice, one in which teams of different professionals brought diverse perspectives on the needs of the students and worked collaboratively to identify children's needs and supports" (p. 18).

This shift toward team-based assessment via a multiplicity of perspectives and practices, regardless of labels, seems particularly relevant for contemporary classrooms. Padilla (2001) suggests that "the study of a specific ethnic group, especially if comparison is likely to be biased, should not examine students from a perspective of their failures in the educational system; rather it should concentrate on how to achieve success regardless of the task or level involved" (p. 23). Such approaches seek to create assessment practices that strive to "ensure that judgments made about behavior of individuals and groups are accurate, and that the decisions made do not intentionally or unintentionally favor some cultural group over another" (Gopaul-McNichol & Armour-Thomas, 2002, p. 10). Goodwin and Macdonald (1997) and Lidz (2001) argue that the information that arises from such assessment practices is much more child-centred and appropriate for Aboriginal students. Darling-Hammond and Falk (1997) herald this approach by calling for a redesigning of assessment measures that are:

> responsive to the differing perspectives of diverse populations; building the capacities of teachers to use a range of strategies that will help students to achieve the standards; designing new forms of assessment that better support and reflect what is being taught; and creating systems for curriculum, assessment and schooling that support student learning rather than merely pointing out deficiencies with new measures. (pp. 51–52)

Philpott (2007b) references this new focus as a contemporary perspective on assessment, shifting from practices that are summative, quantitative, deficit-based, prescriptive, expert-centred and static toward a more process-centred model of learning. He argues that contemporary assessment practices are characterised as being more formative, qualitative, strengths-based, descriptive, child/family centred and fluid. This perspective on assessment highlights multiple views of ability, a goal to empower teachers and parents, and holds a holistic focus on lifespan goals under which differences are embraced. Such a paradigm of assessment is particularly relevant for the inclusive and diverse Canadian context as it seeks to balance factors such as the call for higher achievement, a more rigorous curriculum, and a philosophy of inclusion. Philpott argues that it is particularly sensitive to Aboriginal issues and cultural values and is supportive of a healthy self-identity.

A call to link assessment with teaching can hardly be described as contemporary since a call for more authentic and dynamic assessment to enhance learning opportunities for students has existed for years (Burns, 2002; Chappuis, 2005; Hargrove, 2000; Moore-Brown, Huerta, Uranga-Hernandez, & Pena, 2006; Stanley, 2003; Wiggins, 1993). Stanovich and Jordan (2000) reference it as "interventionist teaching", where teachers embrace the "increasing classroom diversity resulting from changes in the socio-cultural conditions and educational policy, engage in more academic interactions with their students and are more persistent in actively assisting students to construct understanding, and demonstrate more effective teaching behaviors" (pp. 236–237). Lerner and Johns (2009) describe "clinical teaching":

> The goal of clinical teaching is to tailor the learning experiences for the unique needs of the individual student. By using information gathered through the evaluation of the student, along with an analysis of the student's specific learning characteristics, the clinical teacher designs a plan of instruction for that student. Assessment does not stop when teaching begins. In fact, the essence of clinical teaching is that assessment and instruction are interwoven. The clinical teacher modifies the teaching as new needs become apparent. (p. 88)

Cox (2008) references teaching and assessment as "differentiated instruction":

> This requires individualizing learning for each student by arranging the classroom and the entire school for small group, large group and individualized learning. The goal is to maximize the capacity of each learner by teaching in ways that help all learners bridge gaps in understanding and skill and help each learner grow as much and as quickly as he or she can. (p. 53)

More recently, this call to link assessment with instruction is gaining increased support in American schools via the "Response to Intervention" (RTI) model, where accommodations designed to support learning in diverse students are based on displayed need and not prescribed diagnoses. RTI approaches encourage the classroom teachers to try diversifying approaches to instruction and evaluation based on their observations of the child. Assessment is not a pre-requisite to support, but it may be one option if supports aren't working. Gibbons (2004) defines RTI as:

> a problem-solving approach that involves providing quality interventions to at-risk students and providing special education services to those students who fail to respond to well-designed interventions, and do not demonstrate evidence for exclusionary criteria. RTI approaches share three essential components (1) emphasis on universal screening of all students for achievement difficulties, (2) placement in early intervention programs, and (3) careful monitoring of progress and accountability for results. (p. 1)

Gibbons suggests that the approach is particularly effective in addressing the renowned pitfalls of existing assessment practices where students must be categorised prior to support. She states:

There are many advantages to an RTI. First the "Wait to Fail" model is eliminated, and schools can operate under a preventative model focused on early intervention. Second, there is a clear link between assessment and intervention. Third, the emphasis in special education is shifted away from eligibility and focused toward getting children the interventions they need to be successful. Fourth, the model is conceptual as well as practical. Fifth, the model is multidisciplinary and increases teaming. By creating a language of skills and instruction as opposed to disability and pathology, barriers between general and special education may be removed. Sixth, school psychologists will have increased time to focus on functional assessment activities that are directly linked to intervention planning. Finally, the model emphasises serving students in the Least Restrictive Environment. (p. 2)

The RTI model empowers teachers as strategists, and creates team-based approaches to identifying and responding to needs. Such an approach is especially complementary to inclusive practices, and so is appropriate for ethnically diverse populations (Gee, 2001; Klingner & Edwards, 2006; Philpott et al., 2009). Bradley, Danielson and Doolittle (2007) write: "RTI begins with the implementation of scientifically based, school-wide instructional interventions and promotes intervention at the first indication of non-response to traditional classroom instruction … shift of emphasis from process to outcomes" (p. 8). As such, teachers are positioned and supported as the first respond-ers to need. They become experts on both student learning and curriculum. The needed link between assessment and instruction becomes established.

As assessment in the inclusive contemporary classroom becomes increasingly team-based and less prescribed by label, the readiness of teachers to implement such approaches becomes a concern. The shift toward inclusive practice has long identified a need for improved teacher-training as a prerequisite step to successful implementation (Brown, Higgins, Pierce, Hong, & Thomas, 2004; Buysse, Goldman, & Skinner, 2003; Klingner, Vaughn, Schumm, Cohen, & Forgan, 1998; Stanovich & Jordan, 2000; Waldron & McLesky, 1998; Wiener, 2004; Zigmond, 2003). Lyon (2005) states that "teachers are not trained to address individual learning differences in general, and are not prepared to teach students from highly diverse backgrounds with a range of complicated learning difficulties" (p. 142). Taylor and Whittaker (2009) support this call for a renewed focus on training teachers, underscored by the growing ethnic diversity. They write:

The implications for teachers are obvious. Even in areas of the country that remain predominantly White, it is essential that teachers learn about the cultures and languages of many children who are arriving in greater numbers and entering their schools for the first time. Furthermore, many of the jobs available in the next decade will be in urban areas where the population is likely to be even more diverse. All children will need to work and live harmoniously with members of many diverse groups. Teachers will need to develop the knowl-edge, skills, and attitudes necessary to prepare a diverse population of students for success in the mainstream, while also respecting their cultures and languages of origin. (p. 11)

In a Canadian context, teacher readiness is also well documented. Crocker and Dibbon (2008) report that while 90 % of Canadian school principals rank training in educational assessment as very important, only 7 % of them report that current graduates are well prepared in this area. They go on to report that while 81 % of school principals rank training in accommodating diverse needs as important to new teachers, only 8 % felt that current graduates are prepared. Recent provincial reviews of special education policy have contextualised these concerns. Philpott (2007a), in a review of Newfoundland and Labrador's programs, concluded that 87.4 % of teachers report little or no training in the area of diversity (p. 96). In Alberta, concern for initial teacher-training was identified by a provincial Commission on Learning (Government of Alberta, 2006). Their final report recommended improving preservice teacher education programs and expanding post-service training so as to ensure competent teachers who are ready to face the demands of diverse classrooms. A similar review in Nova Scotia (Government of Nova Scotia, 2007) identified "a need for further development of the capacity of school boards and community schools to respond to the special needs of their students" (p. 35).

6.6   Implications for Educational Leaders

A new paradigm of assessment is emerging from the growing debate around the effectiveness of traditional approaches to diversity, the impact of globalisation and the realities of inclusive schools and communities. It is a paradigm that strives to link assessment with learning, avoid the pitfalls of labelling children as different, and empower classroom teachers with the knowledge and skills to accommodate all children regardless of need. It seeks a sharing of perspective, collaborative practice, and open communication. It is a paradigm that views assessment as being part of the learning process and adapting instruction as an integral part of the teaching process. It is a model that responds before failure occurs, implements support without label, and doesn't require categorical approval. While it recognises a role for traditional quantitative assessment practices it balances such with qualitative approaches. It is a paradigm of assessment that is process oriented, relationship centred, and respectful of all individuals involved. It is a practice which is reminiscent, as Wiggins (1993) pointed out, of the Latin origin of the word assessment itself: *assidere*, "to sit beside or with".

Such an approach speaks to the need for innovative leadership in education and calls for renewed professional development of teachers and educational administrators. As educational institutions move to embrace a much broader interpretation of inclusiveness, school leaders must work as diligently at leading this process as teachers must in enacting it in their classrooms (Philpott, Furey, & Penney, 2010). A renewed focus on adopting new approaches to teaching, adapting methods of instruction, and developing a new conceptualisation of 'community' must be made a priority.

In the Canadian context, such a paradigm shift seems particularly relevant as the demographics of schools change dramatically and inclusion becomes the norm. The implications of this shift in thinking and practice are significant for educational leaders who continuously balance ability to deliver with a growing demand for different types of service and need. While Canada typifies the need for this shift as well as the need to prepare teachers to implement it, it is not alone. The global literature predicts that trends toward increased learner diversity will continue and that educators are currently not ready to respond accordingly. As a result, there is an immediate challenge for leaders in policy and programme development to respond. Taylor and Whittaker (2009) state:

> All teachers need intensive training in effective practices to confidently and competently enact such changes. The commitment of teachers increases as they have time to collaborate with others who are enthusiastic and knowledgeable about inclusive practices. (p. 175)

It remains debatable whether a policy shift toward team-based, classroom assessment is new or is actually a return to original good teaching practice. There is little debate that the criticism of approaches that lead to growing numbers of students being misplaced in special education is well-founded. Likewise, the practices of educational psychology, which have often demeaned the input of teachers and families, are increasingly suspect. Today, educators are returning to recognition of the legitimate knowledge and experience of classroom teachers, coupled with the valuable input from parents. Likewise, they recognise that there remains a role for professional opinion, including formalised assessment, but cautions that it should complement the perspectives of the teachers and families. Perhaps what is new in this paradigm shift is the recognition that educational leaders must ensure that the practice of assessment, like the practice of teaching itself, must be a collaborative process, where expertise is shared, devoid of power differentials. Morse (1996) comments on this approach and writes:

> We either find a better way to relate to each other in solving our problems or we go down to defeat. Rejecting collaboration is not an option. Collaboration is a step up in the democratic process, going beyond compromise and cooperation to shared understanding and shared meaning in decision making. This is not a simple upgrading: it is a transformation. (p. xii)

It is the contention of this chapter that Canadian educators understand the need for this transformation, in both policy and practice. As such, they are uniquely positioned to inform debate on this shift at all levels, including pre- and post-service training, policy development, programme planning, and classroom delivery. Canadian educators have the opportunity to articulate a more pragmatic description of effective collaboration for diverse learners as well as informative and empowering assessment practices. The Canadian context can inform and guide the work of all educators as they strive toward finding more effective ways of "sitting beside or with" students.

References

Allan, J. (1996). Foucault and special educational needs: A 'box of tools' for analyzing children's experiences of mainstreaming. *Disability and Society, 11*(2), 219–233.

Alur, M. (2002). Status of disabled people in India: Policy and inclusion. *Exceptionality Education Canada, 12*(2/3), 137–168.

Armour-Thomas, E. (1992). Intellectual assessment of children from culturally diverse backgrounds. *School Psychology Review, 21*(4), 552–565.

Armstrong, F., Armstrong, D., & Barton, L. (2000). *Inclusive education: Policy, contexts and comparative perspectives*. London: David Fulton.

Artiles, A. J. (2003). Special education's changing identity: Paradoxes and dilemmas in views of culture and space. *Harvard Educational Review, 73*(2), 164–202.

Artiles, A. J., & Trent, S. C. (1994). Over representation of minority students in special education. *The Journal of Special Education, 27*(4), 410–437.

Ashman, A. F., & Conway, R. N. F. (1993). Examining the links between psychoeducational assessment, instruction and remediation. *International Journal of Disability, Development and Education, 40*(1), 23–44.

Australian Bureau of Statistics. (2009). *Estimates and projections: 1991-2021*. Retrieved from: www.abs.gov.au/ausstats/abs@nsf/mediareleases by catalogue.

Banks, J., Cochran-Smith, M., Moll, L., Richert, A., Zeichner, K., LePage, P., et al. (2005). Teaching diverse learners. In L. Darling-Hammond & J. Bransford (Eds.), *Preparing teachers for a changing world* (pp. 32–276). San Francisco: Jossey-Bass.

Bradley, R., Danielson, L., & Doolittle, J. (2007, May/June). Responsiveness to intervention: 1997–2007. *Teaching Exceptional Children, 39*, 8–12.

Brown, M. R., Higgins, K., Pierce, T., Hong, E., & Thomas, C. (2004). Secondary students' perceptions of school life with regard to alienation: The effects of disability, gender and race. *Learning Disability Quarterly, 26*(4), 227–238.

Burns, G. E. (1995). Factors and themes in native education and school boards: First Nations tuition negations and tuition agreement schooling. *Canadian Journal of Native Education, 22*(1), 53–67.

Buysse, V., Goldman, B. D., & Skinner, M. L. (2003). Setting effects on friendship formation among young children with and without disabilities. *Exceptional Children, 68*(4), 503–517.

Chappuis, J. (2005). Helping students understand assessment. *Educational Leadership. November,* 39–43.

Chinn, P. C., & Hughes, S. (1987). Representation of minority students in special classes. *Remedial and Special Education, 8*(4), 41–46.

Cox, S. G. (2008). Differentiated instruction in the elementary classroom. *The Education Digest, 73*(9), 52–54.

Crocker, R., & Dibbon, D. (2008). *Teacher education in Canada*. Kelowna, BC: Society of the Advancement of Excellence in Education.

Cummins, J. (1984). *Bilingualism and special education: Issues in assessment and pedagogy*. San Diego: College Hill.

Danforth, S. (1999). Pragmatism and the scientific validation of professional practices in American special education. *Disability & Society, 14*(6), 733–751.

Darling-Hammond, L., & Falk, B. (1997). Supporting teaching and learning for all students: Policies for authentic assessment systems. In A. L. Goodwin (Ed.), *Assessment for equity and inclusion: Embracing all our children* (pp. 51–76). New York: Routledge.

Delaney, J. G. (2002). *Educational policy studies: A practical approach*. Calgary, AB: Detselig.

Donovan, S., & Cross, C. (Eds.). (2002). *Minority students in special and gifted education*. Washington, DC: National Academy Press.

Driedger, D. (1989). *The last civil rights movement: Disabled peoples' international*. New York: St. Martin's Press.

Dunnell, K. (2008). *Diversity and different experiences in the UK*. Retrieved from: www.statistics.gov.uk/articles/nojournal/NSA_article

Duren-Green, T., McIntosh, A. S., Cook-Morales, V. J., & Robinson, Z. C. (2005). From old schools to tomorrow's schools: Psychoeducational assessment of African-american students. *Remedial and Special Education, 26*(2), 82–92.

Dworet, D., & Bennett, S. (2002). A view from the North: Special education in Canada. *Teaching Exceptional Children, 34*(5), 22–27.

Earl, L. M. (2003). *Assessment as learning: Using classroom assessment to maximize student learning* (2nd ed.). Thousand Oaks, CA: Corwin Press.

Edmunds, A. L., & Martsch-Litt, S. (2008). ADHD assessment and diagnosis in Canada: An inconsistent but fixable process. *Exceptionality Education Canada, 18*(2/3), 3–23.

Foucault, M. (1977). Intellectuals and power: A conversation between Michael Foucault and Giles Deleuze. In D. Bouchard (Ed.), *Language, counter-memory, practice: Selected essays and interviews by Michael Foucault* (pp. 205–217). Oxford, UK: Basil Blackwell Press.

Friend, M., Bursuck, W., & Hutchinson, N. (1998). *Including exceptional students.* Scarborough, ON: Allyn and Bacon.

Fuchs, D., & Fuchs, L. S. (1995). What's "special" about special education? *Phi Delta Kappan, 76*(7), 522–530.

Fulcher, G. (1989). *Disabling policies? A comparative approach to education policy and disability.* London: The Falmer Press.

Gee, J. P. (2001). A socio-cultural perspective on early literacy development. In S. B. Newman & D. K. Dickinson (Eds.), *Handbook of early literacy research* (pp. 30–42). New York: Guildford Press.

Gersten, R., Baker, S., & Pugach, M. (2001). Contemporary research on special education teaching. In V. Richardson (Ed.), *Handbook of research on teaching* (4th ed., pp. 695–722). Washington, DC: American Educational Research Association.

Gibbons, K. (2004). *Frequently asked questions (FAQ) regarding Response to Intervention (RTI) and upcoming idea reauthorization.* Retrieved from: http://www.mnase.org

Goodwin, A. L., & Macdonald, M. B. (1997). Educating the rainbow: Authentic assessment and authentic practice for diverse classrooms. In A. L. Goodwin (Ed.), *Assessment for equity and inclusion: Embracing all our children* (pp. 211–227). New York: Rutledge.

Gopaul-McNichol, S., & Armour-Thomas, E. (2002). *Assessment and culture: Psychological tests with minority populations.* San Diego: Academic Press.

Gould, W. T. S., & Findlay, A. M. (1994). *Population and the changing world order.* New York: Wiley.

Government of Alberta. (2006). *Alberta commission on learning.* Retrieved from: http://education.alberta.ca/department/ipr/commission.aspx

Government of Nova Scotia. (2007). *Minister's review of services for students with special needs.* Retrieved from: http://www.ednet.ns.ca/events/special_education_review/documents/review-committee-report-e.pdf

Grobe, W. J., & McCall, D. (2004). Valid uses of student testing as part of authentic and comprehensive student assessment, school reports, and school system accountability: A statement of concern from the International Confederation of Principals. *Educational Horizons, 82*(2), 131–142.

Hargrove, L. J. (2000). Assessment and inclusion: A teacher's perspective. *Preventing School Failure, 45*(1), 18–21.

Hockenbury, J. C., Kauffman, J. M., & Hallahan, D. P. (2000). What is right about special education? *Exceptionality, 8*(1), 3–11.

Holdnack, J. A., & Weiss, L. G. (2006). IDEA 2004: Anticipated implications for clinical practice – integrating assessment and intervention. *Psychology in the Schools, 43*(8), 871–882.

Hutchinson, N. L. (2009). *Inclusion of exceptional learners in Canadian schools.* Toronto, ON, Canada: Pearson Canada.

Kauffman, J. M. (2000). The special education story: Obituary, accident report, conversion experience, reincarnation, or none of the above? *Exceptionality, 8*(1), 61–71.

Klassen, B. (2002). The changing landscape of learning disabilities in Canada: Definitions and practice from 1989–2000. *School Psychology International, 23*(2), 199–219.

Klassen, R. M., Neufeld, P., & Munro, F. (2005). When IQ is irrelevant to the definition of learning disabilities: Australian school psychologists' beliefs and practice. *School Psychology International, 26*(3), 297–316.

Klingner, J. K., & Edwards, P. A. (2006). Cultural considerations with response to intervention models. *Reading Research Quarterly, 41*(1), 108–117.

Klingner, J. K., Vaughn, S., Schumm, J. S., Cohen, P., & Forgan, J. W. (1998). Inclusion or pull-out: Which do students prefer? *Journal of Learning Disabilities, 31*(2), 148–158.

Kozey, M., & Siegel, L. S. (2008). Definitions of learning disabilities in Canadian provinces and territories. *Canadian Psychology, 49*(2), 162–171.

Lerner, J., & Johns, B. (2009). *Learning disabilities and related mild disabilities* (11th ed.). New York: Houghton/Mifflin.

Lewis, J. E. (1998). Nontraditional uses of traditional aptitude tests. In R. J. Samunda, R. Feuerstein, A. S. Kauffman, J. E. Lewis, R. J. Sternberg, et al. (Eds.), *Advances in cross-cultural assessment* (pp. 218–241). Thousand Oaks, CA: Sage Publications.

Lidz, C. S. (2001). Multicultural issues and dynamic assessment. In L. A. Suzuki, J. G. Ponterotto, & P. J. Meller (Eds.), *Handbook of multicultural assessment* (2nd ed., pp. 523–539). San Francisco: Jossey-Bass.

Lipsky, D. K., & Gartner, A. (1997). *Inclusion and school reform*. Baltimore: Paul H. Brookes.

Lipsky, D. K., & Gartner, A. (1998). Taking inclusion into the future. *Educational Leadership, 30*(2), 198–203.

Lupart, J. L. (1999). *Inching toward inclusion: The excellence/equity dilemma in our schools*. Paper presented at PCERA Symposium, Ottawa, ON, Canada, February 16–17, 1999.

Lyon, G. R. (2005). Why scientific research must guide educational policy and instructional practices in learning disabilities. *Learning Disability Quarterly, 28*(2), 140–143.

Macdonald, I. (1981). Assessment: A social dimension. In L. Barton & S. Tomlinson (Eds.), *Special education: Policy, practices and social issues* (pp. 90–108). London: Harper & Row.

McCarthy, C., Rezai-Rashti, G. M., & Teasley, C. (2009). *Race, diversity, and curriculum in the era of globalization*. Oxford, UK: Wiley.

McDonald, T. (2002). Inclusion in Aotearoa/New Zealand: From rhetoric to reality. *Exceptionality Education Canada, 12*(2/3), 53–76.

McLaren, P. (1998). Che: The pedagogy of Che Guevara: Critical pedagogy and globalization thirty years after Che. *Cultural Circles, 3*, 29–103.

McLaughlin, M. W. (1991). Test-based account as a reform strategy. *Phi Delta Kappan, 73*, 248–251.

Migration Watch UK. (2009). *Future migration trends*. Retrieved from: www.migrationwatchuk.org/briefingpaper/document/96

Mittler, P. (2000). *Working towards inclusive education: Social contexts*. London: David Fulton.

Moore-Brown, B., Huerta, M., Uranga-Hernandez, Y., & Pena, E. D. (2006). Using dynamic assessment to evaluate children with suspected learning disabilities. *Intervention in School and Clinic, 41*(4), 209–217.

Morse, W. C. (1996). Forward. In M. Friend & L. Cook (Eds.), *Interactions: Collaboration skills for school professionals* (pp. xiii–xvii). White Plains, NY: Longman.

Muthukrishna, N. (2002). Inclusive education policy and practice in South Africa: Trends, dimensions, and issues. *Exceptionality Education Canada, 12*(2/3), 77–102.

National Center for Educational Statistics. (2009). *Projections of educational statistics to 2018*. Retrieved October 21, 2011 from: http://nces.ed.gov/pubs2009/2009062.pdf

National Commission on Educational Excellence. (1983). *A nation at risk*. Washington, DC: U.S. Government Printing Office.

Noddings, N. (1992). *The challenge to care in schools: An alternative to care in schools*. New York: Teachers' College Press.

Padilla, A. M. (2001). Issues in culturally appropriate assessment. In L. A. Suzuki, J. G. Ponterotto, & P. J. Meller (Eds.), *Handbook of multicultural assessment* (2nd ed., pp. 5–27). San Francisco: Jossey-Bass.

Philpott, D. F. (2007a). *Focusing on students: The final report of the ISSP/Pathways Commission*. St. John's, NL: Queen's Printer/Government of Newfoundland and Labrador.

Philpott, D. F. (2007b). Assessing without labels: Inclusive education in the Canadian context. *Exceptionality Education Canada, 17*(3), 3–34.

Philpott, D. F., & Cahill, M. (2008). A Pan-Canadian perspective on the professional knowledge base of learning disabilities. *International Journal of Disability and Community Rehabilitation, 7*(2), www.ijdcr.ca/

Philpott, D. F., & Dibbon, D. (2008). The evolution of disability studies amidst school reform in Newfoundland and Labrador. *The Morning Watch, 36*(1–27).

Philpott, D. F., Sharpe, D. & Neville, R. (2009). The effectiveness of web-delivered learning with aboriginal students: Findings from a study in coastal Labrador. *Canadian Journal of Learning and Technology, 35*(3). www.cjlt.ca

Philpott, D. F., Furey, E., & Penney, S. C. (2010). Promoting leadership in the ongoing professional development of teachers: Responding to globalization and inclusion. *Exceptionality Education International, 20*(2).

Salend, S. J. (2001). *Creating inclusive classrooms* (4th ed.). Upper Saddle River, NJ: Merrill Prentice Hall.

Samunda, R. J. (1975). From ethnocentrism to a multicultural perspective in educational testing. *Journal of Afro-American Issues, 3*(1), 4–17.

Samunda, R. J. (1998). Cross-cultural assessment: Issues and alternatives. In R. J. Samunda, R. Feuerstein, A. S. Kauffman, J. E. Lewis, R. J. Sternberg, et al. (Eds.), *Advances in cross-cultural assessment* (pp. 1–19). Thousand Oaks, CA: Sage Publications.

Sands, D. S., Kozelski, E., & French, N. (2001). *Inclusive education for the 21st century.* Toronto, ON, Canada: Wadworth Thomson Learning.

Sassen, S. (1996). *Losing control: Sovereignty in an age of globalization.* New York: Columbia University Press.

Sergiovanni, T. (1994). *Building community in schools.* San Francisco: Jossey-Bass.

Shevlin, M. (2002). Special education in Ireland: At the crossroads. *Exceptionality Education Canada, 12*(2/3), 125–137.

Skrtic, T. M. (1995). The special education knowledge tradition: Crisis and opportunity. In E. L. Meyen & T. M. Skrtic (Eds.), *Special education and student disability: An introduction – traditional, emerging, and alternative perspectives* (pp. 609–672). Denver, CO: Love Publishing.

Slee, R. (2002). Developing theories and practices of inclusion in Australia. *Exceptionality Education Canada, 12*(2/3), 103–124.

Smith, J. D. (1998). *Inclusion: Schools for all students.* New York: Wadsworth Publishing Company.

Smith, T. E., Polloway, E. A., Patton, J. R., & Dowdy, C. A. (1998). *Teaching students with special needs in inclusive settings.* Boston: Allyn & Bacon.

Smith, T. E., Polloway, E. A., Patton, J. R., Dowdy, C. A., & Heath, N. L. (2001). *Teaching students with special needs in inclusive settings* (Canadian ed.). Boston: Allyn & Bacon.

Stainback, S., & Stainback, W. (1992). *Curriculum considerations in inclusive schools: Facilitating learning in inclusive classrooms.* Toronto, ON, Canada: Paul H. Brookes Publishing Co.

Stanley, L. D. (2003). Developments in curriculum-based measurement. *The Journal of Special Education, 37*(3), 184–192.

Stanovich, P. J., & Jordan, A. (2000). Effective teaching as effective intervention. *Learning Disabilities: A Multidisciplinary Journal, 10*(4), 235–238.

Statistics Canada. (2007). *Portrait of the Canadian population 2006.* Retrieved March 23, 2007, from: www12.statcan.ca/english/census06/analysis/popdwell/highlights.cfm

Statistics Canada. (2008). *The daily.* Retrieved April 9, 2008, from: www12.statcan.ca/english/070426/d070426a.html

Statistics New Zealand. (2004). *National ethnic population projections 2001-2021.* Retrieved October 9, 2011 from: http://unpan1.un.org/intradoc/groups/public/documents/APCITY/UNPAN016776

Taylor, L. S., & Whittaker, C. R. (2009). *Bridging multiple worlds: Case studies of diverse educational communities.* Boston: Allyn & Bacon.

Thomas, G. (1997). Inclusive schools for an inclusive society. *British Journal of Special Education, 24*(3), 103–107.

Timmons, V. (2002). International perspectives on inclusion: Concluding thoughts. *Exceptionality Education Canada, 12*(2/3), 187–192.

United Nations Development Programme. (2009). *Overcoming barriers: Human mobility and development*. Retrieved from: http://www.undp.org/hdr2009.shtml

Waldron, N. L., & McLesky, J. (1998). The effects of an inclusive school program on students with mild and severe learning disabilities. *Exceptional Children, 64*(3), 395–405.

Ware, L. (2000). Sunflowers, enchantment and empires: Reflections on inclusive education in the United States. In F. Armstrong, D. Armstrong, & L. Barton (Eds.), *Inclusive education; policy, contexts and comparative perspectives*. London: David Fulton.

Weber, K. (1994). *Special education in Canadian schools*. Thornhill, ON: Highland Press.

Wiener, J. (2004). Do peer relationships foster behavioral adjustment in children with learning disabilities? *Learning Disabilities Quarterly, 27*(1), 21–30.

Wiggins, G. P. (1993). *Assessing student performance: Exploring the purpose and limits of testing*. San Francisco: Jossey-Bass.

Wincott, D. (2006). *New social risks and the changing welfare state: Ideas, policy drift and early childhood education and care policies in Australia, the UK and the USA*. Paper presentation at the 2006 annual meeting of the American Political Science Association, Philadelphia. Retrieved from: http://www.asu.edu/clas/polisci/cqrm/APSA2006/Wincott_Social_Risks.pdf

Wink, J. (2005). *Critical pedagogy: Notes from the real world*. Boston: Allyn Bacon.

Ysseldyke, J. E., Algozzine, B., & Thurlow, M. L. (1991). *Critical issues in special education* (2nd ed.). Boston: Houghton Mifflin.

Ysseldyke, J. E., & Shinn, M. (1981). Psychoeducational evaluation: Procedures, considerations, and limitations. In D. Hallahan & J. Kauffman (Eds.), *The handbook of special education* (pp. 418–446). Cliffs, NJ: Prentice Hall.

Zigmond, N. (2003). Searching for the most effective service delivery model for students with learning disabilities. In H. L. Swanson, K. R. Harris, & S. Graham (Eds.), *Handbook of learning disabilities* (pp. 110–122). New York: Guildford.

Part II
Assessment at the District/School Leadership Level

Chapter 7
Current Policies Surrounding Assessment in Alberta: Future Implications

E. Nola Aitken and Art J. Aitken

Policies shape the structure of schools, the resources in schools, the curriculum, the teaching staff, and, to a considerable extent, the round of daily activities. Policies determine how much money is spent, by whom and on what, how teachers are paid, how students are evaluated, and most other aspects of schools as we know them.

(Young & Levin, 2002)

Abstract The authors address student assessment policies in the Alberta context at the provincial and district levels with reference to some international comparisons. The discussion is organised around the topics and issues that emerged from participants in surveys and focus-group forums in the Alberta Student Assessment Study. Participants in the study included superintendents, principals, teachers, government officials, parents, students, and other educational stakeholders. Emerging topics included the politics of assessment, teacher learning, decision making, communication and relationships, leadership, and fairness and equity. Alberta Education policies and regulations formed the basis of the legal mandates that drive assessment practices. Policy handbooks from the largest public school districts in Alberta representing more than 60 % of the student population were examined for student assessment policies and guidelines. A summary of benchmark literature informs the treatment of each issue. The authors found extensive support in policy and in literature for classroom assessment practice, leadership, and professional development. Throughout the policy documents, assessment was consistently positioned as an integral part of instruction and learning. As twenty-first century learning models gain impetus, policy and practice needs to guide fair, balanced, and aligned assessment in a process that represents the interests of students, teachers, parents, and the public.

E.N. Aitken (✉) • A.J. Aitken
Faculty of Education, University of Lethbridge, Lethbridge, AB, Canada
e-mail: nola.aitken@uleth.ca; aitkenaj@telus.net

© Springer International Publishing Switzerland 2016
S. Scott et al. (eds.), *Assessment in Education*, The Enabling
Power of Assessment 2, DOI 10.1007/978-3-319-23398-7_7

Keywords Assessment policy • Politics of assessment • Professional development • Fair assessment practice • Communicating assessment • PISA • Provincial achievement tests • Ontario • Poland • Finland • Singapore

This literature review examines relevant documents and research that inform student assessment policies and practices in the province of Alberta. Policies are examined at two levels — the provincial government policies and regulations, and the policies and practices at the school jurisdictional level. Educational practices and structure of countries with high student achievement are compared to the Alberta system. Additionally, research in the academic community is invoked to inform the discussion about issues that were raised in the assessment forum dialogue conducted by Alberta Student Assessment Study researchers. Those issues include the politics of assessment, teacher learning decision-making, communication and relationships, leadership, and fairness and equity.

7.1 Legislation and Policies

7.1.1 Alberta Legislation

The province of Alberta presides over evaluation of student learning by using a variety of legal and quasilegal legislation. The provincial policies are typically broad, general, and based on principles. School boards are required to implement provincial policy by creating policies of their own. These district level policies are often general as well, but at the same time, they provide a structure for schools to develop specific practices that reflect their interpretation of the school board policy. School boards will also develop administrative procedures for their schools. These procedures are designed to set the operational directions and limits for school principals as they implement school and classroom practices for assessing student performance.[1]

In Alberta there are three significant pieces of legislation that guide assessment practice—the School Act (Alberta Education, 2013i), a Ministerial Order on Student Learning (001/2013), (Alberta Education, 2013h), and the Teaching Quality Standard Applicable to the Provision of Basic Education in Alberta (0016/97), (Alberta Education, 1997). These are supported by and cross-referenced to three other pieces of legislation—a broad Student Evaluation Policy statement (Alberta Education, 2013j), the Student Evaluation Regulation (177/2003), (Alberta Education, 2013k), and the Student Record Regulation (Alberta Education, 2006c). The province also supports this legislation by issuing handbooks, guidelines, and forms that can be accessed from the Guide to Education 2013–2014 (Alberta

---

[1] Most of the information for this discussion has been gleaned from the *Grade Level of Achievement Reporting: Teacher and Administrator Handbook*, Appendix II (Alberta Education, 2008).

Education, 2013g). Under the Student Evaluation Regulation, the Minister of Education administers an external examination programme that requires high school students to write diploma (Grade 12) examinations in all core subjects. These external exams constitute 50 % of the student's grade in each subject. School jurisdictions are expected to create and administer evaluation policies that will guide teachers in assigning a school-based grade that will account for the other 50 % of the student's final grade.

The School Act (Alberta Education, 2013i) generates regulations and guides educational practices in Alberta. It specifies the roles and responsibilities of both teachers and principals with respect to assessing and evaluating students in Alberta classrooms. Under the Act, regarding assessment practices, teachers are required to:

1. provide instruction competently to students;
2. teach the courses of study and education programmes that are prescribed, approved or authorized pursuant to this Act;
3. promote goals and standards applicable to the provision of education adopted or approved pursuant to this Act;
4. encourage and foster learning in students; and
5. regularly evaluate students and periodically report the results of the evaluation to the students, the students' parents and the board. (Alberta Education, 2013i, p. 24)

The Assessment as the Basis for Communicating Individual Achievement policy in the Guide to Education, 2013–2014 (Alberta Education, 2013g) was enacted in the Alberta legislature in 1996 and was designed to distinguish between the interpretation of "grade" as a designation, for example, Grade 4, or Grade 8; and grade as "level of achievement". In other words, in accordance with this policy teachers were required to report to parents on what the student knows, how well the student knows, and the grade level which the student has achieved in any given subject. This policy was intended to ensure that schools specified, not only the grade level at which the student was working, but also the data that were used in assessing the student. It outlined consultation processes (with teacher, principal, parent, and school council), communication requirements (conferences, portfolios, and report cards), and it delved into the realm of Individual Programme Plans (IPPs) for students whose level of achievement fell outside the designated grade level.

Parts of this policy were implemented thoroughly throughout the school districts in the province. Two examples were the use of assessment data to guide placements at the high school level, and the development of IPPs, both of which had funding implications for schools. Reporting the grade level of achievement was not as well implemented in the decade following enactment of the legislation (Webber, Aitken, Lupart, & Scott, 2009), and as a result the province developed its Grade Level of Achievement Reporting handbook to further clarify reporting requirements (Alberta Education, 2008). The need to report Grade Level of Achievement data to Alberta Education has since been rescinded (Alberta Education, 2013f).

In 1997, the Minister of Education exercised his power to order, adopt, or approve goals and standards for the province's education system. The resulting legislation was an order in council, approved by the provincial legislature entitled the *Teaching Quality Standard Applicable to the Provision of Basic Education in Alberta, Directive 4.2.1* (Alberta Education, 1997). This order in council clarified assessment and evaluation practices for teachers holding Interim Certificates and for those holding Permanent Certificates. Extracts regarding assessment that specify requirements from this legislation include the following:

Teachers

- monitor students' actions on an ongoing basis to determine and respond to their learning needs;
- use a variety of diagnostic methods that include observing students' activities, analysing students' learning difficulties and strengths, and interpreting the results of assessments and information provided by students, their parents, colleagues and other professionals;
- select and develop a variety of classroom assessment strategies and instruments to assess the full range of learning objectives;
- differentiate between classroom and large-scale instruments, such as provincial achievement tests, administer both and use the results for the ultimate benefit of students;
- record, interpret and use the results of their assessments to modify their teaching practices and students' learning activities;
- help students, parents and other educators interpret and understand the results of diagnoses and assessments, and the implications for students; and
- help students to develop the ability to diagnose their own learning needs and to assess their progress toward learning goals. (pp. 6–7)

There does not appear to be in existence a policy framework specifically designed to guide the structure of assessment policies for the province and school jurisdictions. However, Alberta Education has crafted a framework for learning that addresses critical components of Alberta's agenda that demand attention (Alberta Education, 2011). The following statement addresses a policy framework for learning in Alberta that becomes a platform for curriculum development and assessment in the future:

> The Framework for Student Learning: Competencies for Engaged Thinkers and Ethical Citizens with an Entrepreneurial Spirit is a foundational element for the review and replacement of the student learning outcomes in the current Ministerial Order (MO) on the goals and standards Applicable to the Provision of Basic Education. The framework and the new MO, along with revised standards, guidelines and processes will provide direction for the development of future curriculum (programmes of study, assessment, and learning and teaching resources). (p. 1)

Alberta Education also has other framework statements: one that focuses on professional practice competencies for school leaders (Alberta Education, 2010b) which addresses the preparation, induction, and practice of school leaders and specifies roles and responsibilities for stakeholders; and another that addresses Aboriginal learning (Alberta Education, 2010c). Although Alberta Education does not have a comprehensive statement regarding a policy framework for assessment, there are individual assessment frameworks that are featured in detail in Alberta Education Curriculum documents, for example, Health and Life Skills Guide to Implementation K—9: Assess, Evaluate and Communicate (Alberta Education, 2002). Curriculum documents typically contain a vision statement, goals, principles, strategies, and performance measures that guide school boards and teachers with direction in assessment practices in Alberta classrooms. Furthermore, the *Guide to Education* (Alberta Education, 2013g) specifies the following:

> To assist in improving programs, establishing and maintaining standards, and improving student achievement, school jurisdictions and accredited-funded private schools shall develop, keep current and implement written student evaluation policies and procedures for conducting continuous assessments and evaluations of student learning in education programs that provide for:
>
> - accurate, fair and equitable student evaluation;
> - the student's right of appeal and procedures for appeal;
> - the role of the student and the teacher in evaluations;
> - the use of evaluation information for the improvement of the quality of educational programs; and
> - timely communication of evaluation information to students, parents and school councils. (p. 22)

The Alberta Assessment Consortium (AAC), with members representing most of Alberta's school boards and postsecondary institutions, two educational organisations, and several out-of-province jurisdictions (AAC, 2010) provides a forum and a resource base for assessment practices for use in Alberta classrooms. Whereas this consortium facilitates a network for assessment-oriented teachers and administrators, it does not have the legislative or regulatory powers that the government possesses. However, the AAC has produced an assessment framework that informs educators about the relationship between the programme of studies, teachers, and assessment practices in Alberta schools (AAC, 2013) (Fig. 7.1).

The government of Alberta has acknowledged that Alberta Education policies and regulations are in need of review. The 2013 School Act is scheduled to be enacted in 2015 and in preparation for that enactment, the Minister of Education has ordered a Regulatory Review of 30 regulations that will support the new School Act. In a minister's report (Alberta Education, 2010d) the matter of changes in assessment practices were directly addressed:

> To measure core competencies, assessment would also change. For example, in community conversations Albertans stressed the need for diverse approaches to assess learner competencies such as innovation and critical thinking, including the use of qualitative measures. (p. 27)

To assess the success of the broader education system, the provincial government looks at indicators like the literacy and numeracy of graduates, high school completion rates, and the percentage of students pursuing post-secondary education. The ongoing dialogue arising from Inspiring Education needs to identify new and additional ways of measuring success from this broader perspective.

AAC KEY VISUAL: ASSESSING STUDENT LEARNING IN THE CLASSROOM

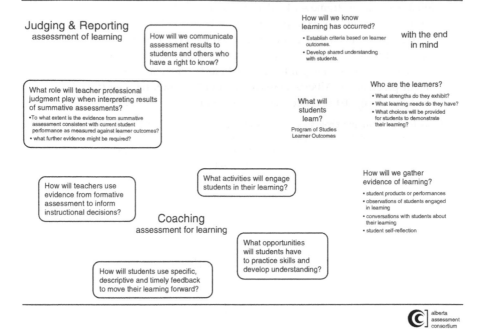

Fig. 7.1 Framework for assessing student learning in the classroom (Copyright © 2012 Alberta Assessment Consortium. Used with permission)

As a further indication that the assessment landscape is likely to change, the Minister has cautioned school boards to delay making changes to policies pending the outcome of the Regulatory Review and the School Act enactment (Alberta Education, 2013e).

7.1.2   School District Policies

Provincial policy documents that inform assessment are typically goals-driven and are an outcome of a larger ministry-designed agenda. Input from stakeholders and the public is largely solicited at the draft paper stage and despite the complexities of developing consensus on a large scale, such input is considered when developing policy details. Alberta Education subsequently sets the agenda for districts by requiring that they develop local policy designed to implement provincial regulations and policies. The Accountability Pillar (Alberta Education, 2006a) shapes or provides a template for districts to develop plans and policies based on a common set of provincial goals. The Accountability Pillar enhances the use of performance management of school jurisdictions by requiring districts to plan and report on performance measures that include the following measurable outcomes:

- Safe and caring schools
- Student learning opportunities
- Student learning achievement (K-9)
- Student learning achievement (10–12)
- Preparing for lifelong learning, world of work, and citizenship
- Parental involvement
- Continuous improvement
  (Alberta Education, 2006a, p. 4)

The Pillar affords school districts the opportunity to allocate resources and implement programs as they see fit. Despite the centrality of student achievement and results when reporting to Alberta Education, districts also account for other aspects that impact student learning—such as safe and caring environments, parent involvement, and satisfaction with the education experience—thereby taking a more holistic view of accountability. Despite the shared purpose implicit in the *Accountability Pillar*, and the guidelines implicit in Alberta Education policies, there are substantial differences among school district assessment policies. In responding to the provincial standards, school boards have discretion in their choice of assessments, grading practices, and student evaluation implementation strategies, but "all jurisdictions measure the same factors in the same way at the same time, creating timely, accurate, consistent data that is publicly evaluated and reported" (Alberta Education, n.d., p. 1). Certainly the districts' political cultures can have a serious effect on how assessment policies are crafted, informed, and implemented at the local level.

This review included an examination of student evaluation and assessment policies in large school districts in the province of Alberta.[2] Two of the districts (i.e., Black Gold, Calgary Catholic) did not have assessment policies listed in their Policy Handbook. In one of those districts officials advised that assessment practices were addressed implicitly in its other policies (i.e., reporting, principal's role, etc.), while the other district responded that they relied on Alberta Education directions to guide evaluation practices in their schools. Others have shifted to developing fewer policies and subsequently to generating quite specific Administrative Procedures that include student evaluation and assessment requirements. School districts included in the study are shown in Table 7.1.

The format for district policies varies. Those districts that have traditional policies (i.e., listed in the District Policy Handbook) incorporate definitions, regulations, and procedures into their policy document. In recent years there has been a trend to move assessment and evaluation matters out of the policy statement into either Regulations or Administrative Procedures—from legal to a quasi-legal format. Those adopting the latter format have definitions, assessment practices, communicating and reporting procedures that are supported by recent research cited in the

---

[2] School districts whose student population exceeded 9000 students were chosen for the study.

Table 7.1 District by student population with online evidence of evaluation policies, regulations, and guidelines included in the review

District	Population	Policy	Reg.
Calgary School District #19	105,665		Yes[a]
Edmonton School District #7	83,433	Yes	Yes
Calgary Roman Catholic Separate SD #1	48,860	Policy paper?	
Edmonton Roman Catholic Separate SD #7	36,205		
Elk Island Public Regional Division #14	16,325		A
Rocky View School Division #41	18,416	Yes	A
Chinook's Edge School Division #73	10,690		A
Red Deer Public School District #104	10,294	Yes	
Parkland School Division #70	9799		A
Black Gold Regional Division #18	9189	Embedded	
Lethbridge School District #51	9050	Yes	Yes
Christ the Redeemer	9097		A

Data available from jurisdiction websites
Reg. Regulation, *A* Administrative procedures based on 2012/2013 September 30th count
Total of 367,032 (60 % of the provincial student population in Public, Separate, and Charter Schools of 616,375)
[a]Calgary School District #19 deleted its regulation June 2013

Alberta Assessment Consortium (O'Connor, 2012; Wiliam, 2011). The premise with these local policy reforms is that assessment plays a central role in supporting student learning—hence the new structure supports an assessment for learning perspective (AfL). These documents provide specific directions to teachers regarding fair, consistent, and reliable evaluation procedures. When changing from an assessment for accountability perspective to an AfL perspective, tensions are common. The government, the teacher association, the local jurisdiction, the parents and the students each have very specific views about the purposes of assessment — and quite often those differing views cause considerable disharmony in the community. It's noteworthy that two Alberta districts attracted widespread media attention — local, provincial, and national — when implementing assessment practices that reflect informed research about supporting student learning. One Edmonton Public School's principal took a hard line in implementing a no-zero mark policy and a teacher was fired for failing to implement the school policy (Zwaagstra, 2012), while Battle River School Division (not included in Table 7.1) drew a massive public response when passing an Administrative Procedure that eliminated the use of percentages or letter grades when reporting to parents ("New Grading System," 2012). Both of these instances illustrate how critically important it is for policy makers to take time to communicate with stakeholders and to balance policy drafts in an attempt to acknowledge competing interests. Policy makers at the government level are focused to a large extent on accountability. Post-secondary institutions see assessment as a way to enhance competitive selection. And local districts are moving toward policies that support student learning, that diagnose strengths and weak-

Table 7.2 Legal cross-references cited in the learning assessment policies in the largest school districts in Alberta

Alberta Education policy references	No. of citations
The School Act, 1999	7
Student Evaluation Policy 2.1.2	5
Student Evaluation Regulation 177/2003	3
Teaching Quality Standard Directive 4.2.1	2
Grade Level of Achievement Reporting: Teacher and Administrator Handbook	2
Standards for Special Education (Amended 2004)	2
Effective Student Assessment and Evaluation in the Classroom	1
Student Achievement ECS to Grade 9	1
Student Achievement in Senior High School	1
Alberta Regulations AR 169/98	1
Alberta Regulations AR 71/99 Student Records	1
Alberta Education Policy 1.6.1 Education Placement of Students with Special Needs	1
Alberta Education Policy 1.6.2 Special Education	1
Alberta Education Policy 2.1.3 Use and Reporting of Results on Provincial Assessment	1
Principles for Fair Student Assessment Practices for Education in Canada	1
The Freedom of Information and the Protection of Privacy Act	1
No legal references	1

nesses, and that align carefully with expected outcomes. These different perspectives illustrate the multi-purpose nature of assessment policy.

Most districts in the study cite the legal references that inform the local policy. Despite this commonality, there is wide variation in the number and titles of provincial policies that are cited in informing the school district assessment policies. Table 7.2 illustrates that the *Teaching Quality Standard Directive 4.2.1* (Alberta Education, 1997), the *Student Evaluation Regulation 177/2003* (Alberta Education, 2003) (amendments 2004, 2005, 2009), and the *Student Evaluation Policy 2.1.2* (Alberta Education, 2013j) were only referenced in two of the district policies while other supporting policies were randomly cited — each on only one occasion. The *School Act* (Alberta Education, 2013i) was acknowledged in five policies; however, the several amendments to the Student Evaluation clause of the Act (i.e., 108/2004, 105/2005, 139/2009) were not included in any of the policies. Similarly, use of policy statement themes was not universally apparent (see Table 7.3). Purpose statements, appeals procedures, reporting, and definitions were among those themes that were addressed more often than others. Interestingly, the calculation and assignment of grades were often not addressed in jurisdiction policies, and when they were addressed, they resulted in a great deal of controversy (Battle River School Division, 2013; Edmonton Public Schools, 2013).

Table 7.3 Prominent themes in policy statements

Policy statement themes	Number
Purpose statement that positions evaluation of student achievement as an integral and ongoing part of teaching and learning and/or aligned with curriculum	8
Appeals procedures	6
Reporting to parents procedures/structure	6
Terms and definitions provided	6
Use of provincial achievement results	4
Grading structure (i.e., A=80+; B=65–80; etc.)	3
Assessment "for & of" practices/procedures	2
Final grade calculation	1

7.2 Some Inter-provincial and International Comparisons

What are the education policies and practices of countries that lead the world in student performance? The underlying premise in posing this question is that student performance is the ultimate criteria for measuring the success of a school system. According to Tucker (2011) a high performing education system is characterised by world-class student achievement: "In short, we defined top performers as nations with education systems that are in the top ranks on quality, equity and productivity" (p. 4). The Programme for International Student Assessment (PISA) is acknowledged as the standard for comparing national school systems on the basis of student performance. The PISA results (2009) reveal that Canada, Singapore, Finland, and Japan are in the top ten countries in the world in literacy, mathematics, and science, based on 15-year-olds who participated in the 2009 PISA tests (OECD, 2010). Other similar international initiatives designed to provide data on student achievement include the Trends in International Mathematics and Science Study (TIMMS) and the Progress in International Reading Literacy Study (PIRLS). The same countries do well on all of these tests (TIMMS and PIRLS, 2013). What are some features of the Canadian system that contribute to its overall success? According to leading informers, three factors may account for Canada's success (Tucker, 2011). First, there exists a common culture of parent support across the provinces. Second, Canada has a strong welfare state where children and adults have access to a strong national health care system, and where there is a norm that society is responsible to protect and foster the right of every child to a quality education. Third, there are three common policy factors that also contribute to Canada's performance—the province-wide curricula; quality candidates in teacher education programs; and equalized funding. Although Canada does not have a national education system, the Council of Ministers of Education issued a report in 2005 that reflected an interest in reforming assessment practices "to strike a balance between large-scale testing and classroom assessment and to use both to facilitate student learning" (Berry, 2012). This report has guided Canadian provinces in their quest for improved assessment practices. Subsequently, Alberta has claimed to be a world leader in achievement results based on performances in PISA tests in recent years. Students consistently score in the upper echelon of results when compared to other provinces and countries. The Alberta results, coupled with other high achieving provinces, Ontario and British Columbia in particular, contribute to Canada's overall success in the PISA programme.

Ontario is the largest province in Canada and has been acknowledged as a world leader in "its sustained strategy of professionally-driven reform of its education system"(p. 65). The two major elements of that reform agenda have been the Literacy and Numeracy initiative in elementary schools and the implementation of strategies to improve the high school graduation rate to 85 %. Both of these initiatives illustrate the profound effect that wide-scale consistent focus and common implementation strategies can have on student achievement. System coherence and leadership coupled with trust and respect are underlying factors in the development of student evaluation policies and practices throughout Canada. These features play a significant role in positioning Canada as one of the highest performing countries in the world of student achievement.

Other countries have also emerged as world leaders in student achievement but for very different reasons. Virtually all of the top ten countries, with Canada being the exception, feature a policy of performance assessment that permeates the system and provides gateways regarding student readiness to progress to the next level i.e., from elementary to secondary, from secondary to university, or from secondary to job-training. This comparison is an example of the practice of "benchmarking" which refers to how countries use features of other successful countries to inform how well they are doing. Tucker (2011) states "Singaporeans may be the most determined and disciplined benchmarkers in the world" (p. 5). Japan has also invested a great deal to learn how others can inform its policies and practices. Finland similarly has researched extensively when developing education policy. Finland also finds itself to be the most "visited" as others seek to learn from the policies of the leading student achievement country in the world.

Finland is a stand-out case of a high achieving country that has held the top position for at least the last decade–2003, 2006, and 2009. Sahlberg states that Finland's dramatic improvement in student learning has emerged from education policies based on equity, flexibility, creativity, teacher professionalism, and trust (Sahlberg, 2007). Finland attracts and employs highly qualified teachers who are considered to have high status in their community – Master's degrees are required for all teachers. Central curricula direction is limited, while teacher autonomy is high. For example, Berry (2012) states, "all assessment of student learning is based on teacher-made tests, rather than standardized external tests" (p. 93). In contrast to other high performing countries, externally administered testing programs are not part of the Finnish education system. Schools, on the other hand, feature closely-knit communities of teachers who create optimal learning conditions and establish learning content designed to meet a broad set of goals. Finnish policy has moved from a practice of external accountability to school-based assessment by professionally prepared educators.

Contrast the Finnish approach to that of Poland–a country whose achievement results have shown considerable improvement. To illustrate, Poland's education system has emerged from the Russian influence of the post-war years to a package of reforms that has focused on enhancing secondary and post-secondary standards, ensuring educational opportunities, and improving the overall quality of education (OECD, 2011d). From a student evaluation perspective, Poland has implemented a heavy dose of external testing at the end of the primary, lower secondary, and upper secondary stages to ensure that students are ready to advance to the next level. The result has been a remarkable turn-around in PISA results. Policies that guide creating common curriculum, new core curriculum, and an accountability system to monitor results have contributed to Poland's emergence in the top achieving countries.

There are some broad policy features in Alberta's practice that parallel those of countries in the upper echelon of student achievement. Like the rest of Canada, Alberta is distinctive in its decentralized structure and in its balance of diversity of language and religious affiliation with its provincial goals (OECD, 2011c, p. 67). Nevertheless, as Tucker (2011) points out, there are commonalities that Canada, and Alberta in particular, share with other successful systems (p. 3). Those broad themes include providing a quality education system for all students, whether they be elite or those struggling with special needs; and teacher recruitment practices that strive for professionally prepared teachers who will be offered competitive compensation packages that compare favourably with other professions. Tucker sums up by describing top performers as nations with education systems that are in the top ranks on quality, equity and productivity.

However, at the international level there continues to be differences in the way that countries view assessment. Berry (2012) suggests that there is still a worldwide dominance of high-stakes summative discourse that permeates issues of accountability; while at the same time there has been some progress in changes to classroom assessment practices. The learning function of assessment is slowly gaining some traction in many education systems. Based on the OECD 2011 report (OECD, 2011b), Canada and Finland appear to be strong supporters of the latter (OECD, 2011a, c).

7.3 Assessment Literature

The review of literature is framed around the initial themes that arose in forum discussions conducted in Stage One and Stage Two of the Alberta Student Assessment Study (Webber et al., 2009). The themes were: Politics of Assessment, Teacher Learning, Decision Making, Communication and Relationships, Leadership, and Fairness and Equity. In Stage One the research team conducted two lecture series for graduate students across the three universities represented. Twenty-four national and international assessment experts presented assessment theories and practices to the 54 registrants.

In Stage Two the research team formed role-alike and cross-role focus group interviews to discuss what they understood about assessment in Alberta schools. Seventy-eight stakeholders were involved in this process from various groups: Alberta Education, College of Alberta School Superintendents, Alberta Teachers' Association (ATA), Alberta School Boards Association, Alberta School Councils' Association, the AAC, provincial government employees, and university faculties from the Universities of Alberta, Calgary, and Lethbridge.

Following the focus group interviews, the researchers coded the data into six themes:

1. The politics of assessment
2. Teacher learning
3. Decision making
4. Communication and relationships
5. Leadership
6. Fairness and equity (later renamed Social Justice).

7.3.1 Politics of Assessment

Alberta Student Assessment Study forum issue:

"This theme encompassed issues related to policy, accountability at all organizational levels, stakeholder mistrust of each other, widespread confusion about student assessment, and a sense of professional responsibility to both the educational and wider communities" (Webber et al., 2009, p. 35). Many educators acknowledged that mistrust was due partly to fear of the unknown, that is, being unable to interpret assessment data and use it appropriately, or as described by one principal, a "statistical literacy" problem (p. 37).

The uncertainty and lack of understanding about appropriate data use caused fear in some educators that triggered "cheating" (Webber et al., 2009, p. 35) and poor instructional practice to somehow "beat the test". The teachers' association provoked some educators further by using value-laden words when describing the provincial assessment; for example labelling provincial tests as "high-stakes", comparing the provincial programme with the testing and the punitive practices (in some cases) based on results in the United States. Dialogue such as this added further fuel to the fire. A senior high school assistant [principal] noted this ploy and said "Very seldom have I seen [unions] operate with the best interest of kids and their learning. It is about teachers" (Webber et al., 2009, p. 133). Levin (2008) acknowledges these complexities and politics of assessment in school systems: "Political leaders promise higher standards and reduced achievement gaps, but delivering these in a large and complex system is a very large challenge" (p. 133).

Since the advent of accountability measures in the 1990s most of the related discussion has centred around critical issues that impact on the requirements to address matters such as assessment, politics, achievement standards, inclusion, and efficiency. An accountable education system "ensures that all children, including those with disabilities, benefit from their educational experience through equal access, high standards, and high expectations" (Ahearn, 2000, p. 14).

In Alberta, the Government Accountability Act (Alberta Education, 1995) required school jurisdictions to report on goal achievement and to demonstrate goal alignment with those of Alberta Education (Burger et al., 2001; Nixon & Kedersha McClay, 2007). The *Accountability Pillar* in Alberta is essentially anchored in results, some of which are test results. Test results, albeit a narrowly conceived view of achievement, are coupled with social and moral values that are profiled as indicators of success (Alberta Education, 2006a).

> The *Accountability Pillar* along with equitable funding and flexibility and [*sic*] the three pillars of the renewed funding framework. School authorities receive equitable funding and have maximum flexibility in allocating funds to meet the learning needs of their students. In return, school authorities are accountable for use of resources and results achieved. (Alberta Education, 2006a, n.p.)

Nevertheless, of the seven categories within Alberta Education's *Accountability Pillar*, only two directly relate to provincial standardised testing (Alberta Education, 2006a).

The Accountability Pillar measures are organised into the following seven categories, each of which reflects dimensions of education of importance to parents and the public. They are:

- safe and caring schools;
- student learning opportunities;
- student learning achievement, K–9;
- student learning achievement, 10–12;
- preparation for life-long learning, employment and citizenship;
- involvement; and
- continuous improvement.
  (Alberta Education, 2006a)

A prevailing political condition over the past few decades in numerous countries is the practice of comparing schools' achievement results. The public's thirst for information coupled with government's penchant for accountability has resulted in a phenomenon known as "league tables" – the publishing of schools' performances on standardised achievement tests and ranking according to level of performance. In the face of this culture, educators are charged with assessing student progress, knowing that their test results will be used to construct league tables (Gronn, 2008). In Alberta, in compliance with the *Accountability Pillar*, school districts report their goal achievement based on student achievement largely supported by provincial achievement test and diploma examination data. Alberta Education's most recent version of its *Accountability Pillar* was implemented in 2006 to support its renewed funding framework.

Although the *Alberta Student Assessment Study Final Report* (Webber et al., 2009) focused on student assessment in its broadest sense, it is important to highlight what members of one focus group articulated, and that is, although student assessment measures are important, a balanced perspective needs to be taken and an overemphasis on student assessment ought to be avoided, and this is evident in the current *Accountability Pillar.*

The politics that surround Alberta's accountability measures are typically responses to the interests of the public, the school boards' responsibilities, and the agendas of the stakeholder groups such as the teacher association and parent councils. The Alberta Teacher Association claims that there is an overemphasis on achievement and diploma results as indicators of school improvement (Nixon & Kedersha McClay, 2007). This stance often places the profession in conflict with the public, a condition not unique to the teaching profession (Perkins, 1990). Consequently, the public importance placed on these results has created unnecessary stress and tension for teachers as they respond by focusing on the provincial test rather than on their teaching (Bruseker, 2006; Simner, 2000). Community demands for purposeful, responsible spending of tax revenues has prompted increased focus on testing in schools (Wiggins, 2006). Wiggins (2010), an early proponent of authentic assessment, claims that government standardised tests reveal critical weaknesses in students' understanding. However, he further states that tests that focus on deep understanding can in a positive sense drive and support effective curriculum and instruction. Moreover, he adds, "Teaching for greater understanding would improve results, not threaten them" (p. 49). Although testing is typically a way to determine how well students have learned particular curriculum outcomes, it is also perceived by some to be a reflection of teacher effectiveness and a principal's performance as an instructional leader. Because these measures are in the public arena (they are required to be reported) they certainly can affect policy and sometimes prompt a comparison of public schools. For example, the Fraser Institute (2010) espouses: "Our School Report Cards include detailed tables for each school that show how it has done in academics over a number of years. This helps parents select a school for their children and evaluate a school's ongoing performance" (n.p.). Some educators recognise the need for the Fraser Institute rankings. A senior high school assistant principal rationalises the need in this way: "Rankings [by the Fraser Institute] are a result of no previous accountability" (Webber et al., 2009, p. 131). In recent years, Alberta Education has displayed school and school authority results on its website annually for the public and stakeholders because as taxpayers, the public has every right to know how schools are doing academically (Alberta Education, 2012a). Moreover, mainstream media often embrace student achievement results as a way to convey issues to their readers (Canada.com, 2008).

7.3.2 Media Influence

In the Fall of 2008, the Edmonton Public School District came under public scrutiny when its provincial achievement and diploma results were released. The local newspaper, the *Edmonton Journal*, ran the story making a direct connection between the results and the quality of teaching in the district. For example, the article's opening sentence read: "Edmonton Public Schools says some of its teaching tactics aren't making the grade" (O'Donnell, 2008, p. B5). Also, the reporter made a more subtle (but nevertheless deliberate) connection between the poor results and the influence of English-as-an-Additional Language (formerly English-as-a-Second-Language [ESL]), and First Nations, Métis, and Inuit, and special education students. The Edmonton Public School District superintendent was cited, stating, "Nearly a quarter of the students [in Grade 3 language arts and math, Grade 6 science, social studies, and math, Grade 9 language arts] either failed the provincial achievement test or failed to write the exam" (Schmidt, 2008, in O'Donnell, 2008, p. B5). The reporter, Sarah O'Donnell, connected the dots for the *Edmonton Journal*'s readership:

> The demographics of Edmonton Public Schools, the second largest school district in the province, have changed as the city's immigrant and aboriginal populations grow. The number of English-as-a-Second Language students alone has more than doubled in the last five years. (p. B5)

In stark contrast, the *Calgary Herald* reported in September, 2006 about the Calgary Public School District's and its Separate School District's (largest and 3rd largest districts in the province respectively) results of an earlier version of the same test that the *Edmonton Journal* had cited. "City students shine in exams", read the headline (Williamson, 2006, p. B1). However, when looking at the Grade 3 reading and math results, the percentages of students not writing and failing were remarkably similar to those of Edmonton Public School District's and indeed, to those of the whole province. After passing accolades to students, teachers, and parents, the article's author drew particular attention to the results of ESL students who "performed admirably, exceeding provincial results on 95 % of all achievement test measures" (p. B1). Admirable indeed! However, neither of the Calgary school districts published a table to help the reader understand such a remarkable statistic.

This contrast in the reporting of results might, in some part, be attributed to contrasting editorial styles; or it may be a result of different perspectives taken by the two school boards in question. But, either way, it is an illustration of the tension and the politics of reporting results of large-scale achievement tests at the school district level and the subsequent effect that atypical students may have on results.

The province is also prone to politicise its achievement results, particularly when it comes to reporting its performance on international tests such as the Programme for International Student Assessment (PISA) that compares the results of 70 countries that make up 90 % of the world's economy (OECD, 2010). An Alberta Education news release read, "These test results confirm that Alberta students are among the best in the world" said the then Minister of Education, Gene Zwozdesky (Alberta Education, 2004, p. 30). "I am very proud of their achievements which demonstrate that students benefit from our province's excellent teachers, high-quality centralized curriculum, outstanding learning and teaching resources, and standardised assessment program" (p. 30). Based on a test that is administered to a random sample of 15-year olds every three years to determine achievement in reading, mathematics, and science, the Minister is unabashedly using a narrow form of data to draw a rather serious conclusion for his public. The Canadian government, whose role, in education, at best is at arm's length, is also willing to use achievement results as a political strategy. Following the 2006 version of the same test, Statistics Canada released their statement:

> When the PISA 2000 and 2003 results were released, the performances of Canadian students were among the highest. Results from this report on PISA 2006 also show that 15-year-old students in Canada performed well in all three domains assessed relative to their international peers. In other words, Canada has retained its high standards over the six-year period relative to other participating countries. (Statistics Canada, 2013, n.p.)

Again in 2009, "Canadian students continue to perform well compared to other countries" (Statistics Canada, 2010, p. 15). However a study of the results indicates that 11 other countries performed as well or better than Canada. The statement also fails to report that Canada opted out of one aspect of the PISA test, namely the reading of electronic text (p. 13). Alberta's Minister of Education, Ron Liepart, matched his predecessor's rhetoric from the previous year when he stated, "Alberta's students are achieving incredible things" (Alberta Education, 2007, n.p.) as he lauded his province's lofty comparative position (in science). Nevertheless, a department official offered a sobering interpretation of the same results in the same news release when he stated that while the results were indeed encouraging, other countries and provinces were closing the gap fast on Alberta in the achievement arena. In 2009 Alberta's PISA results were indeed outstanding and the Minister wasted no time in responding to the public: "I am very encouraged by these results," said Dave Hancock, Minister of Education. "Alberta's education system continues to rank among the best in the world and Albertans can be confident that our schools are succeeding in preparing students to excel on the global stage" (Canadian International Schools, 2013, n.p.).

Each of these public statements (Alberta Education and the Canadian International Schools), although impressive and positive, simply focuses on a measure of performance that allows for a comparison to other countries, but fails to acknowledge that some students continue to fare poorly in a culture that rewards high achievement. Future research that focuses on improved performance of low achievers or disadvantaged children could prompt further improvements to classroom teaching and help the public comprehend the importance of raising achievement levels of students who have traditionally fallen behind their peers.

On a positive note, an accountability-based assessment system can lead to acquisition of much-needed resources to address perceived problems in programme areas (e.g., funding for special needs). Although test data are often perceived as being summative (used for grading purposes) some suggest that test scores that are analysed purposefully can help identify instructional problems and point to potential solutions (Alberta Education, 2012c; Black, Harrison, Lee, Marshall, & Wiliam, 2003, 2004; Nettles, 2007; Stiggins & Duke, 2008; Wiggins, 2010; Wormeli, 2006). When accountability is viewed as a reciprocal arrangement, resources can be directed to areas of need. Furthermore, the notion of reciprocity invokes a team spirit and positive response to a process that otherwise is viewed as a source of conflict (Reeves, 2002).

The Alberta Teachers' Association (2001) has taken an oppositional stance to the provincial assessment programme and rationalises its position citing misuse of data, harm to the emotional well-being of students, and the programme's role in narrowing the focus of teaching practices as harmful side effects. Paradoxically, the opposition to what some see as high-stakes testing has resulted in a positive and significant move toward a more balanced classroom assessment strategy which positions formative assessment practices as critical in meeting achievement expectations (Adamson, 2011; Black & Wiliam, 1998; Priestley & Sime, 2005; Spillane, 1999; Stiggins, 2002; Stoll, Fink, & Earl, 2005; Wiggins & McTighe, 2005). In other words, teachers have researched and implemented broad-based student assessment strategies to illustrate that provincial test data are only one form of assessment data—and perhaps not the best indicator of achievement. Further evidence regarding the move towards a more balanced approach to student assessment can be found in the numerous school improvement projects that address enhanced assessment practices; for example, in Cycle 3 (2006–2009), over 51 % of AISI projects identified assessment for learning as a central theme. The theme continues to be important in AISI Cycle 4 (2009–2012) with over 35 % of AISI projects identifying it as a theme and over 60 % incorporating assessment for learning instructional strategies in their AISI projects (Alberta Education, 2013c).

Polarized discussions about the relative merits of assessment *for* learning as opposed to assessment *of* learning (Earl & Katz, 2006), teacher professional autonomy versus the public need-to-know (Webber et al., 2009), and the use of achievement data for ranking purposes (Fraser Institute, 2010) each fan the flames in the debate about evaluating student learning. Accountability-based political measures and government and district policy initiatives are attempts to ensure that schools adhere to principles of fair assessment (Webber et al., 2009). However, the implementation of policies and directives remain contentious issues. Alberta Education has recently responded to some of these issues by replacing the provincial achievement tests at Grades 3, 6, and 9 with "more student-friendly assessments" (Alberta Education, 2013b, p. 1). The new assessments are intended to provide teachers with formative data to inform their planning and teaching. This would suggest that further study is called for in the area of policy implementation and the difference between parent and teacher expectations and practices where assessment, either formative or summative, is an integrated part of effective teaching.

7.3.3 Teacher Learning

Alberta Student Assessment Study forum issue:

> Teacher learning encompassed preservice education, professional development, mentoring, and professional learning processes that involved student teachers, novice-to-experienced teachers, teacher leaders, school and district administrators, and other community mem-

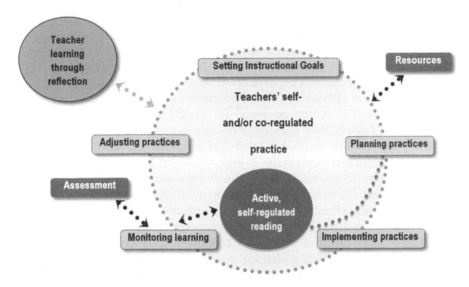

Fig. 7.2 Butler and Schnellert's (2008) model of self-regulated inquiry (p. 39).The use of this figure "Current Policies Surrounding Assessment in Alberta – Future Implications," is protected by copyright and cannot be reproduced in any form without the written permission of the authors or the Canadian Education Association publisher of Education Canada

bers. Collectively, the components of this theme indicated a strong and urgent need for more and more effective learning opportunities related to student assessment. (Webber et al., 2009, pp. 36–37)

There is literally a mountain of evidence indicating that teacher learning is the prerequisite for school improvement (Chung Wei & Darling-Hammond, 2008; Elmore, 2002, 2003; Slavin & Madden, 2000). Similarly the same can be said for the importance of assessment as an integral part of enhancing student achievement (Marshall, 2008; Marzano, 2006; Wiggins, 2006).

Assessment practices are clearly central to changes in understanding about teaching and learning. Correspondingly, reconceptualised models of teacher professional development over the past 50 years are providing momentum for these new understandings about assessment (Burnaford, Fischer, & Hobson, 2001; Eisner, 2002). Whereas teaching was traditionally understood as a technical transmission of knowledge process, it is now redefined as a context-driven decision-making endeavour (Ball, 1995; Butler, Novak Lauscher, Jarvis-Selinger, & Beckingham, 2004) resulting in a form of classroom-level teacher autonomy based on a teacher's beliefs and understandings. "Another trend in recent research on teacher professional development has been the development of collaborative models designed to engage teachers jointly in inquiry-based, longitudinal, and critical examinations of practice" (Butler & Schnellert, 2008, p. 37). Professional development in a collaborative culture becomes a shared practice where teachers are engaged in reflective and self-regulated cycles of inquiry within their learning communities. Figure 7.2 illustrates how teachers' inquiry and assessment practices can intersect.

Research indicates that generally, teachers are not proficient in assessment practice (Black & Wiliam, 1998; Black et al., 2003; Burke, 2009; Earl, 2003; Elmore, 2005; Guskey, 2003, 2004; Lissitz & Schafer, 2002; Nitko & Brookhart, 2007, 2011; Perkins, 1992; Popham, 2004; Reeves, 2002; Smith, 1986; Stiggins, 2002; Stiggins, Arter, Chappuis, & Chappuis, 2004; Wiggins, 2010). Often teachers' poor assessment practice consists of unfocussed curriculum and assessment planning, viewing assessment as an "add-on" purely for grading purposes, and the use of the tried and true methods. Poor assessment techniques do not reap rich or valid data about teaching and learning (Earl, 2003; Wiggins & McTighe, 2005).

Among the opportunities available to improve teacher learning from the outset is preservice teacher education. In 2005, Alberta Education recognised the need for preservice teacher assessment programs to improve their effectiveness and maintain content consistency with one another. After consultation with stakeholders, Alberta Education formed a working group of assessment experts to design a guide, *Effective Student Assessment and Evaluation in the Classroom: Core Knowledge and Skills*, to assist in improving student assessment practice (Alberta Education, 2006b). The purpose of the document was to articulate clearly the student assessment knowledge, skills, and attributes expected under the *Teaching Quality Standard Ministerial Order* of applicants for Alberta interim professional teacher certification (Alberta Education, 1997). The document described for future employers what student assessment principles and core knowledge, skills, and attributes they might reasonably expect of recent Alberta Bachelor of Education graduates as they begin their teaching careers.

Nevertheless, much work has been done in professional development at the professional level in spite of the revamped preservice initiatives. Professional development initiatives, such as the Alberta Initiative for School Improvement (AISI) (Alberta Education, 2013c) and regional consortia, promoted the development of teacher learning in this area. Forty percent of AISI projects in Cycle 3 2006–2009 identified assessment as a project theme (Alberta Education, 2013c). This indicates a demonstrated classroom need for improved student assessment.

7.3.4 Decision Making

Alberta Student Assessment Study forum issue:

> This theme related to assessment-related decision-making at the classroom, school, district, and provincial levels. The school level involved resource allocation, staffing, and student placement. Classroom-related decision-making included formative and summative judgments. An issue that permeated all levels was a perceived lack of clarity about the purpose and data collection uses. (Webber et al., 2009, p. 37)

Assessment data have some universally accepted purposes, most of which are reflected in Alberta school district policies. A policy statement that clearly articulates the purpose of assessment is: "Assessment shall improve student learning, guide effective instruction, provide information for reporting and inform decisions about student learning" (Elk Island Public Schools, 2008, p. 1). In accountability-based schools, data are central to decision making and are the linchpin to what is commonly referred to as a cycle of inquiry (Keeney, 1998). The cycle of inquiry is essentially a decision-making process that uses data as a basis for reflection and planning, and it illustrates the basic steps in the application of data to inform instructional decision-making. The interrelated and interactive steps in the cycle are the following:

1. Establish desired outcomes;
2. Define the question(s) and set criteria related to outcomes;
3. Collect and organise data;
4. Make meaning of the data;
5. Take action; and
6. Assess and evaluate actions.

Using assessment data is also fundamental to the school improvement process throughout—from the planning perspective to measuring progress, to reporting success (Love, 2004; McEwan, 2005; Taylor & Tubianosa, 2001). The Alberta Initiative for School Improvement (Alberta Education, 2013c), although funded from the province, is designed for schools and districts to build educational practices to improve student learning and performance using the collection, analysis, and interpretation of data as fundamental to the Alberta school improvement process.

In the past data were used at the classroom level exclusively to make decisions about student performance—and that process typically involved formative and summative data (Johnson, 1997). The advent of the accountability era and the new understandings about the power of appropriate use of assessments—*for* and *of* learning—has ushered in a movement toward using data for a wider variety of purposes (Earl & Katz, 2006; Reeves, 2002). Accountability reporting systems in most instances attempt to look at a broader set of data than a narrow, test-oriented view of student achievement. Such data include dropout rates, parent satisfaction levels, attendance, career preparation programs, and safety. But, understandably, teachers focus on classroom assessment data because of its high profile with the public, and as a result frequently teachers feel the weight of the world on their shoulders. Similarly school district leaders focus on achievement data as a way of measuring the success of the school system. When such data are used to drive learning and to inform decision making rather than to narrowly focus on comparing achievement to other schools and districts, it is a sign of a school system that is committed to leading and learning (Reeves, 2002).

Members of the acknowledged research community are now looking at ways to connect professional development to classroom assessment data in an effort to undertake and measure professional development based on student achievement (Borko, 2004; Cochran-Smith & Fries, 2005; Darling-Hammond, 2004). Other members of the acknowledged research community are also looking at ways to connect assessment data to decision-making. In particular classroom assessment data are increasingly used as a basis for decisions about teachers' professional development. Darling-Hammond (2010) stresses that professional decisions and effective professional development are driven by, and closely linked to student assessment.

There is clear evidence that high-quality professional development does have a positive influence on teaching practice, school culture, and collaborative learning communities (McLaughlin & Talbert, 2006; Schmoker, 2006). Darling-Hammond states that there is strong evidence that teachers usually have the strongest desire to participate in decisions that most directly affect their work in the classroom (Darling-Hammond, 2010). The work of Joyce and Showers (1996) demonstrated the impact of teachers' professional development on student learning in terms of effect size. This was one of the first studies to demonstrate direct linkages between professional development and student learning outcome improvement. In particular the changes in the classroom assessment practices over the past decade have been supported by a body of literature that cites professional development as an essential factor in driving the change (Popham, 2009; Stiggins & Duke, 2008; Tierney, 2006). Leithwood, Seashore Louis, Anderson, and Wahlstrom (2004) stress that professional development has moved from an independent endeavour to a "school wide culture that makes collaboration expected, inclusive, genuine, ongoing, and focused on critically examining practice to improve student outcomes" (p. 66). Teachers' professional development, in reflecting the depth and scope of shifts in thinking about teaching practice and assessment, could be associated with the level of teachers' engagement in recursive cycles of collaborative inquiry (Guskey, 2002; Schnellert, Butler, & Higginson, 2008). Schnellert et al. found that professional development can result in teachers making changes in teaching practice that foster student achievement when they

- engage in the (co)construction and implementation of situated assessment practices;
- set, tailor, and monitor context-specific goals for students and themselves;
- have opportunities to work collaboratively and recursively through instructional change cycles; and
- are engaged as partners in accountability cycles that incorporate local assessment data. (p. 745)

These findings are supported by other researchers who have found that teachers' reflective practices that result in inquiry cycles produce instructional decisions that can enhance results (Black & Wiliam, 1998; Borko, 2004; Stiggins, 2002).

Nixon and Kedersha McClay (2007) found that collaborative assessment practices can have the dual benefit of enhancing results and fostering professional development simultaneously (p. 162). Collegial practices such as assessing student writing using a shared rubric "sows the seeds for objective and potentially transformative adult learning" (p. 161). Schnellert et al. (2008) conclude with the following:

> teachers, administrators, and policy makers can and should share the common goal of initiating and sustaining cycles of inquiry incorporating careful review of situated assessment data, not only to aid in accounting for outcomes, but also to motivate and guide instructional revision. (p. 747)

In Alberta, the ministry, the school leaders, and the teaching profession have each acknowledged the importance of the wise use of assessment practice and responsible management of test data in their various publications and standards. Such documents include the *Teaching Quality Standard* (Alberta Education, 1997), the *Principal Quality Practice Guideline* (Alberta Education, 2009b), the *Professional Growth, Supervision and Evaluation Policy Model for Administrators* (ATA, 2004), and the *CASS Practice Standard* (CASS, 2013). Each of these statements in one way or another acknowledges and advocates teacher growth, enhanced assessment practices, and appropriate use of achievement data as keys to school improvement. Provincial initiatives that focus on school improvement and capacity building open the doors for researchers to further explore practices that will in turn inform our educators about critical links between professional development, student evaluation, and decision-making.

7.3.5 *Communication and Relationships*

Alberta Student Assessment Study forum issue:

> Effective communication among all stakeholders was a major theme. Key stakeholders were described as teachers, parents, students, postsecondary institutions, and employers. The emotive dimension of student assessment emerged as a strong component of this theme, as did the need for more frequent, timely, and clear communication of student achievement. (Webber et al., 2009, p. 38)

Both parent council representatives and educators expressed their frustration with ineffective communication. They felt that it cultivated mistrust in teacher judgment. Furthermore, it cultivated a distancing of parents from schools. As is often the case, the reverse was true—the difficulty of encouraging some parents to communicate with the teachers. With the advent of the primacy of formative assessment, it is imperative that the student is the recipient of vital information contained in assessment results. Assessment for learning is premised on determining accurate information about each student's learning. That being the case, it is vitally important that the teacher convey the appropriate assessment data to the student such that the student fully understands what next he/she needs to learn and do (Black & Wiliam, 1998; Wolf, 2007). This aspect of communicating results impacts classroom teaching practice in that the teachers need to create space for one-on-one consultation on a regular basis to discuss the student's learning needs. Classroom communication practices if done properly can alleviate much of the potential tension that frequently accompanies assessment when students are unsure of the purpose of the assessment.

Summative assessments are not immune from the communication process – although these types of assessment are fewer and are clear in their purpose. Student report cards, online software, and official transcripts are most frequently used to convey summative results. However, one of those instruments – the student report card – has received a great deal of attention during this assessment revolution (Guskey & Bailey, 2001; O'Connor, 2007; Webber et al., 2009). Many school districts have changed reporting practices in an effort to provide parents with a more accurate picture of what the student knows and can do. As an example, Palliser Regional School Division has developed policy to eliminate using letter grades and percentages on report cards for its K–9 students. Teachers and principals in this revised approach need to report on outcomes in an attempt to provide more information regarding student learning. Elk Island and Battle River are further examples of jurisdictions that have moved away from letter grades and percentages toward an outcome based form of reporting to parents. Changes of this nature require a massive education campaign to inform parents of reporting changes and the thinking behind this practice. Failure to do so can only result in more confusion and distrust.

The stepped-up focus on student assessment over the past decade has clearly placed all aspects of the assessment process under a microscope. Given the changes that have occurred in classroom assessment practice and the renewed demands for accountability, it has become critical that communicating and reporting processes provide accurate and timely information to the various stakeholders. A one-page newsletter to parents is no longer a sufficient way to communicate results to a broad audience. In an age where digital communication has taken its place alongside other traditional forms, it behooves schools to take advantage of all of the communication means at its disposal. Use of web pages, social digital media, news media, annual reports, and targeted releases to stakeholder groups, are each part of the larger communication process. However, what gets reported and how it gets reported are critical components of the communication process.

Educators consistently express concern about a perceived overemphasis on student achievement that is measured, reported, and judged purely on test scores (ATA, 2006, 2008; Couture, 2009). This concern can be at least partially addressed by schools, districts, and the province taking a proactive stance in reporting results. In other words, achievement results that are reported can include data that extend beyond test results. A carefully crafted reporting structure, developed in collaboration with stakeholder groups, that contains key priority information can help alleviate concerns about reporting merely a narrow form of achievement based on a few tests.

Stiggins (2006) stressed that a balanced assessment programme includes communicating results accurately and in a timely manner. Rich descriptions of assessment results will best inform students of their progress and will motivate students to improve. Such importance on accurate descriptions also applies to how schools report their results. Reporting appropriate data through a variety of media can reduce the tensions and conflict that have frequently accompanied achievement reporting in the past.

7.3.6 Leadership

Alberta Student Assessment Study forum issue:

> Focus group participants noted the need for strong, responsible provincial leadership in establishing and maintaining high-quality educational programs. They then stated the need for leadership at the provincial government level "to filter down to the other levels." They acknowledged the quality of the Alberta education system, linking that with ongoing curriculum review, and "maintenance" of standards through provincial student assessment programs. (Webber et al., 2009, p. 39)

School improvement, accountability, and capacity building are the dominant themes that have emerged from the educational literature since the turn of this century. Inextricably intertwined in these conversations are the influences of leadership and the ubiquitous student achievement. How does leadership influence student achievement and how is student achievement measured and interpreted? Recent studies have positioned school leadership as having a significant influence on student achievement – second only to that of the classroom teacher (Leithwood et al., 2004; Leithwood & Mascall, 2008; Marzano, Waters, & McNulty, 2005). Studies involving over 2500 teachers and 90 schools in the United States and Canada pinpoint certain types of leadership as being more influential than others (Leithwood et al., 2004). Findings illustrate that leadership which focuses on creating and sustaining a vision of learning, uses student achievement data as the driving force for instructional decisions, engages teachers in the leadership process, and supports and monitors classroom teaching has the best chance to create a culture that impacts positively on student achievement.

Each of these leadership attributes connects directly to assessment practices and evaluation policies in schools and districts. Murphy, Elliott, Goldring, and Porter (2007) highlight four leadership practices of leaders in effective schools when dealing with student assessment. They are comprehensive in design; they disaggregate the data, triangulate the data, and tightly align classroom assessment practice with school-wide policies. In each of these practices, the leader's presence is integral to the assessment process.

Additionally, effective school leaders are highly skilled at communicating and interpreting data. This focus on data is acknowledged as the heart and soul of the assessment system (Eubanks & Levine, 1983; Murphy et al., 2007; Reeves, 2002). Murphy et al. state that:

> grounded leaders ensure that assessment data are at the heart of (a) mission development, (b) instructional planning, (c) the evaluation of the curricular program, (d) the identification of and the design of services for special needs students, (e) monitoring progress on school goals and improvement efforts, and (f) the evaluation of school staff. (pp. 186–187)

Regarding communication, effective instructional leaders ensure that assessment data are analysed and communicated to the school's stakeholders in a meaningful and purposeful form. It is vital that teachers are included in the data analysis process with a view to adjusting instructional strategies to improve results (Reeves, 2002). The collaborative efforts of teachers and school leaders in designing, implementing, reporting, and analysing assessment practice and subsequent results is explicitly highlighted in all the leadership models that position learning as the central focus of instructional leadership.

7.3.7   Fairness and Equity (Social Justice)

Alberta Student Assessment Study forum issue:

> This eclectic theme covered diverse issues such as problematic assessment practices related to students with special needs and those from cultures outside the mainstream and, additionally, the complexity of assessing for society's diverse expectations for all students. (Webber et al., 2009, p. 40)

A major focus of the literature that addresses social justice and assessment centres on students with special needs, curriculum differentiation, and closing the achievement gap. Alberta Education acknowledges circumstances that impact on students with special needs and subsequently allows students with special needs an array of accommodations that may be used when writing their tests (Alberta Education, 2013a, d). Such accommodations could include use of computers, calculators, readers, scribes, and extra time. It is worth noting that the goal of providing accommodations is to remove obstacles from students with special needs in the interests of creating fairness and equity. Alberta Education policy explicitly states testing accommodations are neither intended nor permitted to:

- alter the nature of the construct being measured by a test;
- provide unfair advantages to students with disabilities over students taking the test under regular conditions; [or]
- substitute for knowledge or skills that the student has not attained. (p. 1)

Alberta Education also allows school authorities to exempt students from writing diploma examinations and provincial achievement tests if, in the view of the superintendent, the student is unable to respond to the test in the current format, or if participation is considered harmful to the student (Alberta Education, 2013k).

Newly minted variations on assessment strategies have been accompanied by a corresponding imperative to differentiate instruction to connect with students in a variety of learning modalities (Ball, 2004; Darling-Hammond & Falk, 1997; Demmert, 2005; Flowers, Ahlgrim-Delzell, Browder, & Spooner, 2005; Gardner, 1999; Nitko & Brookhart, 2011; Tomlinson, 1999; United Nations Educational, Scientific, and Cultural Organization [UNESCO], 2004). The underlying premise in differentiating instruction (and assessment) is that teachers have a social and professional responsibility to address circumstances that mitigate against student learning, whether they be disabilities, economic conditions, or other social inequities. Changing teaching practices, using curriculum differentiation to respond to students' diversity supports classroom inclusion practices by stressing the importance of "providing meaningful learning experiences for all students in their classes" (UNESCO, 2004, p. 6).

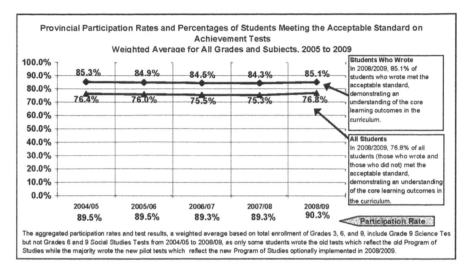

Fig. 7.3 Provincial participation rates and percentages of students meeting the acceptable standard on achievement tests. Provincial Participation Rates and Percentages of Students Meeting the Acceptable Standard on Achievement Tests Weighted Average for All Grades and Subjects, 2005 to 2009 (Alberta Education, 2009c)

Many of the AISI projects in Alberta have focused on building on student strengths using differentiated instruction to close the achievement gap. Examples include "Using Assessment to Improve Student Learning" (St. Albert Protestant); "Integrating UbD (Understanding by Design)";"DI (Differentiated Instruction) to Improve Academic Achievement" (Grande Prairie Public); and "Improving Assessment Practices in High Schools" (Medicine Hat #76) (Alberta Education, 2013c).

In the United States, the *No Child Left Behind Act (NCLB) Executive Summary* (2002), has stimulated an intensified focus on achievement gaps among culturally, linguistically, ethnically, and economically diverse groups (Beecher & Sweeney, 2008). Despite this focus, high-stakes tests continue to reveal lagging achievement in poor and minority populations (Harris & Herrington, 2006; Lutkus, Grigg, & Donohue, 2007). "On March 15, 2010, the Obama administration proposed a sweeping overhaul of the law that would encourage states to raise academic standards after a period of dumbing-down…[and] help states develop more effective ways of evaluating the work of teachers and principals" thereby minimising the propensity to "teach to tests" (Dillon, 2010, n.p). And those are just some of its goals. In Alberta, as in the United States, recommendations for improving schools usually include focusing on curriculum outcomes, aligning assessment with curriculum, data-based decision making, focused professional development, and family involvement (Alberta Education, 2012b). Although these recommendations have considerable value, there have been no discernible changes in student achievement in failing schools in the United States nor in Provincial Achievement Test and Diploma Examination results in Alberta (Alberta Education, 2010a; Lutkus et al.,

2007). For example, Fig. 7.3 illustrates flat-line data over a 5-year period for a combination of all provincial achievement test results.

Perhaps somewhat connected to social justice issues are the consistent numbers of students each year that are either below standard (8–10 %), absent from writing (4–6 %), and excused (4–5 %).[3] Some argue that considerations of socially just pedagogies also must of necessity involve considerations of curriculum, the purposes of schooling, and assessment (Lingard & Mills, 2007). Lingard and Mills further suggest that the curriculum standards may not be appropriate for some students, that the general goals of schooling may miss the mark, and that assessment practices need to change (i.e., the abandonment of high-stakes testing). "Issues of pedagogies, social justice and inclusion cannot be considered in isolation from those of curricula and assessment" (p. 235).

In education systems where high-stakes testing is not the norm (i.e., the Alberta Provincial Achievement Testing programme), it is problematic when assessment, particularly its narrower companion, testing, becomes the main driver of teaching practice (Burger & Krueger, 2003; Guskey, 2003; Popham, 2001; Reeves, 2004; Stiggins, 2002). Remarkably though, the perceived focus on testable curriculum outcomes by the province has led to a corresponding move toward balanced assessment practices in many Alberta classrooms – practices that have been advocated by special interest groups (AAC, 2005; ATA, 2006). Consequently, the limitations of the achievement test have prompted a broader approach to assessment (coined in the phrase "assessment *for* learning") that considers student learning as the driver of the assessment process (Joint Committee on Standards for Evaluation, 2003; Manitoba Education, 2006). This approach is based on the extensive use of formative assessments designed to provide students with feedback regarding their learning, and designed to inform the teacher regarding the effectiveness of teaching strategies. A natural corollary is that students who were previously excluded or "missed" are now identified and supported with enhanced assessment and teaching practices. Because assessment *for* learning directly connects the teaching and assessment process, the literature suggests that the student will subsequently be better prepared for summative assessments and thereby achieve at a higher level.

7.4   Future Directions for Policy Development

According to the *Partnership for 21st Century Skills* (2013), educators of the future will need to focus skills, content knowledge, and expertise that builds understanding across core subjects and also addresses particular interdisciplinary themes (e.g., engaging students using critical thinking skills). Teaching will emphasise a deep understanding as opposed to shallow knowledge, and students need to be engaged with real-world data, tools, and experts (Peat & Allen, 2008). In this culture,

---

[3] See Grade 3 Language Arts Achievement Test Multiyear Report, Provincial Tests: 2005–2009, Alberta Education, 2009a, b, c at http://education.alberta.ca/media/1130929/multiyearprovpat.pdf

assessment practices need to reflect the importance of solving meaningful problems, while at the same time allowing for multiple measures of mastery (Wiggins & McTighe, 2005).

Authentic twenty-first century assessments are the essential foundation of a twenty-first century education (Jukes, 2008). Assessments must measure all five results that matter –core subjects, twenty-first century content, learning skills, information and communication technology (ICT) literacy, and life skills (Eberts, 2008; Richardson, 2008). To be effective, sustainable and affordable, assessments must use modern technologies to increase efficiency and timeliness. Standardised tests alone can measure only a few of the important skills and knowledge that students should learn. A balance of assessments, including high-quality standardised testing along with effective classroom assessments, offers students a powerful way to master the content and skills central to success (Davies & Busick, 2007).

According to the *Partnership for 21st Century Skills* (2013), future assessment practices will do the following:

1. Support a balance of assessments, including high-quality standardised testing along with effective classroom formative and summative assessments;
2. Emphasise useful feedback on student performance that is embedded into everyday learning;
3. Require a balance of technology-enhanced, formative and summative assessments that measure student mastery of twenty-first century skills;
4. Enable development of portfolios of student work that demonstrate mastery of twenty-first century skills to educators and prospective employers; and
5. Enable a balanced portfolio of measures to assess the educational system's effectiveness at reaching high levels of student competency in twenty-first century skills. (p. 8)

The advent of the *Partnership for 21st Century Skills* (2013) list has imperatives for Alberta policy makers and leaders alike (Hollingsworth, 2008). The following recommendations address future policy development and echo the importance of enhanced assessment practice in Alberta classrooms. Alberta Education's visionary education policies can be consistent with integrating twenty-first century skills into education by:

• adopting provincial standards and goals that incorporate twenty-first century tools, learning skills, and technology literacy goals – and reflect these goals in the Alberta Education Accountability Pillar;
• continuing to embed ICT literacy into curriculum outcomes and assessments for core subjects;
• creating provincial and district infrastructure that supports a twenty-first century education by developing a web-based depository on assessments of twenty-first century skills;
• providing professional development that is strategically aligned to support the goal of offering a twenty-first century education to all students;
• encouraging the development of new assessment tools and strategies that address twenty-first century skills; and

- engaging educators, employers, community members, parents, and policymakers in an ongoing dialogue that provides recommendations and advice about twenty-first century education.

In the past decade we have witnessed significant changes in assessment policies at the provincial level in Alberta and across school jurisdictions. Changes in classroom and school assessment practices have been informed by leading researchers across the world. Despite these developments and subsequent improvement in student assessment, some issues continue to result in considerable tension in the provincial education system. Examples include disenchantment with the provincial achievement testing programme, polarized positions on assessment *for* or *of* learning, non-punitive grading practices, accountability data, and communicating achievement to the public. Policy-makers walk a tightrope between government, parent, and teacher demands. In these conditions it is imperative that the province continues to guide the discussion and dialogue by creating policies that acknowledge the paramountcy of student learning, that respect the importance of credible research, that prepare our system for twenty-first century learning, and that recognise that student achievement, while vitally important, is a multidimensional feature. Student learning and student wellbeing are the critical outcomes of the educational system, and well-founded assessment policies are the sole means that we have to measure how well we are doing in those two vital dimensions. Our assessment policies need to reflect the importance of learning and also guide learning in our schools.

Finally, the need to view evaluation through a positive lens is critical for improved student achievement and education systems. The lens must focus on evaluation *for* and *of* learning equally for significant change to take place. The Joint Committee on Standards for Education Evaluation (2003) states this critical importance: "Evaluation of students is central to student learning in every school and classroom. Without evaluation, we do not know if learning has taken place, nor can we plan for future learning opportunities" (p. 1). Educators must embrace accountability for student success in the twenty-first century. What will this take? We believe it will take more than a change of practice and programme. It will mean that educators and stakeholders cease working at futile cross-purposes; instead, they must work collaboratively and genuinely to make the paradigm shift from evaluation as punishment, to evaluation as enlightenment.

References

Adamson, B. (2011). Embedding assessment for learning. In R. Berry & B. Adamson (Eds.), *Assessment reform in education: Policy and practice* (pp. 197–203). New York: Springer.

Ahearn, E. M. (2000). *Educational accountability: A synthesis of the literature and review of a balanced model of accountability*. Final Report Deliverable #2-2.2a under cooperative agreement No. H159K70002. Alexandria, VA: Office of Special Education Programs U.S. Department of Education.

Alberta Assessment Consortium. (2005). *A framework for student assessment* (2nd ed.). Edmonton, AB, Canada: Alberta Assessment Consortium. Retrieved from: http://www.aac.ab.ca/framework_blue.html

Alberta Assessment Consortium. (2010). *AAC member list.* Retrieved from: http://www.aac.ab.ca/memberlist.html

Alberta Assessment Consortium. (2013). *AAC key visual: Assessing student learning in the classroom.* Retrieved from: http://www.aac.ab.ca/resources/Visuals/KeyVisualrev2012.pdf

Alberta Education. (1995). *Government accountability act, 1995.* Retrieved from: http://www.canlii.org/en/ab/laws/stat/rsa-2000-c-g-7/latest/rsa-2000-c-g-7.html

Alberta Education. (1997). *Teaching quality standard applicable to basic education in Alberta.* Retrieved from: http://education.alberta.ca/media/311294/421.pdf

Alberta Education. (2002). *Health and life skills: Guide to implementation.* Retrieved from: http://education.alberta.ca/media/352999/title.pdf

Alberta Education. (2003). *Student evaluation regulation 177/2003.* Retrieved http://www.qp.alberta.ca/documents/Regs/2003_177.pdf

Alberta Education. (2004, December 7). Alberta students show strong results on international tests. *News Release*, p. 30. Retrieved from: http://alberta.ca/release.cfm?xID=173464274E09B-39D4-4CD1-9B54D5C57472F05E

Alberta Education. (2006a). *Accountability pillar.* Retrieved from: http://education.alberta.ca/media/526352/apbrochurefinalnov2006.pdf?

Alberta Education. (2006b). *Effective student assessment and evaluation in the classroom: Core knowledge and skills.* Retrieved from: http://files.eric.ed.gov/fulltext/ED498247.pdf

Alberta Education. (2006c). *Student record regulation.* Retrieved from: http://www.qp.alberta.ca/574.cfm?page=2006_225.cfm&leg_type=Regs&isbncln=0779750381

Alberta Education. (2007, December 4). *Alberta's 15-year olds place among world's best on international tests.* Retrieved from: http://education.alberta.ca/department/newsroom/news/2007/december/20071204.aspx

Alberta Education. (2008). *Grade level of achievement reporting: Teacher and administrator handbook.* Retrieved from: http://education.alberta.ca/media/346277/teachadminhandbook.pdf

Alberta Education. (2009a). *Guide for education planning and results reporting.* Retrieved from: http://education.alberta.ca/media/954726/2009schoolboardplanningguide.pdf

Alberta Education. (2009b). *The principal quality practice guideline: Promoting successful school leadership in Alberta.* Retrieved from: http://education.alberta.ca/media/949129/principal-quality-practice-guideline-english-12feb09.pdf

Alberta Education. (2009c). *Provincial participation rates and percentages of students meeting the acceptable standard on achievement tests.* Retrieved from:http://education.alberta.ca/media/1130954/pat%20graphs_without%20ss%20y1%20to%20y5.pdf

Alberta Education. (2010a). *Achievement testing results: 2012-2013 Provincial results.* Retrieved from: http://education.alberta.ca/admin/testing/achievement-results.aspx

Alberta Education. (2010b). *The Alberta school leadership framework: Promoting growth, development and accountability.* Retrieved from: http://education.alberta.ca/media/2266441/thealbertaschoolleadershipframework.pdf

Alberta Education. (2010c). First nations, Métis and Inuit education: *The Policy Framework.* Retrieved from: http://education.alberta.ca/teachers/fnmi/policies/fnmipolicy/polilcyframework.aspx

Alberta Education. (2010d). *Inspiring education: A dialogue with Albertans.* Retrieved from: http://education.alberta.ca/media/7145083/inspiring%20education%20steering%20committee%20report.pdf

Alberta Education. (2011). *Framework for student learning: Competencies for engaged thinkers and ethical citizens with an entrepreneurial spirit.* Retrieved from: http://education.alberta.ca/media/6581166/framework.pdf

Alberta Education. (2012a). *Diploma examination results, 2011-2012.* Retrieved from: http://education.alberta.ca/admin/testing/diploma-results.aspx

Alberta Education. (2012b). *From knowledge to action: Shaping the future of curriculum development in Alberta*. Retrieved from: http://www.education.alberta.ca/media/6808607/knowledge_action.pdf

Alberta Education. (2012c). Provincial testing: Achievement testing results. Retrieved from: http://education.alberta.ca/admin/testing/achievement-results.aspx

Alberta Education. (2013a). *Achievement general information bulletin*. Retrieved from: http://education.alberta.ca/admin/testing/achievement/achievementbulletin.aspx

Alberta Education. (2013b, May 9). *Alberta empowers more students to succeed*. Retrieved from: http://education.alberta.ca/department/newsroom.aspx

Alberta Education. (2013c). *Cycle 3 and 4 AISI project summaries*. Retrieved from: http://education.alberta.ca/teachers/aisi/leaders/synopses.aspx

Alberta Education. (2013d). *Diploma examination accommodations for students*. Retrieved from: http://education.alberta.ca/media/6446756/08-dip-gib-2013-14_accommodations_2013-08-01.pdf

Alberta Education. (2013e). *FAQ—Education act regulatory review*. Retrieved from: http://www.education.alberta.ca/department/policy/education-act/faqreview.aspx

Alberta Education. (2013f). *Grade level of achievement reporting*. Retrieved from: http://education.alberta.ca/admin/resources/gla.aspx

Alberta Education. (2013g). *Guide to education 2013-2014*. Retrieved from: http://education.alberta.ca/media/7570773/guidetoed2013.pdf

Alberta Education. (2013h). *Ministerial order on student learning*. Retrieved from: http://education.alberta.ca/department/policy/standards/goals.aspx

Alberta Education. (2013i). *School act*. Retrieved from: http://www.qp.alberta.ca/documents/acts/s03.pdf

Alberta Education. (2013j). Student evaluation policy. *Guide to Education 2013-2014*. Retrieved from: http://education.alberta.ca/media/7570773/guidetoed2013.pdf

Alberta Education. (2013k). Student evaluation regulation. *Guide to Education 2013-2014*. Retrieved from: http://education.alberta.ca/media/7570773/guidetoed2013.pdf

Alberta Education. (n.d.). *About the accountability pillar*. Retrieved from: http://education.alberta.ca/admin/funding/accountability/about.aspx

Alberta Teachers' Association. (2001). *The secretary reports*. Retrieved from: http://www.teachers.ab.ca/Publications/ATA%20Magazine/Volume%2082/Number%201/Pages/The%20Secretary%20Reports.aspx

Alberta Teachers' Association. (2004). *Professional growth, supervision and evaluation policy model for administrators*. Retrieved from: http://www.teachers.ab.ca/For%20Members/Programs%20and%20Services/Resources%20For/School-Based%20Administrators/Pages/Administrator%20Professional%20Growth%20Supervision%20and%20Evaluation%20Policy%20Model.aspx

Alberta Teachers' Association. (2006). Student assessment and evaluation: The Alberta teaching profession's view. *Issues in Education, 4*, 1–12.

Alberta Teachers' Association. (2008). *Putreal learning first: The teaching profession's view of student assessment, evaluation and accountability*. Retrieved from: http://www.teachers.ab.ca/Publications/ATA%20Magazine/Volume%2089/Number3/Articles/Pages/PutRealLearningFirst.aspx

Ball, D. L. (1995). Blurring the boundaries of research and practice. *Remedial and Special Education, 16*, 354–363.

Ball, J. (2004). If indigenous knowledge and communities mattered: Transformative education in First Nations communities in Canada. *American Indian Quarterly, 28*, 454–479.

Battle River School Division. (2013). *Administrative procedure 360*. Retrieved from: http://www.brsd.ab.ca/Resources/AdministrativeProcedures/Documents/360%20Student%20Assessment.pdf

Beecher, M., & Sweeney, S. (2008). Closing the achievement gap with curriculum enrichment and differentiation: One school's story. *Journal of Advanced Academics, 19*, 502–530.

Berry, R. (2012). Assessment reforms around the world. In R. Berry & B. Adamson (Eds.), *Assessment reform in education: Policy and practice* (pp. 89–102). London: Springer.

Black, P., Harrison, C., Lee, C., Marshall, B., & Wiliam, D. (2003). *Assessment for learning.* New York: Open University Press.

Black, P., Harrison, C., Lee, C., Marshall, B., & Wiliam, D. (2004). Working inside the black box: Assessment for learning in the classroom. *Phi Delta Kappan, 86*(1), 8–21.

Black, P., & Wiliam, D. (1998). Assessment and classroom learning. *Assessment in Education, 5*, 173–181.

Borko, H. (2004). Professional and teacher learning: Mapping the terrain. *Educational Researcher, 33*(8), 3–15.

Bruseker, F. (2006). *Handle with care: Futures being built.* Retrieved from: http://www.teachers. ab.ca/Publications/ATA%20News/Volume%2040/Number%2011/In%20the%20News/Pages/ Handle%20with%20Care%20Futures%20Being%20Built.aspx

Burger, J., Aitken, A., Brandon, J., & Klink, P. (2001). The next generation of basic education accountability in Alberta, Canada: A policy dialogue. *International Electronic Journal for Leadership in Learning, 5*(19), n.p. Retrieved from: http://iejll.synergiesprairies.ca/iejll/index. php/ijll/article/view/511

Burger, J.M., & Krueger, M. (2003). A balanced approach to high-stakes achievement testing: An analysis of the literature with policy implications. *International Electronic Journal for Leadership in Learning, 7*(4), n.p. Retrieved from: http://iejll.synergiesprairies.ca/iejll/index. php/ijll/article/view/511/173

Burke, K. (2009). *How to assess authentic learning* (5th ed.). Thousand Oaks, CA: Corwin Press.

Burnaford, G., Fischer, J., & Hobson, D. (2001). *Teachers doing research: The power of action through inquiry.* Mahwah, NJ: Erlbaum.

Butler, D. L., Novak Lauscher, H. J., Jarvis-Selinger, S., & Beckingham, B. (2004). Collaboration and self-regulation in teachers' professional development. *Teaching and Teacher Education, 20*, 435–455.

Butler, D. L., & Schnellert, L. (2008). Bridging the research-to-practice divide: Improving outcomes for students. *Education Canada, 48*(5), 36–40.

Canada.com. (2008, October 2). *Edmonton school board releases test results.* Retrieved from: http://www.canada.com/story.html?id=f6022933-9461-403c-b702-0ac9bb6e9b78

Canadian International Schools. (2013). *Facts about the Alberta curriculum.* Retrieved from: http://www.cisamman.com/?page_id=129

Chung Wei, R., & Darling-Hammond, L. (2008). Improving teachers' assessment practice through professional development: The case of national board certification. *American Education Research Journal, 45*, 669–700.

Cochran-Smith, M., & Fries, K. (2005). Researching teacher education in changing times: Politics and paradigms. In M. Cochran-Smith & K. Zeichner (Eds.), *Studying teacher education: The report on the AERA panel on research and teacher education* (pp. 69–109). Washington, DC: American Educational Research Association.

College of Alberta School Superintendents. (2013). *CASS practice standard reflective tool.* Retrieved from: http://o.b5z.net/i/u/10063916/h/Moving%20and%20Improving/CASS_ Practice_Standards_Reflective_Tool.pdf

Couture, J-C. (2009). Collateral damage of government's accountability policies a key focus of 2009 ARA. *ATA News, 43*(18), n.p. Retrieved from: http://www.teachers.ab.ca/Publications/ ATA%20News/Volume%2043/Number18/IntheNews/Pages/Collateraldamageofgovernment% E2%80%99saccountabilitypoliciesakeyfocusof2009ARA.aspx

Darling-Hammond, L. (2004). From "separate but equal" to "no child left behind": The collision of new standards and old inequalities. In D. Meier & G. Woods (Eds.), *Many children left behind* (pp. 3–32). New York: Beacon Press.

Darling-Hammond, L. (2010). *Developing teacher effectiveness: How teacher performance assessments can measure and improve teaching.* Retrieved from: http://www.americanprogress. org/issues/2010/10/pdf/teacher_effectiveness.pdf

Darling-Hammond, L., & Falk, B. (1997). Policy for authentic assessment. In A. Lin Goodwin (Ed.), *Assessment for equity and inclusion: Embracing all our children* (pp. 51–76). New York/London: Routledge.

Davies, A., & Busick, K. (2007). *Classroom assessment—What's working in high schools: Book two.* Courtenay, BC, Canada: Connections.

Demmert, W. G. (2005). The influences of culture on learning and assessment among Native American students. *Learning Disabilities Research and Practice, 20*(1), 16–23.

Dillon, S. (2010, March 16). Array of hurdles awaits new education agenda. *New York Times.* Retrieved from: http://www.nytimes.com/2010/03/16/education/16educ.html

Earl, L., & Katz, S. (2006). *Leading schools in a data-rich world: Harnessing data for school improvement.* Thousand Oaks, CA: Corwin.

Earl, L. M. (2003). *Assessment as learning.* Thousand Oaks, CA: Corwin Press.

Eberts, R. (2008, Fall). Today's students: Reconciling their technology "reality" with their school's rules. *The CASS Connection,* 22–23). Retrieved from: http://o.b5z.net/i/u/10063916/h/CASS%20Magazine/CASB_Fall_08.pdf

Edmonton Public Schools. (2013). *Board policies and regulations: Student assessment, achievement and growth.* Retrieved from: http://www.epsb.ca/policy/hk.bp.shtml

Eisner, E. (2002). From episteme to phronesis to artistry in the study and improvement of teaching. *Teaching and Teacher Education, 18,* 375–385.

Elk Island Public Schools. (2008). *Board of trustees' policy: Learning assessment.* Retrieved from: http://www.bevfacey.ca/files/4/hkab_sept1-08.pdf

Elmore, R. F. (2002). *Bridging the gap between standards and achievement: The imperative for professional development in education.* Washington, DC: Albert Shanker Institute.

Elmore, R. F. (2003, April). *Doing the right thing, knowing the right thing to do: Low-performing schools and performance-based accountability.* Paper presented at the meeting of the National Governors' Association Policy Education Advisors Institute, Los Angeles.

Elmore, R. F. (2005). *School reform from the inside out: Policy, practice and performance.* Cambridge, MA: Harvard Education Press.

Eubanks, E. E., & Levine, D. U. (1983). A first look at effective schools projects in New York City and Milwaukee. *Phi Delta Kappan, 64,* 697–702.

Flowers, C., Ahlgrim-Delzell, L., Browder, D., & Spooner, F. (2005). Teachers' perceptions of alternate assessments. *Research and Practice for Persons with Severe Disabilities, 30*(2), 81–92.

Fraser Institute. (2010). *Compare the academic performance of your child's school.* Retrieved from: http://www.fraserinstitute.org/reportcards/schoolperformance/

Gardner, H. (1999). *Intelligence reframed: Multiple intelligences for the 21st century.* New York: Basic Books.

Gronn, P. (2008). The state of Denmark. *Journal of Educational Administration and History, 40*(2), 173–185. doi:10.1080/00220620802210889.

Guskey, T. (2002). Professional development and teacher change. *Teachers and Teaching: Theory and Practice, 8,* 380–391.

Guskey, T. (2003). How classroom assessments improve learning. *Educational Leadership, 60*(5), 6–11. Alexandria, VA: Association for Supervision and Curriculum Development.

Guskey, T. R. (2004). Zero alternatives. *Principal Leadership (Middle Level Edition), 5*(2), 49–53.

Guskey, T. R., & Bailey, J. M. (2001). *Developing grading and reporting systems for student learning.* Thousand Oaks, CA: Corwin Press.

Harris, D., & Herrington, C. (2006). Accountability, standards, and the growing achievement gap: Lessons from the past half-century. *American Journal of Education, 112,* 209–238.

Hollingsworth, M. (2008). *Excellence in IT/ICT leadership: Building blocks to the future.* Retrieved from: http://education.alberta.ca/media/845012/excellence%20in%20it%20ict%20leadership.pdf

Johnson, J. (1997). Data-driven school improvement. *Emergency Librarian, 24*(4), 9–10.

Joint Committee on Standards for Evaluation. (2003). *The student evaluation standards.* Thousand Oaks, CA: Corwin Press.

Joyce, B., & Showers, B. (1996). The evolution of peer coaching. *Educational Leadership, 53*(6), 12–16.

Jukes, I. (2008, Fall). Educating the digital generation. *The CASS Connection,* 34–35. Retrieved from: http://o.b5z.net/i/u/10063916/h/CASS%20Magazine/CASB_Fall_08.pdf

Keeney, L. (1998, May). *Using data for school improvement.* Houston, TX: Report on the Second Practitioners' Conference for Annenberg Challenge Sites. Retrieved from: http://annenberginstitute.org/tools/using_data/using_data.pdf

Leithwood, K., & Mascall, B. (2008). Collective leadership effects on student achievement. *Education Administration Quarterly, 44,* 529–561.

Leithwood, K., Seashore Louis, K. S., Anderson, S., & Wahlstrom, K. (2004). *How leadership influences student learning.* Paper commissioned by the Wallace Foundation. University of Minnesota, Minneapolis, MN. Retrieved from: http://www.sisd.net/cms/lib/TX01001452/Centricity/Domain/33/ReviewofResearch-LearningFromLeadership.pdf

Levin, B. (2008). What can we expect from politics? *Phi Delta Kappan, 90*(1), 69–70.

Lingard, R., & Mills, M. (2007). Pedagogies making a difference: Issues of social justice and inclusion. *International Journal of Inclusive Education, 11,* 233–244.

Lissitz, R. W., & Schafer, W. D. (2002). *Assessment in educational reform.* Boston: Allyn & Bacon.

Love, N. (2004). Taking data to new depths. *Journal of Staff Development, 25*(4), 22–26.

Lutkus, A., Grigg, W., & Donohue, P. (2007). *The nation's report card: Trial urban district assessment reading 2007 (NCES 2008–455).* Washington, DC: National Center for Education Statistics, Institute of Education Sciences, U.S. Department of Education.

Manitoba Education. (2006). *Rethinking classroom assessment with purpose in mind.* Western and Northern Canadian Protocol for Collaboration in Education. Author.

Marshall, K. (2008). Interim assessments: A user's guide. *Phi Delta Kappan, 90*(1), 64–68.

Marzano, R. (2006). *Classroom assessment and grading that work.* Alexandria, VA: Association for Supervision and Curriculum Development.

Marzano, R. J., Waters, T., & McNulty, B. A. (2005). *School leadership that works: From research to results.* Alexandria, VA: Association for Supervision and Curriculum Development.

McEwan, N. (2005, November). *Using evidence to improve teaching and learning.* Keynote address presented at the Alternative Education Resource Organization Fall Conference, Toronto, ON, Canada.

McLaughlin, M., & Talbert, J. (2006). *Building school-based teacher learning communities.* New York: Teachers' College Press.

Murphy, J., Elliott, S. N., Goldring, E., & Porter, A. C. (2007). Leadership for learning: A research-based model and taxonomy of behaviors. *School Leadership and Management, 27,* 179–201.

Nettles, S. M. (2007). Revisiting the importance of the direct effects of school leadership on student achievement: The implications for school improvement policy. *Peabody Journal of Education, 82,* 724–736.

New grading system sparks controversy in Battle River Schools. (2012). *The Edmonton Journal.* Retrieved from: http://www.ipick.ca/edmonton/new-grading-system-sparks-controversy-in-battle-river-schools

Nitko, A. J., & Brookhart, S. M. (2007). *Educational assessment of students* (5th ed.). Upper Saddle River, NJ: Pearson Education.

Nitko, A. J., & Brookhart, S. M. (2011). *Educational assessment of students* (6th ed.). Upper Saddle River, NJ: Pearson Education.

Nixon, R., & Kedersha McClay, J. (2007). Collaborative writing assessment: Sowing seeds for transformational adult learning. *Assessing Writing, 12,* 149–166.

No Child Left Behind Act (NCLB) executive summary. (2002). Retrieved from: http://www.asha.org/advocacy/federal/nclb/exec-summary.htm

O'Connor, K. (2007). *A repair kit for grading: 15 fixes for broken grades.* Portland, OR: Educational Testing Service. Retrieved from: http://dumais.us/newtown/blog/wp-content/uploads/2013/08/OConnor-K-2007-A-repair-kit-for-grading-15-fixes-for-broken-grades.pdf.

O'Connor, K. (2012). *Fifteen fixes for broken grades: A repair kit*. Toronto, ON, Canada: Pearson.

O'Donnell, S. (2008, October 31). School board to overhaul teaching strategies: Officials want better results on provincial exams. *Edmonton Journal*, B5.

OECD. (2010). *PISA 2009 at a glance*. Retrieved from: http://www.oecd.org/pisa/46660259.pdf

OECD. (2011a). Finland: Slow and steady reform for consistently high results. In *Strong performers and successful reformers in education: Lessons from PISA for the United States*. Paris: OECD. Retrieved from: http://www.oecd.org/pisa/46623978.pdf.

OECD. (2011b). *Strong performers and successful reformers in education: Lessons from PISA for the United States*. Paris: OECD. Retrieved from: http://dx.doi.org/10.1787/9789264096660-en.

OECD. (2011c). Ontario, Canada: Reform to support high achievement in a diverse context. In *Strong performers and successful reformers in education: Lessons from PISA for the United States*. Paris: OECD. Retrieved from: http://www.oecd.org/pisa/46623978.pdf.

OECD. (2011d). Vignettes on education reforms: England and Poland. In *Strong performers and successful reformers in education: Lessons from PISA for the United States*. (pp. 221–226). Paris: OECD. Publishing (data from 2009). doi:10.1787/9789264096660-11-en

Partnership for 21st Century Skills. (2013). Retrieved from: http://www.p21.org/storage/documents/21st_Century_Skills_Assessment_e-paper.pdf

Peat, D., & Allen, B. (2008, Fall). A conversation about 21st century learning. *The CASS Connection*, 14–21. Retrieved from: http://o.b5z.net/i/u/10063916/h/CASS%20Magazine/CASB_Fall_08.pdf

Perkins, D. (1992). *Smart schools*. New York: The Free Press.

Perkins, H. (1990). *The rise of professional society*. New York: Routledge.

Popham, W. (2001). *The truth about testing: An educator's call to action*. Alexandria, VA: Association for Supervision and Curriculum Development.

Popham, W. (2004). *Classroom assessment: What teachers need to know* (7th ed.). Toronto, ON, Canada: Pearson.

Popham, W. (2009). Assessment literacy for teachers: Faddish or fundamental? *Theory Into Practice, 48*(1), 4–11.

Priestley, M., & Sime, D. (2005). Formative assessment for all: A whole-school approach to pedagogic change. *The Curriculum Journal, 16*, 475–492.

Reeves, D. (2002). *The daily disciplines of leadership: How to improve student achievement, staff motivation, and personal organization*. San Francisco: Jossey-Bass.

Reeves, D. (2004). *101 more questions and answers about standards, assessment, and accountability*. Englewood, CO: Advanced Learning Press.

Richardson, W. (2008). WWW: Network building and the new literacy. *The CASS Connection*, 36–39. Retrieved from: http://o.b5z.net/i/u/10063916/h/CASS%20Magazine/CASB_Fall_08.pdf

Sahlberg, P. (2007). Education policies for raising student achievement: the Finnish approach. *Journal of Education Policy, 22*(2), 147–171.

Schmoker, M. (2006). *Results now: How we can achieve unprecedented improvements in teaching and learning?* Alexandria, VA: Association for Supervision and Curriculum Development.

Schnellert, L. M., Butler, D. L., & Higginson, S. K. (2008). Co-constructors of data, co-constructors of meaning: Teacher professional development in an age of accountability. *Teaching and Teacher Education, 24*, 725–750.

Simner, M. (2000). *A joint position statement by the Canadian Psychological Association and the Canadian Association of School Psychologists on the Canadian press coverage of province-wide achievement test results*. Retrieved from: http://www.cpa.ca/documents/joint_position.html

Slavin, R., & Madden, N. (2000). Research on achievement outcomes of "success for all": A summary and response to critics. *Phi Delta Kappan, 82*(1), 38–40, 59–66.

Smith, F. (1986). *Insult to intelligence*. New York: Arbor House.

Spillane, J. P. (1999). External reform initiatives and teachers' efforts to reconstruct their practice: The mediating role of teachers' zones of enactment. *Journal of Curriculum Studies, 31*, 143–175.

Statistics Canada. (2013). *Measuring up: Canadian results of the OECD PISA study.* Retrieved from: http://www.statcan.gc.ca/pub/81-590-x/81-590-x2010001-eng.pdf

Stiggins, R. J. (2002). Assessment crisis: The absence *of* assessment *for* learning. *Phi Delta Kappan, 83*(10), 758–765. Retrieved from: http://electronicportfolios.org/afl/Stiggins-AssessmentCrisis.pdf

Stiggins, R. J., Arter, J., Chappuis, J., & Chappuis, S. (2004). *Classroom assessment for student learning: Doing it right – using it well.* Portland, OR: Assessment Training Institute.

Stiggins, R. J. (2006). Assessment for learning: A key to motivation and achievement. *Phi Delta Kappa International, 2*(2), 2–19.

Stiggins, R. J., & Duke, D. (2008). Effective instructional leadership requires assessment leadership. *Phi Delta Kappan, 90,* 285–291.

Stoll, L., Fink, D., & Earl, L. (2005). *It's about learning (and it's about time): What's in it for schools?* New York: Routledge Farmer.

Taylor, A. R., & Tubianosa, T. S. (2001). *Student assessment in Canada: Improving the learning environment through effective evaluation.* Kelowna, BC, Canada: Society for the Advancement of Excellence in Education.

Tierney, R. (2006). Changing practices: Influences on classroom assessment. *Assessment in Education: Principles, Policy & Practice, 13,* 239–264.

TIMMS and PIRLS. (2013). *TIMMS and PIRLS international study center.* Retrieved from: http://timssandpirls.bc.edu/

Tomlinson, C. A. (1999). *The differentiated classroom: Responding to the needs of all learners.* Alexandria, VA: Association for Supervision and Curriculum Development.

Tucker, M. J. (2011). *Standing on the shoulders of giants: An American agenda for education reform.* Retrieved from: http://www.ncee.org/wp-content/uploads/2011/05/Standing-on-the-Shoulders-of-Giants-An-American-Agenda-for-Education-Reform.pdf

United Nations Educational, Scientific and Cultural Organization (UNESCO). (2004). *Changing teacher practices, using curriculum differentiation to respond to students' diversity.* Retrieved from: http://unesdoc.unesco.org/images/0013/001365/136583e.pdf

Webber, C. F., Aitken, E. N., Lupart, J., & Scott, S. (2009). *Alberta student assessment study final report.* Retrieved from: http://education.alberta.ca/media/1165612/albertaassessmentstudyfinalreport.pdf

Wiggins, G. (2006). Healthier testing made easy: The idea of authentic assessment. *Edutopia.* Retrieved from: http://www.edutopia.org/healthier-testing-made-easy

Wiggins, G. (2010). Why we should stop bashing state tests. *Educational Leadership, 67*(6), 48–52.

Wiggins, G., & McTighe, J. (2005). *Understanding by design* (2nd ed.). Alexandria, VA: Association for Supervision and Curriculum Development.

Wiliam, D. (2011). *Embedded formative assessment.* Bloomington, IN: Solution Tree Press.

Williamson, K. (2006, September 30). City's students shine in exams: Both systems exceed Alberta average [Final Edition]. *Calgary Herald,* B1.

Wolf, P. J. (2007). Academic improvement through regular assessment. *Peabody Journal of Education, 82,* 690–702.

Wormeli, R. (2006). Accountability: Teaching through assessment and feedback, not grading. *American Secondary Education, 34*(3), 14–27.

Young, J., & Levin, B. (2002). *Understanding Canadian schools* (pp. 60–61). Toronto, ON, Canada: Nelson-Thomson.

Zwaagstra, M. (2012). *No-zero grading policies in schools not supported by the evidence.* Retrieved from: http://www.troymedia.com/2012/08/30/no-zero-grading-policies-in-schools-not-supported-by-the-evidence/

Chapter 8
Leading Assessment: The Triple-A Framework for Educational Leaders

Johanna de Leeuw

Abstract At a time when accountability for student performance continues to be a central theme in education reform policy, literacy in student assessment is considered key, if not indispensable for successful educational leaders at every administrative level. Drawing from a wide range of studies published in the last decade on the links between student assessment and educational leadership, three overarching themes are demonstrated to provide a framework for understanding assessment literacy for educational leaders. The 'Triple-A Model' proposes three intersecting points to reflect the complex construction of assessment: aims, approach, and accountability. First, today's leader understands that the **aim** of educational assessment is no longer straightforward but encompasses a wide variety of purposes that are often confused and poorly understood. Second, an intentional, knowledgeable, and visionary **approach** to leadership is shown to be a key factor in the quality of instruction that occurs in classrooms. Third, **accountability** is not only a means for communication between schools and the public, but the result of increasing demands by society and its governments to know and understand what actually happens with students in classrooms.

Keywords Assessment • Formative • Summative • Criterion-referenced • Norm-referenced • Outcomes • Achievement • Leadership • Administration • Instructional • Distributed • Accountability • Policies • Practice • Standardised • Testing • Performance • Reform

8.1 Introduction

Literacy in student assessment is key, if not indispensable knowledge for successful educational leaders at every administrative level in this twenty-first century. Leaders' inadequate knowledge of either the classroom aspect of assessment or the issues surrounding accountability compromises the quality of education (Popham, 2006).

J. de Leeuw (✉)
Founder & President, Instructional Design & Assessment,
Visible Assessment for Learning Inc., Calgary, AB, Canada
e-mail: djohanna@visibleassessment.ca

© Springer International Publishing Switzerland 2016
S. Scott et al. (eds.), *Assessment in Education*, The Enabling
Power of Assessment 2, DOI 10.1007/978-3-319-23398-7_8

Assessment has always been at the heart of teaching and learning, allowing teachers to plan for effective instruction, students and teachers to chart individual progress and plan for academic achievement, and parents and students to become informed decision makers regarding future educational and employment goals (Alberta Education, 2006, p. 9). Today, concern with student assessment is not confined to the instructional setting of the classroom. In Alberta (as in many Western countries), the adoption of standardised government testing to "provide feedback to students and their parents/guardians on how well the students have learned curriculum-based learning outcomes as defined in the programs of study" (Alberta Education, 2006, p. 4) and provide information to teachers on the progress of their students, has become a political platform from which schools, district leaders and government policies are judged (Grobe & McCall, 2004; Marks & Nance, 2007; Moore, Dexter, Berube, & Beck, 2005; Popham, 2006). The larger, politicised implications of student assessment can easily overshadow the primary purpose of student assessment and evaluation – to improve student learning. In an effort to maintain this priority, the Alberta Teachers' Association (ATA) policy states: "Student evaluation has, as its primary function, facilitating the teaching/learning process and, as its secondary functions, measuring the effectiveness of the curriculum and its implementation and recording certain aspects of student achievement" (ATA, 2007, p. 3).

This dual agenda for assessment, individual student learning in the classroom versus political accountability that rates schools or districts (Klinger, Deluca, & Miller, 2008), positions educational leaders in increasingly pressured situations (Møller, 2009). Leaders today balance multiple tasks of attending to classroom instruction, school organisation, local district policy demands as well as delivering tangible 'results' or 'proof' of performance that society has increasingly come to expect (Dinham, 2005, 2007, KI). In an ideal world, standardised test results that provide accountability data could arguably serve as a useful tool that generates additional information for the programming of student learning. Unfortunately, this is not necessarily the case. The growing concern over the last two decades is that the very tests designed to assist and inform are in fact counterproductive to student learning (Slomp, 2008). Included in the charges levelled against these tests is that they are discriminatory (McNeil, 2000, Nichols, Glass, & Berliner, 2006), can be interpreted inaccurately and report on limited learning outcomes (ATA, 2005; Popham, 1999), focus on scores rather than authentic learning, adversely affect student motivation, and result in narrowing the curriculum (Kohn, 2000). According to Wang, Beckett and Brown (2006) the body of research defending the reliance on standardised testing for accountability purposes (Covaleskie, 2009; Phelps, 2005) is slim by comparison. Although there is recognition that standardised tests in some form are unlikely to disappear (Wright, 2009), researchers are proposing with certain qualifications, caveats, and reform, ways in which standardised tests are of benefit to students and teachers (Amrein-Beardsley, 2008; Blanchard, 2003; Parr & Timperley, 2008; Tankersley, 2007; Timperley, 2005; Timperley & Parr, 2007).

Recent developments in curriculum re-design that have or are taking place internationally call for assessment systems that balance formative with summative assessments and are integrated with student learning rather than assessment occurring through isolated events. Recognition that assessment is a complex mixture of finding what students know and can do as well as determining what instructional practices need to change in order to improve student learning is the priority. Central is the engagement and involvement of student, parent and teacher in understanding assessment activities and purposes such as informing learning and measuring achievement. In this redesigned system students have a clear idea of how learning progresses and take responsibility for their learning, parents understand expectations and teachers employ a range of formative and standards based summative assessments. School and district leaders understand the elements and create the conditions for successful learning (Darling-Hammond, 2010).

Although the concept of assessment as learning (referred to as formative assessment) did not originate with Black and Wiliam (1998), it is their studies demonstrating clear connections between student achievement and assessment for learning that spearheaded the movement of placing assessment at the forefront of educational reform. This reconceptualising of assessment has effectively led to a reconceptualising of leadership as focussing on building capacity to implement assessment reform for improved academic achievement (Elmore, 2004a; Leithwood & Mascall, 2008; Leithwood et al., 2004). Because the tools of assessment are used for a wide range of purposes beyond the original intent of making inferences regarding student acquisition of knowledge and skills, it is necessary for leaders to have some understanding of the range of these purposes and the tensions that exist between them (Møller, 2009). The implication that no leader should "dare to be uninformed about [government's] assessment and accountability requirements", and the fact that schools, leaders, and districts are being judged almost completely by how students perform on tests (Popham, 2007), also implies the necessity of increased awareness of the potential negative effects: these same tests can "trivialise education … are constructed on reductionist, simplistic, and decidedly non-intellectual view of education" (Covaleskie, 2009, p. 1). In order to be "players in the political game working to improve not stop testing" (p. 2) and in order to engage in meaningful gains in student achievement and school improvement, an understanding of the principles of assessment and how these inform and impact educational policy and practice is core knowledge for educational leaders.

8.2 Conceptual Framework

The amount of literature published in the last 10 years concerning leadership and assessment is vast and complex. Nevertheless, three overarching themes emerge that provide a useful conceptual framework for discussing the literature on developing assessment literacy and its links to successful educational leadership. Drawing from a wide range of studies published in the last decade, this chapter proposes a triangular model where three points intersect and overlap to reflect the interactive links between assessment and leadership (Covaleskie, 2009; Darling-Hammond, 2004, 2009; Day, Sammons, Hopkins, Leithwood, & Kington, 2008; Elmore, 2005).

They are: aims, approach, and accountability. This tripartite (triple-A) model provides a framework for developing an understanding of proactive policies and practices in student evaluation, and analysing the necessary skills and attributes needed by educational leaders.

First, the contemporary leader understands that the *aims* of educational assessment are no longer straightforward but encompass a wide variety of purposes that are often confused and poorly understood. Newton (2007) points to two major obstacles to effective communication regarding assessment: "(1) the term 'assessment purpose' can be interpreted in a variety of different ways and (2) the uses to which assessment results are put are often categorized misleadingly" (p. 149). Broadfoot and Black (2004) suggest that it is not so much an issue of what the given purpose of a particular assessment activity is, but whether that purpose is evident at all (p. 10). Philosophical and practical clarity regarding formative versus summative assessment, how these concepts may or may not contribute to the same learning goal, where they intersect and where they diverge needs to be understood (Roos & Hamilton, 2005; Taras, 2009), particularly in the context of diametrically opposed expectations that consider assessment as an instructional as well as accountability tool (Ainsworth & Viegut, 2006). Above all, it is important to recognise that assessment is a "social practice, an art as much as a science, a humanistic project with all the challenges this implies and with all the potential scope for both good and ill in the business of education" (Broadfoot & Black, 2004, p. 8).

Second, the contemporary educational leader understands that an intentional, knowledgeable, and visionary *approach* to leadership is a key factor in the quality of instruction that occurs in classrooms. Just as assessment is no longer confined to the narrow interpretation it once had, so too has the concept of leadership broadened to mean more than school organisation, staff deployment, and budget administration. The focus has shifted from the traditional more bureaucratic structures to conceptualising leadership as a structure where the task of managing a school is distributed over a variety of people and roles (Gronn, 2008; Leithwood & Mascall, 2008). Graczewski, Knudson and Holtzman (2009) in their recent study, indicated there is a clear connection between using a distributed model of instructional leadership and more effective teacher performance leading, in turn, to improved student achievement. This has far-reaching implications for leader responsibility. Recent meta-analyses on what constitutes the greatest influences on student achievement (Rowe, 2003, cited in Dinham, 2007; Hattie, 2009, 2011; Mulford, 2006) demonstrated that the student's teacher accounted for 30 % of influence, with the combined influence of home, environment, school, peer group, and student ability accounting for the remaining 70 % (Dinham, 2007). With increased expectations placed on school principals today, a collective or distributed form of leadership has the potential benefit of dividing the labour, and reducing the chance of error (Leithwood & Mascall, 2008). Current research draws attention to how leadership approach is directly related to student achievement (Dinham, 2007; Robinson, 2008). However, in order for a given approach to be sustainable and effective, principals need to understand how shared leadership and trust contribute to a school culture and climate where teachers are empowered to take risks and learn effective instructional techniques based on indepth assessment knowledge.

Third, the contemporary leader understands that *accountability* takes into consideration that "assessment serves as a communicative device between the world of education and that of the wider society" (Broadfoot & Black, 2004, p. 9). However, when media communication becomes the primary source of public information, the limitations of standardised test results as indicators of student achievement may not be apparent. Leaders need to be able to navigate "the political aspect of accountability" and speak knowledgably about the uses and misuses of standardised tests (Scott & Webber, 2008, p. 768). The ability to communicate other indicators of student success, such as increased student engagement and attendance, or involvement in arts and community activities, is essential. Tests are by nature imperfect, reductionist, and limited and provide only one kind of information, but ultimately outstanding teaching and programming "will be reflected in test scores in the same way that we do well on the physical exam if we live fit, nutritious, healthy lives day in and day out" (Wiggins, 2009, p. 36). In recognising that standardised tests "can and should contribute to the democratic governance of schools", educators also need to recognise the importance of continued work to improve them (Covaleskie, 2009). In Alberta, The Alberta Student Assessment Study (Webber, Aitken, Lupart, & Scott, 2009) provided evidence of researchers', educators', government, and other stakeholders' efforts towards this goal.

8.3 Aims of Assessment: Roles and Purposes

An understanding of some of the tensions and potential conflicts of assessment aims is a necessary step to developing a clear leadership vision. The political terrain that educational leaders navigate is a landscape where integration of external assessment events may not be integrated with classroom assessments, where uncovering an unambiguous interpretation of an assessment event or its purpose is not a simple matter (Harlen, 2008). A consideration of the multitude of assessment purposes: improving student achievement, changing curricular focus or priorities, establishing standards, measuring school and district performance for quality control to name just a few, reinforces the degree to which assessment "penetrates social, corporate and political life" (Broadfoot & Black, 2004, p. 11). In the midst of this potential confusion, it is more important than ever for educational leaders to recognise, not only the nature of an assessment event but its intended purpose and whether the event purpose fulfils its intended role.

Fundamentally, assessment purpose as it is understood today can be reduced to two distinct but not necessarily disparate categories: formative and summative, with each category supporting its own set of complex, multi-layered intentions and meanings. Summative assessment, described as assessment *of* learning, refers to the evidence of student learning obtained from completed instructional events. The tests or assignments can be criterion referenced (measured against curricular goals or outcomes) or norm referenced (results are compared with those of other test takers). Summative assessment is both locally and externally situated and the evaluators are usually teachers or external agents. The form of feedback is most often a score or indication of grade level/rank achieved and is usually represented by a numerical or letter grade. Formative assessment or assessment *for*learning is any assessment event (and can potentially include an event used for summative purposes), wherein the priority and primary purpose is to promote student learning (Wiliam, 2006). It is used by teachers to inform and adjust instructional practice and by students to improve achievement (Popham, 2009; Wiliam, Lee, Harrison, & Black, 2004). Newton (2007) traces the development of this dichotomy back to the work of Bloom, Hastings and Madaus (1971) and Scriven (1967), who were the first to shift the focus from using evaluation as a function of selecting and sorting students to improving individual student learning and mastery of educational goals. This work was taken up and further developed by Sadler (1998, 2005, 2007, 2009) whose research centres on feedback and its impact on learning, student self-monitoring, and the debunking of the notion that evaluation is a teacher's prerogative alone (p. 24). The work of Black and Wiliam (1998) put formative assessment at the forefront of the educational discourse on student achievement. Essentially, formative assessment is locally situated in the classroom, and addresses individual student learning and achievement as well as teacher instructional design. The emphasis is on using assessment information to design instruction that meets individual needs, thereby enhancing motivation. The types of tasks used to assess student progress towards mastering a curricular goal range from classroom embedded, performance tasks to teacher created or externally created tests. Characteristically, teachers and students together (including peer and self as assessors), are the agents of judgement and these judgements are always criterion- or standard-referenced. Key to formative assessment is feedback in the form of verbal or written comments, less frequently marks, which are used by students to further their understanding and mastery of a particular learning goal. The key distinguishing factor that has traditionally separated summative from formative assessment is that in the former, results are not used for individual student improvement; rather, the information is used to report to external agents such as parents, district and government bodies for the purposes of curricular decisions (what is taught), student certification, school or district policy making, and accountability. The links between formative assessment and decisions regarding leadership style become apparent when we consider that leadership approach has a direct influence on teacher instructional practices and in turn student achievement.

In an overview of what are now recognised as the important features distinguishing formative purposes from summative uses, Harlen (2008) maintains that the only difference between the two is that they have different purposes: "indeed the same information, gathered in the same way, would be called *formative* if it were used to help learning and teaching, or summative if it were not so utilised but only employed for recording and reporting" (p. 292). Newton (2007) cautions that such confusion may hinder the development of sound assessment practice. His argument is that while formative assessment has a distinct *purpose* (furthering student learning), summative assessment can only have a *use* (decision making, reporting, etc.). For Newton, blurring these distinctions amounts to "dangerous" category errors that could negatively impact policy and decision making, risking the impression that summative assessment results can be used for more than one purpose: "to ensure that wise decisions are made … we need to convey the complexities of assessment design and fitness-for-purpose; we should not allow those complexities to be over-simplified" (p. 161).

Newton's point is an important one for educational leaders to consider in the context of the role that standardised provincial or state testing plays in our schools and classrooms: "Once a system has been designed with an explicit prioritisation of purposes in mind, the operational problem will then become how to ensure that results are not used for inappropriate purposes" (p. 168). Harlen (2008) also points out that evidence from standardised tests is usually not rich enough in detail or readily available at the time of learning to be useful for formative assessment.

The idea that summative tests can be used for formative purposes is debated in the literature. Summative test requirements, which have traditionally dominated teaching practices (Broadfoot & Black 2004), do not support what we know about improving student achievement, as has been graphically depicted in Black and Wiliam's "inside the black box" analogy (1998). The negative impact of summative high stakes testing on teaching practices and the curriculum is well documented (see above), and this points to a pressing issue: formative assessment is clearly recognised as progressive teaching practice, yet the potential conflicts with externally imposed tests are "bound to inhibit and even frustrate" (Broadfoot & Black, 2004). These authors propose that "one way to overcome the severe limitations of external testing clearly must be to use teachers' own knowledge of their students as a source of data for the purposes of certification and accountability" (p. 17).

Leading researchers in assessment are clear that school improvement is undeniably linked to enlightened assessment practices requiring re-evaluation of the role of external standardised tests. Reeves (2007) maintains that "assessment is a leadership issue…our assessment policies put into action our beliefs about the ability of all students to succeed" (p. 8). Leaders need to recognise that the entrenched assessment culture that values summative assessments, normed scoring and grades used for ensuring compliance requires a cultural as much as procedural change (Erkens, 2009). Assessment literacy requires school leaders to create an assessment rich culture where collaboration and sharing of expertise are at the centre. Not only is the focus on formative assessment for academic progress, but traditional norm referenced ways of reporting student achievement are replaced by standards or criterion based models (McTighe & Wiggins, 1999; Popham, 1999, 2003). The recent drive towards curriculum redesign (in countries such as the United States, Canada, Australia, New Zealand, the United Kingdom, Hong Kong, and Singapore) have seen a call for more balanced assessment systems that redirect the focus on school-based assessments. Such redirection places student learning needs at the centre, providing the necessary feedback for high quality learning to occur and enhancing validity by including assessment outcomes that cannot be readily addressed in external examinations (Darling-Hammond & Pecheone, 2010). Leaders have compelling reasons to examine leadership approaches that best facilitate the implementation of these initiatives (Rose, 2009).

8.4   Leadership Approach

Improving student academic achievement, largely driven by an accountability agenda, has been at the centre of school reform research and initiatives for at least the past two decades and has coincided with a virtual revolution in how to think about student assessment. Spearheaded by ground-breaking research that reconceptualises student assessment as an instructional tool for improving achievement (Bloom et al., 1971; Broadfoot & Black, 2004; Reeves, 2007), reformed assessment practice is seen as the basis for school improvement. Fullan (2005a) describes formative assessment as "one of the most high yield strategies" for changing teaching and learning and sustaining this change (p. 54). However, the ability to address the issue of student academic performance on a large scale continues to be confounded by the inability to connect what we have learned about good practice to what actually happens in schools except in relatively isolated pockets. The success of school reform has relied upon the efforts of individuals or groups rather than the collective enterprise of a system at work despite system and district policies and directives (Elmore, 2004a). This points to the thesis that if systemic reform or improvement relies on the efforts and successes of the individual units then these units must function as part of a collective whole and, equally or more important, each individual unit must be aware of how it is part of the collective whole. As suggested by Elmore, "the problems of the system are the problems of the smallest unit … to succeed, school reform has to happen from the inside out" (p. 3). The locus of control is placed at the heart of action – in classrooms.

Elmore (2004a) posits that the reason why so much of what we know about excellence in teaching and learning is practiced in isolated pockets rather than system wide is because of the inherited institutional liability of 'loose coupling'. Detailed educational decisions, specifically instruction and assessment or the "technical core of education … resides in individual classrooms, not in the organisations around them" (p. 44). His concept of "backward mapping" (p. 4) suggests that we need to work from the bottom up, allowing practice to inform policy rather than the reverse: "system-level policymakers and administrators should base their decisions on a clear understanding of the results they want to achieve in the smallest unit – the classroom, the school – and let their organisational policy decisions vary in response to the demand of the work at that level" (p. 5). This has direct implications for school-based educational leaders. If enlightened assessment practice is understood as having the most direct impact on student achievement, then educational leaders have a responsibility to ensure support for teachers to engage in this practice. Stiggins and Duke (2008) list ten specific competencies in assessment for principals and leaders. Two prominent themes that emerge from the literature to comprise leadership competency for sound assessment practice are: building and supporting collaborative cultures that include teacher professional development, and ensuring that school-based instructional leadership involves the distribution of leadership tasks.

8.4.1 Collaborative Cultures for Teacher Professional Learning

Working from the bottom up leads us to re-examine the traditional role of teachers working in isolation as solo practitioners who "operate in a structure that feeds them students and expectations about what students should be taught" (Elmore, 2004a, p. 9). In a culture of individualism, perceived excellence in teaching is seen as an individual trait rather than the professional norm. This fundamental prevents improved techniques, new knowledge and ideas from being disseminated or practiced on any large scale. It results in situations where schools may change in shape and design and new policies may be instituted, but teaching practices remain essentially the same (p. 15). If sound assessment practices rely on common understandings of outcomes and standards and on common pedagogy based on understanding how children think and learn in real life contexts, then educational leadership revolves around finding ways to unleash the powerful and greatly under-utilised resource of teacher collaboration (Fullan & Hargreaves, 1996). Understanding why a culture of individualism exists in teaching is key to changing it. Among the reasons the authors list are: teachers experiencing evaluation under the guise of collaboration, teacher self-imposed high expectations within poorly defined limits, uncertainty, frustration and lack of time to complete the unrealistic goals, reluctance to reveal perceived incompetencies, and reluctance to give and receive help.

There are a variety of interpretations and understandings of what constitutes cultures of collaboration. In Alberta schools, initiatives for school improvement known as the Alberta Initiative for School Improvement (AISI) have placed emphasis on professional learning communities modelled after the work of Dufour and Eaker (1998). These communities are organised around 'SMART' goals intended to focus professional development on specific strategies to improve student learning (Blankstein, 2004). Robinson and Timperley (2007) point out, while collaboration in professional learning communities supports the aim of improved teaching and learning, the type and quality of collaboration needed to create and sustain improvement in assessment on a large scale is in fact very specific. It resists superficiality, contrived collegiality, a 'comfortable' collaboration that is not reflective or critical in its analytical stance, and competing group interests (Fullan & Hargreaves, 1996). Instead, it embraces the long developmental journey of critically reviewing and examining existing practices and seeking improved alternatives. The essential component stresses combined effort that gives voice to individual teacher purpose and values, and at the same time creates strong interdependence, shared responsibility, collective commitment and improvement, review and critique that emerges from team teaching and planning, observation, action research, sustained peer coaching and mentoring. Similar to the action research model, professional collaboration acts on what is learned and continually tests, reviews, and critiques, strategies for their effectiveness.

8.4.2   School-Based Leadership

Despite the plethora of literature on leadership styles and types, it is only recently that research in educational leadership has focused on the links between leadership and student outcomes (Robinson, 2008, 2011). The traditional structure of 'loose coupling' between administrators' tasks at both school and district levels and classroom based instructional practices served to support teaching as an isolated practice ensuring that exemplary practice became localized to individual units rather than a collective or universal norm (Elmore, 2004b). The shift to make schools more publicly accountable for student achievement has led to a re-examination of the role of school-based leaders. Emerging studies indicate that there are strong links between school leadership and student achievement (Leithwood & Day, 2008; Robinson, 2011; Robinson, Lloyd, & Rowe, 2008; Ross & Gray, 2006), particularly when indirect leadership effects, such as leaders influencing teachers' instructional practices, are considered (Leithwood & Mascall, 2008). Robinson's 2011 study in how leadership practices influence student learning outcomes places student learning at the centre and directs a move away from leadership styles such as the "romantic view" or heroic view of leadership (Spillane, 2005; Elmore, 2004a) toward instructional, distributed or collective leadership concepts (Leithwood & Mascall, 2008; Penlington, Kington, & Day, 2008; Robinson, 2008). On the simplest level, it is not difficult to comprehend the differences between instructional practices and distribution of tasks, or to understand how a school leadership approach that centres on improving teaching and learning practices so as to influence student outcomes relies heavily on an instructional leadership structure that utilises a distributed model for implementation. It makes sense that leadership focusing on instruction but still needing to accomplish the expected managerial tasks requires the distribution of roles over a wider number of people in order to accomplish its aims.

8.4.3   Instructional and Distributed Leadership

The words instructional and distributed as applied to leadership styles are often used interchangeably in the literature, yet the two terms imply different emphasis as well as constructs. What follows is an attempt to synthesise the most recent findings on the nature of instructional and distributed leadership, how these constructs have been implemented, and how they have affected student achievement.

A more fully developed notion of instructional leadership first arose in response to the educational reform of the 1980s. The reform agenda recast the goals of education by evaluating success through outcomes rather than inputs, that is, through demonstrations of student learning rather than teacher instructional processes, which in turn, became critical of the absence of attention by management structure to teaching and learning (Murphy, 2004). Since then, the concept of aligning instructional practice for the purpose of improving student outcomes with school leadership has undergone significant changes (Hallinger, 2005). Throughout the 1990s instructional leadership became synonymous with improving student achievement outcomes, ultimately connecting it to teacher performance and professional development (Southworth, 2002). Sheppard (1996, cited in Southworth, 2002, p. 79) outlines the instructional leadership roles as follows: framing and communicating school goals; supervising and evaluating instruction; co-ordinating curriculum; monitoring student progress; protecting instructional time; maintaining high visibility as an instructional leader; promoting professional development.

The implications are that instructional leaders have very specific curricular knowledge which may be more realistic for elementary school principals than for secondary school principals. There is no doubt that focus on instruction may yield significant improvement in student achievement but there is also increasing recognition that the one person, heroic style of leadership cannot accomplish all these aims along with the administrative requirements that school leadership entails. Questioning the conception of leadership as a one-person enterprise arose during the 1980s as leaders were pulled in many directions simultaneously: immersed in curriculum while working directly with teachers, building culture and climate, defining a mission and setting directions, managing instructional programmes, the expectations exceeded what could reasonably be accomplished by one person (Hallinger, 2005). According to Leithwood et al. (2004), there is little evidence to suggest that a distributed leadership model is superior to a vertical or hierarchical one; rather, their evidence demonstrates "that neither is sufficient and that for large-scale reform to be successful both must be provided in a coordinated form (p. 58).

While there does appear to be a general consensus on what instructional leadership entails, this is by no means the case for distributed leadership. As pointed out by Leithwood et al. (2004): "distributed leadership … is, we believe, a more complex orientation to leadership than much of the literature would suggest and one that seems prone to exaggerated claims rooted in democratic ideology" (p. 76). Current literature on the nature and implications of distributed leadership reveals a variety of interpretations. One way of understanding distributed leadership is recognising it as a conceptual or diagnostic tool for analysing and thinking about leadership rather than as a prescriptive term (Spillane & Orlina, 2005); it becomes the umbrella term for the many nuanced forms of leadership that can exist in an instructional setting. Within this theoretical framework, focus on instructional leadership for the purpose of improving academic achievement can be brought to the foreground while other aspects are moved into the background. Most important is that this conceptual framework does not eliminate the variety of roles, structures, and styles that have received attention in the research literature. Rather, it allows for an examination of both the leadership practices by formally appointed leaders (principals, assistant/vice principals) and informal teacher leadership. It investigates how formally appointed leaders may draw upon the strengths of others, creating a space for such leadership to occur within their own specific contexts. Spillane and Orlina (2005) are careful to point out that distributed leadership is not necessarily collaborative and/or democratic. It is the interactions of leaders, followers, and their situation that determine whether these principles inform the distributed model (p. 174).

When leadership is framed as an influence agent by design and intent to either maintain or change an instructional practice, the focus then moves from leadership as an individual enterprise, to leadership practices intended to achieve specific outcomes: "A distributed perspective goes beyond simply enumerating multiple leaders and documenting their contributions; it is foremost about leadership practice (Spillane & Orlina, 2005, p. 8).

To this end, Robinson and Timperley's study (2007) examines how leaders' professional development initiatives intended to change teacher practice influenced student outcomes. Their study revealed five leadership practices that resulted in improved student performance: (1) goal setting or providing direction for change; (2) ensuring strategic alignment of resources to goals; (3) creating a collaborative community that assumes collective responsibility and collective accountability for student achievement that is specific in its focus on the relationship between what is taught and what is learned; (4) engaging in constructive "problem talk" that circumvents "privatised practice and comfortable collegiality" in favour of collective responsibility for, and analysis of student achievement in light of teacher beliefs and practices (p. 253); (5) selecting and developing "smart tools", instruments or resources that in themselves are well designed and "incorporate a valid theory of the task for which they were designed" (p. 256).

Central to the findings in this study is that the design intent was not focused on testing leadership theories but rather on a backward mapping strategy that allowed leadership issues to emerge from the starting point of student achievement. In this context, the authors noted the distributed nature of leadership that facilitated teaching for improved student outcomes emerged from the practical context: "Rather than portrayals of the qualities and activities of a pre-selected group of formal school leaders, these studies provided more subtle and embedded descriptions of a range of leadership practices that were carried out by staff who may or may not have held formal leadership positions" (Robinson & Timperley, 2007, p. 258).

Leithwood and Day's (2008) 3 year study in England explored a number of questions generally related to links between school leadership and student outcomes. Of interest to this review are the questions that specifically explore the impact of school leadership on student outcomes and which leadership practices are linked to improved academic performance. Two papers in this study published so far address the effects of leadership on student outcomes; the first (Day et al., 2008) outlines the mixed methods research approach to garner relevant information within a complex accountability system that encompasses student health and welfare as well as learning outcomes. The second (Penlington et al., 2008) reports on case study data that addresses the role of the principal (headteacher) in: establishing and communicating strong values, vision and direction; models of "widening participation and distributing leadership to other staff; the pivotal role played by the headteacher in setting and communicating a strategic vision for the school within a strong values framework; models of widening participation and distributing leadership to other staff; and building leadership and teaching capacity within the school so as to build a collective commitment, responsibility and accountability for the improvement of pupil outcomes" (p. 65).

Their findings demonstrated that school leaders have a powerful indirect influence on student outcomes particularly when it comes to principals setting a strategic school vision that is responsive to the school culture and community environment, and is also alert to possible future challenges (Penlington et al., 2008). Another key feature is establishing a culture of change that fostered stakeholder voice and participation, one that approached external policy initiatives in a positive manner and simultaneously buffered or prepared teachers for its implementation (Penlington et al., 2008). Of note is the attention paid to the importance of distributed leadership, both "decisional" and "consultative", which was felt by staff and leaders to occur in some way in all schools (p. 70). Building teacher capacities (knowledge and skills) through strategic in-house professional development that was linked to the school development plan and analysis of student assessment data emerged as a key component. The common thread throughout all elements was the close collaboration between the principal and senior leadership regardless of how leadership distribution was applied.

8.5 Accountability

Accountability is arguably the most contentious issue related to assessment. At best, accountability can be seen as governments, districts, schools, and teachers taking responsibility for what students learn; at worst, it carries negative or even punitive connotations when one or more groups are seen as responsible for potential failure. The unprecedented rise in standardised testing, inevitably linked with accountability, has resulted in heated and divisive debate. The purpose of this review is not to discuss the arguments for or against standardised testing as this has been done at length elsewhere (see Burger & Krueger, 2003; Kohn, 2000; McDonald, 2002; Phelps, 2005; Popham, 2001; Volante, 2007; Volante, Cherubini, & Drake, 2008; Wang et al., 2006). Rather, the intent is to explore issues of professional and political accountability and how these link with student assessment, classroom instruction, and school leadership. This discussion will present current thinking by educational researchers and theorists on accountability linked to school reform, as well as some of the recent research on accountability and leadership that relates to international and local contexts of Alberta and other parts of Canada.

The emergence of government accountability policies in American education can be traced back to the 1983 commission on education "A Nation at Risk". The sense that American schools were failing and that the country had lost its economic competitive edge sparked a wave of reform that was highly influenced by the accountability ideas of business elites who saw education as pivotal to productivity (Fuhrman & Elmore, 2003). Standards-based reform rapidly took hold in the US as well as in other Western countries and by the 1990s other business ideas such as the market approach or decentralised site-based management were embraced as part of the reform agenda (Leithwood, 2001). Education reform initiatives in England (spreading quickly to other countries) became inextricably linked with assessment reform primarily due to the work of Black and Wiliam (1998). The subsequent reversal in thinking about teaching and learning as outcomes-based rather than input- or process-based, generated a wealth of educational literature on student assessment. Though the educational emphasis was on assessment as instruction for improved student learning, the outcomes-based orientation of this 'new' assessment concept fit handily into political models of accountability.

By 2001, Leithwood was able to discern four government approaches to account-ability in education that have direct implications for educational leaders. They are the market approach, decentralization approach, professionalization approach and management approach, "each rooted in different assumptions about the basic prob-lems for school reform and the nature of the desirable solutions" (p. 219). Acknowledging that government policies on education are "among the most power-ful influences" on the work of educational leaders, and that these policies are driven by the desire for greater accountability of schools, an understanding of the different leadership responses that each approach calls for provides insight for action (p. 227).

In the market approach school boundaries are relaxed, charter schools are per-mitted or encouraged, funding may follow students, and parents and students become clients able to select a supposedly bureaucracy-free, well-developed prod-uct suitable for their needs (Leithwood, 2001). School leaders in this context would develop strong entrepreneurial skills in addition to their skills as educators. Decentralisation or site-based management, as seen in countries such as New Zealand and Australia, requires leaders to empower parents and community mem-bers to share in the decision making process presumably resulting in a more effi-cient use of resources as well as reflecting the priorities of the local context. School leaders become part of a team and are in the position to facilitate and empower others in decision making (Leithwood, 2001). Professional approaches to account-ability are based on the belief that schooling outcomes are derived from profes-sional practice and that schools need to be held accountable for making use of current knowledge and best practice. Leaders are expected "to create professional learning communities, to assist staff in determining areas for continued professional growth, and assist them in finding the means for such growth" (p. 227). Management approaches hold schools accountable for their decision making. The purpose of Leithwood's outline of approaches to accountability is to highlight that in the recent drive for assessment reform and the consequent demand placed on leaders, reform agendas tend to contain elements of all the conditions outlined above. This places leaders in a quandary as they endeavour to meet expectations: "school leaders attempting to respond to their government's demands for change can be excused for feeling that they are being pulled in many different directions simultaneously. They *are* being pulled in many different directions simultaneously" (p. 228). The past 20 years have seen radical changes in the development of accountability measures in Alberta and subsequently, changing demands made of its educational leaders.

The 1980s saw the development of a comprehensive accountability system in Alberta that introduced standardised tests for Grade 3, 6, 9, and 12 students that claimed to have "reciprocal and mutually beneficial communication links between members of the superintendency and government managers who staffed the network of regional offices of education across the province" (Burger et al., 2001). According to Burger et al., parent satisfaction rates were consistently close to 90 % and student performance was deemed acceptable or better. Unfortunately, another political agenda emerged in Alberta in the mid 1990s when these same initiatives became the levers for downsizing in order to eliminate the provincial deficit and restructuring for more provincial control enabling a market ideology for choice or viability of programmes (Burger et al., 2001; Spencer & Couture, 2009). The new funding framework introduced in 2004 was a model of decentralised control that gave schools and jurisdictions flexibility to respond to local and 'market' needs. At the same time increased emphasis was placed on accountability: "The Accountability Pillar places increased emphasis on achievement of outcomes, reporting of results on a common basis, and using results for informed decision-making for the purpose of improving programs and student results in subsequent years" (Alberta Education, 2006, n.p.). The Accountability Pillar was purported to provide "a new way for school authorities to measure their success, and assess their progress towards meeting their learning goals" as well as ensuring that "Albertans see how their school authority is performing" (Alberta Education, 2009a, n.p.), thus restoring public trust. The data used to measure the success of schools and jurisdictions were derived from seven categories: (1) safety and caring; (2) student learning opportunities; (3) student achievement grades K-9; (4) student achievement grades 10–12; (5) lifelong learning, employment and citizenship; (6) parental involvement; (7) continuous improvement. Perception data were gathered through a combination of parent, student, and teacher surveys, and outcome data included annual dropout rates, high school completion rates, and annual high school to post-secondary transition rates (Alberta Education, 2009b). Receiving by far the most public attention and vigorous debate are the Provincial Achievement Tests (PATs) and Alberta Diploma Examinations.

Accepting the need for accountability and transparency implies that the means by which schools are measured are constantly reviewed and updated. The Alberta Teachers' Association sees the Government's accountability programme, with its increasing demand on teacher time for "implementing, evaluating and sustaining myriad accountability policies" in the context of meeting diverse student needs in an increasingly complex environment, as outdated (Spencer & Couture, 2009, p. xxi). Their "command-and-control testing programmes" emphasis on outcomes-based curricula and standardised reporting undermine core values of public education such as equity, diversity, democracy, and opportunity (Couture, 2009, n.p.). Their view of an outcomes agenda is that it risks standardisation and narrowing of knowledge content and traditional skill development at the expense of creativity, risk taking, and problem solving – educational goals that are deemed necessary and desirable in increasingly complex and dynamic knowledge-based economies. The call is for a "new type of accountability policy that balances qualitative and quantitative measures, and that builds on mutual accountability, professional responsibility and trust" that would see a reduction in test-based accountability in favour of broad, deep learning, and character development (Sahlberg, 2009, p. 10). Within a framework of "intelligent accountability" that stresses mutual responsibility between schools and all stakeholders, learning outcomes are collectively defined and "go far beyond the student achievement results that remain the focus of external standardised tests" (p. 10). Accountability then becomes an response to stakeholders by educators for agreed-upon outcomes and in return, an response by stakeholders to educators for provision of resources and necessary conditions for learning.

8.6 Discussion and New Directions

Leadership and assessment in Alberta has played a prominent role in this review with reason. Hargreaves and Shirley (2012) set out to redefine the features that characterise high achievement by investigating high performance in different school systems across the world. Alberta along with Finland, Singapore, Ontario and California is recognised for high student achievement. Alberta has been Canada's highest performing province on PISA and the highest English-and French-speaking jurisdiction in the world for more than a decade (Hargreaves & Shirley, 2012, p. 97). In attempting to pinpoint the reasons for this success, Hargreaves and Shirley (2012) draw attention to two apparently contradictory provincial initiatives: system wide provincial achievement testing; teacher led innovation and improvement through the Alberta Initiative for School Improvement (AISI) that lasted for 14 years from 1999 to March of 2013. Their analysis, representing the first extended account of change architecture in Alberta, suggests that success is due to several key points. They maintain that Alberta: developed an approach to innovation (the Fourth Way) and collective professional autonomy within a system of test-based accountability (Second and Third way); combined disciplined innovation and continuous improvement; had governments and teacher organisations become educational allies despite occasional conflict; made teacher inquiry and learning permanent conditions; networked with other schools and countries; capitalized on political stability; sustained culture that thrives on risk and trust rather than performance anxiety (Hargreaves & Shirley, 2012, p. 107).

Although teacher based assessments in Alberta have largely remained in the private reporting domain up to this time, significant change is on the horizon. A 2 year government initiative that involved broad public consultation to develop a new long-term vision for education in Alberta resulted in a transformational agenda outlined in the steering committee report, *Inspiring Education: A Dialogue with Albertans* (2010a). The findings were distilled to three outcomes coined "the three E's" of education for the twenty-first Century: engaged thinker and ethical citizen with an entrepreneurial spirit (p. 6). Embedded in this vision are radical policy shifts that can be summarised in seven key points as follows: (1) from system focus to student focus; (2) from focus on content to focus on competencies; (3) from prescriptive curriculum with limited flexibility to local decision making and greater depth of study; (4) from focus on summative assessment to balance among formative and summative assessments; (5) from Ministry led development to collaborative models; (6) from sequential to synchronous development (Alberta Education, 2010a, pp. 22–30).

These policy shifts have radical implications for assessment and leadership. Alberta has now embarked on what could be seen as a risky 2 year journey of curriculum redesign using a rapid prototyping model (Desrosier, 2011) with the intention to see changes beginning in 2015. In addition to the steering committee report, a research foundation that summarises international and national research on curriculum development was prepared by Albert Education (Parsons & Beauchamp, 2012). Prior research included an indepth study of student assessment (Webber et al., 2009). Of particular relevance to assessment is the shift to viewing learning outcomes through the lens of competencies. Competencies are defined as "an inter-related set of attitudes, skills and knowledge that is drawn upon and applied to a particular context for successful learning and living…developed over time and through a set of related learner outcomes" (Alberta Education, 2011, p. 3). How assessment of competencies and balanced assessment practices will relate (or not) to current provincial assessments in Alberta is yet to be determined. In anticipation of change and in accordance with the policy shifts outlined in *Inspiring Education*, Alberta Education (2010a) has introduced a phased approach of replacing the current summative Provincial Achievement Tests (PATs) for Grade 3, 6, and 9 students with computer based Student Learning Assessments (SLAs) that are intended to reflect a more balanced and formative approach enabling "parents and teachers to be aware of a child's strengths or areas needing improvement" over the course of the school year "to support more personalized learning" (Alberta Education, 2013). The intention is that SLAs will provide a blended model as the means for reporting on achievement for Grades 3, 6, and 9, although the means by which this will happen has not yet been addressed.

Clearly, Alberta is articulating a strong stand on progressing toward a balanced assessment approach meaning that: students have varied assessments that provide timely and relevant feedback to help them continue to develop competencies; assessments are compatible with high-quality and engaging learning opportunities with flexible timing and pacing; teachers are skilled and knowledgeable in the administration and interpretation of balanced assessments; assessments are based on learning outcomes for competencies defined by the programs of study; the scope of assessment is expanded to include "assessment as learning", where students learn how to assess their own learning and that of their peers (Alberta Education, 2010b, p. 20). The direction towards a balanced approach to assessment and reporting is equally clearly expressed in a report to the United States Council of Chief State School Officers (Darling-Hammond, 2010). The idea that student assessment is considered as a system which supports a variety of purposes including "informing learning and instruction, determining progress, measuring achievement, and providing partial accountability information" (p. 1).

According to Levin, Glaze and Fullan (2008) a balanced approach has largely been achieved in Ontario. Their article describes how positive partnerships between educators and policy makers demonstrate that "successful large-scale change doesn't require punitive forms of accountability and teacher-proof curricula" (p. 273). They contend that education reform or change has often been informed by wrongheaded approaches, in particular, the increased use of tests as a way to drive improvement. Instead of focussing on the ideological differences surrounding standardised testing, Ontario set ambitious goals for improving elementary literacy/ numeracy outcomes and increasing high school graduation rates and then set about developing and creating specific strategies by which to achieve them. They cite Ontario's education change strategy as representing the fundamental principles grounded in research that are meaningful, sustainable, respectful of professional knowledge and practice, and coherently aligned at the provincial, district and school levels (p. 274). Notable among the many targeted strategies listed is the emphasis on specific teacher professional development to support improved instructional practices, developing strong leadership teams at the district and school levels, adding financial resources to reduce pupil-teacher ratio, adding specialist teachers in the arts and physical education, providing additional time for classroom preparation and professional learning time. A prominent component for sustaining the change over time is the ongoing building of relationships of respect and trust between all stakeholders – government, policy makers, districts, schools, support staff, and the public, in particular between teacher federations and the Ministry of Education: "focus on student outcomes rests on the belief that educators have enormous skill and knowledge to contribute to school improvement" (p. 277). Fullan (2005a, b, 2006a, b) has long been an advocate for seeing sustainability in educational change as a system wide concern where leaders move beyond the immediate focus on increasing student achievement to systemic thinking and capacity building. Two lessons to be drawn from the Ontario experience are, first, that capacity building is the main driver to success and second, "to recognize the fallacy that heavy-handed accountability can create success; instead, getting better results is being more accountable … balancing accountability and capacity building and integrating top-down and bottom-up forces in strong partnerships" (Levin et al., 2008, p. 280).

Volante (2007) suggests that the majority of Ontario teachers and their unions have not widely embraced the recent assessment-led reforms. Similar concerns such as the danger of narrowing the curriculum, issues of reliability and validity as well as suspicion that external testing does not necessarily result in system improvement are listed (p. 6). Most contentious is the reporting of results in a manner that purports to indicate genuine student achievement rather than acknowledging test context and limitations: "over-reliance on large-scale assessment for accountability has been fraught with flawed assumptions, oversimplified understandings of school realities, undemocratic concentration of power, undermining of the teaching profession, and predictable disastrous consequences for our most vulnerable students" (p. 9). Volante argues that large-scale assessment data are only one part of a comprehensive educational accountability framework that should consider all stakeholders as responsible partners, take into account curriculum embedded assessment, and provide assessment literacy training for administrators and teachers. In fact, educational leadership at all levels, school, district, government, and university (research) plays a pivotal role in bringing about multi-level assessment reform

(Volante & Cherubini, 2007). Despite these concerns, Volante (2007, p. 9) acknowledges some positive effects of this reform agenda such as schools using accountability test data to improve learning as well as increased participation in teacher professional development. Barber (2008) describes the Ontario reform as a refinement of the command and control, top-down approach naming it "government-led". Here, "educators have been successfully led by the government to pursue the moral purpose of higher standards of literacy and numeracy" (p. 74). One reason for its success is the development and execution of its "strategic vision" by a small, highly qualified and "courageous" group who were able to adapt to changing circumstances as the process unfolded (p. 80).

National performance-based literacy assessment in New Zealand designed specifically for such formative purposes represents a balanced approach to political accountability purposes and provides policy makers and educators alike with high quality detailed information for instructional improvement (Gilmore, 2002). Their National Educational Monitoring Project (NEMP) replaced in 2010 by the National Standards School Sample Monitoring and Evaluation (NSSSME) is an imaginatively designed rotating system that assesses all curriculum areas (and impressively all six strands of the Language Arts curriculum) and provides New Zealand educators with detailed diagnostic information for improvement of instructional programmes as well as informing national curriculum reforms (Guskey, Smith, Smith, Crooks, & Stockton, 2006). The NSSSME (and the NEMP before it) conceptual model distinguishes itself from other large-scale assessments by placing teaching and learning at its core, assesses a sample of students for this purpose, and uses a comprehensive range of assessment methods such as one-to-one interviews, team, 'hands on' and independent assessment, extensive use of videotaping to record student performance, and engaging teachers to administer or mark the assessment tasks (Gilmore, 2002). Students in years 1–8 are assessed against clearly established national standards in reading, writing, and mathematics. Predictably, the benefits are wide-ranging to both instructional leaders and teachers.

8.7 Conclusion

This discussion presents a Triple-A framework that considers assessment aims, leadership approach, and accountability as an inter-related and integrated way of considering links between leadership and student assessment. In a context where globalisation and technology have changed the face of professions and public service world-wide (Barber, 2005), where there is increasing pressure to reform education instructional practices and improve student performance to reflect that change, student assessment as the central component of instruction and accountability has received attention like never before. As a consequence of performance-based accountability, educational leaders face the imperative to attain indepth assessment literacy requiring the development of new leadership approaches to meet the implied demands. No longer can teachers work as solo practitioners, no longer can schools be single performing entities, and no longer can leaders be manager administrators removed from what happens in classrooms.

This review reveals three central points as important knowledge for educational leaders regarding the *aims* of assessment: (1) understanding how assessment that lies at the heart of instructional practices will improve student achievement and identifying how this aligns with district or provincial standards; (2) knowing how to facilitate the best practices inherent in the formative assessment model; and (3) being critically aware that narrowing the curriculum and teaching to the test not only negatively affects student achievement but is also counter to student motivation and engagement (Ainsworth & Viegut, 2006; Kohn, 2000; Popham, 2006). The distinctive feature that separates how assessment was thought of in the past compared with how it is conceptualised today is that assessment and instruction are no longer seen as separate enterprises. Advocates for standardised testing see value if the results can contribute to providing useful instructional feedback to students (Covaleskie, 2009). Ainsworth and Viegut (2006) refer to "power standards" that are an identified, prioritised subset of district performance standards (p. 35). These power standards are aligned with common formative assessments (collaboratively developed common assessments for each grade level within a school or district) to inform instruction. Formative assessment transforms how we think about teaching and learning and the roles of students and teachers; it simultaneously focuses on process and outcome without privileging one over the other.

Decisions regarding leadership *approach* are directly informed and impacted by the reconceptualising of assessment as instruction. Leaders of today are necessarily highly focused and their roles have become "deliberately de-romanticised" and transformed as they guide and direct instructional improvement (Elmore, 2004a, p. 57). Decisions on how the management tasks of schools are distributed may be site-based but the distribution of responsibilities still requires leaders to create a common culture of expectations around the use of skills and knowledge "holding the various pieces of the organisation together in a productive relationship … holding individuals accountable for their contributions to the collective result" (p. 59). Viviane Robinson's (2011) research confirms the strong links between leadership and student achievement and not just on standardised tests (p. 3). Her research further supports the shift from emphasis on leadership style to leadership practices, identifying specific leadership practices in five key dimensions: goal setting, strategic resourcing, ensuring quality teaching, leading professional learning, safe and orderly environment. Each one of these dimensions requires leaders' deep understanding and knowledge of the effective practices to support them. They are described in three broad leadership capabilities: applying relevant knowledge, solving complex problems, and building relational trust (p. 16). Taken together, the five leadership dimensions underpinned by three leadership capabilities is termed "student-centred leadership" (p.11). Student-centred leadership is not just about understanding what needs to be in place but how to make it happen. It involves the skilful integration of the three capabilities into the work of the five dimensions.

Finally, tensions at the root of the *accountability*debate appear to stem from the differing needs and perceptions of bureaucratic/political accountability versus professional accountability, historically resulting in the pitting of teachers and their unions against government representatives and policy makers (Møller, 2009). The promise of professional accountability "rests on both individual educators assuming responsibility for following standards of practice and on their professional interaction with colleagues and clients" (Elmore, 2005, p. 34). Individuals and groups take responsibility for instructional practices that improve student learning outcomes, and increased professional collaboration becomes the norm as educators seek to learn and share knowledge and skills necessary to fulfil their perceived responsibilities. Assessment aims, measures and practices that are transparent, utilising best professional knowledge on what works for students, teachers, and parents combined with democratic leadership that involves all stakeholders in principles of consensus, trust, openness and equity is key to success (Darling-Hammond, 2009, p. 53).

References

Ainsworth, L., & Viegut, D. (2006). *Common formative assessment: How to connect standards-based instruction and assessment.* Thousand Oaks, CA: Corwin Press.

Alberta Education. (2006). *Renewed framework for authorities funding school jurisdictions.* Retrieved from: http://education.alberta.ca/admin/funding/accountability/works.aspx

Alberta Education. (2009a). *Accountability in Alberta's education system.* Retrieved from: http://education.alberta.ca/admin/funding/accountability/about.aspx

Alberta Education. (2009b). *How the accountability pillar works.* Retrieved from: http://education.alberta.ca/admin/funding/accountability/works.aspx

Alberta Education. (2010a). *Inspiring education: A dialogue with Albertans.* Retrieved from: http://www.inspiringeducation.alberta.ca/LinkClick.aspx?fileticket=BjGiTVRiuD8%3d&tabid=37

Alberta Education. (2010b). *Inspiring action on education.* Retrieved from: https://ideas.education.alberta.ca/media/2905/inspiringaction%20eng.pdf

Alberta Education. (2011). *Framework for student learning: Competencies for engaged thinkers and ethical citizens with an entrepreneurial spirit.* Retrieved from: http://education.alberta.ca/media/6581166/framework.pdf

Alberta Education. (2013). *Information Bulletin: Student learning assessments update.* Retrieved from: http://education.alberta.ca/media/7561878/slainfobulletineng.pdf

Alberta Teachers' Association. (2005). *Accountability in education: Background paper.* Edmonton, AB, Canada: Alberta Teachers' Association.

Alberta Teachers' Association. (2007). *Real learning first: the teaching profession's view of student assessment, evaluation, and accountability.* Edmonton, AB, Canada: Alberta Teachers' Association.

Amrein-Beardsley, A. (2008). Methodological concerns about the education value-added assessment system. *Educational Researcher, 37*(2), 65–75. doi:10.3102/0013189X08316420.

Barber, M. (2005). National strategies for educational reform: Lessons from the British experience since 1988. In M. Fullan (Ed.), *Fundamental change: International handbook of educational change* (pp. 73–97). New York: Springer.

Barber, M. (2008). From system effectiveness to system improvement: Reform paradigms and relationships. In A. Hargreaves & M. Fullan (Eds.), *Change wars* (pp. 71–96). Bloomington, IN: Solution Tree.

Black, P., & Wiliam, D. (1998). Inside the black box. *Phi Delta Kappan, 80*(2), 139.

Blanchard, J. (2003). Targets, assessment for learning, and whole-school improvement. *Cambridge Journal of Education, 33*(2), 257.

Blankstein, A. M. (2004). *Failure is not an option*. Thousand Oakes, CA: Sage.

Bloom, B. S., Hastings, J. T., & Madaus, G. F. (1971). *Handbook on formative and summative evaluation of student learning*. New York: McGraw-Hill.

Broadfoot, P., & Black, P. (2004). Redefining assessment? The first ten years of assessment in education. *Assessment in Education: Principles, Policy & Practice, 11*(1), 7–26.

Burger, J., Aitken, A., Brandon, J., Klinck, P., McKinnon. G., & Mutch, S. (2001). The next generation of basic education accountability in Alberta, Canada: A policy dialogue. *International Electronic Journal for Leadership in Learning. University of Calgary, 5*(19). Retrieved from: http://www.ucalgary.ca/iejll/burger_aitken_brandon_klinck_mckinnon_mutch#top

Burger, J. M., & Krueger, M. (2003). A balanced approach to high stakes achievement testing: An analysis of literature with policy implications. *International Electronic Journal for Leadership in Learning. University of Calgary, 7*(4). Retrieved from: http://www.ucalgary.ca/iejll/burger_krueger

Couture, J.-C. (2009). Collateral damage of government's accountability policies a key focus of 2009 ARA. *The ATA News, 43*(18).

Covaleskie, J. F. (2009). Two cheers for standardized testing. *International Electronic Journal for Leadership, 6*(2). Retrieved from: http://www.ucalgary.ca/iejll/covaleskie

Darling-Hammond, L. (2004). Standards, accountability, and school reform. *Teachers College Record, 106*(6), 1047–1085.

Darling-Hammond, L. (2009). Teaching and the change wars: The professionalism hypothesis. In A. Hargreaves & M. Fullan (Eds.), *Change wars* (pp. 45–70). Bloomington, IN: Solution Tree.

Darling-Hammond, L. (2010). *Performance counts: Assessment systems that support high-quality learning*. Washington, DC: Council of Chief State School Officers. Retrieved from: http://www.hewlett.org/library/grantee-publication/performance-counts-assessment-systems-support-high-quality-learning.

Darling-Hammond, L., & Pecheone, R. (2010). *Developing an internationally comparable balanced assessment system that supports high-quality learning*. Paper presented at the National Conference on Next Generation Assessment Systems. Retrieved from: http://www.k12center.org/events/research_meetings/next_gen_national_conference.html

Day, C., Sammons, P., Hopkins, D., Leithwood, K., & Kington, A. (2008). Research into the impact of school leadership on pupil outcomes: Policy and research contexts. *School Leadership & Management, 28*(1), 5–25.

Desrosier, J. (2011). Rapid prototyping reconsidered. *The Journal of Continuing Higher Education, 59*, 135–145.

Dinham, S. (2005). Principal leadership for outstanding educational outcomes. *Journal of Educational Administration, 43*(4), 338–356.

Dinham, S. (2007). How schools get moving and keep improving: Leadership for teacher learning, student success and school renewal. *Australian Journal of Education, 51*(3), 263–275.

Dufour, R., & Eaker, R. (1998). *Professional learning communities at work: Best practices for enhancing student achievement*. Alexandria, VA: Association for Supervision and Curriculum Development.

Elmore, R. F. (2004a). *School reform from the inside out: Policy, practice and performance*. Cambridge, MA: Harvard Educational Press.

Elmore, R. F. (2004b). Performance vs. attainment. *Harvard Education Letter, 20*(5), 8–17.

Elmore, R. F. (2005). Accountable leadership. *Educational Forum, 69*(2), 134–142.

Erkens, C. (2009). Paving the way for an assessment rich culture. In T. R. Guskey (Ed.), *The principal as assessment leader*. Bloomington, IN: Solution Tree.

Fuhrman, S. H., & Elmore, R. F. (Eds.). (2003). *Redesigning accountability systems for education*. New York: Teachers College Press.

Fullan, M. (2005a). *Leadership and sustainability: System thinkers in action*. Thousand Oaks, CA: Sage Publications.

Fullan, M. (2005b). Turnaround leadership. *Educational Forum, 69*(2), 174–181.

Fullan, M. (2006a). The future of educational change: System thinkers in action. *Journal of Educational Change, 7*(3), 113–122.

Fullan, M. (2006b). Leading professional learning. (cover story). *School Administrator, 63*(10), 10–14.

Fullan, M., & Hargreaves, A. (1996). *What's worth fighting for in your school*. New York: Teachers College Press.

Gilmore, A. (2002). Large-scale assessment and teachers' assessment capacity: Learning opportunities for teachers in the national education monitoring project in New Zealand. *Assessment in Education: Principles, Policy & Practice, 9*(3), 343–361.

Graczewski, C., Knudson, J., & Holtzman, D. J. (2009). Instructional leadership in practice: What does it look like, and what influence does it have? *Journal of Education for Students Placed at Risk, 14*(1), 72–96.

Grobe, W. J., & McCall, D. (2004). Valid uses of student testing as part of authentic and comprehensive student assessment, school reports, and school system accountability. *Educational Horizons, 82*(2), 131–142.

Gronn, P. (2008). The future of distributed leadership. *Journal of Educational Administration, 46*(2), 141–158.

Guskey, T. R., Smith, J. K., Smith, L. F., Crooks, T., & Stockton, L. (2006). Literacy assessment New Zealand style. *Educational Leadership, 64*(2), 74–79.

Hallinger, P. (2005). Instructional leadership and the school principal: A passing fancy that refuses to fade away. *Leadership & Policy in Schools, 4*(3), 221–239.

Hargreaves, A., & Shirley, D. (2012). *The global fourth way: The quest for educational excellence*. Thousand Oaks, CA: Corwin.

Harlen, W. (2008). Teachers' summative practices and assessment for learning – tensions and synergies. In W. Harlen (Ed.), *Student assessment and testing* (Vol. 1, pp. 292–308). Thousand Oakes, CA: Sage.

Hattie, J. (2009). *Visible learning: A synthesis of over 800 meta-analyses relating to achievement*. Oxon, OX: Routledge.

Hattie, J. (2011). *Visible learning for teachers: Maximizing impact on learning*. Oxon, OX: Routledge.

Klinger, D. A., DeLuca, C., & Miller, T. (2008). The evolving culture of large-scale assessments in Canadian education. *Canadian Journal of Educational Administration & Policy, 76*, 1–34.

Kohn, A. (2000). *The case against standardized testing: Raising scores, ruining schools*. Portsmouth, NH: Heinemann.

Leithwood, K. (2001). School leadership in the context of accountability policies. *International Journal of Leadership in Education, 4*(3), 217–235.

Leithwood, K., & Day, C. (2008). The impact of school leadership on pupil outcomes. *School Leadership & Management, 28*(1), 1–4.

Leithwood, K., Jantzi, D., Earl, L., Watson, N., Levin, B., & Fullan, M. (2004). Strategic leadership for large-scale reform: The case of England's national literacy and numeracy strategy. *School Leadership & Management, 24*(1), 57–79.

Leithwood, K., & Mascall, B. (2008). Collective leadership effects on student achievement. *Educational Administration Quarterly, 44*(4), 529–561.

Levin, B., Glaze, A., & Fullan, M. (2008). Results without rancor or ranking: Ontario's success story. *Phi Delta Kappan, 90*(4), 273–280.

Marks, H. M., & Nance, J. P. (2007). Contexts of accountability under systemic reform: Implications for principal influence on instruction and supervision. *Educational Administration Quarterly, 43*(1), 3–37.

McDonald, M. (2002). The perceived role of diploma examinations in Alberta, Canada. *Journal of Educational Research, 96*(1), 21.

McNeil, L. M. (2000). *Contradictions of school reform: Educational costs of standardized testing*. New York: Routledge.

McTighe, J., & Wiggins, G. (1999). *The understanding by design handbook.* Alexandria, VA: Association for Supervision and Curriculum Development.

Møller, J. (2009). School leadership in an age of accountability: Tensions between managerial and professional accountability. *Journal of Educational Change, 10*(1), 37–46.

Moore, A. D., Dexter, R. R., Berube, W. G., & Beck, C. H. (2005). Student assessment: What do superintendents need to know? *Planning & Changing, 36*(1), 68–89.

Mulford, B. (2006). Leading change for student achievement. *Journal of Educational Change, 7*(1/2), 47–58.

Murphy, J. (2004). Leadership for literacy: A framework for policy and practice. *School Effectiveness & School Improvement, 15*(1), 65–96.

Newton, P. E. (2007). Clarifying the purposes of educational assessment. *Assessment in Education: Principles, Policy & Practice, 14*(2), 149–170.

Nichols, S. L., Glass, G. V., & Berliner, D. C. (2006). High-stakes testing and student achievement: Does accountability pressure increase student learning? *Education Policy Analysis Archives, 14*(1), 1–172.

Parr, J. M., & Timperley, H. S. (2008). Teachers, schools and using evidence: Considerations of preparedness. *Assessment in Education: Principles, Policy & Practice, 15*(1), 57–71.

Parsons, J., & Beauchamp, L. (2012). *From knowledge to action: Shaping the future of curriculum development in Alberta.* Edmonton, AB, Canada: Alberta Education. Retrieved from: http://education.alberta.ca/department/ipr/curriculum/research/knowledgetoaction.aspx.

Penlington, C., Kington, A., & Day, C. (2008). Leadership in improving schools: A qualitative perspective. *School Leadership & Management, 28*(1), 65–82.

Phelps, R. P. (Ed.). (2005). *Defending standardized testing.* Mahwah, NJ: Lawrence Erlbaum Associates, Inc.

Popham, W. J. (1999). Why standardized tests don't measure educational quality. *Educational Leadership, 56*(6), 8.

Popham, W. J. (2001). *The truth about testing: An educator's call to action.* Alexandra, VA: Association for Supervision and Curriculum Development.

Popham, W. J. (2003). *Test better, teacher better: The role of instructional assessment.* Alexandria, VA: Association for Supervision and Curriculum Development.

Popham, W. J. (2006). *Assessment for educational leaders.* New York: Pearson.

Popham, W. J. (2009). Assessment literacy for teachers: Faddish or fundamental? *Theory Into Practice, 48*(1), 4–11.

Reeves, D. B. (2007). From the bell curve to the mountain: A new vision for achievement, assessment, and equity. In D. B. Reeves (Ed.), *Ahead of the curve: The power of assessment to transform teaching and learning.* Bloomington, IN: Solution Tree.

Robinson, V. M. J. (2008). Forging the links between distributed leadership and educational outcomes. *Journal of Educational Administration, 46*(2), 241–256.

Robinson, V. M. J. (2011). *Student centered leadership.* San Francisco: John Wiley & Sons.

Robinson, V. M. J., Lloyd, C. A., & Rowe, K. J. (2008). The impact of leadership on student outcomes: An analysis of the differential effects of leadership types. *Educational Administration Quarterly, 44*(5), 635–674.

Robinson, V. M. J., & Timperley, H. S. (2007). The leadership of the improvement of teaching and learning: Lessons from initiatives with positive outcomes for students. *Australian Journal of Education, 51*(3), 247–262.

Roos, B., & Hamilton, D. (2005). Formative assessment: A cybernetic viewpoint. *Assessment in Education: Principles, Policy & Practice, 12*(1), 7–20.

Rose, A. B. (2009). The courage to implement standards based report cards. In T. R. Guskey (Ed.), *The principal as assessment leader* (pp. 175–200). Bloomington, IN: Solution Tree.

Ross, J. A., & Gray, P. (2006). School leadership and student achievement: The mediating effects of teacher beliefs. *Canadian Journal of Education, 29*(3), 798–822.

Sadler, D. R. (1998). Formative assessment: Revisiting the territory. *Assessment in Education: Principles, Policy & Practice, 5*(1), 77.

Sadler, D. R. (2005). Interpretations of criteria-based assessment and grading in higher education. *Assessment & Evaluation in Higher Education, 30*(2), 175–194.

Sadler, D. R. (2007). Perils in the meticulous specification of goals and assessment criteria. *Assessment in Education: Principles, Policy & Practice, 14*(3), 387–392.

Sadler, D. R. (2009). Indeterminacy in the use of preset criteria for assessment and grading. *Assessment & Evaluation in Higher Education, 34*(2), 159–179.

Sahlberg, P. (2009). Learning first. In K. Gariepy, B. L. Spencer, & J.-C. Couture (Eds.), *Educational accountability: Professional voices from the field* (pp. 1–22). Rotterdam, The Netherlands: Sense Publishers.

Scott, S., & Webber, C. F. (2008). Evidence-based leadership development: The 4 L framework. *Journal of Educational Administration, 46*(6), 762–776.

Scriven, M. (1967). The methodology of evaluation. In R. W. Tyler, R. M. Gagne, & M. Scriven (Eds.), *Perspectives of curriculum evaluation* (pp. 39–83). Chicago: Rand McNally.

Slomp, D. H. (2008). Harming not helping: The impact of a Canadian standardized writing assessment on curriculum and pedagogy. *Assessing Writing, 13*(3), 180–200.

Southworth, G. (2002). Instructional leadership in schools: Reflections and empirical evidence. *School Leadership & Management, 22*(1), 73–91.

Spencer, B. L., & Couture, J.-C. (2009). Introduction. In K. Gariepy, B. L. Spencer, & J.-C. Couture (Eds.), *Educational accountability: Professional voices from the field* (pp. 1–22). Rotterdam, The Netherlands: Sense Publishers.

Spillane, J. P. (2005). Distributed leadership. *Educational Forum, 69*(2), 143–150.

Spillane, J. P., & Orlina, E. C. (2005). Investigating leadership practice: Exploring the entailments of taking a distributed perspective. *Leadership & Policy in Schools, 4*(3), 157–176.

Stiggins, R., & Duke, D. (2008). Effective instructional leadership requires assessment leadership. *Phi Delta Kappan, 90*(4), 285–291.

Tankersley, K. (2007). *Tests that teach: Using standardized tests to improve instruction.* Alexandra, VA: Association for Supervision and Curriculum Development.

Taras, M. (2009). Summative assessment: The missing link for formative assessment. *Journal of Further and Higher Education, 33*(1), 57–69.

Timperley, H. S. (2005). Instructional leadership challenges: The case of using student achievement information for instructional improvement. *Leadership & Policy in Schools, 4*(1), 3–22.

Timperley, H. S., & Parr, J. M. (2007). Closing the achievement gap through evidence-based inquiry at multiple levels of the education system. *Journal of Advanced Academics, 19*(1), 90–115.

United States Department of Education. (1983). A nation at risk: The imperative for educational reform. *The National Commission on Excellence in Education.* Retrieved from: http://www2.ed.gov/pubs/NatAtRisk/index.html

Volante, L. (2007). Educational quality and accountability in Ontario: Past, present, and future. *Canadian Journal of Educational Administration & Policy, 58,* 1–21.

Volante, L., & Cherubini, L. (2007). Connecting educational leadership with multi-level assessment reform. *International Electronic Journal for Leadership in Learning, 11*(12).

Volante, L., Cherubini, L., & Drake, S. (2008). Examining factors that influence school administrators' responses to large-scale assessment. *Canadian Journal of Educational Administration & Policy, 84,* 1–30.

Wang, L., Beckett, G. H., & Brown, L. (2006). Controversies of standardized assessment in school accountability reform: A critical synthesis of multidisciplinary research evidence. *Applied Measurement in Education, 19*(4), 305–328.

Webber, C. F., Aitken, N., Lupart, J., & Scott, S. (2009). *The Alberta student assessment study: Final report.* Edmonton, AB, Canada: Government of Alberta. Retrieved from: http://education.alberta.ca/media/1165612/albertaassessmentstudyfinalreport.pdf.

Wiggins, G. (2009). Real-world writing: Making purpose and audience matter. *English Journal, 98*(5), 29–37.

Wiliam, D. (2006). Formative assessment: Getting the focus right. *Educational Assessment, 11*(3), 283–289.

Wiliam, D., Lee, C., Harrison, C., & Black, P. (2004). Teachers developing assessment for learning: Impact on student achievement. *Assessment in Education: Principles, Policy & Practice, 11*(1), 49–65.

Wright, R. (2009). Methods for improving test scores: The good the bad, and the ugly. *Kappa Delta Pi Record, 45*(3), 116–121.

Part III
Leadership Assessment-Related Knowledge and Behaviours

Chapter 9
The Assessment KSA Learning Journey: Expanding the 4L – Life-Long Learning Leader – Framework

Shelleyann Scott, Donald E. Scott, and Charles F. Webber

Abstract Drawing upon two previous research studies – the International Study of Principal Preparation (ISPP) and the Alberta Student Assessment Study (ASAS) – this chapter expands our '4L (life-long learning leader) framework' and 'assessment leader profile' specifically related to assessment and evaluation. We examine the underlying philosophical orientations, values and beliefs, as well as the socio-political acumen leaders must acquire to be successful assessment change agents. We explore specific knowledge, skills, and attitudes/attributes that leaders must cultivate in order to create optimal assessment practices in their schools and systems. Additionally, we describe how leadership development is an ongoing process commencing at the initial preservice education stage continuing throughout an educator's career, that is 4L – a life-long learning leaders' journey pursuing excellence in assessment leadership and we provide a description of the implications for leaders and professional developers.

Keywords Knowledge • Skills and attributes/attitudes • Leading assessment • Life-long learning leader • Visionary capacity • Boundary breaking entrepreneurialism • Professional skills • Instructional design • Assessment literacy • Ethic of care • Courage and commitment • Political acumen • Social acumen • Instructional design • Instrument design • Innovation and change

S. Scott (✉) • D.E. Scott
Werklund School of Education, University of Calgary, Calgary, AB, Canada
e-mail: sscott@ucalgary.ca; descott@ucalgary.ca

C.F. Webber
Faculty of Continuing Education and Extension, Mount Royal University, Calgary, AB, Canada
e-mail: cfwebber@mtroyal.ca

© Springer International Publishing Switzerland 2016   203
S. Scott et al. (eds.), *Assessment in Education*, The Enabling
Power of Assessment 2, DOI 10.1007/978-3-319-23398-7_9

9.1   Introduction

One of our key findings from the Alberta Student Assessment Study (Webber, Aitken, Lupart, & Scott, 2009) was that assessment was one of the most controversial and politically-charged topics within K-12 education systems. There were many reasons for controversy, some of which were identified as tensions surrounding notions of: assessment being closely associated with accountability that impacted teachers' freedoms and system quality through to national competitiveness; parent concerns with their child's motivation, success, and life opportunities; union contentions that educators' assessment capacities and judgements were a measure of professionalism which was considered sacrosanct; and the clarity of purpose and use of different forms of assessment (Webber, Lupart, & Scott, 2012). Even though many of these issues affect teachers, it is school and district leaders who are most impacted by assessment-related controversies. School leaders must navigate and mediate contentions between students, parents, teachers, superordinates, and policy decision makers, all the while maintaining an ethic of care and commitment to social justice for all students. District leaders must mediate the demands from their ministries, strive for continued enhancement of the quality of education within their jurisdictions, and monitor and report on the teaching, learning, *and* assessment outcomes, all while mediating the sometimes competing interests of the stakeholders who look to their leadership for guidance and support. Leadership responsibilities have essentially expanded the current conceptions of instructional leadership – which were predominantly focused on instructional strategies and approaches, and engagement of students – to overtly including assessment purposes, tools, strategies, as well as the importance of *overtly* considering assessment within the instructional design process.

Contemporary schools are very different places to those we attended decades ago (Gray et al., 1999; Scott & Webber, 2013). Globalisation has made an indelible mark on most school systems around the world. For example, with the interconnectedness of nations' economic markets many countries have experienced reductions in financial expenditure on education as a result of global financial crises; this means that many principals and district leaders are having to exercise their entrepreneurial capacities to do more with less (Baker, 2012; Holmlund, McNally, & Viarengo, 2009; Picus & Odden, 2011). Similarly, many nations are encountering the influx of refugees, immigrants, and/or migrants thereby altering the student demographics of many schools and classrooms, which in turn yields new opportunities but also presents complications for leaders in navigating the demands of increased ethnic, linguistic, religious, cultural, and intellectual diversity (Burke, 2002; Fraser, 2009; Hek, 2005; Keddie, 2011;Lupart & Webber, 2002; Rutter, 2006). Information and Communication Technologies (ICT) are further complicating school contexts in our global village. Since the advent of the World Wide Web in 1990, technology integration into, not only the teaching and learning environments but also, administrative processes and communication mechanisms has accelerated and diversified to such an extent that many school and district leaders feel overwhelmed. Educational leaders' concerns include the management of technological investments and the maintenance of ICT infrastructure, learning how to navigate and effectively use new technologically-mediated administrative tools and approaches, communication, collaboration, and evaluation, as well as assuming responsibility for ensuring their teachers adopt these technologies in an increasingly technologically rich world (Afshari, Bakar, Luan, & Sraj, 2012; Berrett, Murphy, & Sullivan, 2012; Cakir, 2012; Polizzi, 2011). Additionally, leaders must address an increasingly technologically sophisticated student body which frequently raises the sometimes sinister dimensions of technology in schools, for example, cyberbullying and sexting (Gordon-Messer, Bauermeister, Grodzinski, & Zimmerman, 2013; Slonje, Smith, & Frisén, 2013), reduction of privacy, and managing educators' socially-mediated public personas (Cam & Isbulan, 2012; Siegle, 2010; Todoric, 2011). Compared to their counterparts' role expectations of two decades ago, leaders of contemporary schools and districts have very different responsibilities and must have more comprehensive and broad knowledge and expertise in order to credibly fulfil their instructional leadership role. No longer is it sufficient for leaders to just know how to undertake essential administrative operations or to be able to create positive school cultures or to organise teacher development (Leithwood, 2012; Leithwood & Strauss, 2009; Leithwood, Seashore Louis, Anderson, & Wahlstrom, 2004; Mulford, 2008; Mulford, Silins, & Leithwood, 2004); leaders must become 'assessment leaders' in order to be effective change agents in this age of increasing accountability for quality educational outcomes (Webber, Scott, Aitken, Lupart, & Scott, 2013). But how do leaders attain the knowledge and expertise they need? What professional, or indeed, leadership development opportunities will facilitate leaders' attainment of the requisite capacities? The following section outlines a selection of key findings to emerge from the International Study of Principal Preparation (ISPP) and the Alberta Student Assessment Study (ASAS) as it pertains to leading enhanced assessment in schools.

9.2 Background

The two main studies which have supported the findings in this chapter were The Alberta Student Assessment Study (ASAS) and The International Study of Principal Preparation (ISPP). We outline in this section the different research foci in these studies and provide an overview of the contexts, participants and research design in each.

The Alberta Student Assessment Study (ASAS) was a large-scale, province-wide study in Alberta, Canada which reported on (1) assessment theory, policies, and practices that inform decision making, (2) leadership approaches that support enhancement in assessment and reporting, and (3) educators' professional development needs and the frameworks that can support ongoing development of educators' assessment capacities. This 2-year study involved a range of educational stakeholders from both the macro levels (external to the school – including district leaders, ministry personnel, union and professional association officials, parent councils, trustee members, university faculty, and professional development consortia members); and the micro levels (internal to the school – students, teachers, leaders, and parents). The study was underpinned by the pragmatic paradigm (Creswell, 2012) thereby utilised mixed methodology encompassing questionnaires and interviews with students, parents, and educators (including school leaders), as well as role-alike and cross-role focus group interviews with educators, and the macro level stakeholder groups (Gay, Mills, & Airasian, 2012). The ASAS involved 3,312 individuals across the province and was the largest, most indepth research about assessment in its broadest sense ever conducted in Alberta. There were 78 individuals who represented macro level stakeholder perspectives who participated in focus groups; at the micro level, there were 2,542 questionnaires collected (n = 195 educators, n = 799 parents, and n = 1,548 students) and 692 individuals who engaged in interviews or focus groups (n = 22 school leaders, n = 163 teachers, n = 462 students, and n = 46 parents). All school levels and types were represented in the data set, including elementary/primary, middle/junior high, senior high, K–9 and K–12 as well as public, separate (Catholic), magnet, alternative, charter schools, and home schooling.

The International Study of Principal Preparation – this research study has continued over 9 years and focuses on novice principals' leadership concerns and leadership preparation and development experiences. Unlike the ASAS study, this research has been conducted across 13 countries around the world – Australia, Canada, China, England, Germany, Jamaica, Kenya, Mexico, New Zealand, Scotland, South Africa, Tanzania, Turkey, and the United States of America. There were four main stages: (1) the mapping of available leadership development opportunities in each cultural context, (2) indepth interviews with novice leaders that led to the creation of a range of case studies, (3) a questionnaire that included both rating-type responses and open-ended items, and 4) analyses spanning the various data sets within the varied national settings, as well as cross-cultural comparisons (Denzin & Lincoln, 2011; Patton, 2002).

Even though the ASAS directly targeted assessment, with one of its foci as 'leadership', it only encompassed one province in Alberta, while the ISPP was international in scope and explored the full range of leadership responsibilities but only with novice principals. Hence, both studies' findings serve as the foundation for this chapter enabling us to examine issues in leading assessment within the overall frame of leadership in complex schooling environments around the world using the real-life experiences and perceptions of teacher-leaders, assistant/deputy principals, novice through to experienced principals, and district leaders.

From the ISPP findings, Scott and Webber (2008) created the 4L (Life-Long Learning Leader) framework which was designed to offer professional developers, university faculty, and system leadership development providers with a framework. The 4L framework included five dimensions – *visionary capacity, boundary breaking entrepreneurialism, instructional design and assessment literacy, professional skills, crisis management* – along with specific leadership responsibility foci that were teachable. Our findings specifically targeting leading assessment from the

ASAS study led to our proposing an assessment leader profile (Webber et al., 2013), which identified four important aspects of assessment leadership: leaders' personal qualities that included "values, theoretical understandings" and their "professional skills, procedural knowledge and a vision that leads to informed action" (p. 11). While reflecting on these two studies we found there was considerable alignment within the findings which afforded us the opportunity to revisit and expand the leadership development foci in the 4L framework to specifically articulate the 'what' and 'how' of developing leadership capacities to enhance assessment in schools. Both the ASAS and ISPP studies were aligned within the pragmatic paradigm as both utilised mixed methodology; therefore, with this paradigmatic and methodological alignment, we felt comfortable in engaging in "warranted assertion analysis" (Ongwuegbuzie, Johnson, & Collins, 2009, p. 119) described by Smith (1997) as "repeated reading of the data as a whole and then arriving inductively and intuitively at a set of credible assertions" (p. 80). In this chapter we focused on extracting the nuances of leading assessment and what that entailed, as this had not been previously examined in the ISPP in any great detail. From our warranted assertion analysis we derived more sophisticated understandings of what leaders need to know, what skills they need to acquire and hone, and what philosophical orientations and values they must nurture that will positively influence their approach to leading principled and sound assessment and evaluation along with their interactions with key stakeholders.

Even though many publications have emerged from the ISPP, there were none that specifically targeted leaders' capacities to promote enhanced assessment and evaluation approaches and practices. Wildy and Clarke (2008) reported on the inadequacies of the largely experiential preparatory experiences of Australian principals which resulted in novice school leaders struggling with adjusting to the social, physical, and professional isolation inherent in the principalship particularly in small and remote communities; the need to develop personal resilience and efficacy; balancing work-life demands; and coping with the visibility of the principalship. Principals reported being unprepared for the many challenges within diverse cultural contexts, and the tensions that they encountered in meeting the needs of the local community, while being constrained by centralised policy mandates. They indicated they needed to develop stronger interpersonal skills in order to effectively partner with parents and other community members as well as to navigate the contentiousness of managing poor performing teachers. Cowie and Crawford's (2008) exploration of Scottish head teachers' preparatory experiences found similar issues to Wildy and Clarke, but they identified that much of the tension for Scottish head teachers revolved around the development of a professional identity and the establishment of principal-efficacy. Slater, Garcia, and Gorosave (2008), in their study of the principalship in Mexico, also reported inadequacy of preparation to cope with the tensions between system demands and local needs. Additionally, they indicated concerns with corruption in the selection of principals which led to a lack of confidence in the system and in the credibility of the leader – an issue which was also identified in principals' reports from Bulgaria (Karstanje & Webber, 2008), Kenya (Okoko, Scott, & Scott, 2012), and Tanzania (Onguko, Abdalla, & Webber, 2008).

Similar to the concerns expressed about system mandates and policy implementation in other settings, Nelson, de la Colina, and Boone (2008) found a high-stakes climate of accountability in the US had led to the socialisation of principals to prioritise administration and management over that of a "lifeworld view [which] is about developing human capital within the school community" (p. 697). Interestingly, only Nelson (2008) and her colleagues and Scott and Webber (2008) reported overt concerns with educational system expectations for efficiency and accountability which directly related to assessment and evaluation in schools, whereas the others discussed policy and system demands in more general terms. When considering the focus in this chapter which explores leadership development, it is useful to consider whether the ISPP participants reported preparation for instructional leadership – specifically leading assessment – as usual in their settings. Generally, principals in Australia, Bulgaria, Kenya, Mexico, South Africa, and Tanzania had largely only experiential preparation, including the roles and responsibilities in other school leadership positions or curriculum leadership roles, which clearly left many feeling unprepared for the complexities of their principalship including leading assessment. Further analyses revealed that these principals may not have had sufficient experience as leaders to necessarily make the direct connection between instructional leadership (particularly leading assessment) and the system expectations related to accountability, and indeed many perceived these to be completely divorced concepts rather than two sides of the assessment and evaluation coin. The following paragraphs provide some useful definitions that explore the nuances of the terminology of assessment and evaluation and how these relate to the responsibilities within the principalship.

9.2.1   Defining Assessment and Evaluation

Barry and King (1998) identified distinct links between assessment and accountability:

> assessment and evaluation can serve such purposes as: … demonstrating accountability for taxpayers' money spent on education … but because of the large amount of government money spent on public education, systems and schools need to demonstrate that the money is being well spent. System wide assessment and evaluation of learning is seen as one way of providing this financial accountability. (p. 331)

To further complicate these issues for leaders in performing their instructional leadership role, our findings from the ASAS indicated there was considerable confusion among educators and associated stakeholders surrounding the proliferation of 'assessment' terminology and purposes, as well as understanding the difference between assessment and evaluation. In this chapter we drew upon Hoy and Hoy's (2013) definition of assessment as a "process of gathering information about students' learning. Assessment is broader than testing and measurement" (p. 263). They included Linn and Gronlund's (2000, cited in Hoy & Hoy, 2013) earlier definition that assessment was "any of a variety of procedures used to obtain information about student performance" (p. 263) which could include both classroom-based assessment activities, as well as standardised tests and examinations. A contentious issue articulated in both the ASAS and ISPP was that assessment naturally includes both formative and summative assessment and there were perceptions emerging from staffroom discussions that placed summative and formative assessment across a polarised continuum. Educators tended to believe summative assessment was negative or destructive and yet a part of a system of accountability imposed through top-down policies, while formative was positive and constructive and the only legitimate form of assessment due to its capacity to guide learning and teaching – thereby reflecting teachers' predominant focus, their instructional approaches and students. The literature identifies that formative assessment, or increasingly pervasively termed, 'assessment *for* learning' (Stiggins, Arter, Chappuis, & Chappuis, 2005) occurs before or during instruction and is designed to provide timely feedback, specific guidance, and is frequently non-graded or assigned a mark therefore designed to inform the learning and teaching process (Arends, 2004; Hoy & Hoy, 2013). Summative assessment, similarly termed assessment *of* learning (Black, Harrison, Lee, & Wiliam, 2004), is designed:

> to provide to all interested parties a clear, meaningful, and useful summary or accounting of how well a student has met the teacher's objectives. ... testing is done for the purpose of assigning a letter or numerical grade ... because its primary purpose is to provide an assessment of learning, to sum up how well a student has performed over time and at a variety of tasks. (Snowman, McCown, & Biehler, 2012, p. 487)

Summative assessment therefore clearly has a place in providing a judgement of how well students have achieved the outcomes within a course of study, as well as providing useful information to guide decisions related to academic progression, higher education gatekeeping, and employment. Hence, when comparing and contrasting these two assessment types, formative assessment is not necessarily superior to summative; rather it serves different purposes. Much of the argument for formative over summative is due to the motivational power that exemplary formative feedback can have on student engagement and learning, and for informing teachers' instructional practices. With the prevailing societal demand for leaders to promote student engagement and learning, it is unsurprising that the overt emphasis in schools is for educators to become more skilled at providing sound formative feedback opportunities rather than focusing primarily on the impact of summative assessment.

Further compounding the complexities within assessment, there are increasing forms and approaches within classroom assessment practices. For example, there has been a trend to move away from the predominant forms of classroom-based assessment in the form of tests and exams to more interesting and diverse forms such as performance-based and authentic assessment tasks due to societal expectations for higher level thinking. Snowman et al. (2012) and Hoy and Hoy (2013) indicated that performance-based assessment and authentic assessment are frequently linked as the same or similar due to the 'realistic' nature of the assessment activities. Snowman et al. defined performance assessment as "assessment devices that attempt to gauge how well students can use basic knowledge and skill to perform complex tasks or solve problems under more or less realistic conditions" (p. 613). Arends (2004) explained that it was having "students demonstrate their abilities to perform particular tasks in testing situations" (p. 535) and identified the nuanced difference with authentic assessment as "students demonstrating their abilities to perform particular tasks in *real-life settings*" (p. 530 emphasis added); hence, the difference Arends identified was in the 'context' of the assessment. Hoy and Hoy mused that authentic and performance assessment arose from the dissatisfaction with the limitations of multiple-choice standardised assessment, however, they offer a cautionary note that this form of assessment is most suited to classroom assessment due to its capacity to capture "complex, important, real-life outcomes" (p. 288). Variability in the level of authenticity may occur, and in its extreme form authentic tasks may be designed in collaboration with external stakeholders (arts, business, and/or industry) who commission the task, jointly (with educators and students) establish the parameters of a quality product or production, and have a role to play in the judgement of the final outcome. These authentic tasks create greater student motivation, participation, and perseverance due to the real-life use of the product and engagement with external experts. As Cumming and Maxwell (1999) stated: "authentic achievement should involve constructive learning, disciplined enquiry, and higher-order thinking and problem-solving. It should also have a value dimension, of aesthetic development, personal development or usefulness in the wider world. The last of these implies transfer of learning" (p. 180). Hoy and Hoy reflected that authentic and performance assessment were innovations in assessment (i.e., new), hence there was a need for more attention to be centred on creating high quality authentic assessment tasks. Considering these innovations in assessment and the complexities abounding in this aspect of teaching, it is little wonder that educators may become overwhelmed by the demands to expand their knowledge about assessment and to diversify their practices in order to more appropriately assess knowledge, skills, and attitudes/values of their students in more effective and valid ways. Similarly, leaders have an even more acute responsibility to maintain their own professional learning about assessment innovations as these directly impact instructional leadership, because if leaders' knowledge, skills and attitudes remain static they cannot effectively lead high quality assessment in contemporary schools.

The term evaluation is frequently used interchangeably with summative assessment in educational discourses due to the embedded 'judgement' dimension within evaluation. In the ASAS research, there was some hypersensitivity, or dare we say paranoia, about words such as 'evaluation' and 'ranking' due to perceptions that making judgements about students, teachers, schools, or systems was automatically a negative or destructive phenomenon. These biases against summative assessment and evaluation denied the unavoidable elements of judgement that occur within the workplace, industry, post-secondary institutions, and indeed everyday life. Evaluation in the macro or overview sense uses a range of assessment data as well as other sources of data from stakeholders and participants to determine whether outcomes have warranted the fiscal investment (Barry & King, 1998; Webber, Lupart, & Scott, 2012). Evaluation, though, can also be applied to different judgements of impact or merit such as that of the effectiveness of a programme of study, resources and materials, and teaching; and in the discipline of programme evaluation it examines the outcomes and worth of courses, programmes, curricula, systems, or initiatives (Smith & Ragan, 2005). Therefore, evaluation of pedagogy and programmes serves a valuable purpose in yielding information that can actually inform teaching and learning, as well as resource (re-)allocation. It is more often the macro form of evaluation that aligns with the administrative responsibilities of principals and system leaders who are charged with monitoring and reporting on programmes, initiatives, and whole-school and district overall performance quality as part of their accountability mandate. Leaders must have knowledge of these varied forms of assessment and evaluation, in order to effectively lead assessment and use the information these elicit to inform learning and teaching, and other decision making processes in their school or district.

In the ASAS project we encountered a number of instructional leaders who were exemplars of leaders of enhanced assessment. These leaders embodied much of what we are exploring in this chapter as essential knowledge, skills, and attributes/attitudes (KSA), and where we encountered a failure of leadership, this was found to be due to deficits in one or more components we have outlined in the 4L framework. Therefore, we note the need for school leaders to embrace the assessment side of their instructional leadership role, but even though there is a myriad of information about instructional leadership, it is frequently difficult for leaders to ascertain the following: what being an 'assessment leader' looks like; what they should know and be able to do in relation to assessment and evaluation; as well as the relationships between seemingly unrelated aspects such as forging trusting relationships with staff and community stakeholders and creating clarity about the purposes of different forms of assessment. In other words, how do leaders acquire the 'big picture' of assessment and evaluation and develop an appreciation of how they themselves and their school community fit into the macro assessment and evaluation landscape? Clearly there is a need to identify what knowledge, skills, and attitudes/attributes (including philosophies and values) assessment instructional leaders must have in order to create a map for leadership development content and approaches.

9.3 Revisiting and Expanding the 4L Framework

This section expands the initial 4L (Life-Long Learning Leader) framework (Scott & Webber, 2008) and our earlier conceptualisations of the 'assessment leader profile' (Webber et al., 2013) to explore the teachable aspects for leaders of assessment and evaluation that may be useful to inform leadership development programming. In the 'assessment leader profile' we highlighted four main aspects that leaders need to have in order to be effective in leading assessment. These four aspects included: knowledge of assessment and evaluation; their values; professional skills; and procedural knowledge. We identified that leaders' values and knowledge were mediated and shaped by their personal qualities which in turn moulded their initial leadership vision. In our original 4L framework, published in Emerald's *Journal of Educational Administration* in 2008, we included dimensions, key components of the dimensions, and leadership development foci. This new expanded version has had 'interpreting leading enhanced assessment' added (see Table 7.1) and integrates the aspects from the 'assessment leader profile'. The following sections highlight the features of leading enhanced assessment within each dimension.

9.3.1   Visionary Capacity

In our initial 4L framework (Scott & Webber, 2008), we explained the importance of a leader's visionary capacity in creating and co-conceptualising frameworks with teachers founded upon principals' fundamental philosophical underpinnings. In interpreting leading enhanced assessment, leaders' attitudes and interactions are influenced by their heightened *ethic of care* for students and a sense of fairness and equity. *Fairness and equity* are actually teachable aspects of assessment and so cross over into the knowledge domain. For example, the Centre for Research in Applied Measurement and Evaluation (1993) developed a document that outlined the principles for fair student assessment practices which serves as an excellent guide, as does Aitken's (2012) work exploring how to incorporate the student voice in the pursuit of increased fairness. Equity is one of the most poorly understood concepts in assessment with non-equitable approaches frequently rationalised by teachers in terms of: preparation of students for the workplace, teaching life skills, perceptions of being seen to be fair to all in the class by treating all the same, and so on. Leaders must understand that equity is not the same as equality; indeed, while equality means being treated the same as everyone else equity means meeting the unique needs of the individual student which may be quite different to others in the class. Leaders need to be able to understand and communicate this simple complexity in order to educate others, especially teachers who do not perceive the nuances of this 'equity/equality' construct.

In leading their school to examine current assessment practices and become more innovative, to interrogate their assumptions, and resolve conflicts that can arise over assessment issues, leaders also need to have *courage and commitment* – courage to stand against the prevailing traditions or norms and commitment to protecting the vulnerable, usually the students – to ensure that educators do the right thing founded upon deep theoretical understandings of principled assessment.

In our previous work (Webber & Scott, 2012), we identified that leaders also need to have a clear understanding of the different purposes of assessment and how these may vary at different levels of the education system, and the appropriate uses of various data. Linked with these 'big picture' (macro) insights, leaders also need to have honed their "multidimensional" thinking where they are able to understand the perspectives of different stakeholder groups and weigh the merits of their rhetoric in relation to assessment (p. 42). Within the assessment leaders' capacity to *plan and implement* is the need to be able to navigate and balance the demands of teachers and students, and indeed, other stakeholders, to ensure conflicting perspectives do not override the potential benefits to students. Integrated into what we described in the assessment leader profile (Webber et al., 2013) as procedural/pragmatic knowledge is leaders' capacity to interpret, analyse, and follow system procedures, manage administrative approaches and paperwork related to assessment, and in some cases, work around restrictive district or system procedures in their pursuit of innovative assessment and evaluation.

9.3.2 Boundary Breaking Entrepreneurialism

Earlier we emphasised the impact of globalisation to illustrate differences in contemporary schools and the increasingly complex role of school and district leaders. Boundary breaking entrepreneurialism emerged originally from the work of Webber and Robertson (1998) and appears highly relevant in explaining our assertion that boundary breaking entrepreneurial assessment leaders must be innovative change agents, must be able to juxtapose the familiar and the foreign in assessment, and challenge accepted practices while embracing ambiguity. Assessment leaders need to challenge 'accepted' tacit knowledge in assessment when it is not founded upon established theoretical knowledge, or where accepted, or maybe 'acceptable knowledge', has been skewed by particular stakeholder groups with the view to winning a political argument or establishing the rights of their stakeholders at the expense of others. The embracing ambiguity may mean that the leader may not have all the answers but is willing and able to continue his/her learning to seek answers. It involves leaders having accurate knowledge of, and the capacity to effectively communicate, the different purposes of assessment to achieve optimal assessment for: the individual student, the whole school, the district, and the nation and society.

Boundary breaking entrepreneurial assessment leaders must also seek to create innovation in the assessment approaches in their school and district. This does not mean that boundary breaking entrepreneurial assessment leaders must know it all, but it does imply that they can access and utilise the expertise of both school-based and external experts within the educational system who can support their vision for innovation and change. Even though these assessment leaders are not expected to know everything about assessment, their theoretical knowledge does need to be sufficiently deep and comprehensive in order to be make sound judgement about the merits of the many 'experts' in assessment to determine if those experts have an appropriate philosophical orientation to support change in the school or district. At the same time, leaders should be able to use a range of quantitative and qualitative data to inform their vision and agency as change leaders for enacting innovation in assessment and instructional practices.

Innovations may include establishing moderation processes within a grade level, across a course/unit, across the school, and even across the district. 'Moderation' may include establishing systems of teaming teachers who have smaller classes with colleagues teaching larger classes in the same subject or year level across schools with the view to sharing assessment tasks, co-creating common assessments, and working together to increase the consistency of teacher judgements and moderate the parity of grading across the larger group. It may involve increasing the transparency of grading practices thereby de-privatising and demystifying marking and grading methods, to interrogate and eliminate poor assessment practices, and increase opportunities for teachers to be exposed to innovations in assessment from colleagues and/or experts.

The other key aspect of boundary breaking entrepreneurial assessment leadership is the cultivation and application of political acumen in the service of principled and courageous innovation and change. This entails the garnering of support and harnessing goodwill in the pursuit of the refinement of assessment practices aligned with whole school/whole district pedagogical innovation. The politically-astute, boundary breaking, entrepreneurial assessment leader (yes you did read that list correctly) is one who understands and navigates the fine balance between being daringly innovative and committing career suicide, or worse, reaching burnout through neglect of personal health and "wellbeing" (Riley, 2013; Webber & Scott, 2013, pp. 111–112).

9.3.3 Professional Skills

We originally identified the *ethic of care* as a professional skill but while not necessarily misplaced, it appeared better situated as part of leaders' philosophical orientation which influenced their beliefs, values, and attitudes and which ultimately shaped their vision for assessment and evaluation. There is no doubt that the ethic of care, in concert with leaders' knowledge of and belief in fairness and equity, is influential in establishing authentic leadership in order to build trusting relationships with students, teachers, parents/caregivers, and the wider community through leaders' appreciation and navigation of alternative perspectives, thereby demonstrating their *social acumen*. Authentic leadership embodies the following characteristics and actions: knowledge of self, being thoughtful and knowledgeable, being informed by one's own and one's followers' values and moral perspectives, an awareness of the context in which one leads, deep knowledge and strength, and being moral, efficacious, resilient, and hopeful (Avolio & Gardner, 2005; Gardner, Cogliser, Davis, & Dickens, 2011, p. 1122). This is not to say that leaders have to agree with everyone or align with dominant cultures in their school but it does mean they would need to effectively *communicate* with their educators and community to establish transparency, set and explicitly communicate high standards for teachers in relation to the leader's assessment vision, *collaborate* with various stakeholders, *solve problems* and *resolve conflicts*, as well as *make sound decisions*. This means leadership credibility hinges upon transparency, visibility, and proactivity in leading assessment.

Apart from *communication* skills, *collaboration* is another professional skill that is essential for an assessment leader. This means that assessment leaders must be able to not only collaborate individually with teachers, parents, community leaders, and assessment experts, but also facilitate the collaborative teaming of their teachers and experts to work on assessment innovations – such as in-class assessments, moderation processes, or discussing the implications of standardised test reports. The capacity to *solve problems* involving assessment can also be linked with engaging teachers in establishing and supporting assessment innovation. When students disengage or perform poorly in assessments it may be because assessments are pointless, meaningless, boring, or demotivating and as a result educators should refrain from automatically blaming students for poor performance and engagement, rather actively become involved in assessment redesign and innovation.

Assessment can frequently cause conflict, particularly between students and teachers or between teachers and parents; therefore, problem solving may be closely related to *conflict resolution* whereby leaders must use their knowledge of sound and principled assessment, along with their values, beliefs, and social acumen to mediate between angry students, parents, teachers or others and negotiate a solution that promotes student learning and motivation. The professional skill of *decision making* can be interwoven with collaboration and discussion. Once leaders have collaborated with educators and other stakeholders, they must have the courage and commitment to actually make a decision that ensures students are not harmed and the right course of action is taken. Sometimes these decisions are not popular but if it is the principled thing to do in the service of sound assessment then the leader must have the strength of character to follow through and clearly explain the decision to the various involved parties. It is in these tense situations where a leader's *social acumen* is best employed to coalesce his/her interpersonal skills, effective communication skills (including active listening, and verbal and gestural communication), and critical and creative thinking to analyse the situation and consider possibilities to create positive solutions and make an appropriate decision, all while remaining true to his/her ethic of care. Finally, leaders need to use *metacognition* to *reflect* upon their strengths and weaknesses, and to understand their personal limitations in knowledge, skills, and attitudes in order to remain humble and willing to seek advice and support from other experts and colleagues.

9.3.4   Instructional Design and Assessment Literacy

Previously we identified the need for leaders to be "highly competent in the area of instructional design and who have sound assessment and evaluation literacies" which would aid their confidence in communicating and working with stakeholders (Scott & Webber, 2008, p. 772). We anticipate that most leaders would have been teachers and teacher-leaders prior to aspiring to the formal school leadership position. Therefore, leaders usually do have a wealth of discipline-specific experience and knowledge about assessment, including a deep understanding of instructional design that encompasses appreciating the important role of assessment in planning teaching and learning, how it drives the selection and attainment of learning outcomes, and the importance of achieving alignment between course/unit outcomes, learning experiences and activities, and the assessment approaches. More recently the emphasis has been on the differentiation of assessment for the inclusive classroom, which means that instructional leaders need to understand how to alter assessment tasks and their assessment approaches in order to accommodate the diverse learning needs of their students (e.g., different approaches for gifted and talented students, altered tasks for cognitively delayed students, etc.). Drawing upon their teaching expertise, leaders need to understand instrument design in terms of the principles of developing effective questions (both multiple choice and open-ended exam questions), how to create useful and informative rubrics, how to establish inquiry projects, and how and why to negotiate assessment with students. A part of leaders' assessment literacy is to acquire a clear and unambiguous understanding of a range of assessment terminology, which is essential in demystifying and deconstructing complex assessment constructs with their staff. They should have deep understandings of the principles of sound assessment including how assessment drives educators' decision making, and students' motivation, engagement, and the depth of their learning approaches; in other words, the psychology that underpins assessment is important knowledge for leaders to be able to create constructive teaching and learning environments in their schools.

The amount of assessment and evaluation data that is collected by schools and which flows back to schools from their district or system leaders is phenomenal. These data-rich reports provide valuable resources for the statistically and interpretively literate assessment leader to use for evidence-based decision making and vision creation. This assumes though that the leader has the requisite statistical and interpretive literacies to be able to validly and credibly collect, process, and analyse a range of statistical and open-ended data in order to make sufficient sense of it so that he/she can explain the implications for change to their staff, students, parents, and community. Frequently these literacies are mediated via technologically sophisticated software, so leaders would also need to either access the technological expertise to assist them or personally expand their IT capacities in order to work with these data. Statistical and interpretive literacies may not necessarily have been requisite for a teacher; hence these literacies may need to be dimensions of assessment leadership that have to be developed beyond the capacities of a teacher or teacher-leader.

9.3.5 Crisis Management

Our original conceptualisation of crisis management was quite a traditional one, wherein principals frequently managed crises which they had to defuse and mediate. The cases that we originally considered included violence aimed at staff or administrators, teacher-student altercations, gang interactions, or student bullying issues that can easily escalate into serious incidents. As we conducted the ASAS, we also found that assessment and evaluation can generate considerable emotion, tension, and outright passionate controversy. Some examples of these 'assessment crises' included: students who reacted angrily due to their perception that teachers had been unfair in their assessment of their work; student fears of unfair or unpredictable school-based grading in their university entrance exam year; parent perceptions of unfairness – particularly where behaviour and learning outcome performance had been coalesced; teachers had not differentiated assessment for special needs students; students' frustration with their inability to access requisite accommodations in assessment situations; teachers' concerns with being evaluated as a result of standardised test reports and discomfort or outright rejection of assessment change processes; and/or community anger over their school's standardised test results reported in the media. What we propose in this *assessment crisis management* dimension is for leaders to use their ethic of care coupled with their courage and commitment to protecting the vulnerable, namely students, by investigating the legitimacy of stakeholder concerns, accessing support agencies in the service of the vulnerable, and by facilitating teachers' professional development in the pursuit of more effective, fair, and equitable assessment. Our final point was that when assessment leadership was strong, leaders demonstrated discernment and social acumen to right wrongs, and took action to ameliorate harm to students from poor assessment approaches, all while remaining respectful of the various stakeholder perspectives – treating all with dignity. We advocate for this form of leadership, perceiving it to be a higher level dimension, as it combines leaders' beliefs and values with their knowledge of principled and effective assessment, the exercise of social acumen, and good communication skills to be able to achieve change agency – the intentional action in pursuit of their goal – namely, more effective and accurate assessment which will optimise student learning and achievement.

In addition to the previously discussed dimensions, the original 4L framework encompassed the dimensions of 'career stage', 'career aspirations', and the 'approaches to leadership development' (not included in Table 9.1). Career stage, career aspirations, and approaches to leadership development varied from the other dimensions (i.e., visionary capacity, boundary breaking entrepreneurialism, professional skills, instructional design and assessment literacy, crisis management) as they did not necessarily relate to specific content or discipline-specific knowledge or skills. Career stage acknowledged that novice principals were likely to have different concerns than those of their more experienced or veteran leader-peers. Likewise, the career aspirations dimension recognised the uniqueness of the individual and identified that leaders may have varied career pathways and be striving for different long-term goals or positions. Therefore, the revisions of the 4L framework in terms of assessment leader knowledge, skills, and attributes/attitudes (KSA) does not directly include the 'career stage' and 'career aspirations' dimensions. We do, however, address some considerations in relation to these dimensions in the next section where we explore the conceptualisation of educators' and leader-aspirants' life-long learning journey and how this might occur, especially related to leadership capacity in assessment and evaluation.

Table 9.1 Revisions to the 4L framework to interpret leading enhanced assessment

Dimensions	Key components of dimension	Leadership development foci	Interpreting leading enhanced assessment
Visionary capacity NOTE: Content *focuses on knowledge attainment and retention and may influence philosophical orientations and development of educationally appropriate values/beliefs – usually the focus of leadership development programming*	Philosophical underpinnings Individual/personal Classroom School District System	Self-reflection and articulation of fundamental beliefs Conceptualising frameworks Implementation planning Evaluation	***Philosophical/Values underpinnings:*** Ethic of Care. Fairness and Equity – develop and share their understanding of equity (meeting the unique needs of the individual) which is not the same as equality (treating all the same). This means leaders explore the nuanced conceptualisation of equity and equality with teachers and support staff to ensure they understand and apply the principles of fairness *and* equity not equality. Courage and Commitment. ***Framework:*** Conceptualising the big picture of assessment – purposes and limitations of different assessments. Understanding different stakeholder perspectives – multidimensional thinking. ***Implementation planning:*** Balancing the needs of teachers and needs of students. Balancing the demands of different stakeholder group. Procedural/pragmatic knowledge – a knowledge of the system, when things need to happen, and how to use the processes and procedures to advance innovation.

| Boundary breaking entrepreneurialism | Political (Acumen) Cross-cultural Technological Theoretical/experiential Global Temporal Spatial | Possibilising Challenging accepted knowledge Juxtaposing the familiar and the foreign Reconsidering space, time, and practice Innovation Embracing ambiguity | *Challenging accepted knowledge:* Challenging established unsound assessment approaches. Challenging unbalanced/skewed stakeholder perspectives. *Innovation:* Seeking to create innovation in assessment approaches (e.g., moderation processes within a grade level, across a course/unit, across schools, and across districts). Across school-teaming of teachers who have small classes with teachers who have large classes for parity and consistency in making sound assessment judgements. Embedding transparency – de-privatising teaching and learning (in the classroom). Encourage/promote the expansion of assessment approaches to, and types of assessment to meet the diverse needs of students. Use both quantitative and qualitative data to inform leaders' vision and approach as change agents for innovations in assessment and instructional practices. *Political acumen:* Understanding the system as well as the perspectives of stakeholders – subordinate, superordinate, and peer/associates – in order to garner support, and harness goodwill to drive innovation and change (unions, professional associations, reporters, parents etc.). The capacity to understand and effectively communicate the different purposes of assessment to achieve optimal assessment for the individual, the whole school, the district, nation, and society. Access internal/external expertise to support innovation in assessment and instruction. Understanding and navigating the fine balance between being a boundary breaking leader and committing career suicide, damaging personal health and wellbeing. |

(continued)

Table 9.1 (continued)

Dimensions	Key components of dimension	Leadership development foci	Interpreting leading enhanced assessment
Professional skills *NOTE:* *Skills are rarely developed or assessed – should be overtly included into leadership development, both formal programming and informal/experiential learning opportunities*	Ethic of care approaches Communication Critical and creative thinking Social acumen	Trust building Conflict resolution Relationships Collaboration Appreciating alternative perspectives Problem-solving heuristics Decision making capacity	Engage in authentic leadership approaches to build *trusting relationships* with teachers, students, and the community by *appreciating alternative perspectives* (uses the Philosophies/Values elements – this involves demonstrating an Ethic of Care). *Communication* – create transparency, set high standards for all teachers and students, be explicit about expectations, and be visible and proactive in leading assessment. *Collaboration* with teachers and experts and coordinate assessment focused professional development with the view to increasing assessment understandings and expertise (not just about statistical literacies with standardised testing results). *Problem-solving* linked with *innovation* – to enhance assessment for a range of groups - individual–classroom–whole-school performance. *Conflict resolution* – mediate and negotiate with varied stakeholder groups to ensure best practices. *Decision making capacity* – once discussion and collaboration is completed the *courage* and *commitment* to actually make the decision and follow through. *Social acumen:* Understand and be able to coalesce interpersonal skills, effective communication (including active listening and verbal and gestural communication), critical and creative thinking, and the ethic of care to create trust and positive relationships with a range of stakeholders. The reflective capacity that engenders humility – to understand the limits of personal leadership knowledge, skills, and attitudes along with the willingness to seek advice and support from experts.

Instructional design and assessment literacy	Principles of curriculum, learning experiences, and assessment	Philosophies of learning and assessment	**Instructional design:**
NOTE: Content focuses on knowledge attainment and retention and may influence philosophical orientations and development of educationally appropriate values/beliefs – usually the focus of leadership development programming	Information analyses Statistical and interpretive literacies	Instructional design Instructional and assessment strategies Communication with stakeholders	As part of a principal's instructional leadership role (and drawing upon his/her expertise as a teacher): develop and share with staff their deep understandings of the role of assessment within instructional design process. Understand how instructional design, including assessment processes and materials, may be differentiated for inclusionary practices – e.g., gifted students need different approaches to assessment. **Instrument design:** Understandings of good practice in designing sound assessment tasks – texts, exams, questions, negotiating assessment with students, rubrics, etc. Avoid confusion and create clarity amongst teachers/students/parents about ambiguous assessment terminology and constructs. **Principles of curriculum, learning experiences, and assessment:** Understand how assessment drives decision making regarding - learning outcomes, instructional practices, and the design of learning experiences. An understanding of the psychology of how assessment influences motivation across various stakeholders. **Statistical and interpretive literacies:** Develop the capacity to read, interpret, and utilise statistical and interpretive data and reports in order to: Determine meaning and implications Communicate the meaning to others Facilitate and guide educators' enhanced instructional approaches (e.g., psych reports) Access expertise to support innovation in teaching and learning Use for evaluative purposes and to create a vision for positive change (e.g., students' learning, teacher development, school development, district innovations, community engagement, etc.) To be able to collect, process, and analyse a range of data using valid/rigorous and/or trustworthy instruments and processes in order to create school-based reports that inform decision making and stakeholders within and external to the school – this may include technological skills in being able to use relevant software to aid the processing and analysis of data.

(continued)

Table 9.1 (continued)

Dimensions	Key components of dimension	Leadership development foci	Interpreting leading enhanced assessment
Crisis management	Internal 　Student 　Teacher 　Parent External 　System 　Community	Processes Legalities System demands Protecting the vulnerable Accessing support services Personal resilience Post-event analyses	Using an *ethic of care*, and *courage and commitment*, ensure leaders are *protecting the vulnerable*, namely students, *accessing support services* in the service of the vulnerable and to be entrepreneurial within the confines of societal legalities and system demands. Having the discernment (*social acumen*) to right wrongs and to ameliorate harm to the vulnerable while remaining respectful of the various stakeholders' perspectives and treating all with dignity.

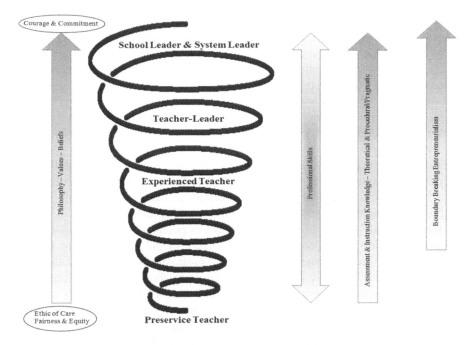

Fig. 9.1 Life-Long Learning Leader Leadership Development Spiral

9.4   Implications for Leadership Development

The 4L framework that we have expanded in this chapter presents an extensive and daunting array of learnable assessment knowledge that school and district leaders must acquire, as well as a range of skills/capacities they must refine, and philosophies, values, and beliefs they must adopt which ultimately influences their leadership approaches. At first glance, an educator who aspires to be a school leader may be tempted to change his/her mind about reaching out for a leadership position if they are expected to know, be able to do, and appreciate all of the aspects previously described. However, in this section we outline how this enhanced assessment leadership capacity can be achieved over time, through various professional development pathways, without running the risk of burning out as a novice leader.

9.4.1   The Spiral of Educator Development

Figure 9.1 depicts our conceptualisation of the pathways of development for enhanced assessment leadership capacity over the course of an educator's life-long learning journey. This encompasses the foundational philosophies, values and beliefs; theoretical and procedural knowledge; professional skills and expertise, as well as boundary breaking entrepreneurialism. We chose an upward 'knowledge and expertise spiral' as this indicated upward movement through the levels of experience, with the outward circling indicating the expansion of an educator's knowledge and skill capacity. The starting point is at the preservice teacher stage wherein aspirant teachers are initially exposed to educational theory and early practicum experiences. Aligned with our life-long learning leader (4L) career trajectory, novice teachers continue their educational learning journey, gaining expertise in instruction and assessment as they engage in various inservice professional development activities until they achieve mastery as experienced teachers. These master teachers can provide leadership (i.e., teacher-leadership) to their less experienced colleagues and share their expertise with others while continuing their own personal 4L journey through engagement in ongoing professional development activities. Teacher-leadership should be encouraged within districts as this can be the first step in succession planning for formal leadership positions. This means that system leaders will have a ready pool of highly expert educators potentially willing to undertake formal leadership roles. Pools of aspiring leaders should be targeted for further, more sophisticated assessment and evaluation professional development that will provide them with requisite knowledge and expertise, thus allowing them to effectively operate in response to system, political, and societal expectations. By the time an aspiring leader actually assumes the mantle of formal leadership he/she will have accrued an extensive knowledge-base in instruction, assessment and evaluation, along with a range of expertise as a result of his/her life-long learning journey as a professional educator. So this raises the question "what knowledge and skills are appropriate at specific stages of an educator's life-long learning journey?"

9.4.2   Philosophical Development

In our expanded version of the 4L framework for enhanced assessment leadership, we posit that the vast majority of prospective educators enter preservice education programmes with a high level of altruism and a strong desire to nurture the potential of their future students. During their undergraduate preparation, preservice teachers' admirable humanistic philosophies would be further expanded and refined to a heightened ethic of care and a deep understanding of fairness and equity, not only in general, but particularly as applied to assessment and evaluation. These philosophical foundations must be consciously nurtured throughout educators' careers as it is easy for teachers to become cynical and jaded when faced with the day-to-day stressors within their role and in encountering the sometimes negative enculturation within schools thereby tarnishing positive values and beliefs, and teacher-efficacy. As educators progress up the spiral they need to maintain and expand their integrity to educator professionalism and expertise which, when nurtured, will ultimately sustain their commitment to 'doing the right thing for students' and, as leaders, ensure they have the requisite courage to challenge poor or unfair practices which harm students.

9.4.3 Professional Skills

Over the past two decades, professional skills (sometimes referred to as soft skills or generic skills) have been highlighted as crucial for professional success. We have identified a range of professional skills that are pivotal for enhanced assessment leadership, namely: critical and creative thinking which includes problem-solving and decision-making (with both encompassing analytical skills); communication – interpersonal and intrapersonal (reflective capacities); collaboration and team working; information literacy (the capacity to access, analyse, and appropriately use information from a range of credible sources); and technology literacy (the capacity to employ a range of software and approaches to generate useful information from raw data). Ultimately one of the most important higher order skills is social acumen which entails a coalescence of interpersonal skills, effective communication (including active listening), collaboration, and mediation and negotiation to resolve conflict. The capacity to build trust, similar to social acumen, is an overview or higher order skill encompassing an individual's positive values and beliefs about people, appreciation of alternative perspectives, ability to work effectively in teams (or in leading teams), and to communicate with clarity and honesty.

Professional skills are an interesting aspect of the 4L framework as they do not necessarily have a uniform starting point (hence the double arrow in Fig. 9.1); that is, individuals who enter preservice education programmes all have different strengths and weaknesses and the same can be posited for all experienced educators. Hence, we recommend that educators engage in targeted reflection thereby facilitating the identification of personal professional skill capacities with the view to develop and refine weaker skills within the set we have articulated as important, while reinforcing those that are already strong. We advocate for this reflection to commence in preservice to enable educators' time and opportunity to engage in professional development activities that will facilitate their 4L skill development.

9.4.4 Theoretical and Procedural Assessment Knowledge

Figure 9.2 highlights the development of *theoretical and procedural knowledge* that teachers develop over the course of their career. It is understood that the knowledge that preservice teachers gain in their undergraduate teacher preparation programmes will continue to be refined from foundational theoretical knowledge – to experienced educator knowledge – to sophisticated teacher-leader knowledge – to sophisticated knowledge for enhanced assessment leadership appropriate for the role and responsibilities of school and/or system leaders. Hence, theoretical and procedural knowledge acquisition is somewhat hierarchical, in that educators as professionals will build on early foundations, continually pursuing professional development in order to know more, to become more proficient, and expand and hone their

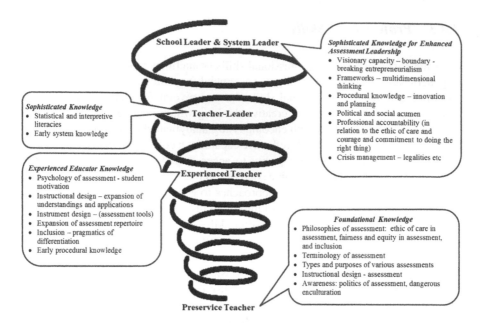

Sophisticated Knowledge for Enhanced Assessment Leadership
- Visionary capacity – boundary - breaking entrepreneurialism
- Frameworks – multidimensional thinking
- Procedural knowledge – innovation and planning
- Political and social acumen
- Professional accountability (in relation to the ethic of care and courage and commitment to doing the right thing)
- Crisis management – legalities etc

Sophisticated Knowledge
- Statistical and interpretive literacies
- Early system knowledge

Experienced Educator Knowledge
- Psychology of assessment - student motivation
- Instructional design – expansion of understandings and applications
- Instrument design – (assessment tools)
- Expansion of assessment repertoire
- Inclusion – pragmatics of differentiation
- Early procedural knowledge

Foundational Knowledge
- Philosophies of assessment: ethic of care in assessment, fairness and equity in assessment, and inclusion
- Terminology of assessment
- Types and purposes of various assessments
- Instructional design - assessment
- Awareness: politics of assessment, dangerous enculturation

Fig. 9.2 Educators' Expanding Theoretical and Procedural Assessment-related Knowledge

assessment knowledge and practices with the view to ensuring they facilitate optimal instructional and assessment practices to the benefit of all students.

9.4.5   Boundary Breaking Entrepreneurialism

Table 9.1 presents boundary breaking entrepreneurialism within the expanded 4L framework as entailing three major components: (1) challenging accepted knowledge, (2) seeking to create innovation in assessment approaches, and (3) using political acumen in order to garner support and harness the goodwill needed to drive innovation and change, while maintaining a balance between entrepreneurialism and burnout. Figure 9.1 depicts this capacity as commencing some time after the novice teacher stage as we felt that it was unreasonable to expect a novice educator to display these capacities, nor would one expect these to be within the purview of a novice; rather, experienced teachers, teacher-leaders, and definitely formal leaders would be advised to engage in and demonstrate these capacities. Leaders' philosophical underpinnings of courage and commitment are interwoven with innovation and change; therefore, boundary breaking leaders challenge teacher complacency and poor practice. Indeed, for innovation and change to occur within such traditional environments as schools, leaders must refine these sometimes uncomfortable or confronting capacities in order to facilitate positive and constructive change to advance the learning outcomes of all students.

9.5 Leadership Development Implications

Although this expanded 4L framework might appear overwhelming in terms of the expectations on leaders to have these aspects of required assessment and evaluation knowledge and skills, we reiterate that much of this knowledge is acquired over a professional lifetime of learning. We posit that the value of this expanded 4L framework is to overtly identify what leaders in schools and systems need to know, be able to do, as well as appreciate and value within the highly politicised and contentious sphere of assessment and evaluation. We advocate that leaders who aim to be enhanced assessment leaders in their school or system reflect on this expanded framework to compare their own knowledge, skills, and attributes/attitudes (KSA) repertoire to identify personal gaps.

Honest reflection is important in guiding leaders' identification of necessary professional development (formal, informal, and/or experiential) that will ensure they have the complete complement of deep assessment and evaluation understandings and expertise needed for enhanced assessment leadership. Professional development may include formal coursework collaboration with experts focused on solving assessment and evaluation problems, professional reading from credible evidence-based literature, webs of enhanced practice (Scott & Scott, 2010), workshops and conferences that explore effective research informed practice and so on. Understanding the complexities and time constraints experienced by principals, it is important that leadership development is targeted, informative, and designed to fill the gaps the leader has identified in his/her own personal knowledge base and/or as a result of a lack of experience.

On a cautionary note, regarding making sound choices of leadership development, it is important for leaders to consider the credibility of the professional development programme in terms of content and provider, keeping in mind that assessment and evaluation are highly politicised with many partisan parties. Hence, professional development that is provided by an organisation which is known to have a partisan affiliation to a particular stakeholder group or indeed to a particular ideology may need to be judiciously evaluated regarding the level of credence and objectivity that can be ascribed to their programme. Another aspect that needs to be carefully considered is the avoidance of inappropriate "cross-cultural borrowings" (Webber & Scott, 2012, p. 41). This means that the lessons learned or findings from other cultural contexts may not be directly relevant, appropriate, or indeed desirable across all nations. Even though there are many similarities in policies, practices, debates, and assumptions within the sphere of assessment and evaluation in educational settings there are also many significant differences. These differences may surface in relation to: the approach to policy implementation, the nuances and unintended outcomes from policies and practices within particular contexts, and cultural mores and understandings that may influence teachers', systems', and communities' expectations and actions. These cultural differences imply the inadvisability of indiscriminate transfer and overlay of policies and approaches that have worked elsewhere directly to different contexts (LeTendre, Baker, Akiba, Goesling, & Wiseman, 2002).

Professional development activities which encourage leaders to identify their own and their followers' assessment misconceptions and misunderstandings, and which promote the interrogation of prevailing political argumentation and controversies are valuable in increasing leaders' critical thinking capacities, thereby expanding their perspectives from more restricted school-based concerns to more macro perspectives. It is important for leaders to seek high quality professional development that overtly promotes objective consideration of a range of theory and practices and multidimensional perspectives, while deconstructing complex and controversial arguments in order to facilitate and reinforce intelligent, balanced, and courageous assessment leadership.

References

Afshari, M., Bakar, K. A., Luan, W. S., & Sraj, S. (2012). Factors affecting the transformational leadership role of principals in implementing ICT in schools. *Turkish Online Journal of Educational Technology, 11*(4), 164–176.

Aitken, N. (2012). Student voice in fair assessment practice. In C. F. Webber & J. L. Lupart (Eds.), *Leading student assessment* (pp. 175–200). Dordrecht: Springer.

Arends, R. (2004). *Learning to teach* (6th ed.). Boston: McGraw-Hill Companies Inc.

Avolio, B. J., & Gardner, W. L. (2005). Authentic leadership development: Getting to the root of positive forms of leadership. *The Leadership Quarterly, 16*(3), 315–338. doi:10.1016/j.leaqua.2005.03.001.

Baker, B. D. (2012). *Revisiting the age-old question: Does money matter in education?* (pp. 1–37). Washington, DC: The Albert Shanker Institute.

Barry, K., & King, L. (1998). *Beginning teaching and beyond* (3rd ed.). Katoomba, NSW: Social Sciences Press.

Berrett, B., Murphy, J., & Sullivan, J. (2012). Administrator insights and reflections: Technology integration in schools. *Qualitative Report, 17*(1), 200–221.

Black, P., Harrison, C., Lee, C., & Wiliam, D. (2004). Working inside the black box: Assessment for learning in the classroom. *Phi Delta Kappan, 86*(1), 8–21.

Burke, G. (2002). *Financing lifelong learning for all: An international perspective* (pp. 1–25). Melbourne, Australia: Centre for the Economics of Education and Training.

Cakir, R. (2012). Technology integration and technology leadership in schools as learning organizations. *Turkish Online Journal of Educational Technology, 11*(4), 273–282.

Cam, E., & Isbulan, O. (2012). A new addiction for teacher candidates: Social networks. *Turkish Online Journal of Educational Technology, 11*(3), 14–19.

Cowie, M., & Crawford, M. (2008). "Being" a new principal in Scotland. *Journal of Educational Administration, 46*(6), 676–689.

Creswell, J. W. (2012). *Educational research: Planning, conducting, and evaluating quantitative and qualitative research* (4th ed.). Boston: Pearson Education Inc.

Cumming, J. J., & Maxwell, G. S. (1999). Contextualising authentic assessment. *Assessment in Education: Principles, Policies and Practices, 6*(2), 177–194.

Denzin, N., & Lincoln, Y. (Eds.). (2011). *The SAGE Handbook of qualitative research* (4th ed.). San Francisco: Sage Publications, Inc.

Fraser, N. (2009). *Scales of justice: Reimagining political space in a globalizing world.* New York: Columbia University Press.

Gardner, W. L., Cogliser, C. C., Davis, K. M., & Dickens, M. P. (2011). Authentic leadership: A review of the literature and research agenda. *The Leadership Quarterly, 22*(6), 1120–1145. doi:10.1016/j.leaqua.2011.09.007.

Gay, L. R., Mills, G. E., & Airasian, P. (2012). *Educational research: Competencies for analysis and applications* (10th ed.). Upper Saddle River, NJ: Pearson Education Inc.

Gordon-Messer, D., Bauermeister, J. A., Grodzinski, A., & Zimmerman, M. (2013). Sexting among young adults. *Journal of Adolescent Health, 52*(3), 301–306. doi:10.1016/j.jadohealth.2012.05.013.

Gray, J., Hopkins, D., Reynolds, D., Wilcox, B., Farrell, S., & Jesson, D. (1999). *Improving schools: Performance and potential*. ERIC Document: ED437740.

Hek, R. (2005). *The experiences and needs of refugee and asylum seeking children in the UK: A literature review*. Birmingham, UK: National Evaluation of the Children's Fund, University of Birmingham.

Holmlund, H., McNally, S., & Viarengo, M. (2009). *Does money matter for schools?* London: Centre for the Economics of Education. London School of Economics and Political Science.

Hoy, A., & Hoy, W. K. (2013). *Instructional leadership. A research-based guide to learning in schools*. Upper Saddle River, NJ: Pearson Education.

Karstanje, P., & Webber, C. F. (2008). Programs for school principal preparation in East Europe. *Journal of Educational Administration, 46*(6), 739–751.

Keddie, A. (2011). Pursuing justice for refugee students: Addressing issues of cultural (mis)recognition. *International Journal of Inclusive Education, 16*(12), 1295–1310. doi:10.1080/136031 16.2011.560687.

Leithwood, K. (2012). School leadership, evidence-based, decision-making, and large-scale student assessment. In C. F. Webber & J. Lupart (Eds.), *Leading student assessment* (pp. 17–40). Dordrecht: Springer.

Leithwood, K., Seashore Louis, K., Anderson, S., & Wahlstrom, K. (2004). *How leadership influences student learning*. New York: Wallace Foundation.

Leithwood, K., & Strauss, T. (2009). Turnaround schools: Leadership lessons. *Education Canada, 49*(2), 26–29.

LeTendre, G. K., Baker, D. P., Akiba, M., Goesling, B., & Wiseman, A. (2002). Teachers' work: International isomorphism and cultural variation in the U.S., Germany, and Japan. *Mensa Research Journal, 33*(Winter), 46–71.

Lupart, J., & Webber, C. F. (2002). Canadian schools in transition: Moving from dual education systems to inclusive schools. *Exceptionality Education Canada, 12*(2&3), 7–52.

Mulford, B. (2008). *The leadership challenge: Improving learning in schools*. Camberwell, VIC: Australian Council for Educational Research.

Mulford, B., Silins, H. C., & Leithwood, K. (2004). *Educational leadership for organisational learning and improved student outcomes* (Vol. 3). Dordrecht, Netherlands: Kluwer Academic Publishers.

Nelson, S. W., de la Colina, M. G., & Boone, M. D. (2008). Lifeworld or systemsworld: What guides novice principals? *Journal of Educational Administration, 46*(6), 690–701.

Okoko, J.M., Scott, S., & Scott, D.E. (2012). *Perceptions of school principals in Nairobi about their leadership preparation*. Paper presented within the symposium "Enhancing leadership development in the international community" at the annual meeting of the American Educational Research Association, Vancouver, Canada, April 13–17.

Onguko, B., Abdalla, M., & Webber, C. F. (2008). Mapping principal preparation in Kenya and Tanzania. *Journal of Educational Administration, 46*(6), 715–726.

Ongwuegbuzie, A. J., Johnson, R. B., & Collins, K. M. T. (2009). Call for mixed analysis: A philosophical framework for combining qualitative and quantitative approaches. *International Journal for Multiple Research Approaches, 3*, 114–139.

Patton, M. (2002). *Qualitative research and evaluation methods* (3rd ed.). Thousand Oaks. CA: Sage Publishing Inc.

Picus, L. O., & Odden, A. R. (2011). Reinventing school finance: Falling forward. *Peabody Journal of Education, 86*(3), 291–303. doi:10.1080/0161956X.2011.578986.

Polizzi, G. (2011). Measuring school principals' support for ICT integration in Palermo, Italy. *Journal of Media Literacy Education, 3*(2), 113–122.

Riley, P. (2013). *The Australian principal health and wellbeing survey* (pp. 1–79). Clayton, VIC: Monash University.

Rutter, J. (2006). *Refugee children in the UK*. Maidenhead, UK: Open University Press.

Scott, D. E., & Scott, S. (2010). Innovations in the use of technology and teacher professional development. In J. O. Lindberg & A. D. Olofsson (Eds.), *Online learning communities and teacher professional development: Methods for improved education delivery* (pp. 169–189). Hershey, PA: IGI Global.

Scott, S., & Webber, C. F. (2008). Evidence-based leadership development: The 4L framework. *Journal of Educational Administration, 46*(6), 762–776. doi:10.1108/09578230810908343.

Scott, S., & Webber, C. F. (2013). Entrepreneurialism for Canadian principals: Yesterday, today, and tomorrow. *Journal of Research on Leadership Education, 8*(1), 113–136. doi:10.1177/1942775112443438.

Siegle, D. (2010). Cyberbullying and sexting: Technology abuses of the 21st Century. *Gifted Child Today, 33*(2), 14–16.

Slater, C. L., Garcia, J. M., & Gorosave, G. L. (2008). Challenges of a successful first-year principal in Mexico. *Journal of Educational Administration, 46*(6), 702–714. doi:10.1108/09578230810908299.

Slonje, R., Smith, P. K., & Frisén, A. (2013). The nature of cyberbullying, and strategies for prevention. *Computers in Human Behavior, 29*(1), 26–32. doi:10.1016/j.chb.2012.05.024.

Smith, M. L. (1997). Mixing and matching: Methods and models. *New Directions for Evaluation, 74*, 73–85. doi:10.1002/ev.1073.

Smith, P. L., & Ragan, T. J. (2005). *Instructional design* (3rd ed.). New York: Wiley Publishing Inc.

Snowman, J., McCown, R., & Biehler, R. (2012). *Psychology applied to teaching* (13th ed.). Belmont, CA: Wadsworth Publishing.

Stiggins, R. J., Arter, J., Chappuis, J., & Chappuis, S. (2005). *Classroom assessment for student learning: Doing it right-using it well*. Kingston, ON: Canada Educational Testing Service.

Todoric, M. E. (2011). Guidelines for acceptable electronic communication with students. *Education Digest: Essential Readings Condensed for Quick Review, 77*(3), 47–49.

Webber, C. F., Aitken, N., Lupart, J., & Scott, S. (2009). *The Alberta Student Assessment Study: Final Report*. Edmonton: The Government of Alberta. Available at: http://education.alberta.ca/media/1165612/albertaassessmentstudyfinalreport.pdf.

Webber, C. F., Lupart, J., & Scott, S. (2012). The ecology of student assessment. In C. F. Webber & J. Lupart (Eds.), *Leading student assessment* (pp. 283–296). Dordrecht: Springer.

Webber, C. F., & Robertson, J. (1998). Boundary breaking: An emergent model for leadership development. *Education Policy Analysis Archives, 6*(21), 1–24.

Webber, C. F., & Scott, S. (2012). Student assessment in a Canadian civil society. *Journal of Management Development, 31*(1), 34–47. doi:10.1108/02621711211190989.

Webber, C. F., & Scott, S. (2013). Principles for principal preparation. In C. L. Slater & S. Nelson (Eds.), *Understanding the principalship: An international guide to principal preparation* (Vol. 19, pp. 73–100). Bingley, UK: Emerald.

Webber, C. F., Scott, S., Aitken, N., Lupart, J., & Scott, D. E. (2013). Leading assessment for enhanced student outcomes. *School Leadership & Management, 33*(3), 240–255. doi:10.1080/13632434.2013.773885.

Wildy, H., & Clarke, S. (2008). Principals on L-plates: rear view mirror reflections. *Journal of Educational Administration, 46*(6), 727–738.

Chapter 10
Grading and Reporting Student Learning

E. Nola Aitken

Abstract The essence of this chapter is classroom grading practice and reporting student learning. Issues with current grading practice and reporting are discussed. This discussion is followed with implications of changing from traditional grading and reporting practices to those that reflect fair assessment practice and accurate communication of student results. The chapter concludes with suggestions and recommendations for implementing outcomes-based reporting of student learning.

Keywords Assessment • Evaluation • Summative evaluation • Formative assessment • Grading practice • History of grading • Punitive grading • Second chances • Bullying and grade inflation • Rewards and awards • Grading options • Assessment for learning • Assessment of learning • Reporting student learning • Grading issues • Fair assessment practice • Outcomes-based grading and reporting • Standards-based grading reporting • Classroom-based assessment • Leadership implications • Teacher bias

10.1 Grading and Reporting Student Learning

The Power of Grading
Like a vulture
the old professor
poises over me
smiling
then cuts and tears
my ideals
severing my values
and grades me
according to
the amount of me

E.N. Aitken (✉)
Faculty of Education, University of Lethbridge, Lethbridge, AB, Canada
e-mail: nola.aitken@uleth.ca

© Springer International Publishing Switzerland 2016
S. Scott et al. (eds.), *Assessment in Education*, The Enabling
Power of Assessment 2, DOI 10.1007/978-3-319-23398-7_10

that is him.
Patti Armstrong, 17
(King & Ranallo, 1993, p. 327)
Reprinted with permission

One of the most discussed and contested topics in education in the twenty-first century is student assessment and evaluation. This topic has emerged largely because of the lack of knowledge of fair assessment and grading practices in classrooms (Nitko & Brookhart, 2007, 2011; O'Connor, 2007; Stiggins, 2008). Two unfair grading practices that surface are (a) punitive grading, such as assigning a zero to work not handed in on time, and (b) inaccurate grading and reporting that results from aggregating student behaviours with student achievement. O'Connor (2007) identified 13 other unfair grading practices that teachers commonly use in schools today that contribute to this contested topic. Currently, however, many teachers in western countries are reviewing their assessment practices and are attempting to make positive changes to evaluation and reporting, to name a few: New Zealand, England, Germany, North America, and Australia (Baird, 2013; Battle River School Division No. 31, 2012; Edmonton Public Schools, 2013; Elk Island Public Schools, 2007; Gill & Bramley, 2013; Guskey, 2011; Guskey & Jung, 2006; Harsch & Martin, 2013; Olson, 2010; Ontario Ministry of Education, 2010; Ronne, 2010; Smaill, 2013; Woods & Griffin, 2013).

In the western educational systems, student assessment review has been overdue. Unfair assessment and confusion about accurate grading and reporting practices in public education have prevailed for over 150 years (Baird, 2013; Brookhart, 2004, 2013; Smaill, 2013). Consequently, reviewing evaluation practices and making a paradigm shift to fair assessment practice and new ways of reporting have been difficult not only for teachers, but students and parents as well (Guskey, 2007, 2011; Guskey & Jung, 2006).

10.1.1   Definition of Terms

The terms "grading" and "marking" are used interchangeably in most education texts. In this chapter, however, I have made a distinction between the two: grading refers to *summative evaluation* while marking refers to *formative assessment*; albeit the two are closely linked.

10.1.1.1   Grading

Grading student work is used with assessment *of* learning, or evaluation: [Assessment] of learning is a summative assessment to make judgments about student learning. Summative assessment is planned for predetermined events that occur at the end of a unit, activity, course, term, or program, and used for grading and reporting purposes to share with those outside the classroom. (Webber, Aitken, Lupart, & Scott, 2009, p. 4)

10.1.1.2 Marking

"Marking" is not grading. Marking means marking students' work with relevant formative feedback using a purposeful rubric to help students recognise their strengths and show them how to improve their work and become independent learners. In other words, marking could be likened as assessment *for* learning. *Evaluative* feedback such as "Good job!" can encourage students but it does little in describing what must be done next for improvement. Marking, when done well, is essentially a focused conversation between the student and the teacher using specific *descriptive* feedback for improving skills, knowledge, and understanding.

The focused conversation, or assessment for learning, "requires a culture in which student and teacher learn together in a collaborative relationship, each playing an active role in setting learning goals, developing success criteria, giving and receiving feedback, monitoring progress, and adjusting learning strategies" (Ontario Ministry of Education, 2010, p. 30). When this practice is carried out, the teacher, acting as a "lead learner", gradually releases more and more responsibility to the student to attain the goal of being an independent learner (Ontario Ministry of Education, 2010).

Sometimes teachers also provide written or oral feedback along with a value (numerical or letter grade) on students' work drafts for a comparison with their next attempt. In this case students are given a "second chance" to improve their work. For individual purposes, that is, using feedback and a grade or some kind of numerical value for comparing against him or herself can be a motivating factor for students to achieve a personal best. In these cases, students are compelled to read or discuss the accompanying feedback to improve their former grade. It is important to understand that this numerical indicator of level of performance or "grade" is used for comparison of the individual student's *prior* work against his or her *next* submission or draft. It is not intended to be used for comparison with other students. Indeed, Black and Wiliam (1998) state that "feedback to any student should be about the particular qualities of his or her work, with advice on what he or she can do to improve, and should avoid comparisons with other students" (p. 143). Further, Black, Harrison, Lee, Marshall, and Wiliam's (2004) research reveals that when a grade is coupled with feedback for improvement and used for comparative purposes with *other* students, the students look only at the grade and disregard the feedback. The purpose of formative feedback that occurs in marking is not used for making comparisons with other students but to inform the student about how to improve and set goals for further progress.

10.2 Review of the Literature

Most teachers dislike evaluating and grading students (Black & Wiliam, 1998; Burke, 2009; Earl & Katz, 2006; Elmore, 2005; Miller, Linn, & Gronlund, 2009; Nitko & Brookhart, 2007, 2011; O'Connor, 2002; Stiggins, 2002). Assigning a grade is difficult at best, and heart wrenching at worst (Barnes, 1985; Thorndike, 1997, cited in Allen, 2005). One reason for teachers' discomfort with assessment practice is their struggle with the perceived competing assessment purposes (Black et al., 2004; Earl, 2003; Earl & Katz, 2006; Elmore, 2005; Guskey, 2004a; Hargreaves, Earl, Moore, & Manning, 2001; Marzano, 2000, 2006; O'Connor, 2002; Stiggins, 2001). Teachers traditionally are poor assessors of student learning; they lack the necessary confidence and skills and therefore are uneasy when making judgment calls about student learning (Brookhart, 1999, 2013; Earl, 2003; Earl & Katz, 2006; Elmore, 2005; Hargreaves et al., 2001). Furthermore, many teachers are unaware of, or cautious about trying new and reliable grading practices (Allen, 2005; Guskey, 2004a; Stiggins, 1993). It is hardly surprising then that "'Grades have long been identified by those in the measurement community as prime examples of unreliable measurement' (Brookhart, 1993; Stiggins, Frisbie, & Griswold, 1989)" (Guskey, Swan, & Jung, 2010, p. 3).

10.2.1 A Brief History of Grading

Examinations, grading, and reporting procedures used in modern times were first developed in schools and universities in Western countries about 1850 AD (Brookhart, 2004, 2013; Guskey, n.d.; New South Wales Department of Education and Communities, 2013; Worsfold, n.d.). From the 1870s onward, more and more children started attending school and the increased enrolment brought with it an increase in diverse skills. Because of the enrolment increase, the need to sort, rank, and grade became necessary to match students' abilities with their appropriate grade levels.

In those early public school years, reporting student learning was carried out in a written narrative form for elementary school students while high school students received percentages and letter grades. Even in those early years debate raged over grading practices and reporting. For example, teachers in the 1800s complained that "assessment and grading were too burdensome and parents complained that the information was difficult to interpret" (Reynolds, Livingstone, & Wilson, 2009, p. 280). Although twenty-first century grading practice has become more consistent, the frustration and debate continue – with no sign of abating (Guskey, n.d.).

Until most recently, few teachers had formal training in evaluation methods and most teachers had limited knowledge of effective grading practices (Gullickson, 1986; Schafer & Lissitz, 1987; Slavin, 1994; Stiggins, 2002; Webber et al., 2009). Left to their own devices, teachers relied on the same methods they experienced as students (Allen, 2005; Guskey, 2004a; Guskey & Bailey, 2001; Stiggins, 1993). Teachers who used these traditional and often ineffective methods unwittingly evaluated unfairly, so it is not surprising that students were nervous when graded work was returned to them.

10.3 Grading Issues

Because of the difficulties in student evaluation much has been written in the past 25 years about the issues of grading practices (Allen, 2005; Black & Wiliam, 1998; Black, Harrison, Lee, Marshall, & Wiliam, 2003; Black et al., 2004; Brookhart, 2004; Chappuis, Stiggins, Chappuis, & Arter, 2011; Loveland, 2005; Marzano, 2000, 2006; Nitko & Brookhart, 2011; O'Connor, 2002; Reeves, 2004; Wormeli, 2006a, 2006b). Some researchers suggest that grades should not be used at all, given the psychological damage they do (Kohn, 1999; Majesky, 1993; Pike, 1991), the competitiveness that results (Brandt, 1995), and their widespread unreliability (Kohn, 1999; Willis, 1993). Others recommend changing grading practices so that student learning is reported more fairly and consistently. But changing grading practice is fraught with obstacles and issues. Dropping grades from report cards has caused a hue and cry from more than a few teachers, students, and parents (Freeman, 2010; Guskey et al., 2010; Olson, 2010), yet assigning grades does not seem to be the answer either.

10.3.1 Teachers', Students', and Parents' Issues: An Overview

Wormeli (2006a) in addressing the current grading issues states that: "A grade is supposed to provide an accurate, undiluted indicator of a student's mastery of learning standards. That's it. It is not meant to be a part of a reward, motivation, or behavioral contract system" (p. 19). Nonetheless, Wormeli's understanding is not necessarily that of all educators, students, or parents. The following provides some insights into why grading has been poorly dealt with these past 150 years or more.

10.3.1.1 Teacher Issues

When dealing with classroom assessment and evaluation teachers have two main purposes: (a) to diagnose students' strengths and weaknesses to provide relevant enrichment and supports for learning, and (b) to grade student work and communicate the results to parents, students, and others. These purposes sound clear and simple enough but in reality teachers are embroiled in a two-hat dilemma. Wearing the assessment feedback-for-learning hat the teacher is the guide, the mentor, coach, and cheerleader who supports students through their learning and achievement challenges; whereas, wearing the evaluation hat, the teacher as judge assigns a value or grade to student work. Both hats are at odds with one another — a binary opposition if you will (Aitken, 1994; Apple, 1979; Grennon Brooks & Brooks, 1993).

10.3.1.2 Student Issues

Students are also confused about the two-hatted teacher. From the students' perspective, which hat is the teacher wearing today? Grader or assessor? Friend or foe? In a nutshell, students are often perplexed about grading procedures. Depending upon the teacher's idiosyncrasies, a student in one class could receive an "A"; however, in another class with a different teacher, he or she could receive a "B" for the same quality of work. Fortunate is the student with the easy grader, but *misfortunate* also for providing the student with a misguided belief in his or her superior skills and knowledge. Research indicates grading is so unreliable that the same work may be given two different grades by the same teacher who reads it at two different times, never mind two different teachers giving different grades for the same work (Kirschenbaum, Napier, & Simon, 1971). Kohn (1999) sums up grading inconsistencies in this way: "In short, what grades offer is spurious precision — a subjective rating masquerading as an objective assessment" (n.p.).

In spite of these dubious grading practices, some students are "addicted" to grades (Kohn, 1999, n.p.). Students are so externally motivated by them that one high school student has admitted, "We've turned into assessment pigs. I love credits and grades. I'll do anything for a bonus project!" (Webber et al., 2009, p. 54). Some students live vicariously through their assigned grade (Brookhart, 2013). Kohn (1999) concurs, citing his experience: "Personally, I've taught high school students who reacted to the absence of grades with what I can only describe as *existential vertigo* (Who am I if not a B + ?)" (n.p.).

Other students despise grades because of teachers' grading inconsistencies. For example, one teacher assigns a zero for late work, a second teacher deducts marks for it, whereas the third gives second chances to complete it (Reeves, 2004). Punitive evaluation and grading disparity among teachers appear to run rampant and leave nervous students at the mercy of their teachers.

10.3.1.3 Parent Issues

If students aren't confused enough, adding parents can exacerbate the confusion. That combination lends itself to heated discussion and further debate and frustration (Webber et al., 2009). Clearly parents – the least involved – are the most confused (Brookhart, 2013; Wiggins, 1994). They feel they can't keep up with the new grading systems and report cards that seem to come and go at will. Although educators make attempts to involve parents in report card change and development, usually the depth of understanding about the reasons for the change is absent (Guskey & Jung, 2006; Olson, 2010; Webber et al.).

One of the grading issues that parents face is comprehending and interpreting reporting indicators. Not surprisingly, many parents still relate to traditional ways of reporting, that is, through percentages and letter grades (Nitko & Brookhart, 2011; Webber et al., 2009). When grades aren't reported this way on their child's report card, "Parents frequently try to take the point system and put a percent to it and that's difficult because those points or numbers don't relate to percentage and they don't understand that" (Webber et al., p. 119).

Some of the parents' lack of confidence in the teaching profession is in part due to the unreliable and unclear information they receive about their child's academic progress (Webber et al., 2009). They feel that ineffective communication fosters "a lack of trust in teacher judgment" and "the distancing of parents from schools" (Webber et al., p. 38). Further, parents noted the "deficiencies in reporting formats, citing problematic use of 'educational jargon' and a lack of comparative information about their children and peer groups" (Webber et al., p. 39). Moreover, "reporting was perceived to be too limited, not capturing students' 'social and emotional growth'" (Webber et al., p. 39). Similarly, Guskey and Bailey (2001) observed that parents want "more and better" information about their child's achievement and progress and on a more regular basis. Guskey and Bailey noted that in addition, parents requested the information they receive be comprehensible, more detailed, and with helpful suggestions about how they can provide a variety of supports for their children in school.

10.4   Grading Practice and Impact

10.4.1   Grades as Punitive Evaluation

Students perceive that classroom-based assessment is a form of reward and punishment particularly where grades reflect good or unacceptable behaviours (Webber et al., 2009). Research indicates that using grades as a disciplinary means has negative consequences (McMillan, Hellsten, & Klinger, 2011; Nitko & Brookhart, 2011; Oosterhof, 2009). One of the most common penalties teachers implement is assigning zeros or reducing marks for work not handed in on time (Webber et al.). In the Webber et al. study, an elementary student reported that he "hates how the teachers scare you with the discipline sheets and say they will dock marks on your report card" (p. 119). The same study showed that about 70 % of elementary students agreed that report card marks change because of "good/naughty behavior" (p. 119). Nevertheless, in some schools the practice of meting out zeros is declining, as one teacher reported: "zero grades [are] a thing of the past and that assignment non-completion [is] virtually eliminated" (2009, p. 92).

Because grading and assessment have been such a fiercely debated issue this past decade, 40 % of the Cycle 3 Alberta Initiative for School Improvement (AISI) projects from public school authorities identified assessment as a project theme (Alberta Education, 2013), resulting in creating more purposeful discussion and study about assessment. This discussion has led to some change according to one elementary school vice principal who reported "her school district leadership had mandated a 'no zero policy' in an effort to promote dialogue about fair student assessment practices" (Webber et al., 2009, p. 97).

Although the practice of giving zeros has been on the decline (Burke, 2005), some teachers continue to give them, their rationale being that they cannot assign a grade other than zero for something they don't have. Other teachers deal with this issue by giving part marks for each day an assignment is late. This begs the question: Is the same piece of work handed in on Tuesday somehow of a lower standard than that same piece of work handed in on Monday? Losing marks for this spurious rationale does not motivate students to do their best if they are late. Why would students work hard and produce a good standard of work for a grade that they know in advance will be low anyway? Wormeli (2006a) believes that "work done without hope for a positive outcome rarely results in significant learning and more often results in resentment and damaged relationships among students, parents, and teachers" (p. 18).

Another problem is grading policy inconsistencies such as the use of punitive or non punitive grading. Inconsistent grading practice permeates Alberta schools and some teachers and administrators worry that there is no dialogue "about why discrepancies exist between classrooms" (Webber et al., 2009, p. 92). For example, as reported in the Webber et al. (2009) study, until about 2012 most schools in Alberta were moving away from awarding zero for work not handed in, and instead using "incomplete" until the work was done. The rationale was that the work must be done and zero is not acceptable, otherwise struggling or unmotivated students soon learn that it is easier to fail than to do the work. Meting out the zero let students off the hook and allowed them to give up, implying that teachers were not interested in student learning (Guskey, 2004b). The "no zero" policy had been upheld in most Alberta school jurisdictions until a high school teacher in 2012 challenged this policy and was fired from the Edmonton Public School Board (Gerson, 2012). The firing resulted in an uproar and massive policy resistance from a significant parent group, teachers, and even students (Staples, 2012). To illustrate this colossal and emotive contention, the "no zero policy" phrase shows at least 350,000,000 hits on Google. Additionally, much of the media supported the retention of the traditional grading system that continues to fuel this controversial topic. Finally, after much debate and public pressure about the "no zero" practice, Edmonton Public School Board rescinded the policy in 2013 ("Draft Policy," 2012; Edmonton Public Schools, 2013).

The Ontario Ministry of Education also considered implementing the "no zero" policy in 2010 but like Alberta, has left such decisions to "the professional judgement of the teacher, [who] acting within the policies and guidelines established by the ministry and board, is critical in determining the strategy that will most benefit student learning" (Ontario Ministry of Education, 2010; "Ontario Schools", 2010, n.p.).

Although opinions are mixed, recent research does not support punishment for work not completed. For example, Nitko and Brookhart (2007) believe that "abhorrent grading practices such as including zero in the achievement grade" should be addressed at the school and district level because "these are not measurement issues per se but matters of educational practice, classroom management, and school policy" (p. 359). Clearly, the assessment conversation will continue as more research emerges about fair student assessment practices.

10.4.2 Second Chances

To add to the stew of mixed expectations, assorted standards, varying grading criteria, and the gamut of teacher idiosyncrasies, some teachers provide students with "second chances" to enable them to improve their work, and ultimately, their grade. The problem with providing second chances or allowing several drafts of a paper before the final grade is assigned is that within one school or grade level alone there can be inconsistencies in the number of chances provided – with some teachers allowing none at all. In defence, teachers will counter by saying second chances depend on a case-by-case need. This sounds fair but how should students be treated when they return to the teacher time and time again to perfect a piece of writing to achieve the coveted A + ? When does the "polishing" end? And finally, whose work is it anyway in the final copy – the student's or the teacher's?

Teachers worry that students won't try to do their best on their first attempt if second chances are allowed. They think that students know as long as they hand something in by the deadline, they won't be punished, and can complete the assignment in a subsequent attempt – and at their leisure. Preparing feedback for learning can be time-consuming on a student's half-hearted first draft. Nonetheless, successive opportunities to demonstrate learning must be accompanied by students engaging in "corrective practice" to improve understanding (McTighe & O'Connor, 2005, p. 17). McTighe's (1997, cited in O'Connor, 2007) findings show that "students will rarely perform at high levels on challenging learning tasks at their first attempt. Deep understanding or high levels of proficiency are achieved only as a result of trial, practice, adjustments based on feedback, and more practice" (p. 96). Using McTighe's logic then, provision of second chances is a legitimate way of ensuring that students are able to demonstrate what they know, understand, and can do. Perhaps even more important, by not expecting students to redo an assignment for a grade, they learn that failure to learn is an acceptable outcome (Wormeli, 2006a). Webber et al. (2009) found that elementary and secondary students were in favour of second chance opportunities instead of receiving a zero, and one senior high teacher reported that he offered "numerous opportunities to complete assignments and retake exams" (p. 48).

In spite of the second chances disagreements, engaging in fair assessment practice does mean providing multiple opportunities for students to show what they know and can do (Alberta Education, 2006; Black et al., 2003; Brookhart, 2013; Centre for Research in Applied Measurement and Evaluation, 1993; Davies, 2000, 2007; Johnson & Johnson, 2002; Stiggins, 2007; Wiggins, 1993). Teachers who do not provide students second chances will not know or be able to report the students' level of understanding or growth. Moreover, allowing students an opportunity to redo an assessment indicates that teachers are "on the students' side" (Aitken, 2012) and care about their students' academic success. In this way, positive student-teacher relationships grow and students are more likely to achieve success.

10.4.3 The Final Grade

O'Connor (2007) believes that only summative evaluations be included in the final grade because students often do not understand the material on the first try, and they should not be punished or pressured into perfecting a task while they are in the process of learning about it. The problem that arises when students are expected to be right on the first attempt is that they resort to memorisation instead of taking the time and risks to understand. Students are expected to take risks and learn from their mistakes only in low-stake situations. Taking risks is part of the learning process. Toddlers making their first attempts at walking take risks at every attempt. They learn to walk in a safe and secure environment with encouragement and praise for their wobbly attempts from adoring parents and siblings. Parents don't expect toddlers to walk perfectly on their first try, so why should teachers expect students to perfect a complex task on their first try? (Aitken, 1994).

Nitko and Brookhart (2011) state that formative assessment, where students are still taking risks in the learning process, should not be used as summative evaluation. The general rule is to "include in the grade the assessments that you establish as useful for summative evaluation and exclude all assessments primarily for formative evaluation" (p. 330). This means that it *is* acceptable to use formative assessment only if (a) the student has already hit the target at the optimum level in the process, and (b) that it is the most recent information of what the student knows and can do. Only then does it makes sense to use that information for grading purposes. Wasting time testing content and skills that the student has already mastered serves no meaningful purpose.

10.4.4 Aggregation of Achievement and Behaviour

To report student learning accurately, Guskey (2004b), O'Connor (2007, 2013), and Reynolds et al. (2009) recommend using a multiple-grade reporting strategy or separate scores where teachers assign an achievement grade (product) and behavioural grades (such as progress and/or process). In this way teachers avoid the inaccuracies caused by a single grade that combines behaviour and achievement, and instead, provide a more accurate picture of student learning by reporting the grades in separate columns. Parents and students see immediately whether or not the student is meeting expectations in work ethic, for example, but needs extra help in the content areas or vice versa. Accurate reporting helps to guide learning and instruction and students' future career plans. Webber et al. (2009) found that secondary teachers believe "effort" should be recognized but also that there be a separation of "behavior from academic and actual learning" (p. 48). Elementary teachers concurred and felt that "marks should reflect understandings, not attitude or effort" (p. 48). Moreover, a United States school district research and assessment director reported, "a national effort was underway to ensure that grades measure only academic achievement and keep effort out of the calculation" ("Policies Differ", 2005).

The negative side of reporting effort and the achievement grade separately is the information it communicates to the academically strong student who exerts little effort and still receives a high achievement grade. What this conveys is that one does not have to work hard to attain a high achievement mark. Kohn (1994) maintains that a teacher should never give a grade for effort. In his view *grading for effort is worse for the academically weak student* who devoted time and commendable effort for work, receiving an "A" for effort but "D" for achievement. What this tells the student is to essentially give up; no matter how hard you work, you will never reach a high achievement standard, or in Kohn's words, "You're just too dumb to succeed" (n.p.).

10.4.5 Grading Effort

The inclusion of "effort" in grading is a North America-wide issue ("Policies Differ", 2005). The main problem is *defining* "effort". First, the criteria could very well differ from teacher to teacher in the same school. Second, how does a teacher know when the student is exerting effort? The assertive student could be graded higher than the quiet student who inconspicuously exerts far more effort. Astute students will also stage or exaggerate their efforts in school if they know they are being graded for it (McMillan et al., 2011). Evaluating effort is tenuous when it is not clear how authentic the student's effort actually is (Aitken, 1994).

McMillan et al. (2011) note that gender and racial/ethnic characteristics and cultures can come into play here also. Some First Nations, Métis, and Inuit (FNMI) students will not appear to be engaging in a lesson or exerting effort because they are not looking directly at their teacher. This does not mean students are not paying attention. Looking directly at a person in authority such as a teacher or an Elder is regarded as disrespectful; therefore, cultural characteristics must be considered in grading (Cota Nupah Makah, n.d.; Kwintessential, 2012; Native American Culture, n.d.).

Although it is difficult to grade effort reliably, many teachers believe effort is a worthwhile behaviour to grade and include in reporting student learning. For example, a teacher from Virginia school district stated: "Grades from assignments indirectly measure effort. ... I tell students that as long as they keep up with projects and homework and make an honest effort on tests and quizzes, they won't fail" (Mathews, 2005, p. A10). Another teacher from the same school district concurred:

> If a student is having a difficult time but works hard and puts forth a great deal of effort, I think that real-life skill should be rewarded. I frankly do not see how struggling students will be motivated to succeed if there are not some short-term rewards for their struggles. (Mathews, 2005, p. A10)

Assuring students that if they try hard and put in "honest effort" they will raise their achievement standard is problematic; for some it might, but it is no guarantee. As Hogge (2009) attests, "[students] also should come to understand, however, that effort and quality are not synonymous. It is achievement, not the effort that led to it, that is rewarded" (n.p.).

10.4.6 Grades as Motivators

One of the reasons often given for grading is to motivate students to work hard for the reward of a high grade (Ebel, 1974, 1979; Oosterhof, 2009). Deutsch (1979, cited in Oosterhof, 2009) refers to grades as "the basic currency of our educational system" (p. 221). Nevertheless, Airasian (1991) notes that this can be a "two-edged sword" (p. 261). Receiving a high grade likely will motivate students to work harder; nevertheless, low grades are more likely to diminish other students' motivation to the point of hopelessness. Wormeli (2006a) argues that teachers mistakenly believe that grading can teach students responsibility and a real-world lesson in working hard for the due reward:

> When secondary teachers record an "F" on a student's poorly prepared project, and think that "F" will teach the importance of working hard, using time wisely, and the tough realities of life, they are incorrect. Letting the low grade do our teaching is an abdication of our responsibilities as educators. (p. 17)

Berger (1991) adds a rejoinder:

> Some critics of giving formal letter grades contend that although letter grades are motivating to "A" students, who get all the positive reinforcement, grades persuade "C" or "D" students that their ability is small and it's a waste of time to try too hard. I would go further: I think grades are destructive even for "A" students. In these students, an emphasis on letter grades encourages a narrow-minded pursuit of conservative and proven strategies to please. (p. 34)

Kohn (1999) observes teachers' misuse of grades:

> You can tell a lot about a teacher's values and personality just by asking how he or she feels about giving grades. Some defend the practice, claiming that grades are necessary to "motivate" students. Many of these teachers actually seem to enjoy keeping intricate records of students' marks. Such teachers periodically warn students that they're "going to have to know this for the test" as a way of compelling them to pay attention or do the assigned readings – and they may even use surprise quizzes for that purpose, keeping their gradebooks at the ready. (n.p.)

Stiggins (2007) believes that it is a myth that grades and test scores motivate learners. What they do learn is that there are "winners and losers". Stiggins recalls his school experiences:

Most of us grew up in schools that left lots of students behind. By the end of high school, we were ranked based on achievement. There were winners and losers. Some rode winning streaks to confident, successful life trajectories, while others failed early and often, found recovery increasingly difficult, and ultimately gave up. After 13 years, a quarter of us had dropped out and the rest were dependably ranked. Schools operated on the belief that if I fail you or threaten to do so, it will cause you to try harder. This was only true for those who felt in control of the success contingencies. For the others, chronic failure resulted, and the intimidation minimized their learning. True hopelessness always trumps pressure to learn. (n.p.)

O'Connor (2007) states that grades can be motivators for successful students but "de-motivators" for students who get lower grades than they expect. He argues "that not only do grades not motivate many students, that they can actually damage both student attitudes toward learning and relationships among students" (p. 11). Clearly, support for grades as useful learning motivators is weak. Extensive research indicates that grades can be harmful to students' disposition toward learning, and can damage social and emotional development.

10.4.7 Low Self-esteem

Nitko and Brookhart (2007) believe that elementary teachers in particular are concerned with the discouraging effects of low grades. When a student is objectified and wears the grade like a "scarlet letter", often the student's self-concept suffers. Jagodzinski (1992) maintains that:

> "Grades" are not lived as plateaus; they become the imprisonment of a letter. This stills the body needlessly. Its life is lost. Educational risk-taking requires that we place the body in a healthy tension. A dichotomous consciousness merely increases anxiety. Desire is perverted so that boundaries are maintained. (p. 161)

Once the grade is assigned, students tend to meet the teacher's expectations: a fail, pass, or distinction (Apple, 1979; Guskey, 2004a; Haberman, 1995; Marzano, 2006; Palmer, 1998; Stiggins, 2001; Wiggins, 1993). Their belief in the assigned grade is stronger than their belief in themselves. Coombs (1976, cited in Burke, 2005, p. 178) states, "We now understand that an individual's self-concept determines his or her behavior in almost everything that person does. It also affects intelligence, for people who are able will try, while those who believe they are unable, will not." Although grades can motivate some students, they can harm others' self-esteem and cause them to give up (Black & Wiliam, 1998; Brandt, 1995; Earl, 2003; Earl & Katz, 2006; Friedman, 2008; Guskey, 2004a, 2004b; Kohn, 1993; Perrone, 1991; Reeves, 2004; Stiggins, 2007). Many students carry the scars of poor grading practice for a lifetime (Marzano, 2000; O'Connor, 2009; Pike, 1991). Some become so depressed over their grades that they cannot face a lifetime of disgrace. The resulting low self-esteem and shame becomes the vehicle for poor choices – and at the extreme – suicide (Aitken, 1994; Chen, 2012; "J&K to Introduce Grading System", 2011; Runeson, 1998).

10.4.8   Teacher Bias

Teacher bias is evident in grading practices although some teachers would refute
that it exists in classrooms today (McMillan et al., 2011; Nitko & Brookhart, 2011;
Reynolds et al., 2009; Webber et al., 2009). Webber et al. reported that both elementary and secondary students experienced teacher bias in grading. One elementary
student confirmed that "teachers play favourites and sometimes think you are cheating when you are not" (p. 48). Similarly, secondary students reported that teacher
bias was a real problem in which favoured students get better marks. Other students
reported that those students who misbehave or disrupt the class received lower
grades. One senior high student remarked that, "If they don't like you, they mark
you more harshly" (Webber et al., p. 127), and another senior high student observed
that "reputation follows the student regardless of ongoing behavior" (p. 119).

10.4.9   Bullying and Grade Inflation

The issue of teachers and professors being bullied for grade increases is rarely discussed openly; however, both parents and students have been reported as being
involved in this practice (Greenberger, Lessard, Chen, & Farruggia, 2008; Roosevelt,
2009; Sonner, 2000). For some students there is a self-entitlement to the grade: "I
attended the lecture – that should earn me an automatic B" (Roosevelt, 2009, p. L2).
For others, the pressure occurs through the push for academic scholarships. Haggling
over grades occurs most often at the college level (Sonner, 2000), but it is also evident in schools where "helicopter parents" (those who "hover" over all aspects of
their child's life) are extremely vigilant in overseeing their child's progress and
achievement (Pytel, 2008). Keeping students and parents happy may mean giving
higher, potentially inflated, grades (Sonner, 2000). Because some teachers feel the
pressure to assign a higher grade than is deserved (O'Connor, 2007) grade inflation
can result, especially when awards are at stake.

The haggling over grades and grade negotiation can be difficult for teachers.
Also, students' focus on high grades can be exasperating and wearisome. For example, consider the following teacher's anecdote about grades:

> I'm getting tired of running a classroom in which everything we do revolves around grades.
> I'm tired of being suspicious when students give me compliments, wondering whether or
> not they are just trying to raise their grade. I'm tired of spending so much time and energy
> grading your papers, when there are probably a dozen more productive and enjoyable ways
> for all of us to handle the evaluation of papers. I'm tired of hearing you ask me, "Does this
> count?" And, heaven knows, I'm certainly tired of all those little arguments and disagree-
> ments we get into concerning marks which take so much fun out of the teaching and the
> learning. (Kirschenbaum et al., 1971, p. 115)

10.4.10   Competitiveness and Relationship Breakdown

Burke (2005) holds that the emphasis on competition for the honour roll, valedictorian, and scholarships "probably weakens the educational system because it separates the 'winners' from the 'losers'" (p. 179). This also weakens relationships not only between teachers and students (Chappuis et al., 2011), but also between students and students. Kohn (1999) asserts:

> Grades spoil students' relationships with each other. The quality of students' thinking has been shown to depend partly on the extent to which they are permitted to learn cooperatively (Johnson & Johnson, 1989; Kohn, 1992). Thus, the ill feelings, suspicion, and resentment generated by grades aren't just disagreeable in their own right; they interfere with learning. (n.p.)

Competition for high grades can result in offensive behaviour. For example, some students have reported having their notebooks stolen before final exams. Others reported student interference in a 3-h biology lab exam that required students to identify specific animal organs on specimens as indicated by label pins. Highly competitive students covertly moved the label pins to different locations on the specimens. This manoeuvre resulted in the subsequent students labelling the organs incorrectly (Aitken, 2007). Reynolds et al. (2009) believed that student competition for high grades can become more important than actual learning and achievement, and some students may have difficulty separating their personal worth from their grades.

10.4.10.1   Rewards and Awards

Unsound grading practices can result in disappointment, frustration, and anger for many reasons, but none more significant than where it influences the result of competition for awards at the "Academic Awards Night". With Academic Awards Night and valedictorian honours in sight, ambitious students are again at the mercy of teachers' grading practices. When one or more of these unfair practices, such as aggregating achievement and behaviour, teacher bias, or punitive grading occur in the same school or department, the grading disparity creates confusion, resentment, and disappointment especially when the chance of being valedictorian is at stake (Allen, 2005).

Some schools are shunning the valedictorian designation completely to ease the competition and pressure that the quest for the top class rankings can place on students (Barboza, 2009). Many teachers and students feel that the over emphasis on honour rolls is unhealthy in that "some incredibly bright students become zombie-like…. They're so worn out by school they don't have much personality left" (Barboza, 2009). Educators report that the celebrations are now "moving to the classroom level and that recognition is given for a greater variety of achievements including student effort and improvement" (Webber et al., 2009, p. 120). In this way, students who would never be recognised for their academic skills could at the very least be recognised for their efforts (Webber et al., 2009).

Black and Wiliam (1998) share that a culture where attaining "gold stars", high rankings, and merit certificates trumps learning is disconcerting. The obsessive focus on competition and awards is debilitating, especially for low-achievers who give up trying to learn because they believe that they will be disappointed. Instead, many low-achievers try to build up self-esteem in other ways (Black & Wiliam, 1998).

10.5   Grading Options

10.5.1   Get Rid of Grades

The research literature suggests that traditional grading must go. Grades have a detrimental effect on elementary and secondary students. Smith (1986) contends that "Grades are the kiss of death; they stigmatize an activity as a pointless educational ritual, worth doing only for the sake of the grade itself" (pp. 182-183). Poor grading practice can devalue learning. When students learn for a test only to forget the material shortly after, learning becomes a futile exercise. It should come as no surprise that given the other social and psychological issues with grading, Kohn (1994) wonders, why bother with grading at all?

10.5.2   Keep Grades

Many schools retain grades because they are important to the students' futures. They are used to place students into academic and non-academic tracks, and that usually has a profound effect on their options for college, career, and income (Grennon Brooks & Brooks, 1993). With students' futures at the forefront, grades cannot be ignored. Parents and students understand the traditional grading system. It is problematic to drop a communication system with which students and parents are comfortable.

10.5.3   A Compromise: Outcomes-Based Grading and Reporting

Undoubtedly, parents, students, teachers, and the public want and deserve accurate information about what students know and can do. This information not only identifies how well students meet curricular outcomes but also indicates where and how students can improve their learning. Accurate descriptors of how well students meet the curricular outcomes result in at least five positive effects. They (a) provide parents with reliable information about student achievement, (b) prevent grades from defining and limiting the students' beliefs of what they can do, (c) relieve the negative pressure that teachers experience in the current grading practice, (d) prevent, or at least reduce competition so students can be more learning-focused, and (e) eliminate the labelling stigma that defines students as winners or losers. Outcomes-based reporting (or standards-based reporting) that reports student achievement according to curricular outcomes and performance reduces the negativity and unreliable information communicated about learning that occurs in a grade-based system.

10.6 Issues in Eliminating Traditional Grades and Moving to Outcomes-Based Reporting

Although arguments for dropping grades are persuasive, those involved at the heart of the matter do have their issues. Traditional letter grades have been around for over 100 years and to change a culture so ingrained in schooling will be difficult to say the least. But Marzano (2000 cited in O'Connor, 2007) challenges, "Why would anyone want to change current grading practices? The answer is quite simple: grades are so imprecise that they are almost meaningless" (p. 1).

Changing the traditional grade reporting system to an outcomes-based reporting system does not mean that performance levels will no longer be evident. It means using comprehensible descriptors that indicate how well students are meeting curricular outcomes. Current research informs us that descriptors that are developed by teachers and leaders for outcomes-based reporting are more accurate and effective in accurately communicating student learning (Guskey et al., 2010). In spite of this research, long-held traditions are difficult to replace unless strong and trusted leadership is available. Leadership that is focussed on student achievement is difficult to argue against. Stiggins and Duke (2008) underscore this point and state: "The principal must be a key player in ensuring the accuracy and effective use of evidence of student achievement at the school and classroom level" (p. 286).

10.7 Outcomes-Based Reporting

Guskey and Jung (2006) argue that a well-planned outcomes-based report card can help parents relate their child's achievement to outcomes and expectations. That said, parents who belong to a different era with different traditions will likely have difficulty in adjusting and understanding the rationale behind the outcomes-based report card, as well as the format and reporting criteria. Aware of this problem, educators caution that parents need to be apprised of the new directions in assessment that are emerging (Brookhart, 2013; Webber et al., 2009). According to one elementary assistant principal, "It's…a change in thinking for parents who reflect on what was done when they were in school. Older kids also are having a tough time about not getting percentages" (Webber et al., p. 119). In other words, educators will face varying degrees of challenge in their quest to change the way they report student learning (Freeman, 2010; Guskey et al., 2010; Olson, 2010).

A requirement for a traditional grading system to move to an outcomes-based reporting system successfully is commitment to fair assessment practice and strong, effective leadership. Many school districts are facing this challenge in the second decade of 2000 (Battle River School Division No. 31, 2012; Zwaagstra, 2013). Consequently, the next 5 years will reveal how successful outcomes-based grading is. Brookhart (2013) contends that currently there are only three empirical studies related to standards-based grading (outcomes-based grading). Although she believes the recent research is promising, she cautions "research on standards-based grading is only in its infancy" (p. 77).

10.7.1   Assessment Leadership

"Leadership is second only to classroom instruction among all school-related factors that contribute to what students learn at school" (Leithwood, Seashore Louis, Anderson, & Wahlstrom, 2004, p. 5). It follows then that for meaningful and sustained change to reporting student learning, and successfully moving from a traditional grading system to an outcomes-based reporting system, school principals or leaders must first be genuine supporters of outcomes-based reporting practice, and second, use student learning results to improve learning. As important, the principal must be working towards the school district's goals and be fully supported by the superintendent. Once the relevant supports are in place, principals must be well prepared to implement change. Some of the requisites that must be in place for principals are the following:

1. *Principals must be assessment literate* (Webber et al., 2009). Teachers have confidence and trust in knowledgeable principals who can comfortably discuss and demonstrate sound pedagogy and assessment practice. When principals are sound in their theory and practice, they will be able to lead their teachers in assessment change confidently and effectively. Stiggins and Duke (2008) deem that the principals' assessment knowledge and understanding is critical for teacher professional development: "The stronger the assessment literacy background for new and practicing school leaders, the more able they will be to develop or arrange for the professional development their colleagues need to find remedies to their problems" (p. 290).
2. *Principals must work with staff to set goals to improve assessment literacy.* Murphy (1990, cited in Nettles & Herrington, 2007) states that one of the most important areas in instructional leadership is "creating focused school goals and communicating them to stakeholders" (p. 278). Once goals are set it is important

that all members are working together in their common mission. Janney, Morris, and Stubbs (2005) concur: "We can only move forward as a school if all parts of the system are moving in the same direction, toward the same target" (p. 9).

3. Principals must plan for change carefully with all stakeholders, articulating the need for change clearly and addressing potential issues before they arise (O'Shea, 2005). Effective assessment literate principals will know of and provide relevant resources to implement successful change to improve assessment and grading practice (Nettles & Herrington, 2007). DuFour and Marzano (2009) claim that effective principals "provide teachers with the training, support, … tools, and templates they need to become effective in this new structure. He or she solicits staff insights regarding obstacles to collaboration and ideas for removing those obstacles" (p. 65).

4. *Principals must involve interested staff in the relevant professional development to effect change successfully* (Nettles & Herrington, 2007). It is particularly important that principals make the effort to "remove all barriers to the development of teachers' assessment literacy" (Stiggins, 2001, p. 24). Teachers need to be assessment literate not only in their practice to make their professional change in grading and reporting student learning, but also for communicating clearly and confidently the rationale for the grading and reporting change to parents and students. Teachers must be confident and clear when discussing the new process with parents to earn their trust and assurance.

5. Principals must be prepared to be patient and provide time for teachers, students, and the community to fully understand the rationale and the need for outcomes-based reporting. This is a critical part of the process because stakeholders need time to come to terms with a paradigm shift. School districts that do not allow adequate time for all stakeholders to be involved in the reporting change process will "find themselves embroiled in controversy, particularly when parents see a standards-based report card for the first time. Discussions about the report card turn into heated debates and unexpected problems thwart their progress" (Guskey & Jung, 2006, p. 1).

6. Principals must allow all parties to have the opportunity to voice their opinions, questions, challenges, and suggestions in changing the grading and reporting practice. Guskey and Bailey (2001) contend that instead of being the last people to be consulted, parents must be alerted early to the grading and reporting change in practice and policies, and involved in the actual planning process. Once the assessment practice and policies are constructed, a carefully designed parent education programme that recognizes parents as key people in their child's education should be included. Davies, Cameron, Politano, and Gregory (1992) state: "Together is better when the way we report includes parents, students, and teachers as valued contributors. Communication is improved when everyone has the opportunity to take part, ask for clarification, see specific examples, and know that they've been heard" (p. 21). Furthermore, Guskey, Swan, and Jung's (2011) standards-based grading initiative showed that once parents actually participated in the programme and understood the initiative, parents favoured the standards-based form of reporting over the traditional form "by a wide margin" (p. 56).

10.8   Recommendations for Reporting Student Learning

As more and more schools are moving to outcomes-based reporting, Guskey and Jung (2006) provide the following suggestions and caveats for making the change in reporting student learning and achievement to parents and students.

The first challenge is to *clarify the purpose* as to why the move to an outcomes-based reporting system is being done. One of the mistakes that schools make is choosing the reporting format first so that the change appears purely cosmetic, resulting in the perception that it is just yet another fad that serves no better purpose than the current one. Changes such as these are not sustained and usually abandoned within a few unsettled and difficult years.

The second challenge is *differentiating grading criteria*. This differentiation is to ensure that aggregation of *products* (specific content achievement or performance standards), *process*, such as effort, behaviour, attitudes, homework and other daily observations of student work, and *progress*, that relates to how much or far students have grown or come in their learning journey to the present time (Guskey, 1996), are clear and distinct.

The third challenge is to *move from letter grades to outcomes* (or standards). As identified previously in this chapter, some parents *and* students would prefer that teachers retain the traditional letter grades instead of outcomes-based grading and reporting because that is what they know and trust.

The fourth challenge is *grading and reporting fairly students with special needs*. Guskey and Jung (2010) point out a dilemma: it seems unfair to fail students with disabilities who have shown remarkable effort and progress but conversely, passing them when they have not met prescribed performance standards also seems unfair. Importantly, however, as long as everyone is clear that these students are working on a modified programme and reported as such, passing them on that programme with different standards is fair if they have met those outcomes (Webber et al., 2009).

Only when those challenges have been met can the reporting content and format be dealt with. For example, teachers will find that the number of outcomes they report must be condensed or reduced so that they, and the parents are not overwhelmed (Guskey & Bailey, 2001; Olson, 2010; Webber et al., 2009). Also, parents want to see a picture of all aspects of their child's growth, achievement, and progress communicated clearly in a jargon-free document (see Appendix for an example of an outcomes-based report card). The reporting system must be presented in user-friendly text, not dense or too complex. Educators' responsibility is to help parents, students, and others to clearly understand what the student knows, understands, and can do, and how the school and home can work together to help the child set goals to succeed (Webber et al.).

Ensuring that the change and policy are sustained, the principal and teachers both have an important part to play. Lingard, Mills, and Hayes (2006) contend that teachers are the key in making certain that change and policy are interpreted and implemented as intended and used in the best interests of student learning. Once the policy and reporting system are in place, principals must monitor the progress. They must "routinely visit classrooms, participate in team-level meetings, and pay close attention to student performance within their school" (Nettles & Herrington, 2007, p. 727). For example, an assistant principal of a kindergarten to Grade 9 school articulates his perception of how best to monitor student progress:

> Being clear about what your outcomes and goals are, you can develop assessment practices that will measure those. Results are easily shared and understood by students, parents and teachers … It has taken time for parents to buy in. They are used to seeing a percent or a letter grade indicating how a child is performing and very often they would compare to their other children or peers so it took time for them to appreciate what is a different system. We no longer give one whole score, instead it is specific outcomes. (Webber et al., 2009, p. 117)

Last, but not least, principals and teachers must listen to the voices of the students and parents to maintain their trust and confidence through respectful, open, and effective communication. Webber et al. (2009) report that:

> For educators, parents, and students alike the report card is the main source of communication about how an individual student is progressing as a learner. This form of communication has been used in schools for decades and since most people, including educators and parents have been on the receiving end of report card feedback as former students, this tradition is held in high regard. As one elementary assistant principal noted, the "report card is still the primary form of communication." (p. 113)

10.9   Conclusion

Assessment and evaluation are integral to instruction. Communicating student learning results and achievement is a critical part of the process. The responsibility no longer rests with the teacher alone; parents, students, and principals are all involved in some way in communicating student learning and results effectively with the purpose of supporting the student. Knight, Aitken, and Rogerson (2000) once declared that "what you assess, how, and why, says a great deal about you as a teacher" (p. 62). Now I would take it further: "What you assess, how, why, *and how you report student learning* says a great deal about you as a teacher." When carried out in a pedagogically tactful way, reporting student learning and results will not be so threatening or abhorred by students and teachers as it has been in the past. Instead, student results based on important curricular outcomes will be communicated and displayed clearly and coherently for all to comprehend with ease. This information will be critical to indicate what the student knows, understand, and can do. It will illustrate progress and process, and ways to improve as a lifelong learner. Grading as we knew it has moved on. As we settle into the twenty-first century now is the optimal time for leaders, teachers, parents, and students to be involved in some meaningful way in moving forward and adopting fair, accurate, and clear grading and reporting practices; practices that serve the best interests of students, and those that allow students to reach their full potential.

10.10   Appendix

Elk Island Public Schools. (2007). Outcomes-based Report Card

Making the Most of Your Child's Outcomes-Based Report Card

The elementary report card used in Elk Island Public Schools is designed to give you a clear, realistic and useful report about your child's learning.

> Read this publication to learn
> - ☑ what outcomes-based reporting is about
> - ☑ how to read your child's report card
> - ☑ how to use the report card to help you support your child's learning

What is outcomes-based reporting?
- ☐ The new elementary report card is tied directly to the Alberta curriculum. Alberta's curriculum is outcomes-based—it describes what your child is expected to know and be able to do each year in each subject. The report card tells you if your child has met these expectations.
- ☐ The report card focuses on clear descriptions of how well your child has acquired the key skills, knowledge and attitudes in each subject.
- ☐ The report card does not involve percentages in elementary school. Instead it uses four levels of achievement to help describe how well your child has met expectations.

How do I read my child's report card?
Here is part of a typical report card:

> The four **achievement Levels** used by teachers are: Excellent, Proficient, Acceptable, Limited. "Proficient" describes the level of achievement that we hope most students will attain.

> These are **learning outcomes** that Alberta students in Grade 6 are expected to achieve.

English Language Arts Grade 6

Identifies and uses organizational structures and text features to enhance understanding	Proficient
Summarizes texts indicating the connections among events, characters, and settings	Proficient
Communicates ideas and information using a variety of formats for specific purposes and audiences	Excellent
Edits for correct sentence structure, capitalization, punctuation, spelling and grammar	Acceptable

> The four **effort levels** used by teachers are: Commendable, Sufficient, Inconsistent, Insufficient.

Effort: Sufficient

Comments: Betty purposefully uses charts, headings, and clues from the author when determining important facts and events in books, articles, and videos. Her responses during the Time Detectives unit were meaningful and supported by evidence in the text. Betty's revised written drafts, such as her persuasive letter to J.K. Rowling, are filled with rich content and voice. Her pieces will improve if she takes time to reread and edit for spelling and complete sentences. The class has enjoyed your many humorous personal narratives, Betty!

> Teachers may use **comments** to provide information about a student's achievement, progress or effort, and to give suggestions about what to do next.

Look at the **learning outcomes** selected by the teacher.
☐ These learning outcomes describe the core of what your child and the class have been learning during the term.
☐ These learning outcomes are important for the continued success of your child in this subject.
☐ Alberta Education publishes curriculum handbooks for parents that further describe what students are expect to know and be able to do in each grade. These handbooks are available at http://www.education.gov.ab.ca/parents/handbooks/

Look at the **achievement levels** determined by the teacher.
☐ Definitions of the four achievement levels are:
  ➤ Excellent—achievement that is commendable. The student demonstrates an in-depth and broad understanding of a subject outcome at this grade. Some students achieve at this level.
  ➤ Proficient—achievement that is competent. The student demonstrates a well-developed and consistent understanding of a subject outcome at this grade. Most students achieve at this level.
  ➤ Acceptable—achievement that is adequate. The student demonstrates a basic and/or inconsistent understanding of a subject outcome at this grade. Some students achieve at this level.
  ➤ Limited—achievement that is not yet at an acceptable level. The student demonstrates inadequate understanding of a subject outcome at this grade. Few students achieve at this level.

☐ The teacher and your child have been collecting the assessment evidence that has resulted in these achievement levels being determined by the teacher. The evidence may include:
  o scores from tests
  o achievement levels from projects, presentations, performances and other significant tasks
  o checklists and notes made by the teacher when observing your child at work
  o actual samples of your child's work

☐ Your child should be able to explain what he or she has learned and how the assessment evidence shows this.

☐ Students achieving mostly at the proficient level are making very good progress. To achieve mostly at this level throughout the year means that your child has reached a strong understanding of the skills and knowledge that are central to the subject. He or she has been solidly completing significant assessment tasks.

Look at the **effort level** determined by the teacher:
☐ Here are definitions of the four effort levels:
  ➤ Commendable—effort is exemplary. The student enthusiastically self-initiates meaningful engagement in learning activities, is highly focused on tasks, and is very productive.
  ➤ Sufficient—effort is appropriate. The student typically begins learning activities voluntarily, is usually focused on tasks, and is generally productive.
  ➤ Inconsistent—effort is sporadic and undependable. Effort is sometimes sufficient or commendable, but is also sometimes insufficient.

> ➤ Insufficient—effort is not yet at an acceptable level. The student is reluctant to engage in learning activities, has difficulty focusing on tasks without prompting and direction, and is sometimes unproductive.

☐ Students sometimes find that more effort results in higher achievement in some subjects, but not in all subjects. In some subjects, additional assistance or support may be the most effective way to increase achievement.

Look at the **comments** written by your child's teacher:

☐ Comments are an important part of your child's report card. The teacher may use comments to provide you with information about your child's achievement, effort or progress, and about what your child's next steps in learning should be.

☐ Comments may give you some ideas about things you might want to discuss at your child's student-parent-teacher conference.

How can I use the report card to help me support my child's learning?

A major factor leading to higher achievement is the use of effective assessment strategies—by teachers, by students, and by parents. Consider adopting some of the following strategies:

➤ Plan not to be surprised by the format of the report card in November—this will leave you with more time to discuss your child's learning at conference time:
  o Read about assessment and reporting in materials available from the school, the district and Alberta Education
  o Talk with your child's teacher about the report card and how it works
➤ Plan not to be surprised by what your child's own report card says in November!
  o A report card should never be a surprise—it is based on key information about your child's learning that has been collected during the term, that your child is aware of and that you have access to
➤ Discuss each of the learning outcomes with your child and the achievement level he or she attained:
  o Your child should be able to explain to you what he or she has been learning, and describe the evidence that has been collected to show the learning
➤ Discuss with your child where he or she believes his or her strengths lie:
  o Focus on the achievement levels shown for each learning outcome. Perhaps your child showed Excellent for one outcome and Proficient for another outcome. Discuss why that might be.
  o Ask your child about his or her hopes and intentions for continuing to learn.
➤ Discuss with your child the level of effort given on the report card for each subject. Effort is the application of energy to learning. The amount of effort students put into learning is often related to the following factors. Discussing these factors with children may help them to apply more effort:
  o Their understanding of the relevance or importance of the learning
  o A clear understanding of what is expected of them
  o Their self-esteem and self-confidence
  o Their desire to learn and their interest in the subject
  o Their personal assessment of what they know and are able to do

       o   Their personal assessment of their own effectiveness, potential and their hope of
          progress
   ➢ Discuss the levels determined by the teacher for your child's learner attributes. Learner
      attributes are the characteristics of students that can help them be successful learners at
      school. This may be a good time to focus on how your child learns and how he or she
      prepares for learning. You may wish to discuss with your child the strategies he or she
      uses for:

       o   preparing for major assessment tasks
       o   learning as much as possible during lessons
       o   managing homework

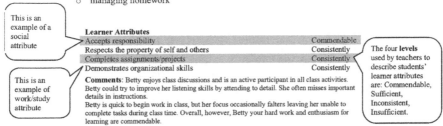

Elk Island Public Schools hereby provides the publisher of Nola Aitken, Springer
Publishing, with permission to use the Elk Island Public Schools Outcomes-based
Report Card (2007) in the book chapter, "Grading and Reporting Student Learning".

Elk Island Public Schools. (2007). *Making the most of your child's outcomes-
based report card.* Retrieved from: http://www.ministikelementary.ca/files/21/
Outcomes%20Based%20Report%20Card.pdf)

References

Airasian, P. W. (1991). *Classroom assessment.* New York: McGraw-Hill.

Aitken, E. N. (1994). *A hermeneutic phenomenological investigation of students' experience of test taking.* Unpublished doctoral dissertation, University of Alberta, Edmonton, AB, Canada.

Aitken, E. N. (2007, November). *The seven deadly sins of assessment—and how to avoid them!* (Sponsored by the Centre for the Advancement of Excellence in Teaching and Learning (CAETL) Teaching and Learning Seminar Series). Lethbridge, AB, Canada: University of Lethbridge.

Aitken, E. N. (2012). Student voice in fair assessment practice. In C. F. Webber & J. L. Lupart (Eds.), *Leading student assessment* (pp. 175–200). Dordrecht, The Netherlands: Springer.

Alberta Education. (2006). *Effective student assessment and evaluation in the classroom: Knowledge, skills, and attributes.* Edmonton, AB, Canada: Alberta Education. Retrieved from http://files.eric.ed.gov/fulltext/ED498247.pdf

Alberta Education. (2013). *Cycle 3 and 4 AISI project summaries.* Retrieved from http://education.alberta.ca/teachers/aisi/leaders/synopses.aspx

Allen, J. (2005). Grades as valid measures of academic achievement of classroom learning. *Clearing House, 78*(5), 218–223.

Apple, M. (1979). *Ideology and curriculum.* London: Routledge & Kegan Paul.

Baird, J. (2013). Judging students' performances. *Assessment in Education: Principles, Policy & Practice, 20*(3), 247–249.

Barboza, T. (2009, December 23). Huntington Beach high schools opt to use Latin honors for top students. *Los Angeles Times.* Retrieved from http://articles.latimes.com/2009/dec/23/local/la-me-valedictorian23-2009dec23

Battle River School Division No. 31. (2012, September). Student assessment. *Administrative Procedures Manual*. Battle River School Division No. 31, Alberta, Canada. Retrieved from http://www.brsd.ab.ca/Resources/AdministrativeProcedures/Documents/360%20Student%20 Assessment.pdf

Berger, R. (1991). Building a school culture of high standards: A teacher's perspective. In V. Perrone (Ed.), *Expanding student assessment* (pp. 32–39). Alexandria, VA: Association for Supervision and Curriculum Development.

Black, P., Harrison, C., Lee, C., Marshall, B., & Wiliam, D. (2003). *Assessment for learning*. New York: Open University Press.

Black, P., Harrison, C., Lee, C., Marshall, B., & Wiliam, D. (2004). Working inside the black box: Assessment for learning in the classroom. *Phi DeltaKappan, 86*, 8–21.

Black, P., & Wiliam, D. (1998). Inside the black box: Raising standards through classroom assessment. *Phi Delta Kappan, 80*, 139–148.

Brandt, R. (1995). Punished by rewards?: A conversation with Alfie Kohn. *Educational Leadership, 53*(1), n.p. Retrieved from http://www.ascd.org/publications/educational-leadership/sept95/ vol53/num01/Punished-by-Rewards¢-A-Conversation-with-Alfie-Kohn.aspx

Brookhart, S. M. (1999). Teaching about communicating assessment results and grading. *Educational Measurement: Issues and Practice, 18*(1), 5–13.

Brookhart, S. M. (2004). *Grading*. Upper Saddle River, NJ: Pearson-Merrill-Prentice Hall.

Brookhart, S. M. (2013). The use of teacher judgement for summative assessment in the USA. *Assessment in Education: Principles, Policy, & Practice, 20*(1), 69–90.

Burke, K. (2005). *How to assess authentic learning* (4th ed.). Thousand Oaks, CA: Corwin Press.

Burke, K. (2009). *How to assess authentic learning* (5th ed.). Thousand Oaks, CA: Corwin Press.

Centre for Research in Applied Measurement and Evaluation. (1993). *Principles for fair student assessment practices for education in Canada*. Retrieved from http://www2.education.ual-berta.ca/educ/psych/crame/files/eng_prin.pdf

Chappuis, J., Stiggins, R., Chappuis, S., & Arter, J. (2011). *Classroom assessment for student learning: Doing it right – using it well* (2nd ed.). Portland, OR: Assessment Training Institute.

Chen, L. (2012, September 12). Tragedies reveal that many schools fail at suicide prevention. *Global Times*. Retrieved from http://www.globaltimes.cn/content/732622.shtml

Cota Nupah Makah, L. (n.d.). The American Indian code of ethics. *Manataka™American Indian Council*. Retrieved from http://www.manataka.org/page1087.html

Davies, A. (2000). *Making classroom assessment work*. Merville, BC, Canada: Connections.

Davies, A. (2007). *Making classroom assessment work* (2nd ed.). Courtenay, BC, Canada: Connections.

Davies, A., Cameron, C., Politano, C., & Gregory, K. (1992). *Together is better: Collaborative assessment, evaluation, and reporting*. Winnipeg, MB, Canada: Peguis.

Draft policy ends 'no-zero' grading in Edmonton public schools. (2012, December 8). *CBC News*. Retrieved from http://www.cbc.ca/news/canada/edmonton/story/2012/12/07/edmonton-grading-policy-zeros-public-schools.html

DuFour, R., & Marzano, R. J. (2009). High–leverage strategies for principal leadership. *Educational Leadership, 66*(5), 62–68 Alexandria, VA: Association for Supervision and Curriculum Development.

Earl, L. M. (2003). *Assessment as learning*. Thousand Oaks, CA: Corwin Press.

Earl, L. M., & Katz, S. (2006). *Rethinking classroom assessment with purpose in mind: Assessment for learning, assessment as learning, assessment of learning*. Retrieved from http://www.edu. gov.mb.ca/k12/assess/wncp/rethinking_assess_mb.pdf

Ebel, R. L. (1974). Shall we get rid of grades? *Measurement in Education, 5*(4), 1–2.

Ebel, R. L. (1979). *Essentials of educational measurement*. Upper Saddle River, NJ: Prentice Hall.

Edmonton Public Schools. (2013). *Edmonton public schools board policies and regulations*. Retrieved from http://www.epsb.ca/policy/hk.bp.shtml

Elk Island Public Schools. (2007). *Making the most of your child's outcomes-based report card*. Retrieved from http://www.ministikelementary.ca/files/21/Outcomes%20Based%20 Report%20Card.pdf

Elmore, R. F. (2005). Accountable leadership. *The Educational Forum, 69*, 134–141.

Freeman, M. (2010, September 20). Letter grades vanishing from some Palm Beach County report cards. District pilots new "standards-based" report card at 13 elementary schools. *The Palm Beach Post News*. Retrieved from http://www.palmbeachpost.com/news/schools/letter-grades-vanishing-from-some-palm-beach-county-926705.html

Friedman, E. (2008, December 5). Are students coddled? Schools get rid of 'F's. *ABC News*. Retrieved from http://abcnews.go.com/print?id=6395403

Gerson, J. (2012, September 19). Teacher who was fired for giving students zeros finds new home at 'old-fashioned' Edmonton private school. *National Post*. Retrieved from http://news.nationalpost.com/2012/09/19/lynden-dorval-captain-zero/

Gill, T., & Bramley, T. (2013). How accurate are examiners' holistic judgements of script quality? *Assessment in Education: Principles: Policy & Practice, 20*(3), 308–324.

Greenberger, E., Lessard, J., Chen, C., & Farruggia, S. P. (2008). *Self-entitled college students: Contributions of personality, parenting, and motivational factors*. Irivne: University of California.

Grennon Brooks, J., & Brooks, M. (1993). *In search of understanding: The case for constructivist classrooms*. Alexandria, VA: Association for Supervision and Curriculum Development.

Gullickson, A. R. (1986). Teacher education and teacher-perceived needs in educational measurement and evaluation. *Journal of Educational Measurement, 23*(8), 347–354.

Guskey, T., Swan, G., & Jung, L. (2010). *Developing a statewide, standards-based student report card: A review of the Kentucky initiative*. Retrieved from http://www.eric.ed.gov/ERICWebPortal/search/detailmini.jsp?_nfpb=true&_&ERICExtSearch_SearchValue_0=ED509404&ERICExtSearch_SearchType_0=no&accno=ED509404

Guskey, T., Swan, G., & Jung, L. (2011). Grades that mean something: Kentucky develops standards-based report cards. *Kappan, 93*(2), 52–57. Retrieved from http://education.ky.gov/school/Documents/Grades%20that%20Mean%20Something.pdf

Guskey, T. R. (1996). Reporting on student learning: Lessons from the past – Prescriptions for the future. In T. R. Guskey (Ed.), *Communicating student learning: 1996 yearbook of the association for supervision and curriculum development* (pp. 13–24). Alexandria, VA: Association for Supervision and Curriculum Development.

Guskey, T. R. (2004a). 0 alternatives. *Principal Leadership, 5*(2), 49–53.

Guskey, T. R. (2004b). Are zeros your ultimate weapon? *Education Digest, 70*(3), 31–35.

Guskey, T. R. (2007). Leadership in the age of accountability. *Educational Horizons, 86*(1), 29–34.

Guskey, T. R. (2011). Five obstacles to grading reform. *Educational Leadership, 69*(3), 16–21. Retrieved from http://www.ascd.org/publications/educational-leadership/nov11/vol69/num03/Five-Obstacles-to-Grading-Reform.aspx

Guskey, T. R. (n.d.). *Grading systems–school*. Retrieved from http://education.stateuniversity.com/pages/2017/Grading-Systems.html

Guskey, T. R., & Bailey, J. M. (2001). *Developing grading and reporting systems for student learning*. Thousand Oaks, CA: Corwin Press.

Guskey, T. R., & Jung, L. (2006). The challenges of standards-based grading. *Leadership Compass, 4*(2), 1–4. Retrieved from http://www.naesp.org/resources/2/Leadership_Compass/2006/LC2006v4n2a3.pdf

Haberman, M. (1995). *Star teachers of children in poverty*. Bloomington, IN: Kappa Delta Pi.

Hargreaves, A., Earl, L., Moore, S., & Manning, S. (2001). *Learning to change: Teaching beyond subjects and standards*. San Francisco: Jossey-Bass.

Harsch, C., & Martin, G. (2013). Comparing holistic and analytic scoring methods: Issues of validity and reliability. *Assessment in Education: Principles, Policy & Practice, 20*(3), 281–307.

Hogge, J. H. (2009). Should university grades be based solely on achievement? *Teachers College Record*. Retrieved from http://www.tcrecord.org/Content.asp?ContentID=15602

J&K to introduce grading system in school education. (2011, January 12). *OneIndia News*. Retrieved from http://news.oneindia.in/2011/01/12/jkto-introduce-grading-system-in-schooleducation-aid0126.html

Jagodzinski, J. (1992). Curriculum as felt through six layers of an aesthetically embodied skin. In W. F. Pinar & W. M. Reynolds (Eds.), *Understanding curriculum as phenomenological and deconstructed text* (pp. 159–183). New York: Teachers College Press.

Janney, K., Morris, L., & Stubbs, N. (2005). A culture of greatness. *Leadership, 34*(5), 8–38.

Johnson, D. W., & Johnson, R. T. (2002). *Meaningful assessment: A manageable and cooperative process.* Boston: Allyn & Bacon.

King, M., & Ranallo, J. (1993). *Teaching and assessment strategies for the transition age.* Vancouver, BC, Canada: EduServ.

Kirschenbaum, H., Napier, R., & Simon, S. (1971). *Wad-Ja-Get? The grading game in American education.* New York: Hart.

Knight, P., Aitken, E. N., & Rogerson, R. J. (2000). *Forever better: Continuous quality improvement in higher education.* Stillwater, OK: New Forums Press.

Kohn, A. (1993). *Punished by rewards.* New York: Houghton Mifflin.

Kohn, A. (1994). Grading: The issue is not how but why. *Educational Leadership, 52*(2), 38–41. Retrieved from http://www.alfiekohn.org/teaching/grading.htm

Kohn, A. (1999). From degrading to de-grading. *High School Magazine.* Retrieved from http://www.alfiekohn.org/teaching/fdtd-g.htm

Kwintessential. (2012). *Malaysia–Language, culture, customs and etiquette.* Retrieved from http://www.kwintessential.co.uk/resources/global-etiquette/malaysia.html

Leithwood, K., Seashore Louis, K., Anderson, S., & Wahlstrom, K. (2004).*How leadership influences student learning.* Retrieved from http://www.wallacefoundation.org/knowledge-center/school-leadership/key-research/Pages/How-Leadership-Influences-Student-Learning.aspx

Lingard, B., Mills, M., & Hayes, D. (2006). Enabling and aligning assessment for learning: Some research and policy lessons from Queensland. *International Studies in Sociology of Education, 16*(2), 83–103.

Loveland, T. R. (2005). Writing standards-based rubrics for technology education classrooms. *Technology Teacher, 65*(2), 19–30.

Majesky, D. (1993). Grading should go. *Educational Leadership, 50*(7), 88, 90.

Marzano, R. J. (2000). *Transforming classroom grading.* Alexandria, VA: Association for Supervision and Curriculum Development.

Marzano, R. J. (2006). *Classroom assessment and grading that work.* Alexandria, VA: Association for Supervision and Curriculum Development.

Mathews, J. (2005, June 14). Where some give credit, others say it's not due. Across the nation, teachers' views vary on whether struggling students deserve points simply for trying. *Washington Post,* (A10). Retrieved from http://www.washingtonpost.com/wp-dyn/content/article/2005/06/13/AR2005061301471_2.html

McMillan, J. H., Hellsten, L. M., & Klinger, D. A. (2011). *Classroom assessment.* Toronto, ON, Canada: Pearson.

McTighe, J., & O'Connor, K. (2005). Seven practices for effective learning. *Educational Leadership, 63*(3), 10–17.

Miller, M. D., Linn, R. L., & Gronlund, N. E. (2009). *Measurement and assessment in teaching* (10th ed.). Boston: Allyn & Bacon.

Native American Culture. (n.d.). *There are many aspects that make up the rich Native American culture that we see today.* Retrieved from http://kb202.k12.sd.us/10/Native_American.htm

Nettles, S., & Herrington, C. (2007). Revisiting the importance of the direct effect of school leadership on students' achievements: The implications for school improvement policy. *Peabody Journal of Education, 82,* 724–736.

New South Wales Department of Education and Communities. (2013). Examinations. *Government schools of New South Wales from 1848.* Retrieved from http://www.governmentschools.det.nsw.edu.au/examinations.shtm

Nitko, A. J., & Brookhart, S. M. (2007). *Educational assessment of students* (5th ed.). Upper Saddle River, NJ: Pearson Education.

Nitko, A. J., & Brookhart, S. M. (2011). *Educational assessment of students* (6th ed.). Upper Saddler River, NJ: Pearson Education.

O'Connor, K. (2002). *How to grade for learning: Linking grades to standards* (2nd ed.). Glenview, IL: Skylight.

O'Connor, K. (2007). *A repair kit for grading: 15 fixes for broken grades.* Portland, OR: Educational Testing Service.

O'Connor, K. (2009). *How to grade for learning K-12* (3rd ed.). Thousand Oaks, CA: Corwin Press.

O'Connor, K. (2013). *The school leader's guide to grading.* Bloomington, IN: Solution Tree Press.

O'Shea, M. R. (2005). *From standards to success: A guide for school leaders.* Alexandria, VA: Association for Supervision and Curriculum Development.

Olson, M. (2010). *Outcome-based progress reporting: Considerations for implementation.* Unpublished paper, University of Lethbridge, Lethbridge, AB, Canada.

Ontario Ministry of Education. (2010). Growing success. *Assessment, evaluation, and reporting in Ontario schools.* Retrieved from http://www.edu.gov.on.ca/eng/policyfunding/growSuccess.pdf

Ontario schools get tough on late assignments. (2010, August 25). *CBC News*, (n.p.). Retrieved from http://www.cbc.ca/news/canada/toronto/ont-schools-will-get-tougher-on-late-assignments-1.953517

Oosterhof, A. (2009). *Developing and using classroom assessments* (4th ed.). Upper Saddle River, NJ: Pearson.

Palmer, P. (1998). *The courage to teach.* San Francisco: Jossey-Bass.

Perrone, V. (Ed.). (1991). *Expanding student assessment.* Alexandria, VA: Association for Supervision and Curriculum Development.

Pike, G. (1991). Reflections of a failing grade. In M. van Manen (Ed.), *Texts of pedagogy* (pp. 201–232). University of Alberta, AB, Canada: Human Science in Education Project.

Policies differ across the region. (2005, June 14). *Washington Post*, (n.p.). Retrieved from http://www.washingtonpost.com/wp-dyn/content/article/2005/06/13/AR2005061301470.html

Pytel, B. (2008, March 9). *Teachers harassed by parents: Parents can be bullies too.* [Web log post]. Retrieved from http://www.suite101.com/content/teachers-harassed-by-parents-a47159

Reeves, D. (2004). The case against the zero. *Phi Delta Kappan, 86*(4), 324–325.

Reynolds, C. R., Livingstone, R. B., & Wilson, V. (2009). *Measurement and assessment in education* (2nd ed.). Upper Saddle River, NJ: Pearson.

Ronne, D. (2010). *Parents' understanding of assessment and reporting: What role can leadership play?* Unpublished paper, University of Lethbridge, Lethbridge, AB, Canada.

Roosevelt, M. (2009, February 17). Student expectations seen as causing grade disputes. *New York Times*, p. L2.

Runeson, B. S. (1998). Child psychiatric symptoms in consecutive suicides among young people. *Annals of Clinical Psychiatry, 10*(2), 69–73.

Schafer, W. D., & Lissitz, R. W. (1987). Measurement training for school personnel: Recommendations and reality. *Journal of Teacher Education, 38*(3), 57–63.

Slavin, R. (1994). *Educational psychology: Theory and practice* (4th ed.). Boston: Allyn & Bacon.

Smaill, E. (2013). Moderating New Zealand's National Standards: Teacher learning and assessment outcomes. *Assessment in Education: Principles, Policy & Practice, 20*(3), 250–265.

Smith, F. (1986). *Insult to intelligence.* New York: Arbor House.

Sonner, B. S. (2000). *A* is for "Adjunct": Examining grade inflation in higher education. *The Journal of Education for Business, 76*(1), 5–8.

Staples, D. (2012, June 4). Public uprising against "No Zeros" policy of Edmonton Public School Board. *Edmonton Journal.* Retrieved from http://blogs.edmontonjournal.com/2012/06/04/public-uprising-against-no-zeros-policy-of-edmonton-public-school-board/

Stiggins, R. (1993). Teacher training in assessment: Overcoming the neglect. In S. L. Wise (Ed.), *Teacher training in assessment and measurement skills* (pp. 27–40). Lincoln, NE: Buros Institute of Mental Measurements.

Stiggins, R. (2001). The principal's leadership role in assessment. *NASSP Bulletin, 85*, 13–14.

Stiggins, R. (2002). Assessment crisis: The absence of assessment for learning. *Phi Delta Kappan, 83*, 758–765.

Stiggins, R. (2007). Five assessment myths and their consequences. *Education Week, 27*(8), 28–29.

Stiggins, R. (2008). *Student-involved assessment for learning* (5th ed.). Upper Saddle River, NJ: Merrill, Prentice Hall.

Stiggins, R., & Duke, D. (2008). Effective instructional leadership requires assessment leadership. *Phi Delta Kappan, 90*, 285–291.

Webber, C. F., Aitken, E. N., Lupart, J., & Scott, S. (2009). *Alberta student assessment study final report.* Edmonton, AB, Canada: Alberta Education\Author. Retrieved from http://education.alberta.ca/media/1165612/albertaassessmentstudyfinalreport.pdf

Wiggins, G. P. (1993). *Assessing student performance: Exploring the purpose and limits of testing.* San Francisco: Jossey-Bass.

Wiggins, G. P. (1994). Toward better report cards. *Educational Leadership, 52*(2), 28.

Willis, S. (1993). *Are letter grades obsolete? ASCD Update, Association for Supervision and Curriculum Development, 35*(7), 1, 4, & 8.

Woods, K., & Griffin, P. (2013). Judgement-based performance measures of literacy for students with additional needs: Seeing students through the eyes of experienced special education teachers. *Assessment in Education: Principles, Policy & Practice, 20*(3), 325–348.

Wormeli, R. (2006a). Accountability: Teaching through assessment and feedback, not grading. *American Secondary Education, 34*(3), 14–27.

Wormeli, R. (2006b). *Fair isn't always equal. Assessing and grading in the differentiated classroom.* Portland, ME: Stenhouse.

Worsfold, A. (n.d.). A history of school examinations. *Wilderspin National School.* Retrieved from http://www.change.freeuk.com/learning/howteach/exams.html

Zwaagstra, M. (2013, April 25). Percentages belong on report cards. *Common Sense Education.* [Online forum comment]. Retrieved from http://michaelzwaagstra.com/?p=329

Chapter 11
Principal Leadership and Challenges for Developing a School Culture of Evaluation

Maria Luz Romay, Constance Magee, and Charles L. Slater

Abstract The purpose of this chapter is to identify how school principals can develop a culture of evaluation that will contribute to improving the quality of learning processes. If this goal is achieved, teachers, administrators and staff will respond more effectively to the needs of students and society in general. The chapter provides an overview of how the role of school principal has changed substantially during the last decade, demanding more rigorous assessment practices and accountability. The authors also discuss the nature and purposes of evaluation, emphasising the importance of integrating evaluation, planning, and decision-making. They describe common problems and attitudes that may impact the effectiveness of evaluations; in contrast, the chapter proposes several conditions that will allow the development of a culture of evaluation in schools. In order to demonstrate how these criteria work, a case study illustrates how they were applied by a school principal to resolve specific evaluation issues. The authors recommend that effective evaluations require cooperation between the school administration and teachers with open communication and active participation. This will not be possible without financial support and adequate training. It is the authors belief that if school principals put these recommendations into practice, it will be possible to develop a culture of evaluation within each educational community.

Keywords Assessment and accountability • Core curriculum standards • Culture of evaluation • Formal evaluations • Ethical issues • Formative evaluation • Summative evaluations • Integration of planning • Decision-making • Methodological capability • Participative dialogue • Principal's role • Programme evaluation • Resistance to evaluation

M.L. Romay
School of Physical Therapy, University of the Incarnate Word, San Antonio, TX, USA
e-mail: romay@uiwtx.edu

C. Magee
Lindbergh Middle School, Long Beach, CA, USA
e-mail: CMagee@lbschools.net

C.L. Slater (✉)
College of Education, California State University, Long Beach, CA, USA
e-mail: Charles.Slater@csulb.edu

© Springer International Publishing Switzerland 2016
S. Scott et al. (eds.), *Assessment in Education*, The Enabling
Power of Assessment 2, DOI 10.1007/978-3-319-23398-7_11

11.1   Introduction

When schools fail, the first person held responsible for the failure is the principal. Principals are coming under increasing scrutiny from the public and private sector to ensure that their schools are meeting the needs of all students. In the United States schools are measured by how well their students perform on yearly state tests.

Principals are critical to school success (Fullan, 2001, 2008a, 2008b; Leithwood, Lewis, Anderson, & Wahlstrom, 2004; Reeves, 2009; Whitaker, 2003). Marzano, Waters, and McNulty (2005) found that principal effectiveness has a direct impact on school progress and student achievement. It is also clear that the job of the principal has changed dramatically over the past decade. Good principals used to be those who took care of student discipline and efficiently managed the site. Today's principals must be agents of change, committed to continuous improvement. They must be masters of finance, human resources, instruction, data analysis, and politics, while balancing the needs of their students, parents, teachers, and district administrators (Wildy & Clarke, 2008; Wohlstetter, Datnow, & Park, 2008). It is no wonder that many view the principal's increased responsibilities as overwhelming and some question whether one person can effectively accomplish everything that is expected (Wildy & Clarke, 2008; Wohlstetter et al., 2008).

Even with all of these expectations, we must add one more. Principals need to be able to evaluate student achievement and determine whether it is increasing in the short-term and in the long-term. As instructional leaders, principals lead teachers in setting goals, planning, and evaluating (Schmoker, 1999). Principals do not need to be experts in evaluation, but they need to have a firm grasp of how it works and how it can be integrated into the school programme (Slater, McGhee, Nelson, & Meno, 2011).

This chapter reviews in its first section how the role of school principals has changed substantially in the United States with the passage of the No Child Left Behind Act in 2001 and the advent of the common core curriculum. These developments have impacted policies related to assessment and accountability. The following sections discuss the nature and main purposes of evaluation in education, emphasising the importance of integrating evaluation, planning, and decision-making processes. Understanding these theoretical principles and factors will enable school leaders to oversee evaluation efforts. Another section of the chapter describes the most common problems of evaluation, in particular potential educators' attitudes or responses when they are called to participate in an evaluation in order to improve the practice of evaluation. To improve the practice of evaluation, several conditions can facilitate the development of a culture of evaluation in schools. Finally, a case study illustrates and elaborates on these evaluation issues.

Different evaluation methods and techniques have been developed based on diverse theoretical models (Hill, 2009; Madaus, Scriven, & Stufflebeam, 1990). Currently a wide variety of resources are available regarding its different concepts and principles; several authors have offered critical perspectives on issues that evaluators encounter as they conduct assessments in diverse environments. The purpose of this article is to guide principals in the development of an evaluation culture.

11.2 Evaluation in Elementary and Middle Education the United States

Since education is not mentioned in the United States Constitution, it has been left to individual states to develop and fund public schools. The role of the Federal Government in education was quite small until the beginning of the twenty-first century, but when the No Child Left Behind Act (NCLB) became effective on January 8, 2002, it opened a new era in educational history and framed the debate about the future of public education (U.S. Department of Education, 2009a). It began as history making bipartisan legislation passed by Congress and signed by the President. The decision to target improvements for public schools led to a high-stakes accountability programme and labelled an increasing number of schools as failing each year. The goals of the legislation require that students from low income families, different racial groups, with disabilities, or who are learning English as a second language, must demonstrate proficiency in mathematics and language arts.

The NCLB legislation (2001) was initially supported as a way to help all groups of students increase academic proficiency. The NCLB legislation mandated that all subgroups meet the national proficiency standard of 100 % by 2014. African American, Latino, and Special Education students from low socioeconomic backgrounds are each looked at as individual groups.

Schools whose students did not meet federal targets are placed in Programme Improvement (PI) and must meet state targets for two successive years in order to exit from the programme. Failure to exit PI came with sanctions that increased in severity for each additional year that a school failed to meet the targets. All sanctions included removing the current principal unless the principal was new to the site. In some cases sanctions also included reconstitution of the teaching staff, closing the school, or re-opening the school as a charter. Programme Improvement schools also lost funding and were required to offer transfers to parents who requested a non-PI school.

Schools were held accountable through annual testing, academic progress, school report cards, and teacher qualifications. The four goals behind the legislation included: (1) assistance for economically disadvantaged students; (2) increasing the pool of highly qualified teachers; (3) increasing the literacy rate of students; and (4) holding schools accountable for the success or failure of their students (Munro, 2008). Schools that failed to meet Annual Yearly Progress (AYP) goals were placed in Programme Improvement. Parents could transfer their children out of low performing schools.

The NCLB required annual testing of at least 95 % of students at each school in Grades 3-8 in reading and mathematics. In addition to overall scores, data were compiled on students from low income families, students from different racial groups, those with disabilities and English language learners. The tests were aligned with state academic standards. Students as a whole and all student groups were required to make adequate yearly progress (AYP) (Slater et al., 2011).

Schools with a high concentration of students from poor families received Title I funds from the Federal Government (U.S. Department of Education, 2009b). Title I schools that failed to meet targeted goals 2 years in a row must offer students a choice of other public schools to attend. After 3 years, students must be offered supplemental educational services. All students were required to reach a minimum level of proficiency by 2013 until the goal was revised. Moreover, states and districts completed a report including reporting on student achievement for all groups and schools. Additionally, all teachers must meet the definition of highly qualified by having a Bachelor's degree, state certification, and proof that they know the discipline. Schools are also expected to provide quality professional development experiences for teachers and paraprofessionals.

11.2.1 Assessment and Accountability

Student assessment in the US has become synonymous with accountability and high-stakes testing. Criterion-referenced assessments replaced norm-referenced tests that were used in many states. The states then measured the extent to which students were meeting state objectives.

In the first years of the legislation, school districts grappled for the first time with an examination of test results that were disaggregated by school group. Previously, a district might have good results overall and not notice or publicise lower results of minority students such as African Americans or Latinos. Achievement is now measured for all students in a school and disaggregated by ethnicity, gender, students in poverty, English language learners, and special programme students. Discussion at all levels has centred on the gap in achievement between the majority and minorities (Ladson Billings, 2006). The system for reporting data is completely transparent so that parents, teachers, citizens, or researchers can consult school and state websites to see complete test results as well as demographic data. In California, each school is compared to overall state results as well as to comparable schools with similar demographics.

Educators have become informed about individual student performance and the public has unprecedented access to data about schools. Many schools have developed careful plans to monitor students, assess, and plan based on test results.

11.2.2 Problems with Educational Accountability

Unfortunately, standardised testing for educational accountability has had several negative effects. The use of standardised tests has driven out more authentic means of instruction. The system has been limited to paper and pencil tests, and there is little room for assessment in which students demonstrate performance in real world settings.

Standardised testing also tends to limit teachers' focus on areas of the curriculum that are not tested such as science, social studies, the arts, health, second languages, and physical education. Testing only language arts and mathematics has resulted in a narrowing of the curriculum to emphasise just what is tested. Even within language arts and mathematics there is often a restriction to content and instruction related to the form of the test.

Students who are most likely to need help in passing the test are assigned to special test preparation classes that are separate from the regular curriculum and may emphasise test taking skills (McNeil, 2000a, 2000b). They may be taken out of music, art, or special education to focus on the state test. There is less opportunity for field trips, extended activities such as library research projects, scientific investigations, or arts performances.

The amount of additional time in test preparation is quite significant and while it takes away from the regular curriculum schedule, it may still not improve test scores, much less make long-term learning gains for students. In Texas superintendents reported requiring students to take practice tests, and in some cases, students were spending up to 35 days, or 7 weeks practicing for accountability system-related examinations (Nelson & McGhee, 2004; Nelson, McGhee, Reardon, Gonzales, & Kent, 2007).

Disaggregating data by income and ethnic group helped to focus attention on students who were not achieving. However, these students have not necessarily been receiving additional resources or an improved curriculum. Rather, they may be receiving a curriculum of test preparation. When compared to the National Assessment of Educational Progress Results, a number of studies have indicated very weak relationships, if any, between accountability testing and student achievement (Nichols, Glass, & Berliner, 2012).

In the worst cases, students who were not likely to pass the test were pressured to leave school. McNeil, Coppola, Radigan, and Heilig (2008) reported that Texas had publicly reported gains in test scores even as additional numbers of students were dropping out of school. Heilig and Darling-Hammond (2008) reported that some school districts tried to obtain higher test scores by testing fewer students at the elementary level and pushing out students at the high school level.

One way to combat some of these problems is to focus on growth targets instead of rigid Adequate Yearly Progress (AYP) percent targets. Individual targets should be calculated for each student and subgroup based on current achievement, rather than using a set percent for proficient or advanced proficient. It is unrealistic to expect that all students in all schools be 100 % proficient in both math and language arts. The system also did not indicate levels of growth, it only signified whether or not the school had made the percent target. Students who qualified for special education and students who were learning English were placed in specific programs, based in part on low test scores, to help them succeed academically. A growth model would more accurately evaluate the progress of the schools and pinpoint the students who are in need of additional services.

11.2.3 Common Core Curriculum Standards

Until recently, each state had different standards, and testing in one state was not necessarily comparable to another state. There was also great variation among school districts within a state. Some districts and schools followed state standards closely while others ignored them.

In 2012, the National Governors Association Centre for Best Practices (NGA Centre) and Council of Chief State School Officers (CCSSO) published a set of national standards that gained wide attention. In a period of only 2 years states began to adopt the new standards to replace their separate sets of standards (NGA & CCSSO, 2012). These standards are intended to emphasise the knowledge and skills that students need to succeed in college and careers, while emphasising complex thinking (Porter, McMaken, Hwang, & Yang, 2011). The Federal Government helped spur the rush to participate when it made participation in the Common Core Curriculum a requirement for states to get funding for Race to the Top grants (U.S. Department of Education, 2009b).

The Common Core Curriculum has pushed school districts toward common assessments as well. States were required to develop new standardised tests by 2014–15. To accomplish this work, states joined either the Partnership for Assessment of Readiness for College and Careers Assessment Consortium (PARCC, 2013) or the SMARTER Balance Consortium (Smarter Balance Consortium, 2013). Common curriculum and assessments bring questions about the nature and role of evaluation to the fore.

11.3 Nature and Role of Evaluation

Evaluation is a natural part of our everyday life: people make evaluations in the form of judgments determining whether something is good or bad, desirable or not. Evaluation seems to be fundamental in our developmental process, as we make decisions that allow us to become mature adults and to assume different responsibilities. Evaluations are also made at the personal or the professional level, and are influenced by personal expectations or preferences. Often those judgments are not made carefully and in an objective manner (Shawn & Greene, 2006).

Formally speaking it is important to acknowledge that evaluation is "a profession, a practice, and a discipline" (Mathison, 2005, p. 1). As the practice of evaluation evolved, it became increasingly professionalized; and it has become entrenched within educational systems in many countries. Applied to different educational problems or areas, evaluation implies an intentional process that responds to different needs of people, groups, or institutions (Martínez Slanova, 1980).

Thus, systematic and formal evaluations require explicit evidence and objective criteria for interpreting data (Kemmis, 1989). These types of evaluations are used to analyse the status of any educational or social program, assess teacher performance, identify what have been the outcomes of learning processes, or to conduct large and complex institutional self-studies (Berk, 1999; Erwin, 1991; Glatthorn, Boschee, Whitehead, & Boschee, 2012; Guerra-Lopez, 2008; Kennedy, 2010; Peterson, 2009; Rueda, 2011). Scientific methods are applied in these cases making clear what sources were consulted before any judgments were made. Usually these evaluations are based on scientific principles that regulate social research. Formal evaluations should demonstrate that the evidence does not rely only in individual opinions, but that information is gathered collectively.

These formal evaluations respond to different purposes. For example, they provide information to public audiences for accountability. They could also be useful for policy making, promoting knowledge through the development of theories, or enhancing specific practices. In each case the choices for the purpose of evaluation and how it is done influences its approach, and validates the process (Nevo, 1986).

Even though the distinction between informal and formal evaluations is important, one needs to recognise that often individuals involved in these processes interpret data in the context of their own practice and knowledge. In other words, informal and formal evaluations may be related in different ways. A formal evaluation could be proposed to offer more explicit and usable knowledge than what is presented informally about a specific situation. Both types of evaluations could be complementary, and could interact providing some reliable knowledge (Patton, 1990).

The root of the word "value" comes from the Latin "valere", meaning "to be worth or to work out the value of something" (Shawn & Greene, 2006, p. 6). Therefore the term itself could lead to measuring the quantitative value of something or estimating its worth. To understand this full meaning, one must accept or use quantitative and qualitative methods.

Most definitions of evaluation include at least one of the following elements: the assessment of worth or merit, its functions, roles, methods, and its purpose. Based on these distinctions we present three definitions that represent these diverse emphases:

> Evaluation is a type of inquiry undertaken to determine the merit and/or worth of some entity, in order to improve or refine what is evaluated, or to assess its impact. (Lincoln & Guba, 1981, p. 550)

> Evaluation refers to the process of determining the value of something, or the product of that process. It normally involves identification of a relevant standard, investigation of the performance of those who are evaluated, and integration or synthesis of the results achieved. (Scriven, 1991, p. 139)

It is not surprising that no single definition is universally accepted by evaluators today. Given the different perspectives and dynamic nature, evaluation as a discipline encompasses several theories, models, and methodologies. Shadish, Cook, and Leviton (1991) in their meta-analysis describe three stages of the development of major evaluation theories: in the beginning, according to Madaus et al. (1990), theorists emphasised a search for truth, looking for solutions to social problems (Scriven, 1967). In a second stage evaluators developed studies aimed to produce politically and useful results based on detailed knowledge of how organisations operate [this stage may be represented by Cronbach (1982), Carol Weiss (1992) and Robert Stake, (1990)]. More recently evaluators have tried to integrate previous contributions insisting on organisational processes and decision-making with a more comprehensive approach [such as the work of Stufflebeam et al. (1971), and Rossi & Freeman, (1992)].

In light of the previous concepts and contributions of numerous authors, in this chapter we adopt a more recent and broad definition:

> Evaluation is an applied inquiry process for collecting and synthesizing evidence that culminates in conclusions about the state of affairs, value, merit worth, significance, or quality of a program, policy, or plan related to educational processes. Conclusions made in evaluations encompass both an empirical aspect (if it is a case) and a normative aspect (judgment about value). It is the value feature that distinguishes evaluation from other types of inquiry. (Mathison, 2005, p. 139)

Generally evaluations in education serve a broad purpose, which is to assess the status and effectiveness of specific policies, programs, students' learning outcomes, or institutional development. According to Álvarez García (1997), the most commonly identified purposes and functions of evaluations are:

(a) **Accountability** – The intention is to demonstrate how far a programme has achieved its objectives, how well it has used its resources, and what has been its impact. This type of evaluation will mainly meet the needs of administrators, programme coordinators, or sponsors from diverse organisations. Often this purpose can be related to control or supervision. It is useful because it allows stakeholders to know what has happened to the resources devoted to specific projects or programs.

(b) **Increasing the efficiency of planning processes or policy making** – Evaluations could be proposed to justify a policy or programme analysing developmental stages to define the next steps in strategic planning processes (Álvarez García, 2008). This type of evaluation mainly meets the needs of planners and policy makers. They could follow a conventional planning process or focus more on innovation (Bridges & Groves, 2000).

(c) **Organisational improvement** – These evaluations allow institutions or schools to enhance or review their performance, structures, and procedures (Schmoker, 1999), in order to determine the level of their effectiveness or assess the strategies used. This kind of evaluation mainly meets the needs of principals or school administrators who want to identify opportunities for change. In today's educational reality research has proven that those evaluations should incorporate the teacher's own reflection on their teaching practice, in other words to include self-assessment practices (Romay & Crispin, 2000).

Table 11.1 Typical questions in evaluation phases

Evaluation phases	Most common questions
Preliminary proposals	What are the current priorities set by governmental agencies related to evaluating quality of school programs?
	Are there specific areas that need to be evaluated?
	What resources are available that can be used in evaluation efforts?
	What problems should be more urgently analysed or studied?
Initial stage	Have the objectives of the planning process been adequate to the needs of the target population?
	Are the goals and policies consistent with the needs of students and teachers?
	What is known about the problem that has been proposed for evaluation?
Processes analysis	Are all members of the institution/programme involved as they need to be?
	Are the existing programs achieving their goals? Are there other alternatives?
	Are the resource allocations transparent and known to those who manage the programme?
	What are the strengths and weaknesses of the programme?
	Have the standards set by leaders been achieved by students?
	How could delivery of the programme be improved?
Implementation/application of the evaluation results.	Have the results of the evaluation been clearly presented and well understood?
	What are the key points that require change or improvement?
	How much may the implementation of these changes cost?
	Who will oversee the implementation of the recommended changes in the study?

Adapted from Shawn & Green (2006) in Chapter 15, Tables 5.1 – 5.4

(d) **Knowledge production** – This type of evaluation is for groups or institutions that want to confirm specific assumptions and theories that they have applied in their practice (Chen, 1990), and determine what lessons can be learned for the future. These evaluations would be particularly important for leaders and policy makers who want to develop new projects or renew existing programs.

Depending on the evaluation's purpose and the stage of the process, one can identify typical questions as Table 11.1 shows.

There are other specific purposes of evaluations such as diagnostic studies, inno-vative projects, or support of particular objectives established by principals or administrators. In these cases, evaluations serve as strategies to facilitate the growth and learning of small groups, communities, or people. Scriven (1967) originally proposed two central functions of evaluations: formative or summative.

(a) Formative evaluation provides information to improve a product or process. For example, a formative evaluation of instructional materials would ideally be con-ducted prior to full-scale implementation (Flagg, 1990), or expert reviews of the content of a programme may provide useful information for modifying or revis-ing selected strategies (Owen, 2006). Therefore, this type of evaluation is pre-dominately used in educational and training settings; it often allows educators to discover issues related to organisational structures, confusions within the learning process, or a need for more illustrations and examples. It may reveal concerns that would lead to revised and improved teaching strategies.

(b) Summative evaluation provides short-term effectiveness or long-term impact information to decide whether or not to adopt a product or process. Summative evaluation can occur just after new materials, programs, or software are imple-mented in full or after they have been in place for a long period of time. It is important to specify what decisions will be made as a result of this type of evaluation, and then, develop a list of questions to be answered. Other times that summative evaluation could be appropriate are: when teachers or administrators would like to know if certain objectives have been met; or if an innovation was efficient in terms of time to completion or had any unexpected outcomes.

Álvarez García (1997) has proposed a list of elements that all evaluations should include:

1. Clear identification of the issues or needs to be studied, analysing whether there is room for change;
2. Contextual factors and resources that may influence the evaluation process;
3. Level of complexity of the study;
4. Analysis and interpretation of data;
5. Initial results and recommendations based on the information gathered;
6. Expected and non-expected results;
7. Positive and negative impact;
8. What resources can be used in the change process; and
9. Follow-up and implementation of recommendations.

An understanding of the broad purposes of evaluation suggests that it should be tied to systematic processes that determine the direction of schools, including planning and decision-making (Álvarez García, 2008). Stufflebeam et al. (1971) maintains that what is important is how evaluation is integrated with those pro-cesses (See Fig. 11.1).

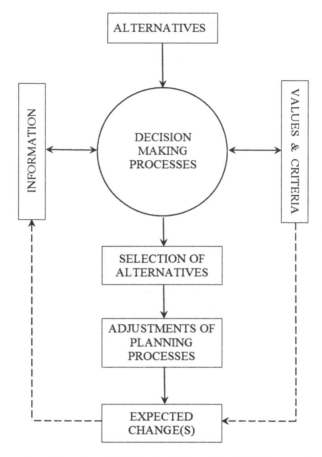

Fig. 11.1 Integration of Planning and Evaluation (Adapted from Stufflebeam et al. (1971)

11.4   Main Issues Affecting Evaluation Processes

Often evaluations face some of the following obstacles or challenges (Calonghi, Gianola, Groppo, Perucci, & Reguzzoni, 1991):

- Lack of clear ideas about evaluation;
- No clear identification of the issues to be evaluated;
- Misunderstanding of some aspects of the purpose and functions of evaluation;
- Confusion of the evaluation process with scientific research;
- Disarticulation of evaluation processes with planning, decision-making and other organisational processes;
- Inadequate methods or techniques applied;
- Not enough knowledge on how to gather valuable information (overlooking aspects of validity, reliability, usefulness);
- Incorrect interpretation or use of findings; and
- Conditions of the social context that make the evaluation not feasible.

In some circumstances defining evaluation criteria may involve negotiations at various levels and throughout the whole process, and it is difficult to get a consensus on relevant decisions. It is particularly problematic if the objectives and purposes of the evaluation are not clear at the outset, or when evaluators find ambiguity between declared and hidden objectives (Álvarez García, 1997), particularly if the organisation is large and complex. It is not uncommon that during evaluations participants feel stressed, even fearful, expending too much time in discussions that waste energy (Spaulding, 2008).

Evaluations proposed at the organisational level require a commitment to participate in interventions that may bring positive changes and define initially specific criteria for measuring success. Also it is important to be aware that in many organisations, members tend to place more value on an external evaluation than when it is conducted by internal resources, arguing that external evaluation is more objective and self-evaluation has the risk of being subjective. However, experienced evaluators recognise that internal evaluations are particularly valuable and truthful if they are conducted in alignment with expected standards. In fact, when members of an organisation are involved in an evaluation more directly, they will have more opportunities for learning and personal development. Of course, there must be controls to assure that administrators, teachers, or students adhere to ethical standards of evaluation.

11.5   Ethical Challenges of Evaluation

Unfortunately, cheating is commonplace in US schools: 56 % of middle school students and 70 % of high school students report having cheated (Decoo, 2002). The pervasiveness of cheating by students requires attention to ethical issues as well as organisational structures to minimise the incidence of cheating.

Cheating by students has been around for as long as schools have administered tests, but the turn of the century has brought a new kind of cheating, cheating by schools. The testing and accountability system that was implemented on a national level in the US was begun in the State of Texas. The Houston Independent School District became known for high-stakes testing that carried financial rewards and punishments for principals and teachers depending on how well students scored (Nelson, McGhee, Meno, & Slater, 2007; Slater et al., 2011).

There have been allegations of several types of cheating. The most straightforward example is when school employees change test results or give students advance information about what is on the test. Several Houston school results have been officially questioned and in 2006 a State audit cited 442 campuses for testing irregularities. In 2010, some Houston employees were reassigned after allegations of cheating (Radcliffe, 2010).

Another type of cheating in Houston is more indirect and is part of the way the system was designed in Texas. Students may show test score gains on the officially reported state measure, but fall far short on other standardised measures that are not reported. Schemo and Fessenden (2003) reported that Houston school gains on the Stanford Achievement Test were far smaller than on the Texas State Test. While there was no wrong-doing that could be traced to any individual, the lack of correlation between the Texas State Test and other measures suggests toleration of systematic deception.

Linda McNeil (1986, 2000a, 2000b) at Rice University in Houston has been a persistent critic of the Houston testing system. She argues that school officials 'game' the system to make the results look good. They systematically exclude some students through manipulation of the rules, provide instruction only for students who are likely to show test score increases, and provide so much testing practice as to harm students' broader learning. Bohte and Meier (2000) have called this type of cheating goal displacement. The organisation operates to maximise incentive rewards based on published criteria while neglecting or even working against the broader intent of the policy.

The largest case of cheating to date took place in Atlanta where 178 principals and teachers were charged with cheating by artificially raising test scores to meet district targets (Winerip, 2011). The superintendent would regularly gather all staff in the Georgia Dome at the beginning of the school year and have school personnel sit in the order of their school test scores. The highest performing schools would sit at the front, and the lowest performing would sit at the back. The superintendent had been named 'superintendent of the year' and was recognised by the Secretary of Education. She collected $600,000 in bonuses over 10 years in addition to her $400,000 annual salary. She said, "Where people consciously chose to cheat … the moral responsibility must be with them."

One of the central issues is who bears responsibility; the school officials who designed and implemented the system, or those who did the actual erasing of scores. In a moral wrong, someone loses and someone gains. Teachers risked being marginalised if they did not participate in "erasure parties". Principals might even lose their jobs if they did not show score increases.

To what extent should the superintendent be held responsible for the cheating? Heads of organisations are quick to take credit for accomplishments but slow to acknowledge a role in failure. Quick and Normore (2004) argue that moral leadership rests with the institution's leader. Not only should the leader act according to a personal code of ethics but he/she must also understand concepts of systems thinking to determine how relationships, support structures, and decisions made by school leaders impact the entire school.

Beyond the school level, we could also look at the accountability system itself. Some organisational structures are much more likely to elicit cheating than others. Several positive cultural qualities can reduce the likelihood of cheating. If teachers are motivated by internal rewards such as satisfaction with class activities and their own professional development are less likely to cheat than those who work for external rewards of salary and bonuses. If they perceive the demands of the school and the district as legitimate, they are more likely to buy into the system of testing. If there are caring relationships and tolerance for error or acceptance of mistakes, teachers are more likely to report results honestly.

Those responsible for designing the system need to take into account the features of the system that can encourage or discourage cheating. A positive culture is crucial to create an ethical environment against cheating, but there also need to be systems in place to guard against cheating. A few incidents of cheating can spread and undermine a positive culture.

Students suffer the most when test results are falsified because they gain their own concepts of truth at least partially from their experiences in school. The message from the 178 teachers and principals in Atlanta was that it is all right to cheat in order to avoid punishment and gain what you want. The truth of the curriculum becomes subject to convenience. We change the facts to fit our beliefs.

11.6 Different Attitudes toward Evaluations

Based on the above difficulties, it is common to find different responses toward formal evaluation processes. Eventually some people will try to ignore what the evaluation may demand from them. These attitudes are self-protective mechanisms that often block the purpose of the evaluation. These responses are similar to what people do when they have to go through a tax audit. Education and communication is required for personnel at all levels of the organisation to convince people of the intended benefits of the proposed evaluation before they are able to modify their assumptions or correct misapprehensions about evaluation.

There are four attitudes that participants involved in evaluation processes could take:

1. **Rejection or resistance**. Often people respond to serious systematic evaluative efforts evading participation, fearing that it will bring more control from management, or negative results. In these cases evaluations are seen then as oppressive actions.
2. **Indifference**. This attitude is a result of misunderstanding the nature of evaluation, or lack of information about the objectives of the project. The attitude could be related to deficiencies of management, or the belief that nothing useful can come from it. In this case people just tolerate what is going on without responding honestly and thinking that there is no other option than to acquiesce.
3. **Passive agreement** due to pragmatic reasons. Another response could be to follow instructions from management but not show commitment to the results of the evaluation. This attitude is common if the evaluation has a conventional approach because it is perceived as part of a routine or a required investigation connected with organisational planning procedures.
4. A positive **collaboration and participation** with a critical perspective. Evaluation projects that generate these attitudes are generally well communicated from the beginning of the process. People realize the importance of getting useful information to improve a problem that has been identified. It is relevant because participants acknowledge opportunities provided by the evaluation for

group development; people who have this attitude will accept more easily the role of values within the evaluation process and change will be welcome (Wholey & Newcomer, 1994).

11.7 Conditions for Developing a Culture of Evaluation

A culture of evaluation requires direct involvement of the principal in a cooperative relationship with teachers. The role of the principal is to work with teachers to present clear ideas about the role and function of evaluation, identify specific needs or problems to be evaluated, select adequate methodology and techniques, and consider contextual factors that may influence the evaluation process. This cooperative relationship is characterised by several conditions that imply actions and beliefs on the part of both the principal and teachers. The following conditions are explained in general and then applied to a case study of a school that developed a culture of evaluation: political support, technical knowledge, administrative feasibility, methodological feasibility, ability to follow up, and participative dialogue.

1. **Political Support**: Teachers must not only be willing to carry out evaluation tasks but ideally, they will embrace the philosophy of evaluation; in other words, they are willing to do it. Principals set up a clear organisational structure and designate responsibilities. They lead different constituencies or groups that might be involved in an evaluation process so that they accept all that the evaluation process implies.
2. **Technical Knowledge**: The principal is responsible for conducting the process and providing training for evaluation projects. A clear purpose and approach will lead to a good understanding of all steps that need to be followed. Teachers will gain a sense that they know how to do it.
3. **Administrative feasibility**: Evaluation projects often require complex and challenging actions. The principal's role is to manage and create a positive atmosphere and space to obtain resources and gain access to information. Before the evaluation starts, the principal may need to analyse and negotiate conditions that arise from power struggles or obstacles to the evaluation. Teachers will feel capable to do it.
4. **Methodological capability**: Teachers will have adequate skills to conduct the process and design instruments. The principal will lead a team to assume the coordination of the evaluation process and assure that they have specific training on the methods that they intend to use and enough statistical knowledge to interpret the results. Teachers will have a sense of competence.
5. **Ability to follow up**: Teachers will know how to use the findings to make use of the information to improve their practice and design new systems. The principal will keep in mind the objectives of improving student achievement, facilitating the quality of instruction, and making ethical decisions. Teachers will be able to apply their knowledge.

6. **Participative dialogue**: The principal will promote two-way communication with teachers in a transparent process. They will receive information and critical comments will be welcomed and encouraged. The principal will integrate the results and actions that may follow within the organisational planning processes and which are supported by management (Álvarez García, I & Romay, 2013). Teachers will feel that their voices are heard.

11.7.1   The Case of Leonard Middle School

The conditions for developing a culture of evaluation can be illustrated by a case study from an urban middle school in Southern California that we will call Leonard Middle School. It is a diverse school with an enrolment of 706 students: 22 % are African American and 64 % are Latino; 88 % of the students are eligible for free or reduced lunch; 22 % are English Language Learners.

California uses the Academic Performance Index (API) as a measure of accountability to determine the extent to which schools are meeting state and federal standards and testing requirements. The scores at Leonard had been decreasing and in 2011, the school API score was down to 702. A year later in 2012 there was a remarkable increase to 750, a 48 point gain. It met its goals school-wide and for all student subgroups. However, it did not meet the federal requirement for Adequate Yearly Progress (AYP) in mathematics and continues to be in Programme Improvement (PI) status.

This extraordinary gain in student achievement was made only 1 year after a new principal was appointed. Ronda Madison was an experienced teacher and assistant principal in the school district and had just spent 5 years as principal of Wentworth, a similar middle school, where she was also able to change the achievement pattern. The API went from 609 to 729 API. The decile ranking at the state level went from 2 to 3 and the ranking among schools with similar demographics went from 7 to 9. Her record of turning around Wentworth school led the superintendent to appoint her at Leonard with the hope that she could do the same thing there.

Madison's philosophy was expressed in her doctoral dissertation in which she said that she started at her first school, Wentworth, by getting to know the staff, students, and parents as quickly as possible. Teachers had asked for many changes and improvements to student discipline at their Change of Principal Workshop. This workshop is conducted by the school district whenever there is a change of principals. Administrators from the district use surveys and interviews to prepare a report of what teachers feel needs to be changed and what needs to be kept as is. The report summarised a school meeting where the staff discussed, openly and honestly, what they wanted to change and keep, for example a specific 'dos and don'ts' list for the new principal. Teachers wanted to change the procedures at Wentworth Middle School.

During her first few months, Madison worked on the list of changes the teachers created at the Change of Principal Workshop. They discussed behaviour standards and created a system of rewards and consequences to help motivate students to improve behaviour. The teachers expressed concern that the students were "running the school" and the teachers did not feel supported by the prior administration. The teachers said they felt blamed for student actions. During her first year as principal, Madison focused on changing student behaviour, modelling expectations, and creating a scholarly climate.

At Leonard, Madison began with a similar report from the Change of Principal Workshop that asked for greater attention to student discipline. She began making organisational changes in the summer before teachers returned to school. By the time they arrived new systems were in place. The changes were widely accepted and allowed Madison to proceed to the next step, developing a culture of evaluation.

She formed a leadership team and delegated discipline and other time-consuming duties that did not directly affect classroom instruction. Visiting classrooms and giving teachers timely and direct feedback was a priority. The more visits and notes she left teachers, the more instruction improved. Visits to classrooms were a critical part of making sure teachers were collaborating, implementing professional development strategies, and working to improve student achievement.

Madison also used teacher data meetings to track student progress. She met with teachers by department to look at the data. These data meetings were scheduled at least once a quarter, and in some cases, they met each month. These meetings gave teachers a chance to share successful practice, while the principal had the opportunity to hear first-hand what teachers were doing to help students learn and help teachers use their data to inform classroom interventions. The data questions that she used were:

1. Tell me about your student results.
2. Where did you see the most improvement? What strategies did you use?
3. Who is continuing to struggle? What is your plan to help these students?
4. Comparing your class results to your English Language Learners (ELLs) and African American (AA) subgroups, what do you see?
5. Who are your students who scored Far Below Basic (FBB), what is the story for each of them?
6. What content are you planning to revisit and why?
7. Let's look at the test and your most-missed items. Show me the ones where most students missed (50 % or more). What did they have problems with? Why?
8. Did you try any new strategies that you would like to share?
9. How do you motivate your classes to improve? How do you display the data in your room?
10. What is your goal for the next assessment?

At the end of the first semester (end of January), she began to plan for the next year. She talked with teachers about evaluating who should be teaching certain classes or grade levels, and they explored changing master schedules to improve

Table 11.2 How the principal looked at school's data

Date	Data & purpose	Frequency
September	Academic Performance Index 9 (API)	Yearly
	Look at results, big picture	
	These data come from California Department of Education (CDE) website – look at subgroups and trends over time, graph API growth and compare to other schools	
September	Grade level data by department	Yearly
	Faculty meeting looking at California Standards Test (CST) data by department	
	Make a list of positive accomplishments, areas that need to change, and prescriptions for change (plus, delta, RX)	
September	CST-Longitudinal data by teacher	Yearly
	Individual	
	Count the number of improved students and the number who decreased (+ – count) and plan for improvement based on results	
Monthly	Classroom data compared to CST and subgroup	Monthly
	Look at student level data, share stories of students and strategies that work	
Quarter data	Quarter exams compared to CST, and subgroup	Quarterly
	Colour graph of class results compared to CST and also separated by subgroups	
Quarter	Comparing Quarter Data across school and teacher, and compare to trends from previous year	Quarterly
	Look at quarter trends, predicting CST	
Mid-year	Similar Schools Rank – CDE website	Yearly
	Compares like schools across the state on 10 point scale	
June	End of Course assessments (EOC) data and CST predictions	Yearly
	Teachers share results and predict CST results based on data trends	

opportunities to learn. These types of long-term planning behaviours signalled that she had enough information to begin changing the instructional programs of the school. Selecting the best teacher for a class or grade level can significantly change the climate and productivity of the school. She weighed the pros and cons of each change as she contemplated how to improve Leonard for the following year. The annual calendar to review data is shown in Table 11.2.

Finally, Madison reviewed summative data to make other decisions regarding student placement, interventions, and resources for the following year. She began setting goals for the next year based on summative results. This cycle repeated itself each year and became part of the school culture.

At Leonard, the principal met with teachers monthly to look at formative assessments. The early gain in API could be attributed to the monthly department data meetings and her visits to classrooms and feedback to teachers each week. She followed a model that suggested a sequence of change starting with discipline, transitioning to classroom instruction, and finally looking at school systems.

Madison's actions at Leonard Middle School and the reaction of the teachers illustrate the conditions necessary for creating a culture of evaluation and suggest additional conditions that are desirable to support principal leadership.

11.7.2   Conditions for Creating a Culture of Evaluation at Leonard School

1. In this case the political support necessary for a culture of evaluation was multi-layered. The data system in the school was required by the federal government after the passage of the NCLB Act that mandated testing and accountability across the grades. The State of California extended accountability and mandated the California Standards Test (CST). The Long Beach School District put into place common quarterly assessments in Mathematics, Science, History, and Language Arts and designed the Change of Principal Workshop. Finally, it was the principal who brought a philosophy of using data to improve instruction and implemented regular classroom observations and data meetings.
2. The principal was attuned to the teachers' need for technical knowledge. She introduced the assessment process in small steps and set up a data wall in her office. In the first year, she required teachers to post their results on a quarterly basis and established a norm of transparency where all teachers could see all class data. In the second year she increased the posting of data to twice quarterly. The district established a new data system called LROIX that allowed teachers to see data across schools. Teachers were able to make comparisons with similar schools and look at each other's data.
3. The principal arranged for **administrative feasibility** by setting aside time for teachers to meet and discuss planning and assessment. Sixth grade teachers were reluctant to discuss data as a group, and the principal responded by mandating a time when teams came together in a common location, the library.
4. The principal became the chief instructor to create **methodological capacity** among teachers. She met with each teacher once a month to review test results on an overall basis. These data ranked students from Advanced to Far Below Basic. She and the teacher looked at specific areas in which students had difficulties. Then she made the teachers responsible for developing plans to address the deficiencies by providing a data form that they could use and suggesting ways that they could display data in the classroom.
5. The principal attended to **follow-up** to make sure that the results of data analysis were being used in the classroom. She also used information from objective data to explore more subjective data. The stories of successful students and those who were struggling were shared and examined in light of school and community factors. Professional development was planned to address common concerns that arose out of the process.

6. The principal communicated in a transparent and timely manner to create **participative dialogue** by establishing a timeline for assessment activities. She met regularly with teachers to work on assessment plans and made sure that teacher concerns were addressed by asking teachers to evaluate each session according positive aspects of the process and areas needing improvement (plus/delta).

The development of a culture of evaluation at Leonard illustrates the main points of this article. The principal paid attention to both formative and summative evaluation processes, making sure that teachers could use data to improve instruction and monitoring the overall progress of students. The key was to integrate evaluation, planning, and decision-making.

The principal addressed teacher attitudes toward evaluation by taking a proactive approach and first understanding their concerns about student discipline, and then putting into place systems that require attention to data. Her work met the conditions necessary to create a culture of evaluation, but it would not have been possible without complementary evaluation systems at the national, state, and district level.

11.8   Conclusions and Recommendations

Evaluation and assessment form the critical strategy for accountability to improve school performance. This chapter has described why the management and use of evaluations, particularly for educational leaders, are not easy, but they are crucial for improving the quality of learning processes.

The globalisation of contemporary society and the need for democratic knowledge require that education more than ever before has to be an integral part of social development and culture. Effective assessment processes include a conscious effort to create and maintain what we are calling a "culture of evaluation".

The role of the principal is to ensure that there is the political will on the part of different actors in the process, and that they are able to learn continually how to conduct an evaluation process with rigour and objectivity. The principal should find strategies to ensure readiness for participation, paying attention to different reactions or personal interests that might be affected. The best way is to communicate objectives clearly and avoid punishment. From the managerial point of view, evaluation efforts always require good organisation skills to assure the implementation of coordinated action.

The most critical conditions of any assessment process are the timeliness and usefulness of results. As this chapter highlights, it is not enough to develop a good design, utilising sound methods or gathering enough data; the evaluation results must probe for validity and indicate how the information obtained can be applied for improvement. An evaluation project can be valuable beyond the school site. Clear processes can be replicated by other schools to enhance knowledge of both the evaluation process and successful practices with students.

There are several recommendations for any school that is undertaking an assessment of students. First, teamwork is essential. Effective evaluations require cooperation between the administration and teachers with open communication and active participation. Second, state and national standards must be adhered to as required by law but they must be developed in a way that is appropriate for the social and cultural context. Third, the justification for assessment must always be related to the improvement of the quality of education. Fourth, assessment cannot be carried out without adequate financial support. Fifth, continuous training is necessary for all staff, and support from specialized personnel is critical to support their efforts.

The principal has the responsibility for the development of a culture of evaluation, but issues of growth, equity, interdependence, and auto-determination go beyond the principal's control. School districts often grow in size with new students to serve and at the same time, districts change demographically often with greater diversity from students of colour, immigrants, and families in poverty. The school is also part of a larger system and is dependent upon enlightened polices on the state and national level. Depending on the system, the principal will have more or less autonomy to carry out an evaluation.

Promoting and developing a culture of evaluation in schools goes beyond technical requirements or traditional functions. The principal does not control many of the large variables and will thus need courage to innovate and advocate for constant improvement. Authentic leadership requires risk, persistence, and dedication to create a culture of evaluation.

References

Álvarez García, I. (1997). Theory of evaluation: Some practical examples (Teoría de evaluación: Algunos ejemplos prácticos). In *Cuadernos de Filosofía y Letras (10)*. UNAM, 1985. Re-edited by UNESCO/CREFAL.

Álvarez García, I. (Ed.). (2008). *Planning and development of educational and social Projects. (Planificación y desarrollo de proyectos sociales y educativos)* (9th ed.). México: Limusa.

Álvarez García, I., & Romay, M. L. (2013). *Challenges for a culture of evaluation in educational institutions (Desafíos para una cultura de evaluación en las Instituciones Educativas)*. Mexico: Limusa-Noriega (Eds.).

Berk, R. A. (1999). *Thinking about program evaluation*. Thousand Oaks, CA: Sage Publications.

Bohte, J., & Meier, K. J. (2000). Goal displacement: Assessing the motivation for organizational cheating. *Public Administration Review, 60*, 173–182.

Bridges, E. M., & Groves, R. (2000). The micro and macro politics of personnel evaluation: A framework. *Journal of Personnel Evaluation in Education, 12*, 321–337.

Calonghi, L., Gianola, L. P., Groppo, M., Perucci, G., & Reguzzoni, M. (1991). *The evaluation issue (El problema de la evaluación)*. Madrid: ITER Editors.

Chen, H. T. (1990). *Theory-driven evaluation*. Newbury Park, CA: Sage.

Common Core State Standards Initiative. (2010a). *Common Core State Standards for English Language arts & literacy in history/social studies, science, and technical subjects*. Retrieved from http://www.orestandards.org/assets/CCSSI_ELA%20Standards.pdf

Common Core State Standards Initiative. (2010b). *Common Core State Standards for mathematics*. Retrieved from http://www.corestandards.org/assets/CCSSI_Math%20Standards.pdf

Cronbach, L. J. (1982). *Designing evaluations of educational and social programs*. San Francisco: Jossey-Bass.

Decoo, W. (2002). *Crisis on Campus: Confronting Academic Misconduct*. Cambridge, MA: MIT Press.

Erwin, D. T. (1991). *Assessing student learning and development: A Guide to the principles, goals and methods of determining college outcomes*. San Francisco: Jossey-Bass.

Flagg, B. N. (1990). *Formative evaluation for educational technologies*. Hillsdale, NJ: Erlbaum Associates.

Fullan, M. (2001). *Leading in a culture of change*. San Francisco: Jossey-Bass.

Fullan, M. (2008a). *The six secrets to change*. San Francisco: Jossey-Bass.

Fullan, M. (2008b). *What's worth fighting for in the principalship?* San Francisco: Jossey-Bass.

Glatthorn, A., Boschee, F., Whitehead, B. M., & Boschee, B. F. (2012). *Curriculum leadership: Strategies for development and implementation* (3rd ed.). Los Angeles: Sage.

Guerra-Lopez, I. (2008). *Performance evaluation: Approaches for improving program and organizational performance*. San Francisco: Jossey-Bass.

Heilig, J. V., & Darling-Hammond, L. (2008). Accountability Texas-style: The progress and learning of urban minority students in a high-stakes testing context. *Educational Evaluation and Policy Analysis, 30*(2), 75–110.

Hill, H. C. (2009). Evaluating value-added models: A measurement perspective. *Journal of Policy Analysis and Management, 28*, 102–109.

Kemmis, S. (1989). Seven principles for programs evaluation in curriculum development and innovation. (pp. 117-140). In E. R. House (Ed.), *New directions in educational evaluation*. Lewes, VA: Falmer Press.

Kennedy, M. M. (2010). *Teacher assessment and the quest for teacher quality: A handbook*. San Francisco: Jossey-Bass.

Ladson Billings, G. (2006). From the achievement gap to the education debt: Understanding achievement in U.S. Schools. *Educational Researcher, 35*(7), 3–12.

Leithwood, K., Lewis, K. S., Anderson, S., & Wahlstrom, K. (2004). *Review of research: How leadership influences student learning*. Minneapolis, MN: University of Minnesota, Center of Applied Research and Educational Improvement.

Lincoln, I. S., & Guba, E. G. (1981). *Effective evaluation*. San Francisco: Jossey-Bass.

Madaus, G., Scriven, M., & Stufflebeam, D. (1990). *Evaluation models: Viewpoints on educational and human services evaluation*. Boston: Kluwer-Nijhoff.

Martínez Slanova, E. (1980). *Principles of evaluation (Los principios de la evaluación)*. Madrid: ICE/UPM. Retrieved from http://www.uhu.es/cine.educacion/didactica/0092principiosevaluacion.htm

Marzano, R. J., Waters, T., & McNulty, B. A. (2005). *School leadership that works: From research to results*. Alexandria, VA: Association for Supervision and Curriculum Development & Aurora: Mid-continent Research for Education Learning.

Mathison, S. (Ed.). (2005). *Encyclopedia of evaluation*. Thousand Oaks, CA: Sage.

McNeil, L. (1986). *Contradictions of control: School structure and school knowledge*. London: Routledge.

McNeil, L. (2000a). *Contradictions of school reform: The educational cost of standardized testing*. London: Routledge.

McNeil, L. (2000b). Creating new inequalities: Contradictions of reform. *Phi Delta Kappan, 81*(10), 729–734.

McNeil, L. M., Coppola, E., Radigan, J., & Heilig, J. V. (2008). Avoidable losses: High-stakes accountability and the dropout crisis. *Education Policy Analysis Archives, 16*(3), 1–45.

Munro, J. H. (2008). *Educational leadership*. Boston: McGraw Hill Higher Education.

National Governors' Association Center for Best Practices (NGA Center) & Council of Chief State School Officers (CCSSO). (2012). *Common core state standards initiative.* Retrieved from http://www.corestandards.org/

Nelson, S., & McGhee, M. (2004). *Time-off task: How test preparation is siphoning instructional time for students of colour and students of poverty.* Paper presented at the annual meeting of the University Council for Educational Administration, Kansas City, MO.

Nelson, S., McGhee, M., Meno, L., & Slater, C. L. (2007). Fulfilling the promise of educational accountability: A unique perspective. *Phi Delta Kappan, 88*(9), 702–709.

Nelson, S., McGhee, M., Reardon, R., Gonzales, K., & Kent, C. (2007). *Supplanting teaching with testing: Does it raise test scores?* Paper presented at the annual meeting of the University Council for Educational Administration, Alexandria, VA.

Nevo, D. (1986). The conceptualization of educational evaluation. (pp. 15-30). In E. R. House (Ed.), *New Directions in educational evaluation.* Lewes, DE: Falmer.

Nichols, S. L., Glass, G. V., & Berliner, D. C. (2012). High-stakes testing and student achievement: Updated analyses with NAEP data. *Education Policy Analysis Archives, 20*(20). Retrieved from http://epaa.asu.edu/ojs/article/view/1048

Owen, J. M. (2006). *Program evaluation: Formative approach* (3rd ed.). New York: The Guilford.

PARCC. (2013). *Partnership for assessment of readiness for College and careers.* Retrieved from http://www.parcconline.org/

Patton, M. Q. (1990). *Qualitative evaluation and research methods.* Newbury Park: SAGE Publications, Inc.

Peterson, K. D. (2009). *Teacher evaluation: Comprehensive guide.* Thousand Oaks, CA: Sage.

Porter, A., McMaken, J., Hwang, J., & Yang, R. (2011). Common core standards: The new U.S. intended curriculum. *Educational Researcher, 40*(3), 103–116.

Quick, P. M., & Normore, A. H. (2004). Moral leadership in the 21st century: Everyone is watching: Especially the students. *The Educational Forum, 68*(4), 336–347.

Radcliffe, J. (2010, March 4). Cheating allegations tighten TAKS test security: State switches exam essay topic, sends monitors to two HISD schools. *Houston Chronicle.*

Reeves, D. (2009). *Leading change in your school.* Alexandria, VA: ASCD.

Romay, M. L., & Crispin, B. M. L. (2000). Self-evaluation and faculty development. In *Faculty evaluation (Evaluacion de la Docencia)* (Chapter 14, pp. 341–364). México: Paidós.

Rossi, P. H., & Freeman, M. (1992). *Evaluation: A systematic approach* (3rd ed.). Thousand Oaks, CA: Sage.

Rueda, R. (2011). *The three dimensions of improving students' performance.* New York: Columbia University Press.

Schemo, D. J., & Fessenden, F. (2003, December 03). A miracle revisited: Measuring success; gains in Houston Schools: How real are they? *New York Times.* http://www.nytimes.com/2003/12/03/us/a-miracle-revisited-measuring-success-gains-in-houston-schools-how-real-are-they.html.

Schmoker, M. (1999). *Results: The key to continuous improvement.* Alexandria, VA: Association for Supervision and Curriculum Development.

Scriven, M. (1967). The methodology of evaluation. In R. W. Tyler, R. M. Gagne, & M. Scriven (Eds.), *Perspectives of curriculum evaluation* (pp. 39–83). Chicago: Rand McNally.

Scriven, M. (1991). *Evaluation thesaurus* (4th ed.). Newbury Park, CA: Sage.

Shadish, W. R., Cook, T. D., & Leviton, L. C. (1991). *Foundations of program evaluation: Theories of practice.* Newbury Park, CA: Sage.

Shawn, I., & Greene, J. (2006). *Handbook of evaluation: Policies, programs and practices.* Thousand Oaks, CA: Sage.

Slater, C. L., McGhee, M., Nelson, S., & Meno, L. (2011). Lessons learned: The promise and possibility of educational accountability in the United States. In C. F. Webber & J. Lupart (Eds.), *Leading student assessment* (pp. 41–58). Dordrecht, The Netherlands: Springer.

Smarter Balanced Assessment Consortium (2013) retrieve from http://www.smarterbalanced.org/

Spaulding, D. T. (2008). *Program Evaluation in practice: Core concepts and examples for discussion and analysis*. San Francisco: Jossey-Bass.

Stake, R. E. (1990). Responsive evaluation. In H. G. Walberg & G. D. Haertel (Eds.), *The International encyclopaedia of educational evaluation* (pp. 75–77). Oxford, NY: Pergamon Press.

Stufflebeam, D. L., et al. (1971). *Educational evaluation and decision making*. Itasca, IL: Peacock.

U.S. Department of Education. (2009a). *Title I — Improving the academic achievement of the disadvantaged*. Retrieved from http://www.ed.gov/policy/elsec/leg/esea02/pg1.htm

U.S. Department of Education. (2009b). *President Obama, U.S. Secretary of Education Duncan announces national competition to advance school reform*. Retrieved from http://www2.ed.gov/news/pressreleases/2009/07/07242009.html

Weiss, C. H. (1992). *Evaluation research: Methods to determine efficiency of programs (Investigación Evaluativa: Métodos para determinar la eficiencia de los programas)*. México: Trillas.

Whitaker, T. (2003). *What great principals do differently?* Larchmont, VA: Eye on Education.

Wholey, J., & Newcomer, K. (1994). *Handbook of practical program evaluation*. San Francisco: Jossey-Bass.

Wildy, H., & Clarke, S. (2008). Charting an arid landscape: The preparation of novice primary principals in Western Australia. *School Leadership and Management, 28*(5), 469–487.

Winerip, M. (2011, July 18). Cracking a system in which test scores were for changing. *New York Times*. http://www.nytimes.com/2011/07/18/education/18oneducation.html?_r=0

Wohlstetter, P., Datnow, A., & Park, V. (2008). Creating a system for data-driven decision-making: Applying the principal-agent framework. *School Effectiveness and School Improvement, 19*(3), 239–259.

Chapter 12
Formative Assessment in High School Communities of Practice: Creating a Culture of Inquiry, Introspection, and Improvement

Dianne Yee

Abstract Although assessment concepts bridge all levels, senior high school educators face pressures regarding assessment of and for learning that are quite different from elementary or middle school educators, particularly in the Alberta context. This vignette of an assessment focus in two very large, urban high schools outlines my perspective as both a principal and a district director – influenced by the conceptual frames of Elmore's (2002) Instructional Core, Wenger, McDermott and Snyder's (2002) Communities of Practice, Conzemius and O'Neill's (2002) SMART Goals, Boudet, City and Murnane's (2005) Data Wise Improvement Cycle, Friesen's (2009) Teaching Effectiveness Framework, and the Galileo Educational Network's (2013) Discipline-Based Inquiry. As a school principal, I eliminated our school professional development committee and gave the days to our individual curriculum department Communities of Practices to meet their needs and support their SMART outcomes. We were very diligent in following the assessment frameworks we designed as a school to improve learning for all ability levels and programs of our students. As a district administrator, I have allocated resources in non-typical ways to allow principals, assistant principals, and learning leaders the time to engage in ongoing conversation about rich task design and formative assessment. I have both enabled and required these instructional leaders to collect and share evidence of student intellectual engagement in their classrooms and throughout their schools.

Keywords Formative assessment • Assessment for learning • Intellectual engagement • SMART goals • Teaching Effectiveness Framework • Data Wise Improvement Cycle

D. Yee (✉)
Director, Area III, Calgary Board of Education, Calgary, AB, Canada
e-mail: DLYee@cbe.ab.ca

© Springer International Publishing Switzerland 2016   285
S. Scott et al. (eds.), *Assessment in Education*, The Enabling
Power of Assessment 2, DOI 10.1007/978-3-319-23398-7_12

12.1   Through My Lens as a Principal and as a District Director

Because I have spent most of my career as secondary educator – as a teacher, a counsellor and a principal – I view assessment primarily through a high school lens. I have worked as a principal in three very different high school settings in Alberta, from a small rural junior/senior high school to a very large urban senior high school. In the 400 student, rural Grade 7–12 setting there were two or three of our teachers working in each curriculum specialty. In the 2300 student, Grade 10–12 setting, we had 15 or more teachers in each curriculum department. Although assessment concepts bridge all levels, senior high school educators face pressures regarding assessment *of* and *for* learning that are quite different from elementary or middle school educators, particularly in the Alberta context. From my experience I would also suggest that as the number of teachers working in a curriculum specialty increases in secondary schools, there are both additional strengths and challenges in terms of developing assessment cultures of inquiry, introspection, and improvement. This chapter is a vignette of an assessment focus in two very large, urban high schools from my perspective as both a principal and a district director.

12.2   Why Focus on Assessment *for* Learning in High Schools?

In an accountability-driven school context such as Alberta, high school educators need to balance the ever-increasing and very public achievement and perception data from the ministry (Alberta Education) with valid classroom-based assessment data. In my 10 years as an Alberta high school principal, I experienced progressively more and more accountability data collected and presented to a sometimes naïve public – who may equate high Diploma Examination (Grade 12 – university/college entrance examinations) scores with high levels of student achievement and engagement and with exemplary teaching. Each year in Alberta high schools, principals receive over 100 pages of text, charts, and graphs, as well as an accompanying colour-coded spread-sheet from the Ministry. This information assists them in understanding current Grade 12 provincial examination (Diploma Examination) results and the Grade 10 parent and student perception data (Accountability Pillar Survey), as well as to track their high school students' completion and post-secondary Rutherford Scholarship Eligibility trends. Certainly, these data are very helpful to principals as they develop a picture of their schools' learning community's strengths and challenges. However, this volume of data represents a small portion of a principal's work and can be a rather simplistic portrayal of the complexity of learning and teaching accomplished in very large urban high schools.

12.3   Conceptual Frames

In developing our high school assessment cultures of inquiry, introspection, and improvement, our district has been guided by the work of a number of contemporary educational researchers which is outlined in the following sections and includes the conceptual frames of Elmore's (2002) Instructional Core, Wenger, McDermott and Snyder's (2002) Communities of Practice, Conzemius and O'Neill's (2002) SMART Goals, Boudet, City and Murnane's (2005) Data Wise Improvement Cycle, Friesen's (2009) Teaching Effectiveness Framework, and the Galileo Educational Network's (2013) Discipline-Based Inquiry.

12.3.1   Supporting the Instructional Core with Teacher Professional Development

Elmore's (2002) focus on the Instructional Core has been central to the work undertaken in our district. Elmore has indicated that school "capacity [is] defined by the degree of successful interaction among teachers and students around content" (p. 23). His view of "instructional practice [as] a collective good – as well as a private and individual concern" (2000, p. 24) has created opportunities for educators, such as myself, to make our individual work transparent to our colleagues. Elmore also has asserted that "internal accountability precedes external accountability and is a precondition for any process of improvement" (2002, p. 20). As a principal, I agree with Elmore that our school must have its own internal system for reaching agreement on what constitutes good teaching practice and for making that agreement visible in our daily work with students and parents. As Elmore suggested, we worked to create "a high degree of alignment among individual teachers about their responsibility for the improvement of student learning" (p. 21). Elmore (2002) also reminded principals – and, optimistically, school systems and ministries – of the necessity to develop a strategy for investing in the knowledge and skills of teachers. "Accountability [for teacher professional development] must be a reciprocal process. For every increase in performance that I demand from you, I have an equal responsibility to provide you with the capacity to meet that expectation" (p. 5).

Elmore's (2002) Professional Development: Consensus View outlined that effective teacher professional development is derived from analysis of student learning of specific curriculum content in the context of our own classrooms:

- Focuses on a well-articulated mission or purpose anchored in student learning of core disciplines and skills
- Derives from analysis of student learning of specific context in an specific setting
- Focuses on specific issues of curriculum and pedagogy

- Derived from research and exemplary practice
- Connected with specific issues of instruction and student learning of academic disciplines and skills in the context of actual classrooms

- Embodies a clearly articulated theory or model of adult learning
- Develops, reinforces and sustains group work

  - Collaborative practice within schools
  - Networked across schools

- Involves active participation of school leaders and staff
- Sustains focus over time—continuous improvement
- Models of effective practice

  - Delivered in schools and classrooms
  - Practice is consistent with message

- Uses assessment and evaluation

  - Active monitoring of student learning
  - Feedback on teacher learning and practice. (p. 7)

Effective professional development in our school context integrated both research and exemplary practice. It required collaboration of curriculum departments within schools, as well as active monitoring of student learning and teacher practice through our SMART outcome process.

12.3.2   Digital Communities of Practice

In my secondary school principalship experience, the term Professional Learning Community (PLC) frequently was interpreted as a book study group – with considerable theorising about "big ideas" but very little action that impacted teacher practice and student learning. When I was principal, we used the term Communities of Practice (CoPs) because a teacher in one of our curriculum departments was pursuing graduate work and found that the communities of practice literature resonated with his high school experience. The teacher was searching for a more positive way to consider professional development because his contention was that often professional development was an activity "done to him" with little or no application to his teaching context. My own experiences with teacher professional development often had been consistent with his view – particularly in large urban high school environments with multiple curriculum departments. As a result, we chose to avoid the term Professional Learning Communities (PLCs) and adopted the Community of Practice framework of Wenger et al. (2002). Consistent with Wenger's view, our CoPs were groups of people who shared a passion for their work as teachers and learned how to do it better through our regular interaction. Wenger explained that CoPs have three key characteristics: the domain, the community, and the practice. In our domain, shared interest and expertise was key;

hence, the focus was on our ten curriculum departments. Community membership implied a shared competence that distinguished specific curriculum department colleagues from other staff members. In our community, teachers engaged in discussions and activities to share information as well as build relationships with their colleagues in order to learn from one another. Our CoPs viewed teachers as active practitioners developing a shared repertoire of resources (experiences, stories, tools, ways of addressing recurring problems etc.) through investment of time and sustained interaction.

Because of my background experience and my doctoral research, I accept that appropriate use of information and communication technology (ICT) can positively impact learning, teaching, and leadership. However, my perspective is that much ICT use in school systems is overly expensive, frustration producing, and not always pedagogically sound. Wenger's work on technology for CoPs began in 2000 when he was commissioned to do a US government study. He initially described the particular roles of specific technology: team work (online project spaces); community management (website communities); online conversations (discussion groups); synchronous interactions (online meeting spaces); online instruction (community-oriented elearning spaces); knowledge exchange (access to expertise); and documenting practice (knowledge repositories). As the technology evolved so did Wenger's research, and there has been a trend towards aggregation into knowledge platforms and hybrid tools that community users can reconfigure (Wenger, White, Smith & Rowe, 2005). As our CoPs developed over the 5 years, we used Wenger's framework to consider the use of ICT in our assessment context.

12.3.3   "Data Wise" and SMART

We worked with the SMART goal process of Conzemius and O'Neill (2002) in an attempt to focus our School Development Plan (SDP) on student learning in our classrooms – as opposed to student results on single standardised tests, or on typical facility and structural issues. The SMART acronym was developed from goal setting processes that were Strategic and specific, Measureable, Attainable, Results-based, and Timebound. Consistent with the key principles of SMART teams, we developed an expectation for whole-school learning and continuous improvement. "Learning happens when theory and practice interact; past experience and new knowledge meet; data confirm or negate perceptions; separate, isolated events or facts emerge into patterns, trends or new ideas; and two or more individuals' creative potentials collide" (p. 3). This SMART format was a relatively simple model to monitor which of our instructional and assessment strategies were making a difference and by how much. Additionally, the format applied across our very diverse curriculum departments.

The Harvard Graduate School of Education "Data Wise" project led by Boudet et al. (2005) highlighted several practical, but often problematic, steps in looking carefully at high school students' assessment data. This eight step "Data Wise Improvement Cycle" as shown in Fig. 12.1 is very similar to the SMART process

Fig. 12.1 The Boudet
et al. (2005) "Data Wise
Improvement Cycle" (p. 5)

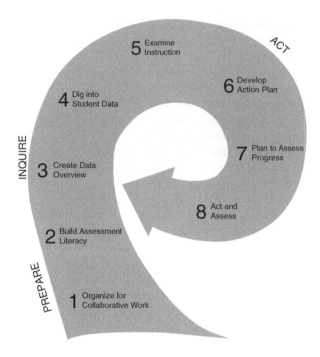

from Step 3 onward – from creating the data overview, to analysis of specific student data, to examining instruction, then developing both an action plan and an assessment plan, and finally implementing the plans. This cyclical process then returns to creating another data overview. In our context, Data Wise Step 1 which is described as "organizing for collaborative work", encouraged us to remove typical high school barriers to working together in large curriculum departments. Also Step 2 which is described as "building assessment literacy", challenged us to address wide differences in individual teacher and curriculum department abilities in order to interpret and understand data. In describing the context for using student data appropriately in the Data Wise format, there was an expectation that the school had a system of interlocking teams and a coordinated information flow between them. Meetings needed to be productive with effective facilitation, and in our context we used specific protocols to guide our professional conversations and to ensure sensitive and respectful commentary. Teachers were encouraged to observe each other teach, and to give each other constructive feedback about instructional and assessment practices and student outcomes. As a result we structured as much time as practicable for these collaborative activities. These key principles aligned with Elmore's (2002) views of internal accountability and Leithwood's (2007) work on teacher efficacy which will be subsequently discussed.

12.3.4 Common Classroom Assessments

Reeves (2004) and others reinforced the value of frequent common assessments to improve student learning. This assessment format, however, was not typical for high school teachers who often have been socialised to value professional autonomy and private practice, particularly if they have been working in high school for a number of years. Reeves' assessment "Gold Standard" advocated for frequent common assessments that have been developed collaboratively and marked by every teacher of a grade level or course. Such assessments promoted consistency in expectations and provided timely, accurate, and specific feedback to both students and teachers. Reeves also articulated a variety of reasons why common assessments were more efficient, effective, and capacity building than creating and using assessment instruments in isolation. Common assessments represented the most effective strategy for determining whether the expected curriculum was being taught and, more importantly, learned. We found that common assessments also had potential to inform the practice of individual teachers as well as build a curriculum department's capacity to improve its whole instructional programme. In addition, common assessments were able to facilitate a systematic, collective response to students who were experiencing difficulty. Our focus was that data from common assessment were used "to improve teaching and learning, not merely to evaluate students and schools" (p. 114).

12.3.5 Focused Professional Conversations

Consistent with the protocol development from the Coalition of Essential Schools, Glaude (2005) created a practical collection of structured questions for professional discussion about student work which proved beneficial in our school's curriculum department Communities of Practice. Her work included four types of protocols for conversations focussed on (1) student work, (2) action research to improve student learning, (3) common text readings, and (4) professional goals or challenges. These protocols included ground rules, guiding questions, and time suggestions for the various processes within each protocol. In our high school, adaptations of these protocols were also used effectively by teachers with their student groups.

12.3.6 Transformational Leadership and Teacher Efficacy

Leithwood's perspective on transformational leadership has guided my thinking on school-based leadership for the past decade. Leithwood's (2007) framework of core leadership practices aligned with the work we did in our CoPs and gave clear direction for leadership development within and across our curriculum departments (see

Table 12.1 Leithwood's (2007) core leadership practices (pp. 52–57)

Core leadership practice	
Setting directions	Building a shared vision
	Fostering acceptance of group goals
	High performance expectations
Developing people	Providing individual support and consideration
	Intellectual stimulation
	Providing an appropriate model
Redesigning the organisation	Building collaborative cultures
	Restructuring
	Building productive relationships with families and communities
Managing the instructional programme	Staffing the programme
	Providing instructional support
	Monitoring school activity
	Buffering staff from distractions to their work.

Table 12.1). His core leadership practices involved (1) setting directions, (2) developing people, (3) redesigning the organisation, and (4) managing the instructional programme. The particular value was the focus the leadership practices brought to the work of our administrative team in an often "undoable" job. Leithwood indicated that enactment of the core practices needed to be sensitive to the context and uniqueness of each school; this resonated with the considerable differences in high school programming and student demographics within our very large school district.

Leithwood's (2007) work on teacher efficacy, or the extent to which the teacher believes he or she has the capacity to affect student performance, made the connection with student achievement which aligned with our CoP framework. His research indicated that "individual teacher efficacy … likely has the largest positive effect on teacher performance and student learning" (p. 47). "Higher levels of teacher efficacy also are associated with higher levels of student achievement, more positive student attitudes toward school, and lower dropout rates" (p. 48), all of which were, and are, current emphases in Alberta high schools.

12.3.7 "What Did You Do in School Today?" and Student Intellectual Engagement

In my recent work as a district director, Willms, Friesen and Milton's (2009) research on student intellectual engagement has provided clear guidance for our school district. Friesen (2009, p. 4) articulated five core principles, which are foundational to effective teaching practices:

1. Effective teaching practice begins with the thoughtful and intentional design of learning that engages students intellectually and academically;

2. The work that students are asked to undertake is worthy of their time and attention, is personally relevant, and deeply connected to the world in which they live;
3. Assessment practices are clearly focused on improving student learning and guiding teaching decisions and actions;
4. Teachers foster a variety of interdependent relationships in classrooms that promote learning and create a strong culture around learning; and
5. Teachers improve their practice in the company of peers.

These five principles are clearly interdependent. Principle 3 of the Teaching Effectiveness Framework which focusses on assessment *for* learning is aligned with the formative assessment perspectives of Reeves (2004) and Popham (2008) as well as the Data Wise [instructional] Improvement Cycle of Boudet and her colleagues (2005). In our high school classrooms, assessment needs to be a significant part of students' learning experience:

> not in the form of separate tests, but as a seamless part of the learning process. The intentional design of assessment for learning that invites students to co-create assessment criteria with teachers is a powerful strategy that enables students to think deeply about, understand the next steps, and become increasingly self-directed in their learning. (Friesen, 2009, p. 5)

Students require teachers to develop clear targets and provide models of quality work. The criteria for evaluating any of students' learning must be made clear to them so they understand both the purpose of their work and what it means to complete it successfully. The clarity in this Teaching Effectiveness Framework has assisted me in my role as Director to continue to develop the assessment skills of our teachers and principals so that our adolescent learners are more intellectually engaged.

12.3.8 Discipline-Based Inquiry

The Galileo Educational Network (2013) has developed a framework for inquiry studies that has assisted our work across the district, particularly at the high school level. From my perspective as Area leader, much of the previous discourse with educators about the value of inquiry-based learning in academic core courses at high school has centred on the lack of time available for teachers to cover content-heavy curriculum, and inquiry studies require more course-time than teachers have available to them. The Galileo framework for inquiry involves authentic tasks grounded in real-world experiences, connecting with experts in the particular discipline, active investigation, academic rigour, sophisticated use of digital technologies, and elaborated communication of student learning outcomes. The Galileo discipline-based inquiry rubric brings structure and clarity to inquiry-based learning that allows our secondary teachers to see the potential of this instructional strategy with their high school students. Assessment *for* learning guides instructional planning and student learning, with on-going assessment woven into the design of the study providing timely, descriptive feedback and utilising a range of methods, including peer- and self-evaluation.

12.4   An Assessment Focus to Improve High School Student Achievement

The preceding conceptual frames have brought clarity to our district collective's work in terms of our high school assessment focus as it has evolved over the past 10 years. We are working to create a culture of inquiry, introspection, and improvement by focusing on teachers as designers of learning, formative assessment, and analysing multiple sources of data to improve instructional practice. The following section outlines my insights on leading enhanced student assessment as a high school principal.

12.5   Through the Lens of a High School Principal – A Case of Whole-School Inquiry into Effective Assessment

12.5.1   Student Achievement Alignment

In the Alberta School Development Plan process, principals are generally required to align expected school outcomes with district and provincial goals. In our school district we have been focussing on our work in schools first, and then "rolling up" the school outcomes into our area and district goals. As principals, our focus on student achievement was clear through the four levels of accountability: from our individual schools, to our area within the district, to the whole district, and finally to the Ministry:

A. *School Priorities*

- Excellence in student achievement in all courses and at all levels of programming
- A personalised learning environment where each student finds success

B. *Area Outcomes*

- Each student's achievement advances

C. *District Ends*

- E-1 – Mega End – Each student, in keeping with his or her individual abilities and gifts, will complete high school with a foundation of learning to function effectively in life, work, and continued learning.

- E-2 – Academic Success – Each student will possess the knowledge, skills, and attitudes required for academic success and will be effectively prepared for life, work, and further learning. Accordingly, each student will meet or exceed provincial grade-level standards of achievement in Language Arts, Mathematics, Science and Social Studies, with priority attention being focused on the attainment of literacy and numeracy skills.

D. *Alberta Education (ministry) Goals*

- Excellence in learner outcomes
- High quality learning opportunities for all

12.5.2 Multiple Sources of Student Data

We used five main types of student data to inform our assessment processes. For many years we had received standardised test data from the Alberta Education Grade 12 Diploma Examinations for our English, Mathematics, Science, and Social Studies courses. For each of our examination sessions in January and June (the school year commences in September – "Fall" semester), we received detailed reports of student performance on the examinations, including specific details on student responses to each question and information on gender trends. We also received a yearly reporting of Diploma Examination Marks, School Awarded Marks, and Participation Rates for each course comparing our school to its counterparts across the province. Our district also aggregated the data for all high schools. For a number of years, Alberta Education has also provided to schools and districts reports on High School Completion Rates. More recently schools have received Rutherford Scholarship eligibility information and details regarding the number of Diploma exams written per student.

At our school, Diploma Examination data analysis was a cyclical investigation consistent with the "Data Wise" process (Boudett, City, & Murnane, 2005). We used a consistent analysis format across the four curriculum departments:

1. Description of Student Performance

   - Diploma Examination Marks
   - Difference between Diploma Examination Marks and School Awarded Marks
   - Difference between Written and Multiple Choice results
   - Diploma Examination Participation Rates

2. Historical Trends in Student Performance (5 year averages)

   - Diploma Examination Marks
   - Difference between Diploma Examination Marks and School Awarded Marks
   - Difference between Written and Multiple Choice results
   - Diploma Examination Participation Rates

3. Specific Implications for Instruction

In our very large school (which included over 2300 students, 120 teachers and 40 support staff members), my four assistant principals each had responsibility for liaison with several of our ten curriculum departments, so a variety of individuals were responsible for this data analysis process. As part of the yearly process, I met with the learning leader of the curriculum department and the associated assistant principal for an initial data review early in the new academic year (in October). Subsequent to this initial data review meeting, the learning leader shared results with individual teachers who had taught the Grade 12 Diploma Examination courses and with the curriculum department as a whole. In January, the four academic core learning leaders met to share their results and discussed commonalities and differences across their departments, and then they created a written report for me as principal. I shared the results in meetings with our whole staff and with our School Council which included parents, as well as student, staff and community representatives. As required by Alberta Education, we published the results in both print and website format for our parent community in our Annual Results Report. We also used the data to inform our subsequent School Development Plan.

In 2003, Alberta Education developed the Accountability Pillar survey to gather perception data from Grade 10 students, as well as from their parents and teachers. These data focused on individual satisfaction regarding school safety, citizenship and career development, breadth of programming, and access to special education resources. In our school these perception data were collected after students and their parents had only 5 months of experience with our school. In my view, schools with a Grade 10–12 configuration often are not accurately portrayed by this perception data; because by comparison, in my previous schools with a Grade 7–12 population or with a Grade 9–12 population, students and parents had more opportunity to understand the services for students and the programs of the schools prior to completing the survey. However, our district created a Grade 12 Exit Survey to collect additional data on student progress. This survey focused on student perception data similar to the Alberta Education Accountability Pillar data. The trend in our school was for graduating students to report considerably more satisfaction with our programs and student services than Grade 10 students who had just entered our large, urban high school from our seven different feeder schools.

At our school, we offered Advanced Placement (AP) courses in a variety of disciplines– English, History, Calculus, Biology, Chemistry, Physics and Art. Each year we received data from the American College Board regarding the performance of our students on the Advanced Placement Examinations that took place in May. In addition, the district provided all Advanced Placement schools with aggregated data. Therefore, this served as yet another data source that informed our leadership team and staff about our students' outcomes.

Finally, we analysed classroom data from our curriculum department SMART outcomes. We used the SMART process for the 5 years that I was principal, and each year we further developed our assessment skills. From our experiences, we learned that this process engendered a valuing of our collective efforts and intelligence, and promoted a sense of teacher efficacy. A SMART outcome was created by each curriculum department, and we focused on the power of classroom assessment and precise teaching to improve student achievement. We modified the Conzemius and O'Neill (2002) SMART format to reflect our assessment focus within our large, urban high school context:

- Specific and Strategic;
- Meaningful and Measurable;
- Action plan including specific strategies;
- Realistic and attainable given time and resources; and
- Trackable with a specific Timeline

Similar to our Diploma Examination data analyses, we used a cyclical yearly process with templates to guide key processes and presentation of essential information from each of our curriculum departments. There was an October meeting between the curriculum department learning leader, the associated assistant principal, and me to review the previous year's results, and then to discuss current year plans. Later in first semester, the learning leader (who included other teachers, if appropriate) shared their results and plans at a whole staff meeting. Over time these presentations, which were initially met with varying degrees of trepidation, became active and engaging learning experiences for our whole staff as we attempted to make teaching and learning more transparent. These meetings typically involved a variety of presentation media, student work exemplars, samples of instructional and assessment material and, on occasion, contests and prizes. They became celebrations of the complex work of the various curriculum departments and an opportunity for our 160 teaching and support staff members to better understand the similarities and differences amongst departments, and thereby played an important role in staff cohesion.

The curriculum department learning leaders also reported interim results to the school Leadership Council early in the second semester and created a year-end written report. (Our Leadership Council, which consisted of 23 learning leaders, 4 assistant principals and me as principal, was responsible for whole school operational decision-making and policy development.) The template for the year-end student data review provoked really engaging discussion about student learning and teacher practice:

1. Measures Used and Results Achieved

   - What baseline and semester-end or year-end measures did you use? (Include a copy of the data collection instrument.)
   - Analysis of the results achieved.
   - Did you meet or exceed your target? Please explain.

2. Timeline and Action Plan Reviewed

   - Did things actually work the way you described in your fall SMART outcome template or what changes were necessary?

3. Promising Instructional Strategies and Changes in Teaching Practice

   • What teaching strategies worked well, and how will they be sustained?

4. What were other *lessons learned* by your CoP that our principals should know about?

12.5.3   SMART Outcome Evolution

Over the 5 years that we worked with the SMART process there was considerable evolution and growth of assessment practice within our curriculum departments. The examples that follow illustrate the diversity and specificity of assessment data that our departments considered.

12.5.3.1   English Department Evolution

• Year 1 (of the SMART process) – Students in English 10–1 (university entrance course) and 10–2 (college entrance course) will improve their writing skills on core assignments.
• Year 2 – Students in English 10–2, 20–2 and 30–2 (college entrance courses) will improve assignment completion.
• Year 3 – Students in all English courses will deepen and widen their vocabulary in both reading comprehension and written expression.
• Year 4 – Students in all English courses will deepen and widen their vocabulary in both reading comprehension and written expression.
• Year 5 – Students in English 10–1 and 20–1 (university entrance courses) will develop critical analytical writing skills through scaffolded practice.

In this curriculum department, teachers worked with outcomes focussing on a particular level of their English courses; for example, assignment completion of the students in the English 10–2, 20–2, and 30–2 college entrance courses. Teachers also worked with all levels of courses as illustrated by the vocabulary development outcomes. In addition, they chose to repeat an outcome for a second year because of their desire to make further adjustments in their instructional strategies and assessment measures.

12.5.3.2   Mathematics Department Evolution

• Year 1 (of the SMART process) – Without using calculators, Pure Math 10 students will improve their basic order of operations, exponent and factoring skills.
• Year 2 – Pure Math 20 students will improve their factoring skills.

- Year 3 – Pure Math 10 students will improve their fraction skills in order to effectively work with algebraic concepts that use fraction manipulations.
- Year 4 – Math 14 and 24 students will improve their employability skills of effective use of class time and good attendance in order to improve their academic achievement.
- Year 5 – Math students will understand rounding in the context of their answers and will be able to do rounding correctly.

In this department, teachers viewed assessment and instruction with considerable precision, considering course specific outcomes such as factoring in Pure Math 20 and employability skills in Math 24 – as well as whole department outcomes such as rounding.

We did not require our programme departments (Guidance, Special Education, English as a Second Language, Advanced Placement, Arts Centred Learning, etc.) to complete the SMART outcome process because of the whole school and multicurricula nature of their teacher groups. However, a number of learning leaders of these departments saw the benefit of combining or working with curriculum departments in order to improve student achievement. Two examples of these collaborations are as follows.

Guidance and Special Education

- Learning disabled students will be able to successfully access their postsecondary education choices by developing self-advocacy skills.

ESL and English

- ESL students in English 10–1 university entrance courses will further develop their skills to independently complete assignments.

12.5.4 SMART Examples from our English and Physical Education Departments

English. This English Department example involved a curriculum research focus, and it resulted in changes in teacher practice and improved student outcomes. The results from the English 30–2 Diploma Examinations from Alberta Education were one source of baseline data. The English teachers also decided to develop an instrument to collect their own data. These data had a significant impact on teacher assumptions regarding student achievement and on the strategies that teachers used to address their concerns arising from student achievement data. Teachers were concerned that the class averages in the −2 college entrance courses at all grade levels tended to be low. In looking closely at the School Awarded Marks for students in our English 30–2 courses, teachers determined that the students who completed the majority of course assignments were successful, but up to 30 % of students were not completing enough work to pass. In English 30–2, the differences between the School Awarded Mark and the Diploma Examination Mark indicated a number of students performed well on the Diploma Examination but entered the exam with a low School Awarded Mark. Our English 30–2 students scored above provincial average in the Reading section, but below in the Written section, often the type of assignment that the students did not complete during the course.

Teachers' essential question then became: "How can we improve the assignment completion rate for students, especially those in –2 courses?" They began by creating and administering an online survey to approximately 200 Grade 10 and 11 students. They were curious to know what factors were impediments to students' assignment completion, as well as what factors were motivators. As an example, when they asked students whether they used aids, such as our agenda books to help keep track of assignments and due dates, 69 % of students said that they rarely used such aids. Teachers found it interesting that when they asked students the reasons for not having completed an assignment, approximately 70 % said they had forgotten about the assignment. Our teachers knew from their own observations that the typical "write it in your agenda book" solution was not working for many high school students. However, this information from students caused teachers to search for more practical solutions, and they began talking with students about sending themselves email, voicemail, or text message reminders for assignment due dates which had a positive effect on assignment completion for a number of students.

Likewise teachers surveyed students regarding why they did not hand in assignments. Teachers knew that students were working on their assignments in class, but frequently the finished assignment was not handed in. Based upon the survey results, 40 % of the students indicated that they "Often" or "Sometimes" had completed the assignments but did not hand them in. Student responses were quite surprising to some teachers and certainly created lively discussion in the department meetings about student perception of only submitting what they perceived to be good work. A sample of student responses follows:

"I either forget … it's not completely done … or I'm not too proud of it."
"If I don't think it's very good. I feel it is a bad representation of my work."
"Well, I usually don't get good marks so what is the point in handing them in if I am going to get a crappy mark."
"It is not up to my standards."
"Sometimes I don't feel like I've done my personal best. Most often I threw it together in twenty minutes, and I just don't care about it."
"Sometimes when I complete assignments I know that they have not been done to the requirements either because I didn't apply myself or the assignment was unclear to me. Instead of handing in a poor assignment and failing, it just seems easier to not hand it in."

These comments also uncovered issues related to student perceptions of self-efficacy, as well as their time management and self-advocacy skills. There was considerable debate in the English Department about our high school students really caring about "good work" – as the students themselves defined it. The survey also inquired as to what encouraged students to complete their work as indicated in Table 12.2.

As a result of the survey information, teachers began to offer students more choice in topic, in method of completion, in opportunities to re-do work to improve it, and in designing assignments.

Physical Education. The example from this department involved their curriculum research focus encompassing an "industry standard" instrument for data collection. There were positive consequences that the teachers had not predicted, and it resulted in changes in teacher practice and improved student outcomes. Physical Education teachers were concerned with low levels of cardiovascular fitness in Grade 10 classes, which all students are required to take by Alberta Education. In their investigation into research trends in physical activity for Canadian youth, teachers found that many teens were not active enough for optimal growth and development and that the number of Canadian children who were overweight had tripled in the last 20 years. The research confirmed teachers' beliefs that moderate to vigorous physical activity would result in increased self-esteem and ability to cope with mental stress, as well as enhanced performance in the classroom engagement. In order to test student fitness levels at the beginning and the end of the semester, the Grade 10 students took the Beep Test – the standard for testing cardiovascular fitness for large groups. The teachers decided that to improve student cardiovascular fitness they would implement an incremental jog twice a week in all of their Grade 10 classes – in September – 6 min; in October – 7 min; and so on.

What they discovered was that at the end of the semester 42 % of the Grade 10 girls were achieving a Max V02 rating of "good" which was a 22 % increase from baseline data. Sixty-nine percent of the Grade 10 boys were achieving a Max V02 rating of "good" which was a 20 % increase from baseline data. Most students were able to go two stages further on their Beep Test, and for many students it was the difference between having a "poor" rating and a "good" rating. Physical Education

Table 12.2 Student perception of english assignment completion factors

Factors in assignment completion	% of students who indicated the factor was		
	Important (I)	Very important (VI)	Both I & VI
Friends	29	25	54
Parents	33	32	65
Mark value	53	14	67
Input in design	41	11	52
Choice in topic	44	26	70
Choice in completion method	45	21	66
Access to computers/ICT	38	25	63
Opportunity to redo the assignment	30	35	65

teachers expected students to react negatively to this strategy, but students did not. In fact, if teachers missed a day, students mentioned they wanted to start class with the jog. As a result, teachers decided to continue the incremental jog in all of their Grade 10 Physical Education classes.

In Year 5 of this SMART strategy, a Physical Education teacher described an incident that illustrated the long-term impact of his classroom assessment focus. For the previous 3 years the teacher had continued the incremental jog with his Grade 10s, but he added an assessment rubric which he created and adapted each year with input from each of his classes. Part of the rubric was student assessment of their performance on the jog. At a parent-teacher conference, the parents of one of his Grade 10 students came to thank him. The student was a shy girl who for many, many years had not enjoyed Physical Education class, particularly running activities. Her parents felt it was important to tell the teacher what a positive impact his class had on their daughter. The previous week she had jogged for 7 min with no stopping. They said that she had never accomplished this before, and she was so excited to see such positive results after only a month in his class. The teacher then asked the parents how their daughter had assessed her work. And they said she had a big smile on her face when she told them she had given herself a 5/5 on the rubric, even though some other students had passed her on the run. For us, as educators, this highlighted the positive impact of our 'assessment *for* learning' focus on both teacher and student efficacy.

12.6   Through the District Director Lens – A Case of Multiple Schools Inquiring into Effective Assessment

In my current role as a district director, I have responsibility for oversight of the teaching and learning environment in 42 schools – including three high schools. One of the high schools has participated in a partnership between our Ministry, our school district, and Galileo Educational Network (an organisation associated with the Werklund School of Education, University of Calgary). Galileo Educational Network was contracted by Alberta Education to design and lead a research and development initiative intended to inform future directions for effective high school education across Alberta. The role of the Galileo team was to collaboratively design and examine the practices that promote increased student achievement and intellectual engagement in high school. The selected high school was chosen because there was a close alignment between the goals of this initiative and those of the school and the district. The school had below provincial average achievement and high school completion rates, a number of high poverty students, large numbers of English Language Learners, and a high percentage of coded (officially identified) exceptional needs students – and the school district was prepared to support this initiative with internal resources and help to lead the collaborative research and development endeavour.

The goals of the research were to investigate:

- Changes in teacher learning when they have been well supported through ongoing professional development that is responsive and specifically designed for their particular context.
- Changes in student and teacher engagement (social, academic and intellectual) when learning environments have been deliberately created to reflect the principles of the Teaching Effectiveness Framework.
- Changes in student achievement when the learning environment has been deliberately designed to reflect the principles outlined in the Teaching Effectiveness Framework.
- Ways teachers and students utilise digital technologies to create knowledge and demonstrate learning.

The research study employed a participatory methodology using design-based research methods. The design-based research was intended to study an innovation as it was being implemented, refined, and adjusted, based on the interpretation of emergent data. It was interventionist in design as emergent data was used to inform the ongoing work of researchers, teachers, and their students. This research method afforded the researchers the latitude that they needed to meet the requirements of the research question, as well as the opportunity to draw upon both quantitative and qualitative data sources which were gathered and analysed throughout the process:

- Audiotaped individual interviews of school and district administrators;
- Audiotaped focus group interviews of students, teachers, and parents/guardians;
- Field notes during interviews;
- Observations of classroom activity by trained researchers using observation protocols;
- Artefacts of teacher planning;
- Artefacts of student work samples and projects;
- *Tell Them From Me*: national online student perception surveys
- School organisation documents, such as the School Development Plan and the Accountability Pillar Survey

In collaboration with the school and district administration, the Galileo team initially analysed school data, designed a plan to increase student performance and student engagement, and designed discipline-based inquiry studies that engaged and challenged students in the classroom. The five principles of the Teaching Effectiveness Framework and the Discipline-Based Rubric for Inquiry Studies from the Galileo Education Network became the guiding documents for this work with Grade 10 teachers and students. The work began with a pilot cohort group of 4 academic core teachers (English Language Arts, Mathematics, Science and Social Studies) and a group of 100 Grade 10 students. The focus of the work was authentic integration of curricula; "real world" application of curriculum content; enhanced off-campus experiences; team teaching; close collaboration with discipline experts beyond the school; emphasis on smoother transition in high school; strengthened student/teacher relationships; effective integration of technology and fostering digital citizenship; and year-long opportunities for learning. The following year 16 academic core teachers and the entire Grade 10 class at the school adopted this framework for teaching and learning.

School staff who participated in the ongoing, on-site personalised and responsive professional learning opportunities provided by Galileo, the University of Calgary, and Mount Royal University indicated that their instructional design and assessment practices were changing. As part of this initiative, teaching staff were required to make the teaching and learning more visible to staff, students, and the community so that professional educators could improve their practices in the company of their colleagues. Bringing forward exemplars of student learning helped to improve teaching and assessment practices. For example, teachers indicated "it's refreshing though and it's challenging ... it's a huge, huge, huge learning curve this year and I think we're all much stronger teachers because of it ... we're rethinking education, we're rethinking semesters, we're rethinking how we teach things, we're rethinking the textbook." They described the impact on students, "we set up and then hand off greater responsibility to the students which, as a teacher, is hard to do – to let them have it. But in the end it's better for them ... I think we're fostering much stronger learners."

In order to support and extend this work across the other schools within my responsibility, it was necessary to design professional learning experiences for all principals, assistant principals, and learning leaders that were aligned with the professional learning of the staff members in the high school research site. In order to accomplish this, I was required, as director, to find additional resources and to allocate typical contingency and discretionary funding in ways that supported professional learning focussed on task design, formative assessment, and instructional leadership.

For the past 3 years we have been able to fund seven full-morning professional learning sessions each year for our 42 principals. Each session has been followed by a principal design team meeting to review feedback and design our next meeting. Because of our focus on success for all learners, but specifically for our Aboriginal learners, we have received support from the United Way to provide funding for our Galileo Education Network facilitators. A mirrored meeting arrangement was established for our 50 assistant principals. The work of Robinson (2011) on student-centred leadership has guided our discussions, and the principals and assistant principals have closely examined evidence of their work as instructional leaders through the lens of the Teaching Effectiveness Framework. Our principals and assistant principals are becoming very intentional about each classroom visit and conversation, with the explicit purpose of engaging with teachers about well-defined instructional practice.

In addition, for the past 3 years we have been able to provide 90 school-based and district learning leaders or lead teachers with seven full-day working sessions per year. With facilitation from the Galileo Education Network, the sessions focus on "teachers-as-designers of learning", and we have designed one group specifically for our secondary school teachers. Working with the principles of the Teaching

Effectiveness Framework and the Discipline-based Inquiry Rubric, participants create intellectually engaging tasks and design formative assessment in the company of their peers. They return to their classrooms and implement the work that they have designed and then bring evidence of student learning to their next sessions to receive peer feedback.

To further create district coherence in assessment practice, this past year we have provided English, Mathematics, Science, and Social Studies learning leaders from each of our 25 high schools with the opportunity to focus on high school teachers as designers-of-learning, again through the lens of the Teaching Effectiveness Framework. This work has been led by school and district administrators with the support of the Galileo Education Network.

12.7   Our Challenges and Strengths

12.7.1   Teacher Perspective: SMART Outcomes in the High School Classroom

When I was a high school principal and initiated our focus on assessment *of* and *for* learning, many of my teachers had three fundamental questions about the SMART outcomes process:

- Will this improve individual and group learning experiences in my classroom?
- Will this improve student achievement? and
- Will I have the time, resources, and the energy to implement this initiative?

As we achieved success, and as individual teachers and whole departments took ownership of the process, many of those original concerns disappeared. The terms Strategic and Specific were part of the original SMART acronym, but our teachers also added the word Shared:

Although the true statement of our character may be dictated by what we do when no one is watching, there is no denying the force of a functional friendship in the face of adversity to make those solitary decisions more sound.

This teacher comment highlighted the importance of relationship building as part of our CoP, particularly for our beginning teachers. As an example, one learning leader had four first-year teachers enter the department together. Because of her careful scheduling and subsequent mentorship, those teachers were able to plan together for a similar teaching load. (After many long hours they began calling themselves, "The Eager Beaver Society"–yes, they were witty, too!) And their group energy and enthusiasm, as well as their willingness to ask critical questions about instructional design and assessment, enriched their curriculum department and our school as a whole.

For our teachers it was critical to embed this classroom assessment in their daily work, as opposed to it being considered an additional task mandated by the principal or the school district or the province. A teacher commented:

> Just as we create learning opportunities for students to engage in the ways they will find most meaningful for themselves, we construct department SMART outcome work such that teachers can access it from varying points in the ways they find most valuable to the work they are already doing.

The process of teachers learning together about student assessment in a safe environment where they could take professional risks was key – "Allow the SMART outcome process to be an opportunity for collegial collaboration that focuses on the process and progress of moving towards the end, rather than focusing solely upon that end." One English teacher explained that was it critical to "recognise that learning happens in ways that can be demonstrated and recorded, though not always measured [numerically]." This comment acknowledged the value of including qualitative data as part of the classroom assessment process, and curriculum departments created or adapted rubrics and other indicators as part of their assessment strategy.

12.7.2   High School Assessment Exemplars

As a high school principal, another challenge was the dearth of high school classroom assessment exemplars, particularly from a Canadian perspective. Because the United States high school context related to assessment is quite different, we were cautious to not adopt strategies that were inappropriate for our provincial curriculum and our Diploma Examination processes. Davies and Busick (2007) developed a two-book series providing vignettes of classroom assessment across a variety of high school curriculum areas, and some of these are Canadian. We provided these books to our learning leaders because we knew their current work would resonate with the exemplars. Popham's (2008) description of transformational assessment also aligned with our high school work and provided guidance for further growth so that assessment-elicited evidence of students' status was used by our teachers to adjust their ongoing instructional procedures, and also by our students to adjust their current learning tactics.

12.7.3   Digital Technologies to Support Effective Teaching and Learning

In my role as principal I was also challenged to provide appropriate ICT access for our teachers and students – in a 6.5-acre, 40-year old facility. Because we had made it a school priority over the 5 years, and because I was involved in district technology planning, we received additional support in terms of providing teachers with laptops, networked multifunction printers/copiers, and interactive whiteboards. Wenger et al. (2005) investigated good technology design from a CoP perspective. Their work indicated that good technology design involved (1) design for ease of use and learning, (2) design for evolution as the community develops and its needs change, and (3) design for "closeness at hand"/mobility access. As would be typical, our school district had selected a learning management platform. We were expected to use it to support our CoP work and to house associated accountability documents. We struggled with using this platform effectively. Part of the dilemma, I believe was reflected in evolving technology issues in CoP as illustrated in Table 12.3.

As is often the case, our district attempted to "select the right solution and expect uniform adoption" when we really needed to be able to configure, adapt, reject, and invent with a variety of pieces of technology. As Wenger indicated, "Good technology in itself will not a community make, but bad technology can make community life difficult enough to ruin it" (p. 9). This was an area of continuing tension for our school.

12.7.4 Leadership Development in Large High Schools

Leithwood (2007) described the complexity of leadership development necessary to support our assessment work:

> These leaders are trying to establish agreement about goals and priorities among a more or less large group of adults with considerable variation in their motivations, dispositions, capacities and aspirations for themselves. They are also helping each of them remain motivated to accomplish those goals and supporting their efforts to develop any new skills they might need to accomplish those goals. The work of leaders also includes making sure the structures and culture of the organization actually assist the work of their colleagues, rather than getting in their way as is so often the case. It would be easy to give up in the face of such complexity. ... Successful leaders have high levels of self-efficacy. They persist. They are optimistic when they really have no right to be. ... Persisting allows the time to learn the way forward. (p. 62)

Table 12.3 An evolving perspective on technology community issues (Wenger et al., 2005, p. 9)

Perspective	From	To
Technology market	A simple market with few options. Single-point "solutions"	Complex choices Ability to integrate and bridge across tools Vendors are users in their own communities
Configuring technology	Selection by "feature shoot out" and comparisons	Mix and match technology to community activities and to multimembership
Technology in use	Select the "right" solution and expect uniform adoption	Members configure, adopt, reject and invent

One of the most daunting challenges in our large high school was leadership development and consistency across our leadership teams. In the school where I was principal, we had 120 teachers, 23 learning leaders, and 5 assistant principals. Each year over the 5-year period we welcomed between 15 and 20 new teachers at the beginning of the year – some who were new to the profession, and some who were new to the building. Of the five-person administration team we initially created, only two of us remained; the others had retired. Several of our learning leaders moved to assistant principal roles in other schools or to district positions, and several of our most experienced and skilled learning leaders have since retired.

Leithwood (2007) expressed concern regarding the transition of staff as a leadership development issue – "instability is one of the most powerful explanations for the failure of most school improvement initiatives" (p. 44). Our school district had a formal leadership development programme that focused on administrative designations at the assistant principal, principal, director, and superintendent levels, but it did not include learning leaders, so we believed we needed to create a programme that would support the district direction but focus on instructional leadership in our specific school context. In addition to the typical school Leadership Council meetings, we purchased books and created leadership workshops with guest facilitators from both education and business. When we first began our assessment work, we also had no role clarity for our learning leaders. With the assistance of our district Director of Leadership Development (and after 4 months of very lively discussion), we created role descriptions to guide the work of our learning leaders which included a focus on instructional leadership and assessment for our curriculum department learning leaders – and on teacher mentorship for all other learning leaders.

It was very challenging to provide adequate time and resources to support our learning leaders in their assessment work. In a public education system, our learning leaders received a district administration allowance of several thousand dollars per year, and as a school we generally allocated them one course equivalent of release time. Each learning leader release period cost our school approximately $12,000, and we needed to balance our budget as well as meet Class Size Initiative targets set by the Ministry. If we could have afforded it, we would have provided more release time for our learning leaders; the leadership that we asked of them was very difficult and time consuming for very little compensation and recognition.

12.7.5   Visible Learning and Teaching for Intellectual Engagement

As a district director, my recent work with school leadership teams has focused on making student learning visible and generating feedback to strengthen teaching practice. As part of this instructional leadership work we are acknowledging the importance of multiple feedback loops and the recursive nature of professional learning. We value the notion of discourse around "works in progress" versus "exemplars". We are going deeper into consistent professional learning rather than moving from one surface level professional development topic to another. For example, professional learning for principals and assistant principals focuses on deeply examining our formative assessment practices for a full school year. We are seeing coherence develop across area schools regarding formative assessment and discipline-based inquiry, and we have a more well-articulated understanding of high quality teaching, learning, and leadership amongst our 200 learning leaders, assistant principals, and principals. We are also observing our students as more intellectually engaged, capable learners; our teachers as more intellectually engaged, capable designers of learning; and, our principals as more intellectually engaged, capable instructional leaders.

12.7.6 District Alignment

Schmoker (2006) and others have described the importance of the district and Ministry alignment in support of student learning. We have been very fortunate to have district directors and superintendents who have helped us focus on student learning and who have minimised other distractions that are often typical in large school districts.

12.8 Creating an Assessment Culture: A Final Word

It requires careful risk-taking to develop high school assessment cultures of inquiry, introspection, and improvement. As a school principal, I eliminated our school professional development committee and gave these allocated days to our individual curriculum department CoPs to meet their needs and support their SMART outcomes. As described previously, we were very diligent in following the frameworks we designed as a school to improve learning for all ability levels and programs of our students. As a district administrator, I allocated resources in non-typical ways to allow principals, assistant principals, and learning leaders the time to engage in ongoing conversation about rich task design and formative assessment. Additionally, I both enabled and required them to collect and share evidence of student intellectual engagement in their classrooms. And, yes, it is still a "work in progress" – as it should be. As a high school principal, I was very encouraged by the work of my teachers, learning leaders, and assistant principals, and how they were willing to engage in the challenging and complex formative assessment processes. Closing their classroom doors and "doing it their way" would have been much easier and certainly less time consuming. Now, as a district director, I am able to observe teachers, learning leaders, assistant principals, and principals continuing to undertake the complex work as designers-of-learning to improve assessment practices that promote student intellectual engagement. We know we must all be learners and teachers — and instructional leaders.

References

Boudett, K., City, E., & Murnane, R. (Eds.). (2005). *Data wise: A step-by-step guide to using assessment results to improve teaching and learning.* Cambridge, MA: Harvard Education Press.

Conzemius, A., & O'Neill, J. (2002). *The handbook for SMART school teams.* Bloomington, IN: National Educational Service.

City, E., Elmore, R., Fiarman, S., & Teitel, L. (2009). *Instructional rounds in education: A network approach to improving teaching and learning.* Cambridge, MA: Harvard Educational Press.

Davies, A., & Busick, K. (2007). *Classroom assessment: What's working in high schools (Book One and Book Two).* Courtenay, BC: Connections Publishing.

Elmore, R. (2000). *Building a new structure for school leadership.* Washington, DC: Albert Shanker Institute.

Elmore, R. (2002). *Bridging the gap between standards and achievement: The imperative for professional development in education.* Washington, DC: Albert Shanker Institute.

Friesen, S. (2009). *What did you do in school today? Teaching effectiveness: A framework and rubric.* Toronto, ON, Canada: Canadian Education Association.

Galileo Educational Network. (2013). *Discipline-based rubric for inquiry studies.* Retrieved from: http://galileo.org/rubric.pdf

Glaude, C. (2005). *Protocols for professional learning conversations: Cultivating the art and discipline.* Courtenay, BC: Connections Publishing.

Leithwood, K. (2007). What we know about educational leadership. In C. F. Webber, J. Burger, & P. Klinck (Eds.), *Intelligent leadership: Constructs for thinking education leaders* (pp. 41–66). Dordrecht, The Netherlands: Springer.

Popham, J. (2008). *Transformational assessment.* Alexandria, VA: Association for Supervision and Curriculum Development (ASCD).

Reeves, D. (2004). *Accountability for learning: How teachers and school leaders can take charge.* Alexandria, VA: Association for Supervision and Curriculum Development (ASCD).

Robinson, V. (2011). *Student-centred leadership.* San Francisco: Jossey Bass.

Schmoker, M. J. (2006). *Results now: How we can achieve unprecedented improvements in teaching and learning.* Alexandria, VA: Association for Supervision and Curriculum Development (ASCD).

Wenger, E., McDermott, R., & Snyder, W. (2002). *Communities of practice: A guide to managing knowledge.* Cambridge, MA: Harvard Business School Press.

Wenger, E., White, N., Smith, J., & Rowe, K. (2005). Technologies for communities. In L. Langelier (Ed.), *Work, learning and networked* (pp. 47–66). Quebec, QC: CEFRIO.

Willms, D., Friesen, S., & Milton, P. (2009). *What did you do in school today? Transforming classrooms through social, academic, and intellectual engagement (First National Report).* Toronto, ON, Canada: Canadian Education Association.

Index

© Springer International Publishing Switzerland 2016
S. Scott et al. (eds.), *Assessment in Education*, The Enabling
Power of Assessment 2, DOI 10.1007/978-3-319-23398-7

Lightning Source UK Ltd.
Milton Keynes UK
UKOW06n1842020616

275488UK00010B/96/P

9 783319 233970